HERO

Also Available

HERO

volume 1
THE SILENT ERA TO
DILIP KUMAR

HERO

volume 2
AMITABH BACHCHAN TO
THE KHANS AND BEYOND

ASHOK RAJ

HAY HOUSE
Australia • Canada • Hong Kong • India
South Africa • United Kingdom • United States

Published and distributed in the United Kingdom by:
Hay House UK Ltd, 292B Kensal Rd, London W10 5BE. Tel.: (44) 20 8962 1230;
Fax: (44) 20 8962 1239. www.hayhouse.co.uk

Published and distributed in the United States of America by:
Hay House, Inc., PO Box 5100, Carlsbad, CA 92018-5100. Tel.: (1) 760 431 7695 or
(800) 654 5126; Fax: (1) 760 431 6948 or (800) 650 5115. www.hayhouse.com

Published and distributed in Australia by:
Hay House Australia Ltd, 18/36 Ralph St, Alexandria NSW 2015.
Tel.: (61) 2 9669 4299; Fax: (61) 2 9669 4144. www.hayhouse.com.au

Published and distributed in the Republic of South Africa by:
Hay House SA (Pty), Ltd, PO Box 990, Witkoppen 2068.
Tel./Fax: (27) 11 467 8904. www.hayhouse.co.za

Published and distributed in India by:
Hay House Publishers India, Muskaan Complex, Plot No.3, B-2, Vasant Kunj,
New Delhi – 110 070. Tel.: (91) 11 4176 1620; Fax: (91) 11 4176 1630.
www.hayhouse.co.in

Distributed in Canada by:
Raincoast, 9050 Shaughnessy St, Vancouver, BC V6P 6E5. Tel.: (1) 604 323 7100;
Fax: (1) 604 323 2600

A catalogue record for this book is available from the British Library.

ISBN 978-1-84850-153-9

Printed and bound at
Thomson Press (India) Ltd.

In memory of my uncle
Shri B. S. Hoogan
one of the founders of Hindi film music

Preface

In my family tradition, made up of the ennobling elements of both the Hindu and Sikh heritage, fine arts such as music, theatre and cinema have received a great deal of critical attention. Sometimes, adulation has been expressed and sometimes criticism.

My grandfather, Shri Ishwar Das, although an engineer by profession was an accomplished singer from Ferozepur (Punjab), specializing in rendering the Gurbani. His eldest son, the late Shri B. S. Hoogan, was one of the leading composers in the Bombay film world of the 1930s. The second son, my father, the late Shri B. R. Hoogan, too was a *shabd* (devotional hymn) singer and often performed popular musical plays based on Hindu mythological tales. For the last two generations, the youngsters in the family have been trained to appreciate the finer points of the aforementioned art forms.

Even as children, we were taken to musical concerts, drama events and cinema halls. We saw many film classics. Later on, there were heated but well-informed discussions and debates on the merits of the cinema of the older generation vis-à-vis ours. Invariably, these discussions and debates – after a thorough dissection of a film (based on its artistic and emotional appeal, directorial treatment, storyline, characterizations, cinematic merits and music) – would finally get focused on the performance of its *hero* as the prime mover of the venture. As the lead actor's role was subjected to a critical appraisal, he was also judged in comparison with his seniors and contemporaries, with the representatives of the two generations arguing passionately in favour of the acting icons of their respective eras: K. L. Saigal-Chandramohan-Prithviraj Kapoor-Ashok Kumar-Motilal-Surendra vis-à-vis Dilip Kumar-Shyam-Raj Kapoor-Dev Anand-Raaj Kumar and later Amitabh Bachchan-Rajesh Khanna-Sanjeev Kumar-Vinod Khanna and the new-age heroes of the 1990s and the new millennium.

As exemplified by the discussions in my family, the popular discourse on cinema and its impact on society have been largely centred around the hero figure – his style, mannerisms, histrionics and the roles he has played in his career. The dynamics of such a discourse and its idiom have also been expressed formally in film reviews (both in the print and electronic media), gossip columns, publicity material, biographies/autobiographies of the heroes, interviews and fan-club hagiographies. In this way, these popular expressions represent a significant part of our cinema's oral, visual as well as written history. Yet, in the amalgamation of these intertextual expressions, which manifests itself as a rereading of the cinema in the public sphere, the very essence of the making of the Indian film hero's persona and the changes it undergoes in different historical points of reference are often lost.

This work, a kind of tribute to my family's film-appreciation tradition, seeks to 'recast' the aforementioned popular discourse on the Indian film hero by retracing and mapping the historic journey of this pivotal figure through different eras of cinema to present the socio-cultural history of the Indian film and also its cinematic context. The first volume covers the silent era as well as Dilip Kumar and his contemporaries. The second volume starts with Amitabh Bachchan and his contemporaries and goes on to highlight the heroes of the 1980s, 1990s and the new millennium.

Given the large canvas and the encyclopedic nature of this work, its publication would never have been possible without the blessings and assistance of a number of people within and outside cinema. I salute these highly knowledgeable and respected individuals who were willing to share their cine-enthusiast spirit (and their inputs) to enlighten me on diverse aspects of what turned out to be a highly challenging task. I am extremely grateful to the following:

- The late B. K. Karanjia, former editor of *Screen*,
- the late Raghava Menon, music critic and writer,
- Firoze Rangoonwalla, a veteran in the field of film writing,
- the late Mohammed Shamim, film critic,
- Geeti Sen, former editor, the India International Centre (New Delhi) journal,
- Ravi Vasudevan, the renowned cinema scholar, associated with the Centre for Study on Developing Societies, New Delhi,
- Har Mandir Singh Hamraaz, the author of the monumental work *Hindi Film Geet Kosh*,
- K. L. Arora, the fabulous one-man encyclopedia and film critic,
- A. K. Balakrishnan, the late Mohan Hari and Pradeep Huda, all film makers,
- Ashok Chopra, CEO and managing director of Hay House Publishers India, for his incredible passion for this work that helped me in developing its perspective and in widening its canvas and thus enabling me to pen the grand saga of four generations of cinema and
- K. J. Ravinder (Ravi), the editor of Hay House, who lent very valuable scholarly and moral support.

My effort was guided by several path-breaking works, which have sought to address Indian cinema as an alternative expression of the wider socio-cultural processes in Indian society. A wealth of information, both hard facts and views on films and heroes, was gleaned from available sources. I specially thank Ashish Rajadhyaksha and Paul Willemen, the compilers of the classic *Encyclopedia of Indian Cinema*, as I gathered a host of insights from their highly fascinating and scholarly compendium.

This work has also made use of film reviews/articles published in the *Hindustan Times, The Times of India, Screen, Filmfare, The Indian Express, The Statesman* and *Jansatta* over past decades. I, therefore, convey my gratitude to the film critics K. M. Amladi, Khalid Mohammed, Amita Malik, Kavita Nagpal and Nikhat Kazmi, who have been associated with these publications (not necessarily in that order).

In formulating the perspective for this book, I received valuable insights from my cousins Pradyuman, the renowned painter, poster designer and film publicity expert, and Puran Chandra Hoogan, who has been associated with the banners of Rajshree, Rajender Singh Bedi and Mahesh Bhatt. I thank the other film lovers in my family: younger brother Ashwini Kumar, doctor by profession and star of Doordarshan's early serials like *Hum Log* and *Phir Wahi Talash*, and his wife Vibha and her film maker sister, my sister Kusum Sood and her husband Colonel R. N. Sood, Aruna Mahendru (another sister of mine) and of course my mother, the late Sushila Devi, for sharing their views and convictions about cinema.

I also thank several film-loving couples for offering their considered views on our films and heroes: Poonam and Mohan Kudesiya, Manju and S. K. Sharma, Shradha and Ravi Kashyap, Apoorva and Biswajit Dhar, Aditi and Rakesh Kapoor, Rumjhum and Girish Kumar (and their children Charu Kartikeya and Sukriti Vinayak), Kanti and Aman Baluni and Seema and Sudhir Sagar. My other friends – Surendra Prakash, Pradeep Biswas, Sangeeta, Abhay Sinha, Satya Prakash, Rahul Kashyap, Shankar Jha and two *bindaas* (happy-go-lucky) pals Rishi Kohli and Himmat Singh – too contributed towards building the information bank for this work.

Thanks also to the library staff of the Film and Television Institute of India, Pune, the Nehru Memorial Museum and Library, New Delhi, Jawaharlal Nehru University, New Delhi, the National Centre for Performing Arts, Bombay, Sangeet Natak Akademi, New Delhi, Chitrabani, Calcutta, the Centre for Study on Developing Societies, the Indian Institute of Mass Communication and the Jamia Millia Islamia University, the last three located in New Delhi.

And, finally, a sentimental hug to my wife Madhu Kumari, who, while bearing the brunt of my uninterruptible involvement in this work and the ensuing anarchy all around, kept inspiring this obstinate dullard with her soulful love and care, sharing along the way the joy of rediscovering and enjoying the romance of cinema. Our son, Pallav, also deserves a pat on his back for stealing my writing sheets and pens and for disturbing my computer work schedule.

– Ashok Raj

Contents

Chapter 1

Dilip Kumar to Amitabh Bachchan:
The Search for Continuity

Dilip Kumar's gradual fading away as the top-ranking hero from the late 1960s onwards left behind a space, which inspired two contenders to try and occupy it: Rajesh Khanna and Amitabh Bachchan. While Rajesh Khanna was the first to fill up this space, staying at the top for about seven years, the entry of Amitabh Bachchan was gradual but far more durable. Within a few years after his arrival, the latter dislodged the former and acquired the permanent status of superstar. This sudden shift in status of the two actors, in fact, marks an interesting development in the annals of Indian cinema.

Post-1975, when the phenomenal rise of Rajesh Khanna was fast losing its steam, Hindi cinema was facing a serious thematic stagnation. The magic of the Gulshan Nanda variety of romantic film stories was proving to be short-lived. Rajesh Khanna, acclaimed as the torchbearer of Hindi cinema's super-romantic era, was now looking far less appealing and worn out. The ageing actors, Dilip Kumar, Raj Kapoor, Dev Anand and Raaj Kumar and others (such as Shammi Kapoor, Shashi Kapoor, Manoj Kumar, Jeetendra and Dharmendra) were unable to rejenuvate the sagging image of the Hindi film. New-generation actors – such as Vinod Khanna, Vinod Mehra, Shatrughan Sinha, Randhir Kapoor, Rishi Kapoor and Navin Nischal – were, by and large, unable to come up with riveting and path-breaking portrayals. Although cinema was performing its routine function of entertainment, it was largely becoming static and was unable to respond to the mood of the people at large. Beneath the exterior were a growing social despair and a sense of pronounced uneasiness among the masses, which the cinema of Rajesh Khanna and other actors was unable to identify and respond to. This situation marked the arrival of Amitabh Bachchan in a big way due to the following changes taking place in society:

- A growing sense of social insecurity and alienation among the people.
- Increasing incompetence of the state apparatus in safeguarding the people against gangsters and hoodlums.
- The prevailing social inequality, in spite of apparently impressive economic growth (among certain segments of society) and development in many areas such as science and technology and industry.
- Amassing of wealth by the dishonest and corrupt (through crime and unfair means) on a scale not seen in the past decades.
- Growing public despair and anger as no substantial improvement in the quality of life of the common man was taking place even almost three decades after independence. Also, the working class and the lower strata of society faced serious shortages of essential commodities, which were sold through ration shops (leading to long queues and frayed tempers), but were available in the black market at exorbitant prices.
- Growing public fantasy about rags-to-riches success stories.
- Seemingly unending suffering of women and the destitute.

Under such circumstances the archetype of Rajesh Khanna's overly romantic image had become unrealistic, as it was unable to articulate the escalating social agonies and the sense of injustice in all walks of life. During this phase, apart from the usual run-of-the-mill romances and family dramas, Indian cinema began to move towards a trend that was to depict an alternative view of reality. This trend projected a curious manifestation of the intense social frustration erupting in the form of full-fledged violence and indulgence in vigilantism by the socially disadvantaged against the representatives of power and wealth acquired through dubious means. The cinema of socially approved violence was about to be formally launched.

The arrival of Amitabh Bachchan amidst such a socio-political setting provided to Hindi cinema a new lease of life, at least for the next 25 years. However, as will be seen later, the making of this superstar was made possible primarily by an extension of Dilip Kumar's cinematic personality interpreted now in a new context. In fact, the Amitabh Bachchan era largely represented a resounding continuity of Dilip Kumar's model of the Indian indigenous film hero. The young artiste exhibited commendable skills by improvising his acting style to suit a variety of situations. In fact, Amitabh Bachchan represents the classical case in the history of Indian cinema where an actor owes his success primarily to his senior by proxy in terms of fame, success and vast mass appeal.

A Comparison of the Formative Periods of Dilip Kumar and Amitabh Bachchan

There is a big difference between these two artistes if we consider the way in which they came to the film industry and the influences that helped them emerge as great actors. As already mentioned in Volume 1, Dilip Kumar's arrival was facilitated by an on-the-spot selection made by an intuitive Devika Rani. Like an apprentice, he was painstakingly trained for many years by some of the best directors of his times. These directors not only worked hard to hone his talent to perfection, but also imparted to him a profound sense of film aesthetics. After a few years of on-the-job training, the actor became his own master and the same directors (and those who came later too) became keen appreciators of his art. They would now look forward to his participation in their creations so as to obtain fresh insights from him for enhancing the scope of their work.

Amitabh Bachchan, on the other hand, arrived in films through an entirely different route. Born (on 11 October 1942) into a celebrated literary family of Allahabad, he had the advantage of parental eminence, as the son of the renowned Hindi poet Harivanshrai Bachchan, who represented the grand classical literary period of the 1930s and 1940s. As Amitabh Bachchan once said: 'My father is immortalized in his work, while I am merely a cinema actor who would be forgotten with [the] passage of time.' The family had strong political connections including those with the Nehru–Gandhi family. The grandsons of Jawaharlal Nehru and the sons of Indira Gandhi, Rajiv Gandhi and Sanjay Gandhi, were Amitabh Bachchan's close friends. Yet, his entry into the film world was not very smooth.

Despite strong recommendations by Nargis Dutt (of *Mother India* fame, who was a friend of Indira Gandhi and later a Rajya Sabha MP), film makers like B. R. Chopra and Mohan Sehgal were not even willing to look at this 'tall, gangly, awkward looking man'. The film industry, dominated as it was then by chocolate-faced heroes presiding over a slick romantic environment, had no place for such an unlikely aspirant. In addition to the above setback, the new aspirant received another jolt when his voice was initially rejected by All India Radio (interestingly, in the case of Dilip Kumar too, the critics found his voice 'too feminine' when his first film *Jwar Bhata* was released in 1944). Disheartened, Bachchan joined a Calcutta freight company as a middle-level executive.

But Amitabh Bachchan was spellbound by the magic of celluloid. Being a keen student of literature and cinema, he obtained his first break in films with a voice-over in the Bengali film maker Mrinal Sen's Hindi film, *Bhuvan Shome* (1969) starring

Utpal Dutt, the legendary acting icon from West Bengal, who was also a writer. His formal arrival was made possible in the same year by K. A. Abbas in *Saat Hindustani*, probably on the personal recommendation of Indira Gandhi. Abbas, a proponent of neo-realist cinema in the mainstream and a camp follower of Nehruvian socialism, was also a close friend of the Nehru–Gandhi family.

Amitabh Bachchan's first few films as hero, released over a period of four years (1969 to 1972), were non-starters and the actor failed to make an impact on the box office. In the case of Dilip Kumar too, his initial films over a period of four years (1944 to 1947) failed to provide him a definite foothold in the film industry.

Like Dilip Kumar, Amitabh Bachchan also faced an identity crisis in his formative period. In this phase, he had two distinct options: either to opt for roles similar to what his contemporaries like Rajesh Khanna, Dharmendra and Vinod Khanna were doing or turn himself into a serious actor in the mould of Dilip Kumar, Balraj Sahni, Guru Dutt or Sanjeev Kumar. Bachchan took the crucial decision to become a student of the Dilip Kumar school, and thus set his career on an upswing, that too, at an awe-inspiring pace!

In the case of Dilip Kumar, three directors – Nitin Bose, Mehboob Khan and Bimal Roy – played a vital role in bringing to full bloom his inherent talent. For Bachchan, it was Hrishikesh Mukherjee (who was deeply influenced by his mentor Bimal Roy) and other movie moghuls, such as Prakash Mehra, Yash Chopra and Manmohan Desai, who transformed potential raw talent into consummate artistry. In fact, what Bimal Roy was to Dilip Kumar, Hrishikesh Mukherjee was to Bachchan.

Amitabh Bachchan: The First Tentative Steps

In Bachchan's formative years, the five films, which broadly moulded (and without anyone realizing this at that time) the basic personality traits of the second indigenous hero of Hindi cinema in the making were: *Saat Hindustani* (1969), *Reshma Aur Shera* (1971), *Parvana* (1971), *Bansi Birju* (1972) and *Bombay to Goa* (1972). Although these films failed to announce the arrival of the new hero in Hindi cinema, the sense of confidence and a refreshing screen presence displayed by the actor in these films showed promise.

The unobtrusive debut of the actor in *Saat Hindustani* inadvertently projected the dominant aspect of his future persona – an ordinary, seemingly directionless youth transformed into a highly motivated crusader for a cause, seen in numerous latter-day films. The film presented the new actor as one of the revolutionaries among the group of seven men from different parts of the country who have embarked on a mission to liberate Portuguese-occupied Goa. In this collective struggle, they give up their religious and regional identities and thus validate, after much suffering and sacrifice, the much-cherished national slogan of 'unity in diversity'. (Goa was integrated into India in December 1961.)

The first glimpse of the new actor in the making was seen in Sunil Dutt's *Reshma Aur Shera*. The film not only earned him good reviews but also established his credentials as a sensitive actor. As the mute witness to the deeds of two warring clans of Rajasthan, Bachchan, in the role of the youngest brother of the hero, captured with commendable skill the agony generated by endless hatred and killings between the two clans.

Jyoti Swaroop's *Parvana* presented Amitabh Bachchan as the obsessed seeker of childhood love (à la Dilip Kumar in *Arzoo* and *Insaniyat*). He is an eminent writer who has been deeply in love with the heroine (Yogita Bali) since boyhood. But when she reveals that she has started liking another man, he feels defeated and devastated. He lays a trap in which he kills the heroine's uncle but creates evidence so that his competitor gets charged with the murder. In spite of his excellent portrayal of an obsessed lover, the critics found Bachchan looking 'gentle' in the role of the scheming villain.

Prakash Verma's *Bansi Birju*, one of the least-known films of Bachchan, cast the young actor in the role of a sensitive, aspiring poet, who is troubled by the socio-economic inequalities all around. The film, which narrates a one-night episode, is about the accidental relationship of the poet with an innocent girl who is being forced into prostitution by a group of people. He comes to the rescue of the traumatized victim and eventually both fall in love. In this powerful narrative, both Bachchan and the heroine Jaya Bhaduri (whom he later married) came up with memorable performances.

Bombay to Goa, produced by N. C. Sippy and directed by S. Ramanathan, on the other hand, showcased Bachchan's talent to portray light romantic roles. He performed, with commendable ease, the role of an easygoing jovial youth, who wins over his fiancée in a thrill- and humour-packed bus journey from Bombay to Goa. The ace comedian Mehmood was the other highlight of this film.

These five films laid the foundation for the screen image of the new hero – a complex mix of immense inner strength and vulnerability. His brooding eyes and a perpetual restlessness reflected an intense turmoil. These personality attributes were soon to become part of his persona of an *angry young man* in the coming years.

Chapter 2

The Colossus Called Amitabh Bachchan

The development of Amitabh Bachchan as the second-generation indigenous film hero of Indian cinema took place along a set of discrete sequences. Interestingly, unlike in the case of Dilip Kumar, these sequences did not follow a chronological pattern (say, from the romantic, to the serious and then to the aggressive-vengeful formations), but took shape more or less simultaneously. These sequences can be broadly demarcated under the following categories (there could be some degree of overlapping):

- The passionate sufferer.
- The angry man as the individual dispenser of justice.
- The angry man as the self-proclaimed liberator.
- The anti-hero awaiting redemption and atonement.
- The rebellious stance as a way of life.
- The simultaneous liberation of the image.
- The trapped man as the individual dispenser of justice.
- The brave man on the side of the law.
- The man in uniform as the defender of the nation.
- The backward-looking patriarch.
- The return of the anti-hero.
- The upholder of lost values.
- The old man as the eternal lover.

The Passionate Sufferer

Hrishikesh Mukherjee – a great admirer of Dilip Kumar's art – was the first director who gauged the hidden talent in this upcoming actor. He took up the task of presenting Amitabh Bachchan as a brooding, melancholic protagonist, a typical Bengali literary stereotype associated with Saratchandra Chatterjee, quite similar to the image of Dilip Kumar in the classical period. Mukherjee established the first formal image of the young Bachchan with two films *Anand* (1970) and *Namak Haram* (1973), juxtaposing him against the reigning superstar, Rajesh Khanna. The director consolidated the image further with *Abhimaan* (1973) and *Mili* (1975).

Anand (with Rajesh Khanna in the title role) became the first turning point for Amitabh Bachchan and marked the arrival of a sensitive, new-generation actor after a long gap. The film projected him as a sufferer who has internalized his painful past and, as a doctor, finds some solace in serving the poor and needy. In his personal life he develops a deep affection for his talkative friend (Anand) who is battling cancer. The doctor is a typical character, who is engulfed by the agony of his helplessness in fighting the dreaded disease, not to mention the anguish caused by his inability to express his love for a charming and considerate woman and also by the suffering all around. He can redefine his identity only by making all possible efforts to cure his friend, who, he knows, is going to die soon. *Anand* was an ideal combination of humour, bonhomie, music, emotional drama and eventual tragedy. The film tugged at the heartstrings of the audiences and made a great impact on one and all. The movie essentially belonged to Rajesh Khanna, but Amitabh Bachchan did make his presence felt.

Mukherjee again paired Khanna and Bachchan in *Namak Haram*, a refreshing portrayal of the industrial working class's struggle against capitalist dominance. The film was loosely based on Peter Glenville's masterpiece *Becket* (1964), starring Peter O'Toole and Richard Burton (as Becket), which was an adaptation of Jean Anouilh's play about the stormy friendship between the Archbishop of Canterbury, Thomas Becket, and King Henry II. On the basis of a contemporary plot, *Namak Haram* attempted to depict hard realism, with the dialogues being studded with Leftist ideology. The story, in brief, is as follows. When the affluent industrialist father (played by veteran Om Shivpuri) falls seriously ill, the son (Bachchan) takes over the responsibility of managing the factory. He has a showdown with the union leader and this event triggers off a strike, which can end only if he tenders an apology to the workers, as demanded by the union. Amitabh Bachchan asks his old friend, a middle-class youth (Rajesh Khanna), to help avenge this 'humiliation'. Rajesh Khanna joins the factory as a worker with the agreed mandate (between him and Bachchan) of destroying the unity of the workers. Rajesh Khanna, however, gets deeply involved with the workers' day-to-day problems and their constant struggle for survival. He sympathizes with the causes of the union and becomes a fellow comrade. The senior industrialist cannot stand this turnaround and arranges to get Rajesh Khanna killed in a truck 'accident'. The son takes the blame, goes to jail and, when released, decides to champion the workers' rights. Bachchan, with powerful interweaving of fiery dramatics and underplay, once again provided a glimpse of his histrionics and reaffirmed his presence as a formidable actor.

Hrishikesh Mukherjee

Born in Calcutta, Hrishikesh Mukherjee (30 September 1922 to 27 August 2006) graduated in science from Calcutta University. For some time he taught in a college and later worked for All India Radio. In 1945, he joined New Theatres, as a laboratory assistant and worked there for about six years. In 1950, he became a film editor with the Bengali film

Tathapi. His association with New Theatres brought him close to Bimal Roy with whom he worked as editor and assistant for many years. He made his directorial debut with *Musafir* in 1957 on the advice of Dilip Kumar and made some of the most memorable films of the 1950s and 1960s including *Anari* (1959), *Anuradha* (1960), *Anupama* (1966) and *Aashirwad* (1968). Later he directed many low-budget family melodramas often produced by N. C. Sippy. Mukherjee introduced many innovations in film editing, for example, the insertion of close-up as a bridge between incompatible shots. His films provided pure and clean entertainment and were notable for their absence of violence and sex.

His Major Films

Musafir (1957), *Anari* (1959), *Anuradha* (1960), *Chhaya* (1961), *Memdidi* (1961), *Aashiq* (1962), *Asli Naqli* (1962), *Sanjh Aur Savera* (1964), *Do Dil* (1965), *Anupama* (1966), *Biwi Aur Makaan* (1966), *Gaban* (1966), *Manjhli Didi* (1967), *Aashirwad* (1968), *Pyar Ka Sapna* (1969), *Satyakam* (1969), *Anand* (1970), *Buddha Mil Gaya* (1971), *Guddi* (1971), *Bawarchi* (1972), *Subse Bada Sukh* (1972), *Abhimaan* (1973), *Namak Haram* (1973), *Phir Kab Milogi* (1974), *Chaitali* (1975), *Chupke Chupke* (1975), *Mili* (1975), *Arjun Pandit* (1976), *Alaap* (1977), *Kotwal Saab* (1977), *Naukri* (1978), *Jurmana* (1979), *Golmaal* (1979), *Khubsoorat* (1980), *Naram Garam* (1981), *Bemisaal* (1982), *Achha Bura* (1983), *Kisise Na Kehna* (1983), *Rang Birangi* (1983), *Jhoothi* (1986), *Hum Hindustani* (1986), *Talash* (1992) and *Jhoot Bole Kaua Kate* (1998).

Abhimaan (1973), a classic directed again by Hrishikesh Mukherjee, provided Bachchan with his long-awaited breakthrough for attaining top-rung status and for doing well at the box office. The film presented him as a complex character, who not only is unable to understand his inner self but also becomes a victim of his ego (à la K. L. Saigal in Nitin Bose's *Lagan*). The hero, who lives in Bombay, is a very famous singer, who has acquired fame and riches and is virtually worshipped by his numerous fans. And yet he is a lonely man not at peace with himself and is unable to overcome his anxieties, which he just cannot understand. During a short visit to his aunt's house

Amitabh Bachchan: Star of the Millennium

(Durga Khote) in a village, he falls in love there with a schoolteacher's daughter (Jaya Bhaduri), who also possesses an inborn talent for singing. They get married and return to the city and soon form a joint musical team. But eventually the wife goes on to become an extremely popular singer, while the husband begins sliding down the popularity graph. This downfall gives a big jolt to his inflated ego and the jealousy syndrome begins to play havoc in the conjugal life of the singer-couple. The film, however, touches only the symptoms and fails to carry out a deeper probe of the hero's psychological aberrations and rushes towards the obligatory happy ending. Both Amitabh Bachchan and Jaya Bhaduri won critical acclaim for their subtle and sensitive performances. The highlight of the movie was the mellifluous music by ace composer Sachin Dev Burman, who bagged the *Filmfare* award for 1973.

Mili was an interesting rework on *Anand* by Mukherjee with a female protagonist. The film presented Bachchan as a melancholic recluse brooding over his highly troubled past and addicted to alcohol, who is shaken out of his negativity by an extremely extrovert personality, Mili (Jaya Bhaduri), who stays one floor below his in a Bombay skyscraper. This jovial, fun-loving girl, like Anand, is a victim of cancer and his deep concern for her well-being rekindles in the recluse a new hope and a new purpose in life. Even though the hero knows that Mili is likely to die, he offers to marry her and provide her a small measure of happiness. Veteran Ashok Kumar, as Mili's father, came up with an outstanding performance.

Apart from the foregoing films, other significant films in the romantic genre were: *Kabhi Kabhie* (1976), *Manzil* (1979), *Bemisaal* (1982), *Silsila* (1981), *Khuddar* (1982), *Armaan* (2002) and *Baghbaan* (2003). (In the last two movies, Bachchan played the role of a senior.)

Yash Chopra's *Kabhi Kabhie* attempted to show that the eternal longing for one's soulmate transcends time and sometimes gets manifested in another generation. The hero (Bachchan) is a poet whose intense creativity is inspired by his beloved (Raakhee). But under pressure from her parents, she marries another man (Shashi Kapoor). The poet gives up his art and marries another woman (Waheeda Rehman) who already has a daughter (Neetu Singh), but she is brought up by foster parents. As the lovers age, the uneasiness between the two families gets resolved when, in the next generation, Raakhee and Shashi Kapoor's son (Rishi Kapoor) chooses the partner he prefers, who happens to be none other than Neetu Singh. Amitabh Bachchan powerfully captured the agony of lost love through the lovelorn poetry of Sahir Ludhianvi, carefully selected from his early anthologies and simplified to suit the theme of the film. In *Kabhi Kabhie*, the musical score by melody maker Khayyam (full name Mohammed Zahoor Khayyam Hashmi) was truly captivating and was instrumental in providing his career with a new lease of life.

Basu Chatterjee's *Manzil*, one of the offbeat films of Bachchan, was a scathing attack on the monopoly practices of Indian business. It showed how the traditional business class uses unfair means to thwart the development of a new class of professional entrepreneurs in the changing corporate environment. The protagonist is a young entrepreneur who, with his optimism and zeal, starts an enterprise dealing in scientific instruments. He represents the ambitious enterprising youth with no family background in business and industry working to succeed as a professional. He thus dreams big and even acts rich to impress his beloved and her parents, who belong to the affluent stratum of society. However, the big shark in the trade buys off the source of Bachchan's technical expertise, the seasoned technician (A. K. Hangal, a respected character actor), resulting in failures to fulfil orders and his inability to ensure the high quality of the instruments. In the climax court scene, the hero is tried for malpractices, but is defended by a socially conscious lawyer (Shreeram Lagoo, another respected character actor). Bachchan, with a rare naturalness and a sense of underplay, negotiated the dilemma of the character: his inability to reconcile his ambitions with the harsh realities of the outside world.

Hrishikesh Mukherjee's *Bemisaal*, like Navketan's 1971 venture *Tere Mere Sapne* (featuring Dev Anand and younger brother Vijay Anand as doctors), explored the issue of medical ethics and the social responsibility of a medical practitioner. A tale interwoven with greed and sacrifice, *Bemisaal* presented Bachchan in the memorable role of a socially conscious doctor, strongly opposed to the commercial mindset of his college-time doctor friend (played by Vinod Mehra) regarding their profession. The friend, who is married to the girl (played by Raakhee), with whom the hero was in love earlier, is obsessed with making big money with scant regard for the ethics of the profession. When a patient dies in an abortion case in his hospital, it is the hero (Bachchan) who takes the rap and goes to jail. Vinod Mehra now realizes his folly and decides to turn a new leaf. The two friends join hands (after the hero's release) to serve the poor.

Yash Chopra's opulently mounted fiim, *Silsila* (1981), which falls into a category of its own and created quite a sensation when it was released, marked a distinct shift of Hindi cinema to the adult terrain (one important predecessor was his elder brother B. R. Chopra's *Gumrah*, 1963). *Silsila* depicted the man–woman relationship in a new, mature perspective. This new formation challenged the traditional conceptions about the mystical and soulful love and the agony and the pining that were the trademarks of the classical film. Celebrated as the liberation of love from the clutches of morality, this film underlined a new kind of 'violence', going all out for self-gratification, far less mentally but more physically, and at the expense of others who just happened to be trapped in the obsession of the two lovers for each other. The plot of the film was rather unusual. Bachchan is a poet deeply in love with Rekha, while his elder brother (Shashi Kapoor), an air force officer, has an affair with another girl (Jaya Bhaduri). As the elder brother dies in the course of war, leaving his beloved pregnant, the hero opts to marry her to save her honour and reputation. Rekha, for her part, marries a doctor (Sanjeev Kumar) but soon the ex-lovers meet as a result of an accident and start their romancing all over again. They cause a great deal of suffering to their respective partners by secretly running away to a hill station, wandering amidst the beauty of nature. They eventually realize the meaninglessness of their passion in their present context. The climax featured high melodrama, in which Bachchan and Sanjeev Kumar come together to save the victims of a serious accident. Incidentally, most of the cinegoers believed that *Silsila* was based on the *real-life* romance between Amitabh Bachchan and Rekha. Two maestros, *santoor* wizard Shiv Kumar Sharma and ace flautist Hariprasad Chaurasia, came together to compose the music for this film as Shiv Hari.

Khuddar (1982), directed by Ravi Tandon, was about the self-respect and pride that the urban poor have despite their intense suffering and agony. The bases for such traits are the virtues of honesty and hard work. Amitabh Bachchan is an illiterate, self-made individual, a taxi driver, who cannot tolerate dishonesty and immoral conduct. Interestingly, as in Ritwik Ghatak's Bengali classic, *Ajantrik* (1957), he is shown having an intimate companionship with his mode for making a living, his taxi, which would even sing a song with him in his lighter moments. The protagonist toils hard to support his younger brother's (Vinod Mehra) education, but the young lad's life falls into the wrong hands; he marries into a rich family and becomes part of a smuggler's empire. In a twist to the tale, the hero is accused of murder. Soon the eldest brother (Sanjeev Kumar), an eminent lawyer, who was separated from his brothers many years ago, enters the scene and saves the hero from being wrongly convicted. In spite of its stereotyped plot, the film had memorable performances by Bachchan and Sanjeev Kumar.

Bachchan's less significant films in the passionate sufferer genre were: *Faraar* (1975) and *Kasme Vaade* (1978).

Director Shankar Mukherjee's *Faraar* (starring Sanjeev Kumar and Sharmila Tagore apart from Bachchan) was a suspense thriller. Bachchan, on the run from the police, takes shelter in a house. Coincidentally, the lady of the house, Sharmila Tagore, happens to be his former lover, but is now married to Sanjeev Kumar, a police officer. (They have a child, who befriends the fugitive.) After a series of dramatic developments, Bachchan is eventually captured. The film, unfortunately, sank without a trace despite noteworthy inputs by the three main actors.

Kasme Vaade (1978), directed by Ramesh Behl, was a critique of the violent nature of society and professed to provide a pacifist approach to the social deviants losing their lives in sadistic occupations. Bachchan plays a college professor who cherishes and propagates high moral conduct. He has a young college-going brother (Randhir Kapoor) who wants to avenge the humiliation meted out to him by a bunch of college toughies by fighting it out. He is regularly admonished by his professor-brother to stay away from such behaviour but to no avail. The professor eventually gets physically involved in a scuffle with the miscreants in an attempt to save his brother and gets killed. His fiancée (Raakhee) is shocked and is unable to get over the trauma. This incident brings the younger brother to his senses and both of them (Raakhee and Randhir Kapoor) decide to move over to another town. Here, they meet the look-alike of the professor, who turns out to be a ruffian. Randhir, with his goodness and patience, takes up the mission of reforming the hooligan and persuades Raakhee to forget the past and consider this man for matrimony.

In contrast with the aforementioned films, our hero's five films in this genre – *Pyar Ki Kahani* (1971), *Raaste Ka Pathar* (1972), *Sanjog* (1971), *Kasauti* (1974) and *Ganga Jamuna Saraswati* (1988) – hardly made any impact aesthetically or commercially.

In *Pyar Ki Kahani*, directed by Ravikant Nagaich, the new actor appeared to be experimenting with his screen image. This time he is a lover charmed by the idiosyncrasies of the tomboyish heroine (Tanuja) who is also being passionately loved by his bosom friend (Anil Dhawan). Although Bachchan gave a fairly good account of himself, he failed largely in highlighting the comic content in his role. *Raaste Ka Pathar* (directed by Mukul Dutt) was about the first-hand exposure of a common man – an ordinary employee in a ruthlessly managed advertising firm headed by the villain Prem Chopra – to the sleazy world of crime. Bachchan is an innocent man, who inadvertently gets trapped in the ugly environment of deceit and intrigue. As he uncovers the nefarious activities of the 'bad boys', he becomes a stumbling block in their game plan. However, being the hero, he finally brings all of them to book.

Gemini's *Sanjog* (a remake of the Tamil film *Iru Kodugal* and directed by S. S. Balan) presented Bachchan in a typical role of a young man inexorably caught up in the ups and downs of life and the resultant uncertainties. The story is essentially about a fairly well-to-do young man marrying a poor girl (Mala Sinha) and their eventual separation caused by the evil designs of his status-conscious mother. Mala Sinha stakes her independence and soon becomes a highly placed bureaucrat, whereas the hero's family suddenly sinks into poverty and he lands up as a subordinate in his ex-wife's office.

Kasauti, directed by Arvind Sen, a somewhat contrived drama, tended to undermine the persona of Bachchan during this period. He plays an educated taxi driver struggling for survival in the big city but is shown more as the conventional romantic film hero. He is in love with the slum-dwelling, but glamorous, heroine (Hema Malini) who gets involved with a gang of smugglers. They get temporarily separated when the heroine becomes a famous stage actress before her final happy reunion with the hero. The saving grace of *Kasauti* was villain-turned-character actor Pran, who stole the show in the unforgettable role of a Gurkha.

In *Ganga Jamuna Saraswati*, director Manmohan Desai took up a multiple love theme instead of his usual 'family-members-being-separated' concoctions. He wove his story around the popular Indian myth about three sacred rivers (as per the film title). Ganga (Amitabh Bachchan), a truck driver, and Jamuna (Meenakshi Sheshadri), a local belle, are in love with each other, while Saraswati (Jaya Prada), a nautch girl, is obsessed with Ganga. Ganga and Jamuna marry, are separated temporarily and finally rejoin, while Saraswati dies, disappearing (like the mythical river) as a symbol of unfulfilled love.

Manmohan Desai

Manmohan Desai (26 February 1934 to 1 March 1994), the pioneer of masala spectacles in Hindi cinema of the 1970s, belonged to a family of film makers. His father, Kikubhai Desai, was the founder of Paramount Studio and elder brother Subhash Desai was a producer. He started as assistant director to Babubhai Mistri in the late 1950s. The first film he directed independently was *Chhalia* (1960), starring Raj Kapoor and Nutan. In the 1960s, he continued making run-of-the mill musical romances relying largely on the Elvis Presley model evolved by Subodh Mukerji and Nasir Hussain using Shammi Kapoor (*Bluff Master*, 1963, and *Badtameez*, 1966) and also Biswajeet (*Kismet*, 1968). In the 1970s, Desai started making films with good-bad dual roles and used the lost-and-found genre extensively with Rajesh Khanna (*Sachcha Jhootha*, 1970), Jeetendra and Shatrughan Sinha (*Bhai Ho To Aisa*, 1972) and Dharmendra and Randhir Kapoor (*Chacha Bhatija*, 1977). In *Roti* (1974), he even attempted to portray Rajesh Khanna as an angry young man.

The turning point in Desai's career was the 1977 mega-hit *Amar Akbar Anthony*, which placed him among the leading directors of the 1970s. With this film and later *Parvarish*, *Suhaag*, *Naseeb*, *Coolie* and *Mard*, he led Bachchan into a cinema which was as meaningless as it was entertaining. In contrast with other Bachchan directors, Desai presented the actor's persona as a kind of street show of lumpen power. In most of Desai's films, the urban hero's aggressiveness is more diffused and less targeted and he is more of an earthy humorist than an angry crusader.

His Major Films

Chhalia (1960), *Bluff Master* (1963), *Badtameez* (1966), *Kismet* (1968), *Sahcha Jhootha* (1970), *Bhai Ho To Aisa* (1972), *Rampur Ka Lakshman* (1972), *Shararat* (1972), *Aa Gale Lag Jaa* (1973), *Roti* (1974), *Amar Akbar Anthony* (1977), *Chacha Bhatija* (1977), *Dharam Veer* (1977), *Parvarish* (1977), *Suhaag* (1979), *Naseeb* (1981), *Desh Premi* (1982), *Coolie* (1983), *Mard* (1985) and *Ganga Jamuna Saraswati* (1988).

The Angry Man as the Individual Dispenser of Justice

Amitabh Bachchan could have easily got typecast in films of the foregoing category, and might have even faded into oblivion. However, the actor soon broke this mould and began to play a historic role in bringing about a complete transformation of the dominant concerns of Hindi cinema, especially with reference to its social context and its impact.

Such a transformation was evidently facilitated by the singular influence of Dilip Kumar's cinema on Bachchan's screen persona, resulting in the metamorphosis of his image from the unglamorous, passionate sufferer to the powerful, melodramatic anti-hero reincarnation – he became 'the angry young man'. This image very soon superimposed itself on the collective imagination of the masses with unprecedented rapidity and force. In fact, it was this makeover that provided a new lease of life to Bachchan in the film world. By donning the mantle of the traditional angry rebel, the *baghi* – from the feudal rural boondocks to the urban setting – the young incumbent took up Dilip Kumar's style with renewed energy and imagination and reinterpreted it in the light of the swiftly changing socio-political milieu. However, the remarkable success of Bachchan's angry cinema (which undermined all other themes for the time being) had deeper reasons. Like the cinema of Dilip Kumar, that of Bachchan had also its own social basis, which influenced its content, style and mass appeal.

During this transformation of Bachchan's image, Hindi cinema itself was struggling to come out of its thematic stagnation. The redemption came from an entirely unexpected quarter. A pair of non-conformist scriptwriters – Salim Khan and Javed Akhtar – entered the scene and came up with a significant breakthrough for the Hindi film. They modulated their creativity keeping in mind the socio-political realities of those times (early to mid-1970s). And their highly innovative ideas worked. Indian cinema was to be largely resurrected by the imaginative work of the duo. In developing their paradigm, Salim-Javed were evidently inspired by the films of the earlier decades and by international cinema, mainly Hollywood. The two scriptwriters as well as the producers who bought their scripts were set to strike gold.

Salim-Javed basically focused on of the growing popular discontent and disillusionment among the masses and the failure of the state apparatus in ensuring their welfare and well-being. Prices were swiftly spiralling upwards. Even essential commodities became scarce. Public institutions were being stripped of their legitimacy and smugglers and gangsters with political patronage seemed to call the shots. The only options left were either for the individual to fight against the system or for the people to launch a collective struggle. The two writers, who emerged as the new ideologues of Indian cinema, worked out the design of a vigilante people's hero, a superman-incarnate who would wage war against all kinds of atrocities, injustice and discrimination.

Salim-Javed identified three essential inputs for their new mission:

- A new generation of directors who had acquired a high degree of specialization in making wholesome formula films, but were willing to experiment with new themes;
- various success points such as plots, scenes, characterizations and dialogues from the classical era films; and
- an actor who could establish in his portrayals an emotional identity with the audience as the first indigenous hero – Dilip Kumar – of the classical period had done earlier.

Amitabh Bachchan, who happened to be the right man in the right place at the right time, spearheaded the new trend by effectively utilizing the opportunities on hand. Salim-Javed thus became the main instruments in building up a new image for this new volcano of talent.

The 'Bachchan methodology' adopted by Salim-Javed for developing the new indigenous hero was based on a set of well-designed strategies:

- An extreme sense of social vulnerability as a child; the hero is often an orphan or becomes one.
- A feeling of personal invulnerability; the hero is a symbol of complete omnipotence (like mythological giants) possessing immense physical strength, great intelligence and masterly techniques to eliminate the all-encompassing evil forces that are destroying society.
- A stereotype rags-to-riches story for the hero, who often succeeds in achieving pelf and power through unfair means not approved by law or society.
- The protagonist's complete lack of faith in the state's law-and-order apparatus as well as in the legal system.

This methodology repositioned the typical melodrama associated with Hindi cinema around the rebel-vigilante hero, caught in the triangular clash among the traditional family kinship, the law of the state and the anti-people forces. The hero, who dons the mantle of the outlaw, defined for himself a higher moral order above the family (representing obedience and conformity) and the state machinery (responsible citizenship) in order to avenge all the wrongs and injustices.

Salim Khan and Javed Akhtar

Salim Khan and Javed Akhtar, the creators of Bachchan's angry young man persona, represent the most successful script writer duo in Indian cinema. Javed Akhtar, born on 17 January 1945 in Gwalior, began his career in cinema in the 1960s as a small-time dialogue writer in films like S. M. Sagar's *Sarhadi Lutera* (1966).

Salim Khan (the father of macho hero Salman Khan) came into prominence as a scenarist with the Rajesh Khanna starrer *Haathi Mere Saathi* (1971). The first time the two teamed up was for writing the dialogues for Ramesh Sippy's

1972 hit *Seeta Aur Geeta* (the film is often referred as the petticoat version of *Ram Aur Shyam*). Nasir Hussain's hit *Yaadon Ki Baraat* (1973) announced their arrival in cinema.

Salim-Javed set the trend of vigilante cinema with Prakash Mehra's *Zanjeer* in the same year, quickly followed by *Deewar* (1975), *Sholay* (1975), *Don* (1978) and *Trishul* (1978). However, the two separated in the 1980s with each becoming an independent scenarist.

Bachchan's cinema in this genre brought about a qualitative change in the way this medium depicted society, thereby redefining the social context of a commercial film. Building its narration around the all-powerful hero as the pivot, this cinema created an overwhelming spectacle for the audiences, which made them a part of a much-desired crusade of vengeance against the highly oppressive forces, which appeared to be in total control of society. In this process, the introvert Bachchan of the earlier phase got radically transformed into the extrovert, the enraged campaigner, who would funnel all his pent-up anger into a sharply focused sudden surge of energy to destroy all manifestations of social and political evil and its practitioners.

The new paradigm and its methodology introduced, for the first time in Hindi cinema, a cold-blooded full-blown brand of violence, going several steps beyond the anger and the disquiet of the earlier period. This cinema, in sharp contrast with the slick crime thrillers of Navketan (which invariably depicted the handling of crime within the legal and normative parameters), challenged the state apparatus and gave a kind of social sanctity to the dissemination of justice through an individualized form of vendetta. This new form of highly romanticized radicalism being dispensed within the urban context (different from that articulated through the traditional dacoit in the rural context) indeed flew in the face of the so-called traditional Indian philosophy of *Panchsheel* – non-violence, tolerance, respect for others, cooperation and peaceful co-existence – which the earlier cinema was communicating to its audience.

One point worth noting is that the design of the clash between the vigilante hero and the forces of evil and the formation of the new image were not totally original. They were derived from the archetype of the militant, self-proclaimed liberator of *Mother India* (1957) and *Ganga Jumna* (1961). Bachchan's angry young man was no different, except that his cinema provided a powerful and potent political language to the same old plot on which most of Indian films had been based. Dharmendra, for instance, had already played 'the angry man' in the urban milieu with commendable skill in *Phool Aur Patthar* (1966).

The public acceptance of this new paradigm construct was announced in 1973 with the supersuccess of the first prototype of the angry cinema – *Zanjeer* (meaning chain). This film was produced and directed by Prakash Mehra, who started as an assistant director and a lyricist, formally launching Amitabh Bachchan as the vigilante hero. The narrative is built around the transformation of an honest police officer into a self-proclaimed upholder of justice who would not accept anything wrong. As a child, the protagonist Vijay has witnessed the murder of his parents by an individual wearing a chain with a white horse around his wrist, but whose face has been hidden. Haunted by the image of the chain, the adult Vijay (Bachchan) becomes a police officer determined to clean up the Bombay underworld. Although reluctantly involved with Mala (Jaya Bhaduri), a roadside knife sharpener, Vijay single-mindedly destroys all evil-doers and finally identifies his parents' killer Teja (Ajit), an embodiment of sinister wickedness. Taking the law into his own hands he avenges the murders. In his mission, Vijay is assisted by the Pathan Sher Khan (played by Pran to perfection), with whom he initially has a dramatic confrontation – one of the highlights of the film. Salim-Javed's pithy dialogues, delivered with a great deal of panache by the new hero, had the audiences cheering wildly. *Zanjeer* stands out as a milestone in Hindi cinema.

Zanjeer: Crime Drama that Pricks Conscience

Zanjeer ... comes up with an unusual hero for the Hindi screen – a police officer with a chip on his shoulder and a bee in his bonnet.

Vijay (Amitabh Bachchan), the young officer in question, is no ordinary pinion in the law enforcement machine. He is an overaggressive man whose nervous system tenses up at the mere sight of criminals and suspected criminals.

In dealing with the criminal world he is inclined to overstep the boundaries of legitimate official conduct, an inclination which has brought him nearly a dozen transfers during his six years of police service. The officer's abnormal trait the film suggests is related to a childhood trauma – the witnessing of the simultaneous murder of both of his parents at the hands of a gangster.

It is essentially a crime drama that the film presents but what distinguishes it from routine exercises in the genre is among other things a dash of sincere concern for innocent victims to criminal violence. The familiar attitude of apathy, which drives many to prefer a conveniently bind eye to a nagging conscience also comes in for passionate denunciation ...

As the easily combustible hero Amitabh suffuses the character with the dark fury of a man in the grip of an explosive obsession. He gives a powerful performance not foreshadowed by his earlier films ...

Source: *The Times of India*, 12 May 1973.

Prakash Mehra

Prakash Mehra, born on 13 July 1939, in Bijnaur, Uttar Pradesh, started in films as an assistant to Dhirubhai Desai at Vishnu Cinetone in the late 1950s. After working as a lesser known lyricist in the 1960s, he made his directorial debut in 1968 with *Haseena Maan Jayegi* (in which Shashi Kapoor played a double role). He continued making some run-of-the-mill films till the instant success of *Zanjeer* (1973) brought him among the top directors of Hindi cinema. He directed as many as seven Bachchan films including superhits *Muqaddar Ka Sikandar* (1978), *Lawaris* (1981) and *Namak Halal* (1982). He passed away on 17 May 2009.

Select Filmography

Haseena Maan Jayegi (1968), *Mela* (1971), *Aan Ban* (1972), *Samadhi* (1972), *Ek Kunwari Ek Kunwara* (1973), *Zanjeer* (1973), *Haath Ki Safai* (1974), *Hera Pheri* (1976), *Khalifa* (1976), *Aakhri Daku* (1978), *Muqaddar Ka Sikandar,* (1978), *Desh Drohee* (1980), *Jwalamukhi* (1980), *Lawaris* (1981), *Namak Halal* (1982), *Sharabi* (1984), *Muqaddar Ka Faisla* (1987), *Mohabbat Ke Dushman* (1988), *Jaadugar* (1989), *Zindagi Ek Jua* (1992) and *Bal Brahmachari* (1996).

Apart from *Zanjeer*, the other five most significant films, which became the building blocks for the persona of Amitabh Bachchan over the years as the vigilante anti-hero, were *Roti, Kapda Aur Makaan* (1974), *Deewar* (1975), *Adalat* (1977), *Aakhri Raasta* (1986) and *Agneepath* (1990).

In Manoj Kumar's *Roti, Kapda Aur Makaan*, although Bachchan appeared in a supporting role, it laid the basic design parameters for another aspect of the actor's persona – a contemporary, unemployed, frustrated youth, who, when given an opportunity, would direct his built-up anger against the villainous rich who are playing havoc with the lives of ordinary people.

Deewar, directed by Yash Chopra, was a rework of *Ganga Jumna* with the narrative now set in a metropolitan milieu.

Yash Chopra

Yash Chopra (born on 27 September 1932), who directed quite a few of Amitabh Bachchan's films and helped the star in many ways to acquire his screen persona, was a product of the classical era. He started as assistant to elder brother B. R. Chopra. He made his directorial debut with *Dhool Ka Phool* (1959) under the B R Films banner and made other important films for the company including the classic *Dharamputra* (1961, based on the novel by Chatursen Shastri) and *Waqt* (1965). He set up his own company in 1973, the first film being the Rajesh Khanna starrer, *Daag* (1973). Although he has largely been preoccupied with upper-class love stories involving triangles and even quadrangles, the real turnaround in his career was *Deewar*. This film and others in this genre – *Trishul*, *Kala Patthar* and the Dilip Kumar starrer, *Mashaal* – once again introduced a strong social orientation to his cinema. In the early 1990s, Yash Chopra used his style for grooming the screen image of Shahrukh Khan as the disllusioned sufferer in love as in *Darr* (1993).

Select Filmography (as director)

Dhool Ka Phool (1959), *Dharamputra* (1961), *Waqt* (1965), *Aadmi Aur Insaan* (1969), *Ittefaq* (1959), *Daag* (1973), *Joshila* (1973), *Deewar* (1975), *Kabhi Kabhie* (1976), *Trishul* (1978), *Kala Patthar* (1979), *Silsila* (1981), *Mashaal* (1984), *Faasle* (1985), *Vijay* (1988), *Chandni* (1989), *Lamhe* (1991), *Parampara* (1992), *Darr* (1993), *Dil To Pagal Hai* (1997), *Mohabaatein* (2000) and *Veer Zaara* (2004).

In *Deewar*, Vijay (Amitabh Bachchan), the elder brother, puts in tremendous physical effort, initially as a shoeshine boy and later as a coolie in the Bombay harbour and is subjected to a lot of humiliation by the rich and mighty. His aim is to ensure that his younger brother Ravi (Shashi Kapoor) gets a good education. Helpless and angered by the prevailing social inequities, Vijay joins a dockyard gang of smugglers and soon becomes their leader. As he is about to marry his pregnant lover, a club dancer (played by Parveen Babi), also alone in the alien metropolis, she is murdered by his rival gang. He now becomes a ruthless vigilante. Through its saga of rags-to-riches story (apparently inspired by Bombay underworld don Haji Mastan's life), the film humanizes its protagonist and thus puts the stamp of respectability on the high-flying smuggling icon (the same way the media built up conman Charles Sobraj's image). Such respectability is far more than that given to the poor rural rebel, who later becomes the stereotype dacoit in Hindi cinema. As in *Ganga Jumna*, Vijay is finally shot by his brother who is an honest police officer. Again, Salim-Javed worked their trademark magic, and *Deewar* became a landmark film.

Narendra Bedi's *Adalat*, made two years after *Deewar*, firmly established three key features of Amitabh Bachchan's cinema, which were to largely govern the thrust of his films and characterizations in the coming years:

- the typical father–son conflict over values and attitudes;
- the actor's versatility and abilities exploited by film makers to cast him in double and triple roles; and
- the narrowing of the anti-establishment stance from the larger social context to merely destroying the sadist villain who has wronged his family members.

The story of *Adalat* was about the transformation of an honest and hard-working poor farm hand into a powerful mafia don, who

makes it big in Bombay. Dharma (Bachchan) leads a hand-to-
mouth existence in a village with his wife (Waheeda Rehman),
younger sister (Heena Kauser) and newborn son. Nevertheless,
despite the meagre income, the family is relatively content. As
the conditions in their village worsen due to a long drought,
Dharma takes up the job of supervisor in a factory in Bombay
owned by three brothers. When a police raid reveals that the
factory is a cover for drug- and gold-smuggling operations,
Dharma is arrested and sentenced to serve a term in jail. His wife
starts working as a maidservant and his sister ends up a victim
of rape by one of the villainous brothers. On his release from jail,
a vengeful Dharma sets up his own underworld empire and begins
his vendetta against the three brothers. Soon he enters into a
conflict with his now grown-up son (also played by Amitabh
Bachchan), who rebels against his father's unlawful deeds and
lifestyle. Bachchan, as the father exhibits immense ability in
underplay, internalizing his trauma, contrasted ably with the son
who is jovial, often comic, and goodhearted. The film, however,
failed to project cogently the vengeful mood of the angry young
man of *Zanjeer*, *Deewar* and later *Trishul* (1978).

Aakhri Raasta (1986, directed by K. Bhagyaraj), which
presented Amitabh Bachchan in a double role, as father and son,
was one of the most realistic treatments of the vengeful crusade
of a wronged man. With a great sense of underplay to express
the undercurrents of stabilized anger building up in the human
mind over the years, the actor virtually single-handedly infused
life into a movie consisting of the usual elements of crime and
punishment.

The protagonist, a simple-hearted, dedicated party worker
is deceived by his mentor, the politician (played by Sadashiv
Amrapurkar), who rapes his wife (played by Jaya Prada). The
politician has two other supporters (a crooked police officer
and an unscrupulous doctor). She dies and the worker is
implicated for her murder and sent to prison. Their son, who is
brought up by the jailed man's bosom friend (played by Anupam

Kher), becomes a police officer. After his release from jail (where he spends many years), the aged protagonist coolheadedly designs three different foolproof plots to kill one by one those who had destroyed his life. The upright son follows the course of law to arrest his killer-father. The film had an obvious resemblance to the Dilip Kumar starrer *Duniya* (1984), but Bachchan managed to surpass the senior actor in depicting the agony of a ruined man.

Bachchan's cinema depicting him as a vigilante hero came to a conclusive end by taking sadism to unprecedented heights with *Agneepath* (1990), directed by Mukul Anand. This movie exemplified a complete 'Hollywoodization' of Indian crime films with the overworked and less convincing one-man army as the agency. *Agneepath* (path of fire), which took its title as well as the inspiration from a poem by Harivanshrai Bachchan, Amitabh's father, showed that man's emancipation from the brutalized world is only possible when he traverses the 'path of fire' and then attains 'liberation'. The film, very much different from others in this genre in its treatment of the subject, portrays innocence (represented by the hero's simple schoolmaster father, mother and foster-brother, who live in a village) juxtaposed with widespread social brutality (villagers lynch the hero's father, who has been falsely implicated in a scandal). The hero seeks to avenge this killing. He himself becomes a gangster and is pitted against the villain (Danny Denzongpa), who had instigated the villagers to kill Bachchan's father.

In *Agneepath*, Amitabh Bachchan appears as Vijay Chauhan aka 'Bhai'. In various scenes showing the the hero's protracted battle (marked by some grisly scenes) with the brutal don and his minions, Bachchan has captured successfully the 'fire' metaphor. He looked more at ease with himself in *Agneepath* than in his earlier films. The crowning glory of *Agneepath*, however, was a memorable performance by Mithun Chakraborty in the role of a South Indian foster-brother (a serious but equally impressive version of Mehmood's comic role in *Padosan*, 1968).

Mukul Anand

Mukul Sudheshwar Anand (11 October 1951 to 7 September 1997), the designer of Amitabh Bachchan's comeback vehicles in the early 1990s (*Agneepath*, *Hum* and *Khuda Gawah*), represented – along with Ramesh Sippy, Subhash Ghai and Mehul Kumar – the new generation of young film makers in the post-classical cinema. Son of a chartered accountant and nephew of famous scenarist and film maker Inder Raj Anand, he started as an assistant to Chetan Anand and Ravi Tandon. He made his directorial debut in 1984 with *Kanoon Kya Karega*, based on J. Lee Thompson's *Cape Fear* (1962), followed by *Aitbaar* (1985), 'inspired' by Alfred Hitchcock's 1954 thriller *Dial M for Murder*. The success of big-budget films like *Sultanant* and *Insaaf* in the 1980s helped him gain his place among the top directors. In his cinema, Mukul Anand attempted a reproduction of Hollywood's crime genre in its spirit, scale and style, and far more than his many camp followers, his films carried a highly disturbing infusion of blood, gore and sex.

Filmography

Kanoon Kya Karega (1984), *Aitbaar* (1985), *Maa Ki Saugandh* (1986), *Main Balwan* (1986), *Sultanat* (1986), *Insaaf* (1987), *Mahasangram* (1988), *Agneepath* (1990), *Hum* (1991), *Khoon Ka Karz* (1991) and *Khuda Gawah* (1992).

In Bachchan's repertoire, the less significant films (as compared to those discussed above), which projected the angry man as the ultimate dispenser of justice were: *Trishul* (1978), *Andha Kanoon* (1983), *Giraftaar* (1985), *Hum* (1991) and *Khuda Gawah* (1992).

Trishul, scripted by Salim-Javed, and directed by Yash Chopra, saw Amitabh Bachchan in a very similar role to *Deewar*. Here again, the protagonist is obsessed with his mother (Waheeda Rehman), who has been abandoned by his father, played by Sanjeev Kumar, who goes on to become a construction company magnate. Sanjeev Kumar marries a girl from an affluent family and inherits a fortune. The hero, in league with his father's competitors, takes revenge on his parent by separating him from his family and bringing him to the brink of financial ruin. After a series of dramatic sequences, eventually a family patch-up takes place. Forceful dialogues and superb screenplay made watching *Trishul* a unique experience.

In *Andha Kanoon* (directed by T. Rama Rao), Bachchan articulated his anti-establishment stance at a more complex level – an upholder of the law getting disillusioned with the very law enforcement system of which he is a part. His rejection of the system is triggered off when his wife is raped by a gang of criminals who then murder her and their child. The pro-establishment point of view is upheld by the heroine (Hema Malini), a police officer, who strongly believes in the sanctity of the system. Interestingly, the hero is a loner and mostly fights his battles alone. The South Indian superstar Rajnikanth (real name Shivaji Rao Gaekwad) also played a significant role in this movie as Hema Malini's brother.

Giraftaar (directed by Prayag Raj), another addition to lost-and-found melodrama involving three brothers, repeated the Bachchan stereotype. He is a small-time criminal who meets his lost youngest brother (played by another South Indian hero, Kamalahasan) in jail. The third brother (Rajnikanth) is an honest police inspector and finally they collectively come up with a scheme to corner the villain. The wronged-mother syndrome is also conveniently included to bolster the stereotype. However, the film took up an interesting subject as a subplot – the extreme inequalities prevalent among the people working in the film world. Kamalahasan, film stuntman, protests to the producer when paid a meagre amount for enacting dangerous scenes, demanding that he be treated on par with the hero.

Mukul Anand's *Hum*[1] was set against the backdrop of exploitation of dockyard workers of Bombay by the local mafia. Going beyond the concerns of *Deewar*, it intended to show the impregnable nexus among the dons, the police and the lumpen class. Bachchan this time is a true lumpen to begin with, in the role of Tiger, who lives by collecting petty protection money from the workers. He abandons his friend, the workers' leader (Romesh Sharma), when the latter leads them against the chief villain (Danny Denzongpa). Finally, he realizes his folly and the hero and his two brothers (Rajnikanth and Govinda) team up to annihilate in quick succession the various villains who represent anti-national and anti-worker forces.

Khuda Gawah, directed again by Mukul Anand, was a complicated tale narrated with tribal Afghanistan as the background. Essentially, the film presented Bachchan as the traditional vengeful but simple-hearted Pathan, Badshah Khan, who would die for the honour of his kin. He leaves his home and comes to India to avenge the killing of his wife's (Sridevi) father but is jailed for the murder of a policeman, for which he is not responsible. On his release, the aged Pathan returns but is unable to reconcile with the victimization he has to face. His daughter (also played by Sridevi), whom he has never seen, helps him overcome his painful past. Finally, he takes his revenge against the villain, a narcotics lord, with the help of two young committed police officers.

The least significant films in this category, which marked the diminishing stature of the angry man, were: *Besharam* (1978), *Kaalia* (1981), *Mahan* (1983), *Coolie* (1983), *Indrajeet* (1991), *Mrityudaata* (1997) and *Lal Badshah* (1999).

Devan Verma's *Besharam* was another run-off-the-mill addition to the long series of vigilante films of Bachchan. In this moth-eaten venture, he off starts as a righteous young man who takes up arms against the lord of the underworld (Amjad Khan) to avenge the death of his kith and kin.

In *Kaalia* (directed by Tinnu Anand) Bachchan once again

took up the heroic transformation from a meek lower middle-class youth Kallu into an elegantly dressed and street-smart vengeful crusader now called Kaalia. The turning point in this transformation is the death of his brother, a trade union leader, who is murdered despite the hero's appeals for mercy to the hard-hearted villain, the head of a smuggler-industrialist syndicate. He takes on a horde of underworld gangsters as well as the country's elaborate police force. After being jailed, he clashes with the prison authorities led by the jailer played by Pran. He eventually flees from jail and traps the villain. Bachchan carries off his role with his usual panache but with much less impact than before.

Mahan (directed by S. Ramanathan), yet another lacklustre lost-and-found drama, presented the actor in a triple role. As in many other films, the enmity of the father with the villain leads to the separation of the family. The father goes over to Nepal and becomes a rich businessman, while one son becomes a policeman and lives with the mother and the other son, brought up by dotting foster parents, is an aspiring theatre actor. Finally, the police officer, while investigating cross-border smuggling, reaches out to his father and the narrative brings in the rituals of the family reunion and the punishing of the guilty. The triple roles were earlier played by Raj Kumar (different from Hindi cinema's Raaj Kumar) in the Kannada original, *Shankar Guru* (1978) and by Sivaji Ganesan in the Tamil version, *Tirisulam* (1979).

Coolie, along with its successors *Inquilab* (1984) and *Shahenshah* (1988), marked a big quantitative leap in the bloodshed-and-gore depiction in Bachchan's portrayal of the superhero, which reached its finale later in *Agneepath*. The protagonist, to begin with, is a jovial railway coolie whose mythical status as the platform hero is highlighted by his pet, the menacing falcon riding on his arm. He becomes a natural leader of his fellow workers, takes a dig at the vulgarities of the rich and finally wages a vengeful war against the villainous gangs. In the process, he finds his long-lost mother (played by Waheeda Rehman). It was on the sets of *Coolie* that Amitabh Bachchan suffered a near-fatal injury. Fortunately, he bounced back with fresh vigour after recovery.

Indrajeet (directed by K. V. Raju) was virtually *Zanjeer* revisited, with the vengeful drama spread over two generations. This time the narrative is built around the business–police–politics crime nexus. The vigilante hero, whose father has been murdered by powerful villains when he was a child, joins the police establishment to disseminate justice and take care of the helpless people. He sacrifices his love (Jaya Prada) for his convictions and remains single to bring up the orphaned daughter of a trade union leader who has been killed by goons hired by the factory owner. When his only emotional link, his foster daughter, is molested and killed by a group of rowdies belonging to rich families, the hero, who has by now become old, takes up his vigilante avatar and carries out his act of revenge. Bachchan in this stereotyped role looks rather fatigued and rundown.

Mrityudaata (directed by Mehul Kumar) added a new dimension to the genre of chilling sadism in Bachchan's cinema. The sheer magnitude of its violent content seemed to show that, in a highly dehumanized society, human life is far less real than the ever-hovering shadow of death. The extremely unimaginative tale was about the misfortunes of a famous and highly respected surgeon, Ram, who has become an alcoholic because his brother has been killed by the sadist villain. The surgeon turns avenger and finally burns the villain alive on a burning pyre, indicating, through unconvincingly, that the supreme life-saver can also become the most cruel life-taker if one dares to tread wrongly in his scheme of things. Bachchan looked desperate in his attempts to evoke his trademark mannerisms from the 1984 hit film *Sharabi* (discussed later) and other films and to rejuvenate his dying charisma. The film also made references to contemporary issues like the Enron power project fiasco and the fodder scam (involving the former chief minister of Bihar, Laloo Prasad Yadav), but without making much of an impact.

In K. C. Bokadia's *Lal Badshah*, the actor made a desperate attempt to revitalize the magic of his angry young man image. He appears once again in a double role of father and son. The son, Lal Badshah, grows up as the vengeful crusader for justice after seeing his humble father and mother (Nirupa Roy) being wronged by the powerful don (Amrish Puri), who has perpetuated a reign of terror among the local people. Bachchan once again employs his celebrated Poorabiya (eastern Uttar Pradesh) accent to regenerate his trademark humour. However, the film's weak script and the stereotyped treatment of the protagonist failed to lend any feel of authenticity to the reconstruction of the rebel's persona.

The Angry Man as the Self-proclaimed Liberator

Driven by growing disillusionment with his social position, Bachchan's angry man also trod another path. Apart from internalizing the wrongs inflicted on him, the protagonist, through an introspection of his experiences, would proceed to relate his frustration with the social reality around him. As he gains political consciousness, he would immediately focus his energies to bring about, single-handedly, a radical change for the wider social good. The birth of this mythical revolutionary on celluloid was significantly depicted in *Khoon Pasina* (1977), *Ganga Ki Saugandh* (1978), *Main Azaad Hoon* (1989), *Aaj Ka Arjun* (1990) and *Ajooba* (1991).

   Khoon Pasina (directed by Rakesh Kumar), in its basic design, drew in many main elements of Bachchan's standardized formula – a street-smart hooligan becoming socially conscious and emerging as the people's hero, a wronged mother (Nirupa Roy, this time foster) trying to rein in her deviant son, her real son (Vinod Khanna) lost in childhood and the message of Hindu–Muslim togetherness as depicted by the poor (irrespective of their religion) facing oppression perpetuated by a lecherous villain (Kadar Khan) and his minions. Set amidst the exploitative environment of a tree plantation, the film presented Bachchan as a mythical hero (Shiva) with a pro-poor stance, who is being pursued by another mythical figure Shera (Vinod Khanna) at the behest of a feudal lord. Moved by the plight of the plantation workers, the hero takes up a crusade against the feudal lord and, with the help of Shera, overpowers the villain who had also killed their respective fathers, Ram and Rahim, in their childhood. Bachchan's standard comic antics and compulsive violent disposition were very ably juxtaposed with the characteristic confident underplay of Vinod Khanna.

Sultan Ahmed's *Ganga Ki Saugandh* attempted to reconstruct the formation of the rebel (*baghi*) in Indian cinema by transporting Bachchan's vigilante urban hero to a rural setting. The protagonist is a rustic rural youth who swears vengeance in the name of Ganga Maiyya (Mother Ganges), after his mother has been humiliated and killed, and becomes an outlaw. His mission is to destroy a lascivious zamindar's son (Amjad Khan) who has been playing havoc with the lives of the harassed villagers. Some scenes, mainly those showing the exodus of people, were reminiscent of Raj Kapoor's *Jis Desh Mein Ganga Behti Hain* (1960).

Main Azaad Hoon, directed by Tinnu Anand and scripted by Javed Akhtar, was one of the near-realist films of Bachchan. This venture presented him as the people's hero in letter and spirit. Taking a firm stand against the hypocrisy of the self-styled progressives and political activists as its theme, the film was about the creation of a mythical character, 'Azaad', representing the common man's aspirations for an equitable and caring social order. In the whole narrative, the protagonist moves as if in a dream – seeking an unattainable political consciousness while being caught in the mire of political opportunism.

Azaad is an aimless wanderer, who is promoted by a group of commercially minded journalists (with the major contribution made by the heroine Shabana Azmi) as a mass leader. They do so at the behest of a politician in order to win the political support of the people. Azaad, on the basis of his idealism, leads a successful combined struggle waged by the industrial workers and the farmers against the powerful nexus between the politicians' lobby and the industrialists' lobby. When he becomes popular and a symbol of people's unity, his own mentors now want to eliminate him from the scene. He is accused of being an impostor and not the real Azaad so that his own people become his enemies (as happened to the people's poet Guru Dutt in *Pyaasa*, 1957, and to Dilip Kumar in *Sagina*, 1974). Azaad, in order to validate his truthfulness, finally jumps from a building to his death. In the memorable climax, people gather in a big stadium to listen to their hero where his last message is played on a large video screen and the visibly moved audience members spontaneously raise their hands to salute the martyr.

Devoid of songs (except for one chorus number), dances and unnecessary comedy elements, Bachchan's memorable performance was marked by excellent underplay and a poignant melancholy, which led to a powerful emotional catharsis in many touching scenes in the film. However, the uneven pace of the narrative and unimaginative camera work weakened the overall impact of the work. Moreover, the protagonist donning a long overcoat throughout the movie looked misplaced in the hot and dusty Indian environment. He looked more like a character in an English film set in a cold climate.

In K. C. Bokadia's maiden directorial venture, *Aaj Ka Arjun*, Bachchan stuck to his conventional image – a simple villager self-transformed by the fire of revenge into a city-slick crusader against the perpetrators of evil. The transformation this time takes place after the hero's sister is duped by the local exploiters, triggering his emergence as the natural leader of the suffering peasants. Bachchan's comedy looked tedious in the first half of the film but he managed to regain his usual élan as the people's hero in the second half. The film had a strong cinematic resemblance with Anil Sharma's *Hukumat* (1987, with Dharmendra in the lead) and Manmohan Desai's *Ganga Jamuna Saraswati* (1988).

Shashi Kapoor's directorial venture, *Ajooba*, was a rare experiment in Hindi cinema in that it was a film for children with a big star cast. It followed the archetypal plot of a fairy tale: a good king (Shammi Kapoor) is deposed by an evil *wazir* or minister (Amrish Puri). The main hero (Bachchan), in the title role as Ajooba, like Zorro, appears as the saviour of the masses. The heroine (Dimple Kapadia) wants to rescue her father from jail. The second hero (Rishi Kapoor) is a loverboy for whom the princess (Sonam) defies her father the *wazir*. Also, the film focuses on the queen, who is reduced to begging in her own kingdom. It is inevitably Ajooba who sets things right for everybody. The film, however, largely failed to help Bachchan in making an impact in the realm of fantasy films.

The less significant films in the 'engineered transformation' genre were *Mr Natwarlal* (1979), *Kala Patthar* (1979), *Pukar* (1983) and *Mard* (1985).

Directed by Rakesh Kumar, *Mr Natwarlal* took Bachchan once again on a trip of wishful vengeance, this time to a far-flung mountainous area, with beautiful landscapes, but whose inhabitants were reeling under the terror unleashed by the local feudal tyrant (Amjad Khan). And once again, the agenda of personal vendetta was suitably superimposed over the pro-poor stance of the omnipotent hero. The only relief in the film was the excellent comedy rendered by the actor, particularly the hilarious song he sings (in his own voice) for the village children (*Mere Paas Aao Mere Doston*, penned by Anand Bakshi and set to tune by Rajesh Roshan).

Mr Natwarlal: Mythical Image of an Anti-hero (excerpts from a review)

He is the newest Messiah in the shape of a gun-slinging Western hero to have transcended on his people in a God-forsaken village and, since greatness is thrust on him from the moment he sets his foot there, he finally condescends to deliver them from bondage ... he soon proves himself to be a tower of strength amidst all-round helplessness and while everyone adores and worships him, the queen-bee (Rekha) without a second thought mortgages her body and soul to the descending Messiah. Sky seems to be the only limit to which hack writers can fit the theme of personal vendetta and twist script situations to suit the mythical image of an anti-hero.

No one knows wherefrom such 'stalwarts' fell to earth and one can be pretty sure even the story-writer does not have a clue to it. But this Mr so and so is there and who else can don the mantle except the current superstar Amitabh Bachchan? As always what brings the Messiah to the village is to settle old scores with the sadist-maniac slave trader (Amjad Khan) whose method of recruiting slaves is indeed a novel one. He lets a tiger run amuck and as the villagers flee in panic they are captured ...

Source: *The Indian Express*, 10 June 1979.

Yash Chopra's *Kala Patthar* was inspired by the 1975 Chasnala (Bihar) coal mine tragedy in which about 350 miners lost their lives. This fast-paced and tightly scripted movie presented the experiences of three protagonists with different backgrounds in the dark world of the mines. They have come to work here so as to overcome their individual afflictions. The first hero (Bachchan) is a courtmartialled ex-Merchant Navy officer, who wants to forget his past guilt of abandoning his ship during a storm. The second (Shatrughan Sinha) is a dacoit who is hiding from the police among the miners. The third protagonist (Shashi Kapoor) is a mining engineer who wants to forget a failed love affair. They get transformed as they witness the plight of fellow miners and subsequently save them from the disaster engineered by the greedy mine owner (Prem Chopra). The photography and the technical inputs were superb, especially with relation to the underground filming. However, the film failed to capture convincingly certain vital issues such as the nexus among the political system, the bureaucracy, the organized mafia and the trade unions in playing havoc with the country's mining industry. Bachchan as well as fellow-miner Shatrughan Sinha emerged as the rough-hewn toughies packing a powerful punch in their respective roles. Shashi Kapoor carried off his role with his characteristic élan.

Pukar (directed by Ramesh Behl), released more than a decade after *Saat Hindustani*, placed Amitabh Bachchan for the second time amidst the liberation struggle against the Portuguese who had occupied Goa. This time, the seasoned actor donned the mantle of an anti-hero – he is an ardent supporter of colonial rule and even works for its representatives as an informer. The reason for this anti-nationalistic position is that, as a child, he had witnessed his father, a freedom fighter, being killed by his compatriot, although his father had compelled his comrade to kill him because he did not want to be killed by the enemy's bullet. The film, consequently, depicted the ideological transformation of the hero from a quisling to a high-spirited nationalist, unfolding the influences on him from various quarters including that of his lady friend, a journalist. The politically conscious hero now wages a war against the colonial power.

Manmohan Desai's *Mard* was a tacky caricature of the anti-colonial struggle. This movie presented Bachchan as the invincible crusader against imperial and feudal arrogance and oppression, his virility being symbolized by the name 'Mard' (meaning man) tattooed on his chest. He is the son of the local king who has been taken captive by the scheming British. He grows up as Raju Tangewala in a poor family and takes up the mission of freeing his father from the clutches of the English tormentors (they are called Dyer, after Reginald Dyer the general responsible for the 1919 Jallianwala Bagh massacre in Amritsar, and Simon, after the head of the infamous Simon Commission, headed by Sir John Simon). The heroine (Amrita Singh), the arrogant daughter of a doctor in the service of the British, first whips the hero and then falls in love with him (in the same way as in the classic *Aan*, 1952, in which the heroine Nadira, treats Dilip Kumar, the rebellious clan leader).

The least significant films in this category, which, in fact, undermined the quality of Bachchan's crusader image were: *Inquilab* (1984), *Shahenshah* (1988), *Toofan* (1989), *Major Saab* (1998) and *Kohram* (1999).

T. Rama Rao's *Inquilab* was an insipid addition to the 'easy-to-make celluloid revolution' genre in Indian cinema, in which the wronged angry protagonist lashes out at the pro-rich, politically corrupt system of governance and then destroys it single-handedly. The tale is about a roadside *bhelpuri* seller (Bachchan) who is picked up by a racketeer politician (Kadar Khan) with the intention of making him a pliable police officer. Eventually, he becomes a pawn in the game-plan of his godfather to usurp power. The unexpected twist takes place at the fag end of the narrative when the hero, now anointed as the chief minister-designate, guns down the entire cabinet before the swearing-in ceremony. With the mass slaughter over, the rebel comes out in the open and addresses the huge crowd with handcuffs on.

Tinnu Anand's *Shahenshah* marked the introduction of the typical split personality feature in Bachchan's persona. At one extreme, he is a comically lethargic and spineless policeman, and at the other, he dons the gleaming attire of an intrepid liberator of the people – he becomes the Shahenshah, the one-man army against the corrupt and anti-people forces. Bachchan performed the comic acts with his usual finesse, but in the serious role, he looked rather stiff and lacking the spirit of a people's hero.

Toofan (directed by Ketan Desai) marked the linking of Bachchan's superman hero with Indian mythology *per se*. Here he is not the usual omnipotent heroic figure destroying evil by mobilizing his mental and physical energies, but merely an instrument of Hanuman, the monkey god of Ramayana, for punishing the *rakshasas* (demons) in society. The protagonist is a village simpleton who, being an ardent worshipper of Hanuman, acquires mythical physical powers at the time of need and thus becomes the people's hero for settling scores with the tyrannical feudal lord. However, the unimaginative use of mythology to deliver the social message resulted in a highly unconvincing characterization of the hero.

Tinnu Anand's *Major Saab*, one of the most pretentious films of Bachchan in a senior role, reworked his larger-than-life image by transporting him this time into the professional Indian Army environment and pitting him very crudely against some corrupt anti-national civilians. Bachchan, the officer-in-charge of the National Defence Academy (NDA), is a tough disciplinarian and hard taskmaster, who is obsessed with the pride and reputation of the Indian Army and demands complete obedience from his cadets. As in many of his films, the protagonist has a painful past – he had to forgo his child when his wife's life was to be saved in childbirth. And since then he has dreamt about having a son who would be a disciplined soldier like him. The major comes into sharp conflict with one cadet (Ajay Devgan) who openly defies his authority. But soon the major becomes a crusader and takes the civil law in his hands in order to help this cadet to rescue his beloved from the clutches of local mafia dons. In this rather unconvincing role, marked by sweeping rhetoric, Bachchan keeps on barking orders at an extremely loud pitch virtually throughout the film, making him a caricature of his own histrionics.

Mehul Kumar's *Kohram* added another dark layer to the by-now tired image of our hero. Designed as a saga of comparative histrionics of two seasoned actors – Bachchan and Nana Patekar – the film attempted to delineate the paradox faced by upright, disciplined army men as they are committed by their duty to serve and uphold their corrupt political bosses. Bachchan takes up the role of a colonel, who is angry with the lecherous and anti-people deeds of a minister and attempts to assassinate him. He then disappears. His superior (Kabir Bedi), a disciplined soldier, tries to track him down but in vain. As time rolls by, he is presumed dead. After many years, Bedi, in a chance encounter, spots a commoner who bears a striking resemblance to the absconding colonel. On his instructions, one of his officers (Nana Patekar) goes on a mission to find out the real identity of this man. In the double role of the colonel and the impostor, Amitabh Bachchan once again repeats his celebrated 'split personality' syndrome – the silent vengeful upholder of justice and the comic, eccentric and benevolent Poorabiya immigrant, who becomes a natural leader of the city's poor around him.

The Anti-Hero Awaiting Redemption and Atonement

In this category, Bachchan's protagonist is often a greedy individual or a mercenary or a non-conformist with no scruples about morality, law or human relationships, at least initially. He also, in some cases, carries within himself a strong undercurrent of evil, which is seeking release. But this self-oriented anti-hero, who also had his predecessors in the classical period of Indian cinema, is rather contemplative (in contrast with the projection of Ashok Kumar in *Kismet*, Dev Anand in *Jaal* and Raaj Kumar in *Waqt*). He often awaits his final redemption and goes in for atonement. Apart from *Parvana* (1971), discussed earlier, other significant films in this category were: *Saudagar* (1973), *Jurmana* (1979) and *Shakti* (1982). In this classification can also be included films such as *Bandhe Haath* (1973), *Faraar* (1975), *Zameer* (1975), *Sholay* (1975), *Do Aur Do Paanch* (1980) and *Desh Premi* (1982).

Sudhendu Roy's *Saudagar* was another example of Bachchan's initial affiliations with the Bengal school of film making. Based on Narendranath Mitra's Bengali story, *Rus*, the film was about the commodification of women in Indian society. It presented the actor in a true anti-hero role, an opportunist upstart who is the least bothered about finer human feelings and is obsessed with his immediate material gains and carnal gratification. Moti (Bachchan) is a rural entrepreneur who climbs tall palm trees and collects their *rus* (juice), which is the source for making jaggery. He uses the expertise of Mahjubhi (Nutan), a widow, and the best jaggery maker in the village. While he makes a name in the trade for himself by exploiting the know-how of the widow, he also falls in love with the enticing Phoolbano (Padma Khanna), a village belle. But he is unable to pay the dowry her father has demanded. The unscrupulous young man marries Mahjubhi with the intention of earning that amount. Within a year he saves the requisite sum, divorces Mahjubhi and marries Phoolbano. However, soon he comes to know about Phoolbano's inability to make *gur* (jaggery). His reputation in the marketplace suffers and so does his love life. He again turns to Mahjubhi but she is already settled with a rich widower Nadir (Trilok Kapoor). Amitabh Bachchan exhibited fine underplay in his performance but was largely overshadowed by the intensity of the senior artiste's (Nutan's) histrionics.

Jurmana, one of the lesser known films of Hrishikesh Mukherjee, presented Bachchan in a credible anti-hero role. The film intended to juxtapose the innocence of ordinary people with the moral decadent ways of the spoiled urban rich and the unwarranted turmoil caused in the aftermath. The two conflicting aspects in the narrative are represented by Bachchan, a wealthy playboy, and by the family of a professor settled in a village. The egotistical hero arrives in the village and, from the moment he sets his eyes on the professor's (Shreeram Lagoo) daughter (Raakhee), he gets obsessed with her. He starts pursuing her but his vanity is hurt when he finds that he cannot have her despite his wealth and his charm. Instead of adopting a more aggressive course, he deeply falls in love with her, which makes the girl withdraw further away from him. Bachchan portrayed the playboy with unusual calmness, capturing well the dimensions of his obsession. But his portrayal got weakened in the latter part of the film where the narrative lost its breezy pace and got stuck in a melodramatic morass. The film was noteworthy for the excellent performance by Raakhee, who a played her role with immense dignity.

Shakti represented in the world of cinema a singular example where an old master, facing severe competition from a new-generation actor, reaffirms his status of being the number one in his field of specialization and demonstrates a clear-cut superiority over his younger colleague. The much-awaited clash between the two titans indeed proved unequal. The senior actor deftly offset the disadvantage of being placed against the reigning superstar of the day by simply resorting to his superbly controlled sense of underplay seen in his earlier films. Bachchan attempted to work up his typical alienation and the pent-up anger against his father (Dilip Kumar) using his own melodramatic style, but looked quite ill at ease and self-conscious, features not witnessed in any of his earlier films. However, he was also at a disadvantage, considering the relative strengths of the two characters. While the father's role was built around a multifaceted personality, the son merely depicted the typical angry young man.

O. P. Ralhan's *Bandhe Haath*, built around extreme improbabilities, presented a crude transformation of an anti-hero to a respectable citizen. Bachchan manages to impersonate a well-known writer who is his look-alike and has died recently in complete obscurity. The impersonation brings the hero in touch with a stage actress (Mumtaz), who falls for the impersonator. He now decides to turn a new leaf and takes a painfully torturous route to his destination. The film, unfortunately, sank without a trace.

Ravi Chopra's *Zameer*, inspired to some extent by Raj Khosla's classic, the Dev Anand–Suchitra Sen starrer *Bombai Ka Babu* (1960), was a film devoid of any aesthetic sensibilities. Bachchan played a small-time criminal who aspires to join the big league by impersonating the long-lost son of a millionaire (Shammi Kapoor). He has a serious competitor in Vinod Khanna. Bachchan in this film emerged as a poor caricature of a superhero. One wonders how a down-and-out pickpocket (who is also simultaneously an expert guitar player, a sharp shooter and a skilled horse rider) displays the uncanny ability to adjust to the opulent world of the superrich.

Sholay (which drew its inspiration from several internationally acclaimed movies such as *The Seven Samurai*, 1954, *The Magnificent Seven*, 1960, and *The Secret of Santa Vittoria*, 1969), instilled newer levels of sadism and mayhem in Indian cinema. No other film has done so much damage to Indian sensibilities than *Sholay*, although the movie went on to become a superhit and one of the all-time great box-office successes. In writing this film, the scriptwriters Salim-Javed simply inverted the themes of *Ganga Jumna* and *Mother India* so as to bring the villain, the dacoit Gabbar Singh (a role immortalized by Amjad Khan), into the central focus and tearing off from his characterization the social basis that would have forced him to take up arms. This extremely unsympathetic and dehumanized treatment of a rebel, in fact, goes against their own formations of the anti-hero in films like *Zanjeer* and *Deewar*.

Sholay, however, has influenced the course of Hindi cinema in yet another way: it took up the destruction of the sadistic feudal mores of the rural society by bringing in two city-bred, small-time gangsters (who were far superior, well-equipped and highly motivated mercenaries than the local dacoit, Gabbar Singh, and his minions). Dharmendra and Amitabh Bachchan played these gangsters. Bachchan came up with a creditable performance despite being pitted against Sanjeev Kumar and Amjad Khan among others.

Do Aur Do Paanch (directed by Rakesh Kumar), among the least appreciated films of our hero, presented him once again as a small-time conman, who joins a boarding school (in a hill station) as a teacher in order to kidnap the child of a rich family for ransom. The innocence of the child finally transforms him into a good human being (as also another impostor-teacher Shashi Kapoor who, too, is in the pursuit of the child). (The metamorphosis through the innocent child was also depicted earlier by Sheikh Mukhtar in *Do Ustad*, 1959, and by the Pran–Ajit–Anwar Hussain trio in *Nanha Farishta*, 1969.) Bachchan came up with his by-now-familiar heroic antics and the film comprised the usual humorous anecdotes, all of which, however, seemed to fall flat. In one scene, he repeated, in a drunken state, his patented talk about his orphan background, and the way he had to struggle to survive in a cruel and harsh world. But this sentimental outpouring was out of context vis-à-vis the narrative and was included only to strengthen his character, which was otherwise on a weak footing.

Manmohan Desai's *Desh Premi* was about the clash of values between two generations. Bachchan played a father-and-son double role. The father is an old-time idealist, a humble teacher who has participated in the freedom struggle, whereas the son, representing the new generation, is a compulsive conman. The son is compelled to marry the heroine (Hema Malini) in a community marriage ceremony in order to save himself from the police. He, however, refuses to accept the new bride, but the father takes her home. The hero becomes a gangster, but gradually realizes the futility of his criminal life. *Desh Premi* was certainly not one of Manmohan Desai's better ventures, despite his efforts to forge national unity through the film.

Shankar Mukherjee's *Faraar* has already been discussed earlier in this chapter.

The Rebellious Stance as a Way of Life

Apart from Bachchan's belligerent rebellious stance in the angry young man portrayals, this stance was also seen in a rather passive form in some of his films. Representing broadly a continuity from the classical period to the post-classical one, these portrayals underlined the protagonist's position as a rebel against the decadent social values and practices. The most significant films that belonged to this category were: *Ek Nazar* (1972), *Alaap* (1977),

Muqaddar Ka Sikandar (1978), *Laawaris* (1981) and *Nastik* (1983), while *Sharabi* (1984) can be considered less significant.

B. R. Ishara's *Ek Nazar*, an important film of the era, dealt with the contemporary moral decadence in society and the seemingly unending misery faced by women. Inspired by B. R. Chopra's classic *Sadhana* (1958, starring Vyjayanthimala and Sunil Dutt), the film took up the cause of a nautch girl (Jaya Bhaduri), who is determined to change her destiny and her fallen status, and who clashes head-on with her exploiters. Although her lover, a socially conscious young poet (Bachchan) who defies the social conventions, is her main source of solace as well as inspiration, it is her sheer determination that leads to her final emancipation. *Ek Nazar* witnessed the full blooming of the histrionics of both Jaya Bhaduri and Amitabh Bachchan. This film was studded with some melodious *ghazals* that flowed from Majrooh Sultanpuri's pen and were tuned by Laxmikant Pyarelal.

Hrishikesh Mukherjee's *Alaap* presented Bachchan as a practitioner and a connoisseur of Indian classical music. He develops great admiration for an aged lady classical singer of a bygone era, now a destitute, and begins understanding the cultural milieu of her times. In this appreciation and concern for the singer, he rebels against his rich father who wants to remove her and her people from his land on which they have lived for generations. Bachchan very ably captured the nuances of this role set in the classical film era mould. Old-timer Jaidev's musical score did full justice to the theme of the movie.

Prakash Mehra's *Muqaddar Ka Sikandar*, which witnessed the emergence of Amitabh Bachchan as the ultimate urban hero, presented him as a lonely homeless urchin who receives his name, Sikandar, from his foster-mother (Nirupa Roy). Since childhood he has worked as the servant of the heroine (Raakhee), the same way as did Dilip Kumar's protagonist in *Hulchal* (1951) and *Dil Diya Dard Liya* (1966). He falls in love with the heroine, but her father accuses him of theft and he is thrown out of the house. Sikandar finds his new identity under the patronage of a rich lawyer (Vinod Khanna), who is also in love with the heroine. There is also a nautch girl (Rekha), whom Sikandar visits regularly, but is unable to accept her love for him. She eventually commits suicide. The hero now expresses his gratitude by arranging his benefactor's marriage with the heroine. Finally, he is killed by the villain (Amjad Khan), a former lover of the nautch girl. Bachchan has given a memorable performance as the slick, carefree, yet sensitive, lower class youth.

Prakash Mehra's superhit *Laawaris* presented Amitabh Bachchan as a protesting man caught in the turbulent domain engendered by the clash between the urban rich and the urban destitute. He is the illegitimate son of a rich playboy, Amjad Khan, who has disowned him and his mother. The mother (Raakhee) dies and the son is brought up by the down-and-out alcoholic (played admirably by Shreeram Lagoo), who Bachchan thinks is his real father. When he comes to know the truth, he is stunned. He then goes in search of his real parents and manages to find his father. Amjad Khan, meanwhile, has become a kind of saint-patron. The hero demands that he must be accepted by his father and fights his opponents in order to gain credibility in his father's eyes. Bachchan lived up to expectations and performed with his characteristic élan, especially during the song *Mere Angne Mein Tumhara Kya Kaam Hai* ... (in which he appears as a 'female').

In Pramod Chakravarty's *Nastik*, our hero took up an entirely different rebellious position – he is a non-believer, who considers religiosity a sign of human backwardness. His mother (Nalini Jaywant) lambasts him for his attitude and believes that the family's unending misfortunes are because of her son's atheism. When his father is falsely implicated in a temple robbery, the mother throws the son out of the house. The hero begins working for a villainous landlord (Amjad Khan). The hero's sister is shot by the villain and is in a critical condition. The hero finally kneels before an idol in a temple and begs for her life. And like in a typical mythological film, Lord Krishna's divine aura lights up the screen, thereby accepting the heart-rending appeal of the new convert.

Prakash Mehra's other film *Sharabi*, made in the same vein as *Laawaris*, attempted to capture the acute isolation and alienation caused by deteriorating family relationships. The protagonist is a rich youth who, as in *Shakti* (1982), has sought, from childhood, love and warmth but his extremely busy father (Pran, who is a business tycoon) fails to realize his son's yearnings. The son becomes an alcoholic amidst the riches and comforts and looks for love on the streets. However, the film (inspired perhaps by Dilip Kumar's characterization in *Daag*, 1952) failed to dissect the central issue meaningfully and became no more than a collage of Bachchan's drunken antics enlivened by a few catchy songs.

The Simultaneous Liberation of the Image

Amitabh Bachchan would have been immensely satisfied with the supersuccess of his angry young man image. He would have continued with this kind of cinema at the risk of becoming stale and stereotyped and getting overpowered by the image. But the artiste, like his predecessor Dilip Kumar, took up a complete liberation of this image by introducing two major innovations in his screen persona. By assimilating in his serious image two other genres, light romance and comedy, Bachchan imbibed all the necessary characteristics required to form a complete indigenous film hero. This upgradation of his screen persona – after the initial passionate sufferer and then angry young man – virtually finalized the manifestation of the actor's histrionics in full splendour, with the three facets – angry, romantic and comic – fully realized. This changeover, in fact, brought him into his natural self – highly witty, spontaneous, confident and yet marked by an undercurrent of controlled anxiety. As the central piece of entertainment, he, like a successful acrobat or a magician, transformed a movie into a virtual one-man show, whose success was based on personal charisma and showmanship rather than on the overall quality of the film.

To complete his image of urban hero, Bachchan carried out

another significant innovation in his persona – the street dance form associated with the urban poorer classes. Far less formal and highly spontaneous, this dance style is built on minimalist body movements, without much elaboration in pace and rhythm. This style is far different not only from the standard folk forms of, say, Uttar Pradesh, Punjab or Maharashtra, but also from the step-dancing in the traditional Western street dance. For evolving this dance style, Bachchan this time did not look for inspiration from Dilip Kumar, Raj Kapoor or other leading stars, but from legendary actor-director Master Bhagwan, Indian cinema's first true hero of the downtrodden, especially in cities and towns. Bhagwan, who rose to instant fame with *Albela* (1951), enjoyed far more popularity among the urban poor, and as veteran actor Balraj Sahni once pointed out, the working class saw in him their own image and what endeared him to them was that he was a fellow member of the proletariat. Film chroniclers Ashish Rajadhyaksha and Paul Willemen[2] have observed that the Bhagwan–Bachchan dancing style over time, in fact, has become a major behavioural influence on people indicated by how they move or dance on the streets during wedding or religious processions.

Apart from *Bombay to Goa* (1972, a rib-tickling comedy with in-built elements of crime), the liberation of Bachchan's image was facilitated by three very significant films: *Chupke Chupke* (1975), *Amar Akbar Anthony* (1977) and *Namak Halal* (1982). Much later came *Bunti Aur Babli* (2005). This liberation was somewhat similar to what *Aan, Azaad, Kohinoor* and *Leader* did for Dilip Kumar. With these films, Bachchan virtually reinvented the formula of seemingly mindless entertainment, originally founded by none other than Bhagwan with Raj Kapoor and Kishore Kumar making their own contributions later.

Hrishikesh Mukherjee's *Chupke Chupke* is one of the greatest comedies thrown up by Hindi cinema. Based on a story by Upendranath Ganguly, the film (a remake of a successful, earlier Bengali version) celebrates life as a mix of hilarious situations involving false identities, apparently scandalous romances, mock threats to the newly weds and other complications. A botany professor (Dharmendra) falls in love with and decides to marry a college student (Sharmila Tagore) whose fascination with the botany textbook written by the professor (and by extension with the author himself) is of a kind that young heroines in many films usually reserve for poets. They eventually get married in Allahabad.

The central piece of the comedy is the heroine's intense admiration for her elder sister's (Usha Kiran) husband (Om Prakash), who believes in, and vehemently advocates, the preservation of the Indian tradition by the purity of the spoken language and thus wants people to speak chaste Hindi. She is obsessed with the 'greatness' of her brother-in-law and keeps on praising him. The professor, somewhat fed up with his wife extolling the virtues of the man, executes a plan in collaboration with his friend, an English professor (Amitabh Bachchan) to pull the sister's husband's leg and teach him a lesson or two. Bachchan, whose flair for comedy came to the fore, has to impersonate the botany professor and playact as Sharmila Tagore's husband when she goes to visit her sister and brother-in-law in Bombay. Dharmendra, as the driver of the household, speaks pure Hindi and really bugs Om Prakash at every possible opportunity. When Bachchan goes to his friend's (Asrani) house, he gets attracted to Jaya Bhaduri, his friend's sister-in-law. But he cannot express his love for her because he is already 'married'. She wants to learn botany from him but he wants to talk about English literature and poetry as he is totally unfamiliar with botany! Anyway, after a series of uproarious comic sequences, all's well that's ends well.

Manmohan Desai's *Amar Akbar Anthony*, far more than being a fantasy spectacle in the lost-and-found genre, was a curious synthesis of various features typical of Indian cinema, including a city-bred hooligan with a heart of gold, who is unrefined in his language and manners and, like Guru Dutt in his early films, speaks the colloquial Bombaiya Hindi. He is Anthony (played by

Bachchan), who infuses his role with impressive dollops of comedy. Next, we come across a clumsy, paan-chewing tailor Akbar (played by Rishi Kapoor), whose main pastime is qawwali singing and who represents the traditional Muslim milieu. The third hero is Amar, the middle-class upright professional young police officer (played by Vinod Khanna). They are three brothers separated at childhood due to circumstances beyond their control. The plot also involves their suffering mother and her lifelong search for them. The father (Pran), separated from the mother and the three children, who becomes an influential gangster, is another important character. As the title implies, the movie also carried an implicit message of religious tolerance and communal harmony.

The three separated brothers, unaware of their blood ties, manage to corner the villains after many twists and turns. Interestingly, *Amar Akbar Anthony* was very different from the dominant trend of violence and vengeance of this period. As the basic objective of the film was to celebrate the crazy antics of its three protagonists, the crime elements and the villains were largely incidental to the narrative. As writer Tarun Tejpal (of *Tehelka* fame) observes: *'film makers had always bandied this particular formula about. With Manmohan Desai it found its feel.* Amar Akbar Anthony *was unabashedly moronic. Desai was the magician conning the audience right, left and centre, pulling out rabbit after rabbit from his top hat. The film was a superhit and laid the foundation for the edifice of mindless entertainment ...'* [italics added] ('The Mirror Has Two Faces', *Outlook*, 20 July 1998).

Prakash Mehra's *Namak Halal* took up the oft-repeated theme of juxtaposing the innate honesty and simplicity of rural people with the evil world of the urban ultrarich (a theme that has remained an all-time favourite of our film makers). The hero (Bachchan) arrives in the metropolis from his village and takes up the job of a personal assistant-cum-bodyguard with a rich hotelier (Shashi Kapoor). With his straightforwardness, obedience and sense of humour, he wins over his employer and finally protects him from the greedy 'sharks' in his circle plotting to kill him. The comic highlight of the film was the crazy sentimental relationship between the hero and his grandfather (Om Prakash) who has arrived in the hotel disguised as a Westerner to track down his grandson and to inquire whether he has given up his good old values. Bachchan, with a great sense of spontaneity, excelled in his comic acts in the film.

Bunti Aur Babli (directed by Shaad Ali) was another significant film that employed Amitabh Bachhan's persona to add comic as well as humane appeal to the narrative. (The film was 'inspired' by the 1967 classic *Bonnie and Clyde*, directed by Arthur Penn and starring Warren Beatty and Faye Dunaway.) Here, he was in the company of his son Abhishek Bachchan and Rani Mukherji. The committed detective cop (the senior Bachchan), despite his apparent craziness and devil-may-care attitude, keeps following the runaway young couple (who are on a conning spree). Finally, when he nabs them, he shows his magnanimity by letting them go so that they can start their lives all over again. The highlight of the film was an 'item number' (*Kajrare, kajrare ...*) performed by Aishwarya Rai whose exuberant dancing companions were the two Bachchans!

In the comedy genre, the less significant films were: *Hera Pheri* (1976), *Imaan Dharam* (1977), *Yaraana* (1981), *Naseeb* (1981), *Satte Pe Satta* (1982) and *Jaadugar* (1989).

Hera Pheri (directed by Prakash Mehra) presented the antics of two small-time conmen-in-arms (Amitabh Bachchan and Vinod Khanna). After indulging in a range of deceitful activities, which are marked by touches of humour, the two finally emerge as valuable helping hands for the law in bringing to book the corrupt and the evil.

Imaan Dharam (directed by Desh Mukherjee), more of a sequel to *Hera Pheri*, presented Bachchan once again as a small-time conman, this time in the comic company of Shashi Kapoor. The two loafers, who make a living by specializing in giving false evidence in courts, inadvertently, become the upholders of the law after being influenced by a Good Samaritan, played by Sanjeev Kumar. They expose the evil deeds of the crime mafia and help in saving Sanjeev Kumar, who is wrongly accused of murder. The experiences of Bachchan and Kapoor provided some interesting insights into the trials and tribulations of the typical poor urban youth. Sanjeev Kumar was his usual accomplished self.

Yaraana (directed by Rakesh Kumar), a revisit to the much-exploited theme of eternal friendship in Indian cinema, presented Bachchan in a well-designed comic-romantic role. A rural simpleton having rudimentary music talent is brought to the city by his rich childhood friend (Amjad Khan) to be trained as a professional singer. The friend spends his fortune to commercially promote the budding singer and eventually goes bankrupt. The hero, in turn, mortgages his voice (the idea apparently borrowed from the old-time 1956 classic *Basant Bahar*) in order to save his benefactor from the impending economic downfall. The romantic angle was provided by the heroine Neetu Singh, who initially deprecates the hero, but later comes to appreciate his talent and potential.

Manmohan Desai's *Naseeb*, like some of his other films, was again a somewhat crass celebration of the world of crime, in which criminal dispositions and actions are projected in a glorified way. The film was a rework of *Amar Akbar Anthony* but far more convoluted in plot and was packed with a multitude of characters. Desai foretells the change in the destiny of three ordinary workers' families because the fathers have jointly won a huge amount in a lottery. The acquisition of sudden fortune and the rampant greed among the winners dislocate the families, with the second generation later being forced to work out its own destiny in the world of crime perpetuated by the upstart squabbling fathers. Bachchan, as one of the sons, plays the role of a waiter in a five-star hotel. But even his presence failed to salvage the film, which stumbled due a weak narrative structure. His portrayal of a boxer in the latter part of the film was a poor caricature of Charles Bronson's celebrated role as a street fighter in *Hard Times* (1975). The other two heroes, Shatrughan Sinha and Rishi Kapoor, seemed to plod through the movie, and the three mandatory heroines (Hema Malini, Reena Roy and Kim) were more symbolic than effective. Veterans like Pran and Jeevan appeared stilted and repetitive; their traditional impact was not felt.

Satte Pe Satta, directed by Raj N. Sippy, a loose adaptation of *Seven Brides for Seven Brothers* (1954), underlined the influence of a feminine presence in reforming uncouth male behaviour. Bachchan played the role of an overpowering, strong-headed simpleton, the eldest among seven unruly brothers living in a commune beyond the pale of the civilized world. The turning point in the lives of these brothers arrives when the unsophisticated hero pursues the heroine (Hema Malini), a nurse in a hospital, and finally brings her as the first bride in the household. Bachchan, inspired perhaps by the character of Shyam in *Ram Aur Shyam* (witness the way he hogs food), carried the film with his instinctive sense of breezy, uninhibited comedy. However, the overall jovial mood of the film is ruined in its latter part when suddenly Bachchan is introduced in a second role of a serious looking wronged man so as to infuse the crime elements into the narrative.

Prakash Mehra's *Jaadugar* had a socially important theme – it stressed the need for inculcating rational thinking among people so as to free them from being controlled and manipulated by unscrupulous godmen. In this film, the godman (Amrish Puri) is idolized and worshipped by people for his miraculous powers. His son (Aditya Pancholi) gets disgusted with his father, who swindles his innocent believers, and he (the son) hires a magician (Amitabh Bachchan) to expose him. Bachchan tackles the godman on an equal footing with his own expertise in the science of magic and finally lays him bare. The film, by and large slipshod, failed to create the desired 'magical' effect on the audience.

The least significant films, which did not particularly help Bachchan much, now a senior artiste, to reaffirm his enviable excellence in comedy in the changed milieu of Hindi cinema, were *Bade Miyan Chhote Miyan* (1999), *Hum Kisi Se Kum Nahin* (2002), *Kabhi Alvida Naa Kehna* (2006), *Jhoom Barabar Jhoom* (2007), *Darna Zaroori Hai* (2007) and *Bhoothnath* (2008).

Bade Miyan Chhote Miyan, David Dhawan's joint venture with Amitabh Bachchan and the young actor Govinda, emerged as another hallmark of mindless entertainment (which Manmohan Desai may have approved) with a minimum concern for sense and sensibility. The two clumsy protagonists, with a complete lack of common sense, take Bombay's world of crime for a ride! However, the extremely elemental story and the use of double roles for the two actors, combined with a sloppy script and a meandering narrative, undermined the overall value of the film.

In *Hum Kisi Se Kum Nahin*, again directed by David Dhawan, Bachchan reconstructed his comic persona in a senior role, employing his typical confused look reinforced with the matter-of-fact type dialogues spoken in his native Allahabadi lingo. (This film was loosely based on *Analyze This*, released in 1999 and directed by Harold Ramis. The cast included Robert De Niro and Billy Crystal.) Bachchan is a simple-hearted medical practitioner, who has to perform the dutiful task of providing complete moral and strategic support to a close friend, an underworld don (Sanjay Dutt) who has taken a fancy to Bachchan's sister (played by the gorgeous Aishwarya Rai). The lovelorn goon is unable to win over his object of desire, and thus loses interest in his professional work. The film attempted to drum up comedy by transforming a don into an obsessed lover, and in a way tended to lend social sanctity to the underworld operators. In fact, it seemed to show their ready acceptance among the common people with whom they interact without any social stigma. Further, the intended humour remains more or less stuck at one plane in the film, unable to grow and create more hilarious episodes.

In Karan Johar's *Kabhi Alvida Naa Kehna*, Bachchan played the role of 'Sexy Sam', who constantly seeks the company of young women. But when he suffers a heart attack (due to extreme indulgences in life), he advises his daughter-in-law to leave his son as their marriage falls victim to extreme incompatibility.

In Shaad Ali's *Jhoom Barabar Jhoom*, he essayed the role of an oldish gypsy dancer sporting a trimmed white beard, but his dancing lacked his trademark style.

Ram Gopal Verma's *Darna Zaroori Hai*, a curious package of six horror stories directed by different directors, presented Bachchan in the role of an old professor who is spooked by an unseen presence.

Bhoothnath, a film directed by Vivek Sharma produced under the B. R. Chopra banner, presented Bachchan as a suffering ghost awaiting his deliverance. Highlighting the power of innocence and the pure love of a child in healing troubled souls (even from the other world), the narrative is built around the curious relationship between the ghost wandering around in a uninhabited house and a seven-year-old child (Aman Siddiqui) whose family has recently shifted to this haunted mansion. The ghost is in limbo, and he won't let anyone live inside the house, where he had spent his life. The child in his innocence mistakes the ghost for an angel and befriends him. The ghost, in turn, entertains him by performing magical feats.

The Trapped Man as the Individual Dispenser of Justice

From the 1970s onwards, amidst the rapid criminalization of society and the resulting problems accompanied by misgovernance, Bachchan's protagonist also often inadvertently became a trapped man caught amidst highly surcharged circumstances. As a result, the only course left for him was to energize his inner self and dispense justice at least for his and his family's own safety. *Benaam* (1974), *Majboor* (1974), *Do Anjaane* (1976), *Viruddh* (2005, in a senior role) and *Ek Ajnnabi* (2005, in a senior role again) were the most significant films in this grouping, while *Gehri Chaal* (1973) was on a lower stratum of film quality rating.

Benaam, directed by Narendra Bedi, an important film of Bachchan in this period, is about the typical paradox faced by a common law-abiding man, who, while discharging his duty as a responsible citizen (he carries an injured man to a hospital in his car), gets trapped in traumatic situations not of his making. The hero is a company executive, and one night while he and his wife (Moushumi Chatterji) are on their way to attend a party in their car, they suddenly see a man being stabbed on the road. The assailant manages to escape. The hero then picks up the victim and takes him to a hospital. And as a result of this simple humane gesture, he has to face many trials and tribulations. First, he finds himself, in a rather true-to-life scene, on the verge of tearing his hair out at the callousness of the government hospital staff. Later, he begins to receive ominous phone calls from the mysterious assailant who is worried that his victim in the hospital would reveal his identity. The assailant kidnaps the hero's son and tries to bully him into killing the injured man. Although the film, in the development of the plot looked promising, it finally gets bogged down in the typical long-drawn-out violent drama of one-upmanship between the hero and the villain. Bachchan's role demanded controlled aggression and he lived up to it superbly.

In Ravi Tandon's *Majboor*, Bachchan's protagonist echoed the perennial problems of helplessness and vulnerability that often engulf the urban middle class. He is a lowly paid employee in a travel agency who has to support a family consisting of his widowed mother (Sulochana), younger brother (Master Alankar) and invalid sister (Farida Jalal). Suddenly, he is subject to periodic migraine attacks, which, a doctor points out, are due to a brain tumour, which needs to be removed by surgery. However, the doctor does not guarantee success; hence, Bachchan is reluctant to go in for surgery. He gets extremely worried about his family's future in case he dies. He then offers himself to the police as the man who is absconding after committing a murder (on whom there is a big cash reward). He thinks that this reward would help his family financially. However, as a convicted prisoner, he has to undergo the operation that he has been avoiding. The surgery is successful and the tumour is removed. Now cured, he frantically wants to escape the gallows. He manages to escape from prison and finally tracks down the real murderer with the help of one Michael D'Souza, admirably portrayed by Pran. Some of the scenes during the climax were 'inspired' by the Charles Bronson thriller *Cold Sweat* (1970).

In Dulal Guha's *Do Anjaane*, 'inspired' perhaps by two similar films of B. R. Chopra – *Afsana* (1951) and *Dastaan* (1972) – Bachchan portrayed the agony of a middle-class man whose values of a simple life clash with those of his wife, an ambitious woman (Rekha), aspiring to be a film actress. She falls for her husband's rich and indulgent friend (Prem Chopra), who finally throws the hero out of a running train after a brawl. The deceived man somehow survives and, over the years, becomes rich. He takes on a new identity and hatches a plot to avenge his tormenters. The touching relationship between the sorrowful child of the couple, studying in a boarding school, and the stranger-father greatly enhanced the emotional appeal of the film.

In Mahesh Manjrekar's *Viruddh* (2005), a film about the devastating impact that the anti-social lifestyle of today's well-connected neo-rich youth has on the lives of common citizens, Bachchan portrayed with absolute finesse the painful transformation of an elderly, peace-loving middle-class man into an extremely reluctant dispenser of justice. His peaceful retired life goes haywire when his son (John Abraham) is killed by the villainous son of a politician when John intervenes to prevent a criminal act from being committed. The grieved and desperate father fails to get justice despite numerous attempts to do so, and, finally, after pleading in vain with the murderer to surrender, Bachchan shoots him dead.

Gehri Chaal (directed by C. V. Sridhar) also a depicted a trapped man (Amitabh Bachchan). The protagonist is the son of a bank official who is blackmailed by a gang of bank robbers to help them in looting the bank. His close friend (Jeetendra), an officer of the intelligence department, comes to the city to investigate the crime and stays with him. The scared hero creates such situations that the officer would be forced to leave the city in disgust. Finally, the truth is revealed and the trapped man regains his confidence and joins hands with the officer-friend to nab the criminals. The film did not create much excitement and has fallen into the abyss of obscurity.

In Apoorva Lakhia's *Ek Ajnnabi*, Bachchan portrayed very ably the transformation of a hardened man into an understanding human being through the innocence of a child. As a colonel in the army, he had accidentally shot dead two children during an engagement with terrorists in Kashmir. This act has made him a profoundly unhappy man, who seeks to drown his pain in alcohol. But when he is commissioned to be the bodyguard of an eight-year-old (Rucha Vaidya), the feisty child enlivens his existence, making him discover a new purpose in life. Eventually, the child is kidnapped and shot dead by the kidnapper (Raj Zutshi). With a broken heart, but with fierce determination, he now draws upon his reserves of courage and perseverance and, in a vengeful mission, destroys the kidnapper. This film was based on Hollywood's *Man on Fire* (2004, directed by Tony Scott), starring Denzel Washington.

The Brave Man on the Side of the Law

The notable films in this category are *Parvarish* (1977), *Don* (1978, double role), *Suhaag* (1979), *The Great Gambler* (1979, double role), *Shaan* (1980), *Dostana* (1980), *Ram Balram* (1980), *Barsaat Ki Ek Raat* (1981), *Akalya* (1991), *Khakee* (2004), *Dev* (2004), *Shootout at Lokhandwala* (2007) and *Zamaanat* (2008). (In the last four films, Bachchan appeared in senior roles.)

Manmohan Desai's *Parvarish* was an obvious remake of the Raj Kapoor–Mala Sinha–Mehmood starrer of the same name released in 1958, but much more glitzy in its format and presentation. A disgruntled bad man (Amjad Khan), in order to take revenge on an honest police officer, plants his newly born son in his household who grows up with the latter's son. Mistaking his own son as that of his enemy, the villain trains him to become a hard-core criminal. The other lad becomes a police officer (Bachchan), who finally reveals the birth identity of his foster brother (Vinod Khanna). Bachchan played this role with his characteristic élan and stood his own against Vinod Khanna and stalwart Shammi Kapoor (who played the father's role). All the mandatory ingredients of a typical Manmohan Desai potboiler were included.

Don, directed by Chandra Barot, reflected Bachchan's excellence in the art of impersonation. A clumsy, simple-hearted, paan-chewing Poorabiya (a person who hails from eastern Uttar Pradesh) is asked by the police to impersonate Don, the powerful commander of a mafia set-up, who has apparently been killed. A police officer (Iftekhar) grooms him and guides him at every step. Bachchan's live-wire performance provides a much-needed boost to an ordinary crime tale. Salim-Javed's punchy dialogues and Kalyanji Anandji's enjoyable music added more verve to the movie. (The film was remade by Farhan Akhtar, Javed Akhtar's son, in early 2006 with Shahrukh Khan in the lead. A whole lot of modern-day gizmos were bunged in to create a more sophisticated ambience.)

Shakti Samanta's *The Great Gambler* projected Amitabh Bachchan's persona in a double role – twins separated in childhood. Following the stereotype of such roles in the actor's cinema, one brother is an ace gambler having magical powers of stacking playing cards in his favour (à la Raj Kapoor in *Shri 420*) and is patronized by a mafia don, Madan Puri. The other brother is an intrepid police inspector, committed to destroying the spy syndicate (represented by Utpal Dutt and Madan Puri) collecting information on India's defence secrets. As per the standard narrative of such films, the two look-alikes recognize each other, change places and then, after many dramatic sequences, together wage a war against the enemy. The film was largely shot in Europe, with a melodious number (*Do Lafzon Ki Hai Dil Ki Kahani*... sung by Asha Bhosle and Sharad Kumar, with Amitabh Bachchan speaking in between, and tuned by Rahul Dev Burman) picturized on a gondola (carrying the hero and one of the heroines, Zeenat Aman) in Venice.

Suhaag, yet another Manmohan Desai concoction, was a repeat of the lost-and-found melodrama becoming common in the actor's portfolio. One of the heroes (Bachchan), a street-smart ruffian, is a loner who is separated from his estranged parents in childhood. Unknowingly, he becomes a close friend of a police officer (Shashi Kapoor), who turns out to be his long-lost brother. The villain, their father (Amjad Khan), who is unaware of his sons' identities, hires the ruffian to kill the police officer but later changes his mind and decides to blind him. The blind police officer then motivates the hero to join the police force and thus fulfil his mission of capturing the villain. The sons finally apprehend their father who has turned to evil ways.

In Shakti Samanta's *Barsaat Ki Ek Raat*, Bachchan is a police officer who starts living in a village disguised as a jovial local. The film is set in the picturesque hill areas of Darjeeling. The hero's mission is to break the nexus between the exploitative local traders and the anti-national spy ring operating in the region. Attired in a *farlong* (a kind of smock) and a jute hat, the actor gave a memorable performance in a breezy comic-action role. One major highlight of the film was his tender love affair with a local blind girl (Raakhee).

Ramesh Sippy's *Shaan* presented Bachchan, along with Shashi Kapoor (who plays his brother), initially as small-time conmen, who, after a series of rollicking episodes, turn into crusaders out to punish the sadist mafia don Kulbhushan Kharbanda, who stood out in the role of Shakaal, modelled on the lines of the villain Ernst Stavro Blofeld in some of the James Bond movies. Shakaal is responsible for killing their elder brother (Sunil Dutt), a brave and honest police officer. A sharpshooter, played by Shatrughan

Sinha, also pitches in and helps the brothers in their quest. The movie was packed with action sequences, catchy songs and hi-tech gadgets (controlled by Shaakal). But the character who stole the show was Mazhar Khan, who appeared as a physically handicapped individual with acumen for picking up all sorts of information with regard to crime and criminals.

Raj Khosla's *Dostana* intended to interpret the Indian law from two diametrically opposite viewpoints. Amitabh Bachchan, a police officer, is an alert and sincere upholder of the law, while his bosom friend, Shatrughan Sinha, is a highly successful lawyer who has no scruples about setting free the criminals arrested by the former by finding loopholes in the law. They both love the heroine (Zeenat Aman), which leads to friction between them. As the film races to its climax, the friends, who have fallen apart, manage to clear all misunderstandings and join hands to foil the sinister plans of the villain and his cronies. However, the film lacked the earlier magic touch of the veteran director.

In *Ram Balram*, directed by Vijay Anand, Bachchan played the stereotype of an upright, brave police officer, who, in collaboration with his friend (Dharmendra, his brother in reality), confronts the smuggling kingpins. Dharmendra is forced to become a petty crook by his mentor (Ajit), who is also instrumental in making Bachchan a policeman so that he (Ajit) can manipulate Bachchan. Ajit wants Bachchan to follow his directives but the latter refuses to do so. In between the fight sequences with an assortment of villains, the heroes take time off to perform their usual comic capers and sing a few songs with the heroines (Rekha for Bachchan and Zeenat Aman for Dharmendra). And again the sorrowful past is conveniently tagged on to the narrative – a wronged mother separated from her sons in their childhood.

In *Akalya*, Amitabh Bachchan once again portrayed the lone and angry crusader against the forces of evil. Director Ramesh Sippy designed the film as a new edition of sadism and brutality after his 1975 mega-hit *Sholay*. The maniac villain tries to break the hero, an upright police inspector, by killing first his bosom friend and then his younger brother. The hero does not cower and becomes the one-man avenger in pursuit of the villain who uses his twin brother (a woolly headed character) to hide his real identity. Amitabh Bachchan, in a memorable performance, transcended the limitations of a weak script and the film became a grand display of his histrionics.

Rajkumar Santoshi's *Khakee* was a scathing indictment of the country's police system. In a towering role as DCP (deputy commissioner of police) Anant Shrivastav, Bachchan appeared as a dutiful but brooding police officer frustrated with the callous attitude of, and rampant opportunism among, the police force. Caught in the murkiness of deceit and astounded by acts of treachery of his fellow cops while leading a police team (including Akshay Kumar and Tusshar Kapoor) in a mission to chase a dreaded terrorist (Ajay Devgan) from Chandigarh to Bombay, he draws upon his inner strength to transcend his seemingly uncontrollable despair. He very ably captured the anguish, which a principled man has to undergo, to make his way very carefully through the highly placed and powerful people around him.

Dev, directed by Govind Nihalani, presented Bachchan in one of his most memorable roles. As Dev Pratap Singh, joint commissioner of police, the upright but tortured cop, he gave a mind-blowing performance. Apparently designed as a revisit to the highly acclaimed *Ardh Satya* (1983), by the same director, the film, set against the backdrop of communal riots, is a scathing attack on political opportunism and social decadence and shows that a principled man cannot find peace in today's new-age India. Dev performs his duty as per the rule book, and his senior and close buddy, Tejender Khosla or Tej (Om Puri), is a zealous representative of Hindutva in the law-enforcement apparatus of the state. While Dev strives to bring back the honour of the minority community in general and that of Farhan (Fardeen Khan), a Muslim youth, in particular, Tej, with the tacit support of the ruling party, is bent upon ensuring this community's complete alienation, and even elimination. The two close friends would often indulge in debates on the system of governance and the position and status of minorities in the country, as they spend their evenings over a bottle of whisky. In the character of Dev, Nihalani very ably foretells the fall of a nation and also of those in a small minority who, with their strong sense of conviction, have been able to uphold their ideals so far. The riot scenes and their aftermath, along with the conspiracies hatched by scheming politicians and their henchmen, have been powerfully captured on celluloid.

In Apoorva Lakhia's *Shootout at Lokhandwala* (2007), inspired by the massacre of the Maya Dolas gang by a police task force in 1991, Bachchan, as the chief of operations, merely listens to the presentations made by the cops and makes sarcastic comments.

In S. Ramanathan's *Zamaanat* (2008), the director helps Bachchan in employing a physical disability to dramatize a seemingly helpless individual's crusade against injustice. Bachchan appears as a prominent lawyer, who has lost his vision in an accident and decides to lead a secluded life. He has also lost track of his beloved (Vijayshanti), a doctor by profession. This recluse is shaken out of his agonized existence by a college girl (Karisma Kapoor), who approaches him to secure justice for her lover, a poor youth falsely implicated in a murder case. The lonely man reluctantly takes up the case and, despite his disability, launches a long and arduous struggle to bring the real culprit, a rich, spoilt brat, to book.

The Man in Uniform as the Defender of the Nation

The awe-inspiring screen persona of Amitabh Bachchan propelled many film makers to cast him in war films in larger-than-life portrayals. His was the archetype of a highly professional armed forces man, who is suffused with a lifelong dedication to defend the nation. The major films in this category are *Hindustan Ki Kasam* (1999), *Deewar – Let's Bring Our*

Heroes Home (2004), *Lakshya* (2004) and *Ab Tumhare Hawale Watan Saathiyo* (2004).

Hindustan Ki Kasam (directed by Veeru Devgan) presented Bachchan in a small but dominating role of a freedom fighter woven unimaginatively into a tale told against the backdrop of the 1971 Indo–Pakistan conflict. He is an old-time nationalist who is troubled by the present-day decadent political culture and the unending enmity between the two countries. The story is largely centred round his twin sons (both played by Ajay Devgan) – one is a writer of political thrillers and the other, who got lost in the 1971 war, becomes an officer in the Pakistani army. In its seemingly unending twists, intrigues and recourse to violence, the film loses the message it intended to deliver. Bachchan, in the cliché-ridden, overdramatized role, uses his familiar baritone to deliver long patriotic discourses but looks stale and fatigued.

Milan Luthria's *Deewar – Let's Bring Our Heroes Home*, set against the backdrop of the 1971 Indo–Pak war, cast Bachchan in a role that enabled the seasoned actor to exhibit the true depth of his time-tested histrionics. Ostensibly inspired by real-life events and also by the 1963 Hollywood classic *The Great Escape* (directed by John Sturges), the film is about the daredevil escape of Indian prisoners of war, led by Major Ranvir Kaul (Amitabh Bachchan), from a Pakistani concentration camp where they are forced to suffer the atrocities inflicted by the Pakistani officials. Although the narrative was replete with several implausible scenes, Bachchan's powerhouse performance, marked with unusual felicity and physical energy, saves this grossly unevenly paced film.

In *Lakshya*, directed by Farhan Akhtar, Bachchan takes up the role of a 'thinking' army officer, who is upset with the death and destruction caused by war but yet is a duty-bound soldier. He becomes the inspiration for the hero, Hrithik Roshan, a rich boy who joins the Indian Army to find a purpose in his otherwise meaningless life. He begins to find some meaning in the army discipline, decorum and regimen. He also takes part enthusiastically in a war. Although the film sought to explore the serious existential problem of today's alienated youth, its overstretched jingoist stance, as seen in the personality of the senior officer, and also in the young hero seeking his identity in the glamour of army culture, undermined the other possibilities available to the youth to take up a number of socially useful vocations in present-day India.

In Anil Sharma's highly contrived story, *Ab Tumhare Hawale Watan Saathiyo*, Bachchan essayed the role of Major General Amarjeet Singh, a dedicated officer of the Indian Army, who is has lost his son in action during the 1971 Indo–Pak war, but now he is extremely disappointed as his grandson, also an army officer, lacks the professionalism he and his son had in them while serving the country selflessly.

The Backward-looking Patriarch

The Amitabh Bachchan magic continued to cast its spell even during the late 1980s, but the actor's reign *as a hero* virtually came to an end in the early 1990s. Soon, however, he staged a commendable comeback through senior roles. In this phase Bachchan again drew inspiration from Dilip Kumar's powerful performances in the 1980s as a character actor. In this category of films, he appeared as an upright, upper-class, omnipotent patriarch, who exercises his complete authority most of the time. Another repetitive role was that of a feudal lord intoxicated with his own sense of power. But the viewers, who had loved the rebel image of their star in the younger days, could not fully accept this transformation in his image. That is perhaps why his highly dominating roles failed to impress much of the audience in films like *Suryavansham* (1999), *Mohabbatein* (2000), *Kabhi Khushi Kabhi Gham* (2001) and *Aetbaar* (2004).

The most important movie in this category, *Suryavansham* (directed by E. V. V. Satyanarayana), a typical family drama based on an earlier Tamil film, marked this portrayal change. Bachchan is an obstinate aristocrat, who is obsessed with the pride of his lineage and with his power. Thus, his towering presence dominates all family members. His son (also played by Bachchan) is a docile man, in complete awe of his father, and yet unlike his feudalistic father, he is forward looking and responsive to the changing times. He is compelled by circumstances to rebel and opts for his independence, while the patriarch becomes a lonely man imprisoned within his own self. Although Bachchan very ably expanded his persona, covering the two characters at the extremes of the human personality, the film's impact was undermined by a not-so-refreshing treatment of a clichéd theme and the forced inclusion of villainy to resolve the father–son conflict.

The other films in this category (*Mohabbatein, Kabhi Khushi Kabhi Gham* and *Aetbaar*) together presented the transformation of Amitabh Bachchan's persona into the archetype patriarch, the modern moghul, who, in spite of his acquired modernity, is unable to overcome his feudal attitudes. He is now a revised model of the anti-hero, representing the past, projected as the main roadblock in the affairs of the new age. In these films, Indian modernity is simply looked at from the viewpoint of the upper-class youth, the lead pair, who demand a complete transformation of values in the new globalized world and its culture. Their affluence, opulent lifestyles, both in India and while living abroad, and, above all, the presentation of the ultrarich NRIs (non-resident Indians) as the ultimate symbol of trans-national Indian success, tend to create a make-believe world that a common man is expected to simply observe and appreciate. However, the young protagonist in the films of this genre, as the upholder of this modernity, is not the 'new man' rebelling against the patriarchal order, but an ambitious and money-driven individual who wants to please the 'old' to ensure the sybaritic pleasures in his present. Sadly, such big-budget, technically glossy multistarrers lack the substance of meaningful cinema, which is essential for any film to make an impact or set a trend.

Aditya Chopra's (Yash Chopra's son) *Mohabbatein*, which

took up the debate of tradition vis-à-vis modernity in the context of the present cultural and social milieu, presented Bachchan as a reverse image of his earlier live-wire anti-establishment persona. He is a traditionalist who has envisioned a modern Indian society that is technologically slick and thus prosperous but driven by the age-old Indian values of high moral conduct and commitment to tradition. To validate his model of development, this visionary initiates a project in the form of a *gurukul*, an ancient institution of the Vedic times, where he takes up the mission of developing the necessary human resources as per his ideals. A group of his students, representing the new-age youth led by the hero, Shahrukh Khan, plays havoc with his sentiments, and questions his extremely puritan approach to life. The conflict builds up as the old-world teacher opposes the highly Westernized lifestyle of his pupils and their explicit love affairs. Shahrukh Khan is in love with Aishwarya Rai, Bachchan's daughter, but the affair ended tragically due to the patriarch's strict opposition to it. Aishwarya kills herself as a result of her father's rigid stance. The clash between Bachchan and Khan marked the highlight of the film.

However, in its superficial treatment of the theme and in a somewhat less-than-convincing turnaround on the part of Bachchan, *Mohabbatein* comfortably deconstructs this idealist and his values hailing the victory of new-age culture, thus validating implicitly the growing cultural subjugation of the Indian culture by the West. As in *Suryavansham*, Bachchan exhibited in this film remarkable ability in underplay (particularly the use of a low-tone voice and intentional compression of words in dialogue delivery) and an aura reminiscent of Dilip Kumar in many senior roles.

Karan Johar's *Kabhi Khushi Kabhi Gham* looked like an urban follow-up of *Suryavansham*, presenting Bachchan in the role of a business tycoon, who, in spite of being at the helm of a modern business enterprise, is highly rigid in his attitudes, which seem almost feudal. Highly conscious of his class and status, he gets extremely agitated when Shahrukh Khan, his foster son, dares to defy him by bringing to the palatial home a bride (Kajol) who belongs to a social stratum far below that of the Bachchan clan. As the conflict mounts, there is a dramatic verbal exchange between the father and son, reminiscent of that in *Mughal-e-Azam* (1960) and *Surayavansham*, the only difference with respect to these two films being that the docile-looking son does not declare war but smartly parts ways. Bachchan carried his underplay well but otherwise his mannerisms looked rather contrived and out of tune with the undeniably stale theme. The film was studded with opulent indoor sets and fabulous outdoor locales apart from a wide variety of costumes donned by the characters. The obligatory song-and-dance sequences were like fairy-tale escapades.

In Vikram Bhatt's *Aetbaar*, which can be considered an unimpressive sequel to *Mohabbatein*, Bachchan portrayed an old-fashioned man perturbed by the onslaught of the new-age yuppie culture. A protective father, he abhors the lover (John Abraham) of his haughty upmarket daughter (Bipasha Basu) whom he considers wild, unpredictable, overpowering and obsessive. But he has all the qualities that the girl always desired in her life partner: handsomeness, magnetism and sensitivity. Bachchan's performance was noteworthy, especially in the scenes when he tries to safeguard his daughter.

The Return of the Anti-Hero

In this category of films, the transformation in our hero's persona has been represented by his characterizations in the following films: *Aks* (2001), *Aankhen* (2002), *Kaante* (2002), *Boom* (2003), *Sarkar* (2005), *Family – The Ties of Blood* (2006), *Ram Gopal Verma Ki Aag* (2007) and *Sarkar Raj* (2008). From a closed-minded patriarch in 'feel-good' cinema, he now swiftly moved to an entirely new arena in order to expand further his cinematic space. Some of his roles in this category were bizarre. These roles seem to have been designed to create a new genre for the Indian film hero, a protagonist trapped in the 'compulsive obsession behavioural syndrome', a major psychiatric disorder. With these roles, Bachchan's vigilante hero leaves behind his social concerns and virtually, like Albert Camus' *The Outsider*, he is a 'being in nothingness', plundering and killing at random.

Rakeysh Omprakash Mehra's *Aks* was a sleek political thriller and a study on dual human behaviour patterns in a class of its own. The film is mainly set in Budapest with Amitabh Bachchan playing Mannu Verma, who is responsible for ensuring national security. Verma has accompanied India's defence minister to the Hungarian capital to obtain a floppy disk in which are stored the names of some potentially dangerous individuals. During the trip, Mannu learns that the minister's life is in danger. He is being targeted by Manoj Bajpai (named Raghavan in the movie), a cold-blooded and sadistic assassin. Unfortunately, the minister is killed and the disk has also disappeared. Verma manages to track down Raghavan, who is taken back to India and is to be executed by hanging. But his spirit enters into Mannu Verma and the villain now starts manipulating Verma to perform acts on his command. Bachchan excelled himself in this changeover of personality. The major highlight of this movie was the extraordinary photography by Kiran Deohans.

In Vipul Shah's *Aankhen* (based on a popular Gujarati play, *Andhalo Pato*), the new anti-hero hires three blind men (somewhat similar to *Sholay* and *Karma*, where the reasons were different) to loot, ironically, a bank he had originally set up, but from which he has been dismissed. These three are Akshay Kumar, Paresh Rawal and Arjun Rampal. This act indicates a clear indictment by the protagonist of the sanctity of the public institutions and his love for anarchy. In this context, the noted film trade expert Komal Nahata writes: 'Bachchan should learn that there are certain kinds of films he should keep away from. Vipul Shah's bank robbery drama was one such film Amitabh should never have lent his name to. But either he is least interested in the quality of films he is doing or he has lost his sense of judgement. Either way, it is bad. Of course, no actor can expect a 100 per cent track record, but there are certain films, which when you hear the subject itself, you realize it would not be worth the while to get associated with.' ('Big B's Performance Falls Flat in *Aankhen*', *The Hindustan Times*, 11 April 2002.)

In *Kaante* (directed by Sanjay Gupta), a film set in the back lanes of America's business world, Bachchan takes up the near-real-life portrayal of a middle-aged entrepreneur who wants to earn fast money in the land of opportunities to pay for the medical treatment of his ailing wife. When his efforts in making a legitimate entry into the corporate world fail, he becomes an accomplice in an audacious bank robbery project thought up by a gang of five renegades (Sunjay Dutt, Kumar Gaurav, Suniel Shetty, Lucky Ali and Mahesh Manjrekar) who have lost their bearings and sensibilities in a world driven by greed, get-rich-quick attitudes and jet-set opulence. They are nabbed by the police because one of them is an informer. Though the film intended to capture the various problems that the hordes of immigrants face as they are caught up in the vagaries of an indifferent or rather materially superior society, it could not rise above its overall tenor of an ordinary crime thriller stereotype.

Bachchan, in a highly subdued role, was denied the opportunity of articulating the transformation of his protagonist from a well-meaning professional to a full-fledged mercenary in full action. Only in one scene in the later half of the film does the seasoned actor provide a glimpse of his trademark ability in depicting emotions when he talks about the suffering and the eventual death of his wife.

In Kazaid Gustad's *Boom*, Bachchan sought to deploy his acting skills to extend the persona of the Indian film protagonist to psychologically complex negative characters, not much seen in earlier films (the few exceptions being K. L. Saigal's *Lagan*, Prithviraj Kapoor's *Pagal*, Dev Anand's *Jaal* and Dilip Kumar's *Aadmi*). Driven by their deep sense of existentialism, these characters seek solace and identity in obsessive preoccupations, thus attempting to display their masculinity with criminally challenging acts. In *Boom*, Bachchan portrayed Bade Miyan, a kinky mafia don based in Dubai who seems to be enjoying the unresolved duality of his personality. He is an elderly, powerful, unscrupulous underworld monarch and yet a teenager at heart, spending most of his time reading comic books and fantasizing about the sensuous Hollywood heroine Bo Derek.

The highlight of *Boom* is the daredevil operation that Bade Miyan and two other dons – Medium Miyan (Gulshan Grover) and Chhote Miyan (Jackie Shroff) – launch to filch diamonds from the Nizam's famous treasure collection and smuggle them out of India. However, the three supermodels (Katrina Kaif, Padma Lakshmi and Madhu Sapre) employed by them to carry out the job unwittingly run away with the booty. In Navketan's *Jewel Thief* (1967), the danseuse (Faryal) and her accomplices used the same ploy to steal various ornaments. Finally, the three dons, as in *Kaante*, kill each other.

Although conceived as an innocent crime thriller, *Boom* primarily projected the alluring world of overwhelming affluence and sensuality ruled by gangsters as a natural extension of life. Denounced as one of the most incredibly bad films made in recent times, *Boom* sought to bring together, and exhibit, the power and glamour of the two strata of 'high society' – fashion modelling and the underworld. Given Bachhan's talents, *Boom* was a complete waste. With a shoddily developed characterization, apart from a weak script and somewhat sloppy direction, the film failed to offer the artiste an opportunity to deploy his histrionics to live up to the pathologically complex role. This failure once again showed that, unlike their Hollywood counterparts, the Indian acting icons, cast as they are in the classical mould, are often not very comfortable in portraying extremely negative characters. This drawback was also noticeable in the case of Dilip Kumar in films like *Dil Diya Dard Liya*, *Aadmi* and *Qila*.

Ram Gopal Verma's *Sarkar*, designed as an Indian prototype of Francis Ford Coppola's 1972 classic *The Godfather* (in which Marlon Brando played the title role), presented Bachchan in the role of a cool-headed patriarch Subhash Nagre, the centre of unconstitutional power and a mass leader worshipped by the masses for his philanthropic acts. (The character had some similarities with the Shiv Sena supremo Bal Thackeray.) The tussle of power between his two sons is triggered by Sarkar's rejection of a deal (on moral grounds) sought by a Dubai-based don. The don tries to eliminate Sarkar with the help of his eldest son (Kay Kay Menon), a movie producer who is a debauched but ambitious man. His highly educated second son (Abhishek Bachchan) rises to the occasion to counter his father's rivals and finally kills his brother to help his father regain his powerful status.

Bachchan, with his restrained acting and meticulous underplay, superbly portrayed the frail but yet all-powerful man who negotiates everything, whether business or humanitarian issues, with a rare sense of finesse and conviction. He re-creates the aura of his protagonist's power and glory not through screaming and highhandedness, but through a kind of simplicity and naturalness. The sequel, *Sarkar Raj* (like *The Godfather*, Part II), was released in mid-2008, with Abhishek Bachchan in the lead role.

Family – The Ties of Blood, a lacklustre movie and a box-office catastrophe directed by Rajkumar Santoshi, had Amitabh Bachchan as Viren Sahai, a mafioso blessed with a very happy family. Although his life revolves around murder and crime, he cannot tolerate any harm to his family. When he accidentally kills Shekhar (Akshay Kumar), a simple, hard-working chef who adores his younger brother Aryan (Aryeman Ramsay) and is willing to die for him, the younger brother unleashes a revengeful crusade against the don.

In *Ram Gopal Verma Ki Aag*, a contrived urban version of Ramesh Sippy's blockbuster *Sholay*, Bachhan sought to diversify his image by appearing as a sadistic villian by taking up the legendary role of Gabbar Singh, played with deadly effect in the original by a young Amjad Khan. Unfortunately, the film sank into oblivion.

Sarkar Raj (directed by Ram Gopal Verma) depicted on screen the shady and violent power politics behind setting up a multimillion-dollar power plant in rural Maharashtra. In this sequel to *Sarkar*, Subhash Nagre aka Sarkar (Amitabh Bachchan) is caught in a terrible power struggle and seeks to assert his control over this project planned by an international electrical power firm with the support of the deputy chief minister Karunesh Kaanga (Sayaji Shinde), a middleman Hassan Qazi (Govind Namdeo), an ambitious rural leader Somji (debutante Rajesh Shringarpure), an unscrupulous businessman Kantilal Vora (Upendra Limaye) and Sarkar's own trusted lieutenant Chander (Ravi Kale). After his second son Shankar, a supporter of the project is killed, Sarkar sets off on a path of bloody revenge. The film ends with Sarkar going and sitting at Shankar's desk, symbolizing that he has reclaimed the title of 'Sarkar' himself after his son's death.

The Transitory 'Decline' of the Maha-Nayak

The making of Amitabh Bachchan as the second-generation indigenous hero had many serious repercussions for Indian cinema. The initial skyrocketing success of the Bachchan phenomenon began to adversely affect the very quality of many of his later films. As the film makers went berserk to cash in on his immense popularity, they began to forsake the basic logic in the storyline, narrative and treatment. The films now became terribly formula-ridden, extremely violent – with the lead protagonist doing his earth-shaking *tandav* (a vigorous dance form associated with Lord Shiva) – and sometimes even ridiculous.

As the megasuperstar preferred to work only with a limited number of directors, this factor imposed serious limitations on his growth as an actor. Even stalwarts such as Yash Chopra, Manmohan Desai and Prakash Mehra soon became blasé over the years. A major part of the 1980s, dominated by Bachchan, in fact, became a period that witnessed highly commercially motivated cinema with quality plummeting to an all-time abysmal low. Now, neither Bachchan's films nor his roles came up with anything really new.

Bachchan's angry young man image also completely changed the face of the hero in Hindi cinema. This cinema was conceived and designed with the hero as the focal point. One simple approach to multiply this focus was to cast Bachchan in double, and sometimes, triple roles so that the whole film revolved around the histrionics of the superstar. Such an approach invariably made every other creative ingredient in a film redundant. Sidekick comedians, hitherto so indispensable in a Hindi film, lost their relevance. Music and songs also became mere fillers. With cinema in its dominant genre thus becoming one-dimensional rather than a composite whole, it steadily slid downhill.

From 1985 onwards, for about a decade, the audience's acceptability of Bachchan's movies (for example, *Jaadugar*, *Toofan* and *Akayla*) became markedly low as evident from the fact that many big-banner films failed at the box office. For the actor, the liability of failed ventures was higher than apparent. Such a downfall, unmistakably, marked the beginning of mainstream cinema's journey towards a big disaster. As the overall quality of cinema reached its nadir, even the grand presence of Amitabh Bachchan could not save it.

This qualitative decline was largely caused by the opportunism exhibited by the directors of the day, who made it big by simply exploiting this vigilante hero's image to the hilt. They proved to be totally incapable of providing creative inputs to carry his legend forward and instead used this great actor only monochromatically, ignoring his vast range and potential. In fact,

Bachchan's image was so powerful and so seductive even for the man himself that he steadily slid down the chute. In spite of the continuing fall during this period, Bachchan could never either overgrow or redefine the angry man image. He kept on doing tacky repetitions of the set routines of comedy-vengeance-dance · combinations. As he lost his earlier depth and authenticity, these characterizations now looked like caricatures of his own without a soul of their own. According to veteran Hrishikesh Mukherjee, the first mentor of the actor, 'the image had fallen prey to the law of diminishing returns. Film makers were still bogged down by Bachchan's earlier films. What they needed to do [was to] give him a new role, create a new image for him'.

As the trends and tastes have changed in the new millennium, Bachchan, frozen in his image of the 1970s, became an inevitable victim. The overexposed, hard-hitting protagonist had lost his social relevance and appeal because, in the post-liberalization and globalization phase, his stance was out of tune with the emerging 'feel-good' cinema centred round a new horde of highly glamourized treadmill heroes. These heroes, with Shahrukh Khan and Aamir Khan in the lead, began to define Indian cinema in an entirely new context. Bachchan, in his desperate search for a new cinematic identity and acceptability, took his patented screen persona many steps backwards. Instead of enriching the scope of his anti-establishment protagonist by linking him with the challenges of the rapidly emerging socio-political complexities of the post-liberalization period, the actor conveniently opted for the pro-establishment roles, and, in some of his latest films, he has appeared in extremely negative roles.

The actor's own association with art cinema was even less than symbolic. Bachchan did only two voice-overs: in Mrinal Sen's *Bhuvan Shome* (1969) and Satyajit Ray's *Shatranj Ke Khiladi* (1977). Like Dilip Kumar, he also does not have to his credit a single art film. Thus, the actor, in spite of having a strong intellectual background, failed in harnessing his immense talent in the parallel cinema genre. Bachchan also did not take up films inspired by literary works; the only exception being *Saudagar*.

In spite of acquiring the enviable status of the indigenous film hero, Bachchan could not save himself from the influences of the brave new globalized world. His roles in *Aks*, *Aankhen*, *Kaante* and *Boom* not only offended one's sensibilities, but also appeared dangerous in a society that is increasingly becoming violent and sadistic. Bachchan in these films thus further alienated himself from the trends of meaningful cinema and also undermined his status as the indigenous hero. The artiste has also become the highly priced advertising anchor and brand ambassador for many top multinational companies; he was even involved in organizing mega beauty pageants. In the new millennium, he also conducted a very popular quiz programme on TV, which gave him a new lease of life. The icon of Indian cinema has inadvertently become a supporter of the present-day consumerist culture. The legends of the earlier graceful period, Dilip Kumar, Raj Kapoor, Dev Anand, Balraj Sahni and Raaj Kumar, indeed would have shuddered at the very idea of using their image for commercial purposes to ensure their popular appeal and its saleability for a few more years.

Thus, the intellectual and cultural decline of his persona *seemed* to have hit rock bottom vis-à-vis his status as the indigenous hero, who was once hailed as the ultimate icon of our times: the rebellious, pro-poor and anti-status quoist *par excellence*. But Amitabh Bachchan has this uncanny ability to bounce back, whatever be the odds stacked against him.

The Upholder of Lost Values: The Actor Reaffirms Himself as the Ageless Superhero

Despite all the negativism, there is still a ray of hope. Significantly, a string of impressive films – *Ek Rishta* (2001), *Baghbaan* (2003), *Armaan* (2003), *Dev* (2004), *Veer-Zaara* (2004), *Waqt: The Race against Time* (2005), *Black* (2005), *Ek Ajnnabi* (2005), *Babul* (2006), *Last Lear* (2008) and *Aladin* (2009) – projected our seemingly ageless hero as the upholder of the social concerns, principles, values and virtues being rapidly being forgotten in today's so-called modern society as a result of their rapid delinking from the family and, by extension, the community. This iconic cinematic figure, promoted by its inherent mass appeal and also by adulation garnered by the actor over the years, now represents a rare dissemination in the popular consciousness of the basic tenets of humanism and the essence of heroic survival amidst the widespread trend of self-gratification and a narrowly held worldview.

Ek Rishta (directed by Suneel Darshan) presented the senior actor once again in the role of a patriarch struggling to come to terms with the changing times. It perhaps marked a well-conceived response of some Indian film makers while taking up themes of critical contemporary importance. This stance was in sharp contrast with the usual conflict in a rich family caused by a love affair set along the class divide as was to be seen soon in *Kabhi Khushi Kabhi Gham*. Set against the backdrop of the present era of globalization and liberalization, *Ek Rishta* sought to capture the conflicting perceptions between the old and the new schools of business management regarding the issue of industrial productivity vis-à-vis the labour–management relations. The other members of the cast included Raakhee, Akshay Kumar, Juhi Chawla and Karisma Kapoor, all of whom pitched in with creditable performances.

Bachchan appeared again as a disillusioned sufferer who is struggling to keep up his ideals in two highly significant films: Honey Irani's (who was once a child artiste) *Armaan* and Ravi Chopra's *Baghbaan*.

Armaan marked Bachchan's 100th film. Apparently inspired by Akira Kurosawa's *Red Beard* (1965), Kamal Amrohi's *Dil Apna Aur Preet Parai* (1960) and Hrishikesh Mukherjee's *Anand* (1971), the film attempted to capture the ideals of the 'Hippocratic Oath', providing a glimpse into the goings-on in a highly authentically created (on celluloid) world of modern science and medicine.

In this movie, Dr Siddharth Sinha (Bachchan), an elderly doctor, is the frontal figure in the narrative, the modern saint/missionary in pursuit of the ideals of his noble profession in the current dehumanized and commercial milieu. In his life-long mourning over love lost in his youth, the doctor transforms this loss into a twofold socially productive mission: raising an orphan (Anil Kapoor) as his doctor-son and setting up a hospital in a far-flung hilly area. Recognizing the immediate need for modernizing his hospital with state-of-the-art technology, he works out a grand project and seeks funding support from financial institutions. In the execution of this project, the film very ably juxtaposes the deep neuroses of the 'vulgarly rich' class with the idealism of the few to serve the society. The love triangle (involving the adopted son and two women) is also built into the story, without disturbing the flow of the narrative.

Baghbaan signified the return of Bachchan to the classical vulnerable protagonist, typical of the cinema of the 1950s and the next couple of decades. Taking a cue from the numerous family melodramas starring Balraj Sahni (especially *Bhabhi*, 1957, and *Ghar Sansar*, 1958, among others) and Rajesh Khanna (*Avtaar*, 1983), the film sought to highlight the cruel economic and emotional delinking of the old and new ways of life in a rapidly disintegrating Indian middle-class family. It thus inadvertently raised the problem of rehabilitation of old people whose numbers are going up rapidly over the years because of increase in longevity. In this film, the angry old man of Indian cinema was seen transformed into an ordinary fallible man whose well-cherished idealism for family harmony and old-age comfort falls apart, given the craze for materialistic and sybaritic acquisitions with scant regard for human relationships.

Raj Malhotra (Bachchan) is an elderly man who has slogged all his life to raise his four sons. With no financial backup to rely upon after retirement, he and his wife Pooja (Hema Malini) become completely dependent on their sons. But the four black sheep are reluctant to take up the responsibility of looking after their aging parents. Eventually, they work out a plan of dividing the responsibility, with each one keeping one parent at a time for six months in rotation. The old couple gets separated, expressing their anguish through songs and over the telephone. The director now uses a familiar ploy devised by Indian cinema – the good old foster relationship – to lend a quick-fix remedy to the old couple's predicament. The foster son (Salman Khan) brought up by the benevolent couple, who has achieved financial success and also greatly adores both, finally brings them together under his caring fold.

The film thus highlighted the growing dehumanization of family relationships in the new-age culture propelled by self-centred individualism, perpetuated, in turn, by the hard economic compulsions of self-preservation. It also raised the core issue of parenthood: is it merely for a reproductive function or is it to raise a responsible generation driven by compassion and social and family responsiveness? The film also seems to conclude that it is in through one's linkages with the benevolent undercurrents of the present-day society (the foster son in this story) that one can hope to obtain help and solace in times of distress and insecurity.

In Yash Chopra's *Veer-Zaara*, a grand spectacle displaying a shared culture and interreligious tolerance between Indian and Pakistani people, Bachchan portrayed a visionary but aging farmer, projected in the narrative as the symbol of Indian benevolence and big-heartedness. When his son Veer (Shahrukh Khan) brings Zaara (Priety Zinta), a Pakistani girl, to his village, the elderly farmer receives her with heart-felt warmth and pure spontaneity. He exclaims: 'Oh! It is so wonderful! You are our special guest! I have served my country so very earnestly. Now I get my first chance to offer hospitality to the neighbouring country.' Veer now presents his father a bottle of army rum, which he hurriedly grabs and while rushing away with the bottle, he joyfully exclaims: 'Neighbouring country: Cheers!' The girl is immensely impressed with their warm hospitality and the common culture that nourishes the land on both sides of the border. Zaara now comes to take leave to return to her home country. The elder puts his hand on her head and says in an emotional tone: 'Daughter, please convey to your parents that this sixty-year-old Indian salutes the values they have nurtured in you!' (The rest of the film is discussed in Chapter 8.)

Vipul Shah's *Waqt: The Race against Time* (2005), a saga about a dying man's desire to complete his worldly duties before death, presented Bachchan in the role of an industrialist suffering from cancer. He wants to see his directionless and irresponsible son (Akshay Kumar) settled in life. But the son elopes with his girlfriend (Priyanka Chopra), whom he later marries, and she becomes pregnant. The father, in order to make his son realize his responsibilities, throws him and his wife out of the house. The distraught son begins to hate his father and becomes a recluse. He eventually succeeds in becoming a responsible man and also finds out about the illness of his father. His desperate prayer to god that his father be granted a few minutes of life until his grandson's birth is answered.

After *Armaan*, Bachchan further expanded his image as the heroic healer with Sanjay Leela Bhansali's *Black*. He came up with a truly impressive performance as the archetype of a lonely, cynical scientist-experimenter who gets obsessive pleasure by venturing into the domain of the unknown and the seemingly impossible.

Like the highly acclaimed Marathi film *Shwaas* (2004), *Black* represents the cinema of hope. It depicts the journey of the healer (Bachchan) and the healed (a visually handicapped girl, who cannot hear or speak) into uncharted territories as they surmount the mental and physical barriers and arrive at the destination they have set for themselves. Presented subtly as a modern-day reincarnation of Jesus Christ, the healer attempts to tackle the disability not by miraculous powers but with strong positive affirmations and moral support. The film tends to show that it is not the visual ability alone that defines sight, but how we illuminate our minds with a vision of compassion and understanding, thus imparting a larger purpose and dimension to life. Although the protagonist is witty and cynical, he is forthright in challenging the stereotypical attitude of society towards the handicapped (as seen in the initial reluctance of the parents of the deaf-dumb-blind girl) and fervently demands reinstating the dignity of the disabled as human beings.

In today's highly competitive world marked by acute self-centredness and one-upmanship all around, *Black* proclaims the victory of compassion and goodwill for those disadvantaged people (especially children) who are being increasingly ignored by society. Equally significant is another message: deaf, dumb and blind society, particularly the new-age materialistic youth, can only be reformed and 'rehabilitated' on a humanistic path by the vision, zeal and discipline of an idealist. In this emphasis, the film reached great heights, virtually restating the concerns of cinema in its formative and classical periods, as in V. Shantaram's *Dr Kotnis Ki Amar Kahani* (1946), Hrishikesh Mukherjee's *Anuradha* (1960) and later Tapan Sinha's *Ek Doctor Ki Maut* (1991). *Black* also seemed to be inspired by *Khamoshi* (1969) in which the nurse protagonist (Waheeda Rehman) herself loses her mind as she works diligently to bring back the hero (Rajesh Khanna), a psychotic patient, to the world of sanity.

Black applauds mankind's victory over disability through the discovery of sign languages and numerous other rehabilitation tools developed over the centuries and also the missionary zeal and prolonged efforts of those unsung messiahs – the doctors, physiotherapists and social workers – who have dedicated their life to serve the disabled. It thus symbolizes a grand tribute to the national rehabilitation programmes and those under the aegis of numerous voluntary organizations that have been working among the disabled. The film also questions the oppressive medical care system when the old healer, who keeps on roaming in the ward of the hospital, is mercilessly chained to his bed, and finally freed by his rehabilitated disciple.

However, in *Black*, the extremely Westernized milieu and the photographic grandeur and glitter somehow seemed to undermine the spirit of the narrative. Like Bhansali's other opulent offerings, this film has also been designed for the global audience. It has completely sidelined the thousands of disabled individuals and their teachers from the lower strata of society who spend virtually their entire lives in blind schools and other institutions where they strive to develop socially productive individuals who can lead dignified lives.

Bachchan's protagonist in this film also underlined a powerful resurrection of the hero of the classical period. He is a lonely sufferer, who broods over his lost past, looking forlorn, often seeking solace in alcohol. And, above all, he is a rebel who, despite his own suffering, challenges the status quo and nurtures an alternative vision of empowered human existence. Ayesha Kapoor, as the eight-year-old, and Rani Mukherji, as the grown-up handicapped girl were stunning in their respective roles.

Black: A Review...

We get an extraordinarily moving film, full of moments which resonate, and superb performances ...

As the middle-aged teetering-on-the-edge-of-alcoholism, eccentric teacher, Bachchan [as Debraj Sahai] falls into the trap of posturing a little, but as soon as he gets into the same space as Rani, he sheds the gestures. The interactions between them are mesmeric, especially when the older Alzheimer-ridden Debraj starts to forget himself, and loses his memories: Some of those sequences are his career-best ...

But the actor who really lights up Bhansali's movie is Rani. The tilt of the head, the face, alternating between animation and vacuousness, the slightly open mouth, he bewildered lost look, the jerky gait – any or all of it could have turned Michelle into a caricature. But Rani overcomes the handicap of being 'normal', and nails all of it down with an unsparing, unsentimental starkness.

A word of applause for Bhansali and his co-producers ... for believing in a film which has no songs, which bucks convention, and which doesn't use schmaltz to falsely glorify disability ... the filmmakers redefine what Hindi cinema can do, and do it with as much finesse as the rest of the world.

Source: *The Indian Express*, 6 February 2005.

Aladin (under production), directed by Sujoy Ghosh and a contemporary depiction of the classic fairy tale, has Amitabh Bachchan in the role of Genius the genie. Riteish Deshmukh appears as the title character while Jacqueline Fernandez plays Jasmine.

The Old Man as the Eternal Lover

Two of Amitabh Bachchan's films *Nishabd* and *Cheeni Kum*, both released in 2007, brought into Hindi cinema's domain an entirely modernist discourse on love, not seen earlier. These works were about socially forbidden love perpetuated not by the class or caste difference so typical of our cinema, but by far more socially alarming factors: a large age gap and the attitude towards life of the lovers.

In Ram Gopal Verma's *Nishabd*, a powerful discourse on loneliness and insecurity in contemporary times among the older generation, Bachchan came up with a dignified portrayal of an elderly man with whom a teenager (Jiah Khan) falls in love. As the two physically incompatible individuals seek solace in each other beyond the usual perceptions of difference in age, appearances and life experiences, the man is caught up in a dilemma: on the one hand are social and familial responsibilities and on the other are an individual's freedom to seek happiness. His kitchen-bound wife (Revathi, who was once a famous danseuse) and daughter (Shraddha Arya) are, predictably, enraged by his uncalled-for adventurism.

Cheeni Kum (directed by R. Balakrishnan) is about an elderly man's reluctant but sure entry into the world of conjugal love to rediscover the long years lost in committed bachelorhood. This film was yet another tribute to the popular saying that 'love has no bounds'. Bachchan is an acclaimed master chef and the owner of an Indian restaurant in London. Being a cynical, 'confirmed' bachelor, he has virtually submerged his libido in his cuisine, which he develops like a work of art. His acute cynicism, powered with overwhelming life energy, impresses the heroine (Tabu) some 30 years younger to him. They gradually begin to fall in love with each other. The sequences are impressive and the dialogues sprinkled with liberal doses of humour. Bachchan once again exhibited his usual expertise in portraying this non-conformist comic role apparently designed for him.

In Ravi Chopra's (B. R. Chopra's son) *Babul* (2006), Bachchan appears as an enlightened modern man, who makes his grief-stricken daughter-in-law (Rani Mukherji) remarry when his son dies young. However, according to a review, 'the subject of rehabilitating widows was treated with far [greater] conviction in [B. R.] Chopra banner's own *Ek Hi Raasta* (1956) and Raj Kapoor's *Prem Rog* (1982). Ravi Chopra uses a tame, ponderous tone for a subject which needed much more fire and brimstone.' (*The Hindustan Times*, 10 December 2006). Another powerful film on the subject was V. Shantaram's classic *Subah Ka Tara* released way back in 1954.

Vidhu Vinod Chopra's magnum opus *Eklavya: The Royal Guard* (2007) recounted a tale wrapped around the conflict between feudalism-rooted loyalty and the shallowness of the princely class. Amitabh Bachchan pitched in with a towering performance as the royal guard with life-long devotion to the erstwhile royal family that has been served for many generations by his forefathers. He has to kill his illegimate son (Saif Ali Khan) borne by the queen (Sharmila Tagore) and raised as the prince of the state. The son is accused of murdering his mother, while the real murder was her husband, the king.

The Last Lear (2008), the masterpiece directed by Rituparno Ghosh, cast Bachchan in one of his career- best performances. Based upon Utpal Dutt's famous play *Aajker Shahjahan*, the film presented a captivating study of the comparative merits of theatre and cinema as art forms. An impatient young auteur wants to cast a veteran theatre thespian of the bygone era, Harish Mishra (Amitabh Bachchan), in his film. But as an outsider in cinema, the cynical thespian keeps on dismissing the technology-driven film medium as unrealistic and fake and far below the dignity and aura of the theatre. He rages against the ways of the modern world. Sporting a medieval silver mane, Bachchan exhibited his vast range of histrionics in negotiating the Shakespearean character with all its vanity, disillusionment and cynicism.

Amitabh Bachchan's Indigenous Hero and Hindi Cinema

The transition of the indigenous film hero from Dilip Kumar to Amitabh Bachchan represented the rapidly changing ethos of Indian society in the 1970s and its renewed interpretation by cinema. While Dilip Kumar's cinema was predominantly located in the feudal setting, gradually witnessing the moving on to modern times in later films, the cinema of Bachchan brought the urban milieu centre-stage (with a few exceptions), projecting essentially the same traditional conflict (good versus evil) in a far more slick and sophisticated environment, but largely ignoring the concerns of the rural settings. As a result, the dominant concern of Hindi cinema gradually shifted to the easily recognizable urban milieu (which included the slums and shanty towns), highlighting the nexus among corrupt politicians, the government apparatus and the archetypes of the underworld.

Bachchan's indigenous hero model encompassed virtually the same the ideological positions represented by Dilip Kumar's prototype. At one level, this revised model, once again, was built around the unresolved clash between tradition and modernity, which is resolved finally in the narrative only through a legitimization of pre-industrial social relationships in a highly commerce- and industry-driven environment. At another level, the new hero emerged as an intrepid crusader against capitalist exploitation of the urban proletariat, who was constantly taking on the villains and their minions. However, eventually his violent crusades went haywire, with vigilantism and vendetta becoming the order of the day.

***

The zooming success of Amitabh Bachchan as hero in the 1970s and the 1980s accurately reflected the public mood, which had become increasingly disillusioned with the political class and the bureaucracy for ignoring the basic tenets of democracy and for not providing responsible leadership and proper public governance. As already mentioned, the masses were also deeply resentful of the hoarders and blackmarketeers, whom they tended to equate with businessmen. Hindi cinema quickly responded to capture this growing mass disillusionment and resentment through the creation of the so-called 'angry man syndrome'. It is ironical that whereas Manoj Kumar's cinema was completely in tune with the populism of the Indira Gandhi-led Congress (I), Amitabh Bachchan (a close associate of the Nehru–Gandhi family) caught the people's imagination by providing a highly compelling insight into the country's highly corrupted political system and its linkages with the privileged sections of society. In a wider sense, this cinema thus helped to some extent in swinging the people's mood in favour of new political formations from the middle to late 1970s.

This new prototype of the indigenous hero clicked because a majority of the viewers were suffering intensely in their daily life and many were unable to acquire their basic necessities. The villains in the new situation were not local zamindars or moneylenders (as in *Ganga Jumna* or *Mother India*) but members of a well-equipped and wealthy crime syndicate or a gang of hoarders/backmarketeers with a gigantic infrastructure for mass oppression and other related nefarious activities. For the most insignificant individual in the audience, about whom society at large was the least bothered, the mission of vengeance taken up by the hero against the status quo was highly comforting, even redeeming. Tormented by a perpetual sense of insecurity, he felt convinced that 'this is the man who cares for me and this is how even I should be!' As writer Tarun Tejpal observes, 'the new hero's final cathartic explosion left him [the common man] grateful and a slave for life'. ('The Mirror Has Two Faces', *Outlook*, 20 July 1998.)

This hero's violence was essentially an act of intimate communication with the toiling masses; it was to assert the pride of the poor, a reaffirmation of their dignity as poignantly brought out by the dialogue in *Deewar*: '*Main gire huye paise nahi uthata*' (I don't pick up money thrown for me) and their new awakening to go against the status quo. However, in-built in this role model were a kind of sanctity and approval for resorting to unbridled aggression. Slum children and youth began to take up body building and performing exercises and could be seen sporting a red scarf tied around the neck, just like their hero. They carried their aggression on their sleeves, thus becoming ready to indulge in vandalism on any pretext.

For the haves among the viewers, Bachchan's cinema was 'mythology retold'. The larger-than-life mythological hero depicting his rational thoughts or irrational fancies, his extreme sense of authority (in spite of being a rebel) to hold sway over the others, the evident signs of his success in quick get-rich operations and other similar missions, the passion for attaining his goals, his controlled fury and his dedication to his mother (on par with Durga Ma, the omnipotent goddess) suited them as nothing before did. For the 'moralistic' middle class and, of course, the intellectuals, the new hero was a dream-come-true among the prevailing social conditions that reeked of complete moral and political decadence.

Whatever the differences in the responses among different strata, the new hero was truly a class apart. He appeared really serious in his mission and cogent while expressing his ideas and opinions. He was poised in his style and mannerisms. In spite of his herculean strength and roughness in his methods, his performance appeared sophisticated.

Amitabh Bachchan also performed another very useful social function. The hero virtually became the entire community's psychologist who would mesmerize his viewers and interpret their dreams and their realities. He would also try to fulfil their desires. Nowhere in the world had a matinee idol created this kind of emotional relationship with his audience. This relationship created an innate sense of dependence of the viewers on their hero-therapist for the release of their tensions and for rekindling self-confidence in themselves, so much so that the therapist finally became their messiah!

The high drama of unbridled on-screen violence also performed another important function. It jerked most viewers out of their own somewhat monotonous existence, forcing them to come to terms with the violence shown on the screen. And they invariably realized that their lives were still better off, far more peaceful and did contain some love and intimacy. The vicarious violence provided by Bachchan's angry cinema helped the viewers to accept life as it came, despite all the trials and tribulations. Thus, it is an irony that his powerful characters were juxtaposed against the growing impotence within society, being reflected in the growing self-gratification among the upper and middle classes and their increasing depoliticization. This state of affairs made them passive spectators who just watched the growing decadence of the socio-political culture all around.

In spite of this passivity on the part of certain sections of the populace, violence in almost all spheres of life was rapidly increasing: in personal relations, in families, in workplaces and in the streets. It was getting reflected in gestures, words or in the flexing of muscles on the slightest provocation. Bachchan as the protagonist in several films interpreted for the viewers their subconscious desire to physically vent their anger, thereby providing a sense of gratitude to their hero for enabling the release of their tensions and frustrations.

But soon this kind of collective psychotherapy became unsustainable. As the actual social conditions started becoming increasingly harsher, the people became increasingly immune to the hero's pent-up anger. The hero's actions now began to appear no more than a fantasy being repeated again and again. Thus, by the mid-1980s, the grand success formula of violent cinema patented by Bachchan and his camp followers began to lose its initial appeal so much so that nearly all his films of this genre in this period were received with much less enthusiasm both by the viewers as well as the critics.

The ingredients employed for the development of the second-generation indigenous film hero were also far less original in their form and content than those of the first one. The fundamental inspiration came from the globally successful Hollywood genre of violent cinema along with borrowing many elements from the films of the classical period. Although uncouth violence had formally made its way into Hindi cinema through Dharmendra, Amitabh Bachchan appeared far more overpowering, reflecting the rapidly changing perceptions of the new moghuls of Hindi cinema. In fact, in Bachchan, they found a new film icon who proved handy in finally replacing the overworked classical film format with a truly fast-paced film structure, which contained the necessary quota of violence and racy dialogues, not to mention sex.

Within the ambit of the foregoing influences on the form and content, apart from the symbolic socio-political references in Bachchan's films, his anti-establishment hero would often define his indigenous context by employing some cultural idioms and motifs but symbolically. The different communities (including the rural ones) were presented only superficially. In many films (*Don, Toofan, Lal Badshah* and *Kohram*, for example), he would attempt to project himself as the typical Hindi-heartland man adorning his eyes with *kaajal* and sporting a long red *teeka* on the forehead and speaking the lingo of that region, albeit in an exaggerated manner. Very few, if any, of the film makers ever attempted to transform the fantasy of the superhero into a realistic entity by adopting tales either from history or literature. The end result was that this new brand of cinema, in its dominant form, was rather limited in its impact when it came to awakening the social consciousness in comparison with the films of the classical period.

In such 'deculturization' of cinema, the worst victim was the music. The film song lost its earlier soothing texture, literary content and soul-stirring appeal perfected by a curious blending of Indian classical music, folk tunes and Western rhythm by the pioneers in this field. Its context in the narrative was also totally transformed. The melodies earlier had a definite aesthetic function, and were used to enhance the beauty of films through their integration with the narration and the depiction of the characters. But now the songs had very little scope in films. Thus, Bachchan's angry cinema undermined, and eventually destroyed, the classical compositions in Hindi films evolved so earnestly by great masters in the classical phase.

However, in spite of certain negative traits, Bachchan's indigenous hero was imbued with two definitive qualities. The first was his distinct indifference, by and large, to any kind of deep religiosity (as was also the case with regard to Raj Kapoor, Dev Anand and Guru Dutt). This image stands out in sharp contrast to many characters portrayed by Dilip Kumar, who, in spite of his suffering and railing against the status quo, would finally bow down before god and accept his supremacy (for example, as in *Insaniyat, Ganga Jumna, Gopi, Bairaag* and *Vidhata*; the only exception being *Daag*). Bachchan, on the other hand, was obviously casual, if not aloof, about the presence of god. And yet this attitude was not indicative of the eventual delinking of the indigenous film hero from the traditional moorings of faith and worship, as reflected in movies such as *Deewar*, *Coolie* and *Toofan*.

Only in *Muqaddar Ka Sikandar* does the hero himself become an iconoclast as he rebukes god and proclaims that he would be the maker of his own destiny rather than remaining a victim of circumstances. In *Nastik*, he is initially projected as a non-believer, but ultimately is compelled by circumstances to accept the supremacy of god.

The second definitive attribute of Bachchan's urban hero was that he represented diverse categories of the urban working class mostly engaged in menial occupations – dockworker, railway station coolie, taxi driver, waiter and bodyguard among others. He also played a bootlegger with great aplomb (as in *Amar Akbar Anthony*).

Notes and References

1. The highlight of *Hum* was the *Jumma Jumma Dede Chuma* dance sequence. Picturized amidst a dockyard, this sequence, which starts unexpectedly, builds up gradually towards a climax and provides an entertaining diversion for the dock workers in their oppressive environment. In this sequence, a seductive dancer (Kimi Katkar), willingly presents herself as the focal point of the workers' desire, articulated on their behalf by the hero. Pretending to be oblivious of what they want, she dances merrily on top of a deck, while the hero and the animated crowd of workers below, who are caught up in a great gush of implicit sexual arousal, keep on asking her for a kiss. Towards the end of the song, the hero and his friends drench the dancer with a hosepipe till the whole crowd is drenched, representing a collective orgasm of all the participants.
2. Ashish Rajadhyaksha and Paul Willemen, *Encyclopedia of Indian Cinema*, London: British Film Institute, and New Delhi: Oxford University Press, 1994.

Chapter 3

Film and Portrayal Diversity in Amitabh Bachchan's Cinema

Film Diversity

Table 3.1 gives the distribution of Amitabh Bachchan's films according to their genre. For comparison, the figures relating to the films of K. L. Saigal and Dilip Kumar are also given.

In the case of Amitabh Bachchan, as many as 81 out of a total of 125 films were socials, 42 were crime thrillers and only two were fantasy/costume dramas (*Ajooba* and *Eklavya*). Like Dilip Kumar, Bachchan too has also not yet deployed his talent in biographical films; nor does he have a historical movie to his credit so far. None of the three heroes took up a mythological role, although Amitabh Bachchan, who is still active, may do so in the future.

Table 3.1
Types of Films of K. L. Saigal, Dilip Kumar and Amitabh Bachchan

Type	Number of films		
	K. L. Saigal	Dilip Kumar	Amitabh Bachchan
Social	15	54	84
Crime thriller	Nil	Nil	42
Costume drama/fantasy	4	4	2
Historical	3	1	Nil
Biographical	3	Nil	Nil
Mythological	Nil	Nil	Nil
Total	25	59	128

Portrayal Diversity

Table 3.2 presents the profiles of the roles played by Bachchan in terms of the five attributes: portrayal, social milieu, dominant character persona, genesis of the character and final manifestation of the character.

Table 3.2
Profiles of Roles by Amitabh Bachchan*

Film	Portrayal	Social milieu	Dominant character	Genesis of character	Final manifestation of character
1969–80					
Saat Hindustani (1969)	Young nationalist	Semi-urban	Ordinary youth-turned-revolutionary upholding the ideology of non-violence	People's hero – crusader for nationaal liberation	Successfully delivers the freedom message
Anand (1970)	Doctor	Metropolis, middle class	Socially conscious and caring introvert, pained and driven by sense of concern for others	Upholder of friendship and other human relations	Establishes social commitment of profession
Reshma Aur Shera (1971)	Rural youth	Rural	Humble and dumb youngster, tormented by enmity and violence around him	Anti-establishment – opposed to family authority; vengeful attitude	Silent and passive observer of the mayhem
Pyar Ki Kahani (1971)	Urban youth	Urban	Upbeat/romantic humorist	Upholder of love	Positive; reset on happy course
Parvana (1971)	Writer	Metropolis	Obsessed seeker of childhood love	Anti-hero	Confession through self-realization
Bansi Birju (1972)	Poet	Urban	Socially conscious and caring introvert; pained and driven by sense of concern for others	Upholder of love	Positive; discharges his moral duty

* Does not include films in which Amitabh Bachchan put in a special appearance, guest appearance or played minor roles.

(contd.)

Film	Portrayal	Social milieu	Dominant character	Genesis of character	Final manifestation of character
Bombay to Goa (1972)	Urban youth	Urban	Upbeat romantic and adventurer/ humorist	Upholder of love	Positive; reset on happy course
Ek Nazar (1972)	Poet	Urban	Seeker of socially unacceptable love	Anti-establishment, rebelling against exploitation of women	Positive; reset on happy course
Raaste Ka Patthar (1972)	Company executive	Metropolis	Upright professional trapped in high-crime environment; crusader against criminal forces	Upholder of law	Victorious
Sanjog (1972)	Rich youth/office clerk	Urban, middle class	Sufferer due to lost love	Victim of circumstances	Positive; takes life in stride
Abhimaan (1973)	Singer	Metropolis	Romantic overtaken by negative disposition and self-obsession/ professional climber	Both hero and anti-hero	Overcomes negative attitudes through self-realization
Bandhe Haath (1973) (double role)	1. Writer 2. Small-time criminal	Metropolis	1. Warm, creative man 2. Anti-social youth in conflict with good values	1. Upholder of love 2. Anti-hero	1. Dies 2. Personal transformation through self-realization
Gehri Chaal (1973)	Bank manager	Metropolis	Trapped man caught in a blackmail trap due to his family's improper past	Upholder of family's honour and law	Transformed in the end
Namak Haram (1973)	Industrialist	Urban	Indulgent young industrialist with anti-worker attitude/upholder of friendship	Anti-establishment; rebelling against parental authority	Becomes socially conscious

(contd.)

Film	Portrayal	Social milieu	Dominant character	Genesis of character	Final manifestation of character
Saudagar (1973)	Rural entrepreneur	Rural	Self-centred schemer; manipulating others for selfish ends	Anti-hero	Overcomes negative attitudes through realization
Zanjeer (1973)	Police inspector	Urban	Sufferer due to painful past/ angry and vengeful against perpetrators	Anti-establishment rebelling against ineffective justice system	Victorious in mission of vengeance
Benaam (1974)	Company executive	Urban, middle class	Commoner troubled because of sense of responsible citizenship	Anti-establishment; rebelling against ineffective public institutions	Victorious
Kasauti (1974)	Taxi driver	Urban poor	Upbeat, romantic and caring	Upholder of love	Positive; reset on happy course
Majboor (1974)	Office employee	Metropolis; lower middle class	Sufferer due to painful, insecure present/crusader against criminals	Upholder of family welfare and law	Victorious
Roti, Kapda Aur Makan (1974)	Educated youth	Urban, lower middle class	Unemployed and insecure youth in search of a socially useful role	People's hero	Victorious
Chupke Chupke (1975)	Professor	Urban, upper middle class	Upbeat romantic/ humorous	Upholder of love and friendship	Positive
Deewar (1975)	Dock worker-turned-smuggler	Urban poor/urban rich	Sufferer due to lost family ties/ angry and vengeful against perpetrators	Anti-establishment; rebelling against ineffective justice system	Dies for his convictions
Faraar (1975)	Painter-turned-fugitive/ murderer	Urban, middle class	Trapped man unable to come to terms with his crime	Anti-hero	Transformed due to self-realization

(contd.)

Film	Portrayal	Social milieu	Dominant character	Genesis of character	Final manifestation of character
Sholay (1975)	Convict	Rural/ semi- urban	Mercenary/ caring man driven by sense of concern for others	Dispenser of justice	Dies for a just cause
Zameer (1975)	Small-time criminal- turned- wealthy heir	Rich business class	Mercenary and schemer/upbeat romantic	Anti-hero	Transformation through self-realization
Mili (1975)	Rich youth	Urban, upper middle class	Angry, self- indulgent recluse, trapped in the past	Anti- establishment; rebelling against inhuman attitudes of others	Transformed through self-realization
Adalat (1976)	1. Honest farmer- turned mafia don (father) 2. Rich youth (son)	Rural poor/ metropolis	1. Wronged man turning vengeful 2. Upbeat romantic/ troubled due to family's present	1. Dispenser of his own justice 2. Upholder of moral values	1. Dies 2. Positive; reset on happy course
Do Anjaane (1976)	Middle- level office employee- turned- rich man	Urban middle class/ metropolis	Sufferer due to painful past/ vengeful against perpetrators	Dispenser of justice	Victorious
Hera Pheri (1976)	Small-time conman	Metropolis	Romantic/ humorous crusader against anti-social elements	Dispenser of justice	Victorious
Kabhi Kabhie (1976)	Poet	Metropolis	Romantic, trapped in the past	Upholder of love	Overcomes past through self-realization
Alaap (1977)	Classical singer	Semi- urban	Sensitive, artistic youth dedicated to upholding Indian cultural traditions	Anti- establishment; rebelling against parental authority	Victorious

(contd.)

Film	Portrayal	Social milieu	Dominant character	Genesis of character	Final manifestation of character
Amar Akbar Anthony (1977)	Small-time bar owner	Metropolis	Upbeat/romantic/humorous/easy-going non-conformist not bothered about social etiquette/crusader against underworld forces	Dispenser of justice	Victorious
Imaan Dharam (1977)	Small-time conman	Urban, poor	Upbeat/humorous	Dispenser of justice	Victorious
Khoon Pasina (1977)	Village street-smart character-turned plantation worker	Hilly areas	Upbeat/romantic/humorous/crusader against feudal oppression	People's hero	Victorious
Parvarish (1977)	Police officer	Metropolis, upper class	Upright law enforcer motivated by a sense of duty/crusader against crime world	Upholder of law	Victorious
Besharam (1978)	Urban youth	Metropolis; middle class	Upright man suffering due to lost family ties/angry and vengeful against perpetrators	Anti-establishment; rebelling against ineffective justice system	Victorious
Don (1978) (double role)	Urban youth impersonating mafia don	Metropolis	1. Simpleton/humorous 2. Upbeat romantic/crusader against underworld forces despite appearing to support them	Upholder of law	Victorious
Ganga Ki Saugandh (1978)	Village simpleton-turned-dacoit	Rural poor	Vengeful crusader against feudal oppression	Anti-establishment; rebelling against ineffective justice system	Dies for his convictions

(contd.)

Film	Portrayal	Social milieu	Dominant character	Genesis of character	Final manifestation of character
Kasme Vade (1978) (double role)	1. Professor 2. Roadside ruffian	Metropolis/ small town; middle class	1. Good-hearted academician strongly opposed to mindless violence prevalent in society. 2. Mercenary unable to look beyond himself but becomes socially responsible through feminine presence	1. Upholder of responsible citizenship 2. Anti-hero	1. Dies 2. Transformed
Muqaddar Ka Sikandar (1978)	Poor youth	Metropolis	Easy-going, non-conformist not bothered about social etiquette/ humorous/seeker of childhood love/ vengeful against anti-social elements	Upholder of law, love and friendship	Dies for a just cause
Trishul (1978)	Real estate dealer/ builder	Metropolis	Sufferer due to betrayal/angry and vengeful against perpetrator	Anti-establishment; rebelling against ineffective justice system	Dies
Jurmana (1979)	Rich playboy	Rural middle class	Overconfident romantic/ obsessed seeker of unfulfilled love	Anti-hero	Overcomes negative attitudes through self-realization
Kala Patthar (1979)	Coal mine worker	Rural industrial	Upright; vengeful crusader against exploitation	People's hero; champion of workers' rights	Victorious
Manzil (1979)	Technical entrepreneur	Metropolis; lower and upper middle class	Professional becoming victim of dominant business culture	Upholder of modern business practices and ethics	Overcomes negative attitudes through self-realization

(contd.)

Film	Portrayal	Social milieu	Dominant character	Genesis of character	Final manifestation of character
Mr Natwarlal (1979)	Small-time conman	Urban/ rural	Mercenary/ romantic/ humorous vengeful crusader against oppression	People's hero	Victorious
Suhaag (1979)	Roadside ruffian-turned-police officer	Metropolis	Romantic/ humorous/ broken family ties/upright law enforcer motivated by a sense of duty against evil doers	Upholder of law	Victorious
The Great Gambler (1979) (double role)	1. Gambler 2. Police inspector	Metropolis rich	1. Mercenary 2. Upright law enforcer motivated by a sense of duty against anti-national forces	1.Anti-hero 2. Upholder of law	Victorious
Do Aur Do Paanch (1980)	Small-time conman	Urban	Mercenary/ romantic/ humorous	Anti-hero	Transformed due to self-realization
Ram Balram (1980)	Police inspector	Urban/ middle class	Romantic/ humorous/ upright law enforcer motivated by a sense of duty against underworld/ broken family ties	Upholder of law	Victorious
Shaan (1980)	Street-smart youth/ small-time conman-turned-avenger	Metropolis	Upholder of family ties/ vengeful crusader against perpetrators of crime	Dispenser of justice	Victorious

(contd.)

Film	Portrayal	Social milieu	Dominant character	Genesis of character	Final manifestation of character
Dostana (1980)	Police officer	Metropolis	Upright law enforcer motivated by a sense of duty and with a strong concern for personal relationships	Upholder of law and friendship	Victorious

1981-90

Film	Portrayal	Social milieu	Dominant character	Genesis of character	Final manifestation of character
Barsaat Ki Ek Raat (1981)	Police inspector impersonating street-smart village youth	Rural hills	Upbeat romantic/ humorous/ crusader against anti-national forces	Upholder of law	Victorious
Kaalia (1981)	Small-time criminal-turned-mafia don for avenging killing of brother	Urban	Upholder of family ties/ vengeful crusader against killers	Anti-establishment; rebelling against ineffective justice system	Transformed
Laawaris (1981)	Street-smart youth-turned manager	Metropolis	Sufferer due to lost family ties	Upholder of personal rights	Victorious
Naseeb (1981)	Waiter/ fighter	Metropolis	Upbeat romantic/ humorous	Dispenser of justice	Victorious
Silsila (1981)	Writer	Metropolis	Indulgent and obsessed lover	Anti-hero	Overcomes negative attitudes through self-realization
Yaraana (1981)	Village youth-turned-popular singer	Rural/ metropolis	Strong-headed simpleton/ humorous, with a deep sense of concern for others	Upholder of friendship	Victorious

(contd.)

Film	Portrayal	Social milieu	Dominant character	Genesis of character	Final manifestation of character
Satte Pe Satta (1982) (double role)	Urbanized rural youth/ criminal	Rural/ urban	1. Overpowering family head without sense of social etiquette/ humorous 2. Vengeful	1. Upholder of love and family ties/ dispenser of justice 2. Rebel	1. Victorious 2. Dies
Bemisaal (1982)	Doctor	Metropolis	Socially conscious medical professional suffering due to painful past	Upholder of professional ethics	Victorious
Desh Premi (1982) (double role)	1. Nationalist (father) 2. Small-town conman (son)	Urban	1. Socially conscious man perturbed by deceitful character of son 2. Unscrupulous, deceitful and self-centred youth	1. Upholder of moral values 2. Anti-hero	1. Successful 2. Transformed into a good human being
Khuddar (1982)	Taxi driver	Urban	Law-abiding commoner with strong sense of self-esteem, with pride in honesty and hard work.	Upholder of moral values and family ties	Positive; reset on happy course
Namak Halal (1982)	Personal assistant-cum-bodyguard	Metropolis	Strong-headed simpleton/ humorous	Dispenser of justice	Victorious
Shakti (1982)	Educated youth-turned-criminal	Metropolis; upper middle class	Loner/ sufferer due to lost family ties/ self-oriented in thinking and actions	Anti-establishment; rebelling against parental authority	Dies
Andha Kanoon (1983)	Police officer	Metropolis	Disillusioned, upright law enforcer becoming vengeful crusader against anti-social and criminal elements	Anti-establishment; rebelling against ineffective justice system	Victorious

(contd.)

Film	Portrayal	Social milieu	Dominant character	Genesis of character	Final manifestation of character
Coolie (1983)	Platform porter	Urban	Romantic/ humorous/ vengeful crusader against anti-social and criminal elements	Dispenser of justice	Victorious
Mahan (1983) (triple role)	1. Lawyer-turned-businessman 2. Police inspector 3. Actor	Urban-rich/middle class/lower middle class	1. Wronged man separated from his family 2. Upright law enforcer suffering due to lost family ties/crusader against anti-social and criminal elements 3. Simple-hearted comic upstart, obsessed with acting	1. Upholder of professional ethics 2. Upholder of law 3. Theatre aficionado	Victorious
Nastik (1983)	Rural youth	Rural/ urban	Atheist; upholder of rational thinking/crusader against criminal forces	Anti-establishment	Transformed in the end
Pukar (1983)	Ordinary youth-turned-smuggler	Colonial period (Portuguese)	Disillusioned man-turned-opportunist; negatively disposed towards people's struggle, but changes stance later	Anti-hero	Transformed into a good human being
Inquilab (1984)	Roadside vendor-turned-police officer and politician	Metropolis	Simple-hearted commoner deceived by the apparent charisma of public figures/ vengeful against the politically corrupt	People's hero	Surrenders after the vengeful act
Mard (1984)	Tonga driver-turned-freedom fighter	Colonial period	Clan heir separated from parents, becoming crusader against British rule	People's hero	Victorious

(contd.)

Film	Portrayal	Social milieu	Dominant character	Genesis of character	Final manifestation of character
Sharabi (1984)	Rich youth	Urban	Indulgent, self-obsessed/sufferer due to lost family ties	Anti-establishment; social deviant	Reformed in the end
Giraftaar (1985)	Police officer-turned-criminal	Urban	Loner suffering due to disillusionment with law-enforcing system and lost family ties/crusader against underworld forces	Dispenser of justice	Victorious
Aakhri Raasta (1986) (double role)	1. Police inspector 2. Ex-prisoner	Urban	1. Upright and dutiful 2. Vengeful sufferer due to painful past.	1. Upholder of law 2. Anti-establishment; rebelling against ineffective justice system	1. Victorious 2. Dies for just cause
Shahenshah (1988)	Police inspector-turned-community leader	Urban	Romantic/humorous/disguised crusader for ensuring people's welfare and rights	People's hero	Victorious
Ganga Jamuna Saraswati (1988)	Truck driver	Semi-urban	Lover in pursuit of eternal relationship	Upholder of love	Positive; reset on happy course
Toofan (1989)	Rural youth-turned-bandit	Rural	Simpleton blessed with mythical powers/crusader against feudal oppression	People's hero	Victorious
Jadugar (1989)	Magician	Urban	Slick, confident professional offering services for debunking godmen using magical skills/humorous	Dispenser of justice	Victorious

(contd.)

Film	Portrayal	Social milieu	Dominant character	Genesis of character	Final manifestation of character
Main Azaad Hoon (1989)	Roadside inhabitant-turned-political activist	Urban	Idealist in search of social identity/ demagogue, propagating the ideal of equitable society	People's hero	Dies; victim of political opportunism
Agneepath (1990)	Gang leader	Urban	Upholder of family ties/ vengeful crusader against criminal elements	Anti-establishment; rebelling against ineffective justice system	Dies for just cause
Aaj Ka Arjun (1990)	Village youth	Rural/ urban	Vengeful crusader against feudal oppression	Anti-establishment; rebelling against ineffective justice system	Victorious
1991–2000					
Hum (1991)	Small-time, street-smart hooligan-turned-family man	Urban	Romantic/ humorous/easy-going non-conformist with concern for others/upholder of family ties	Dispenser of justice	Victorious
Ajooba (1991)	Clan leader	Royal; medieval	Disguised crusader for ensuring people's welfare and rights	People's hero	Victorious
Indrajeet (1991)	Police officer-turned-rebel	Urban; middle class	Upholder of law, suffering due to painful wronged past/disillusioned, becoming vengeful crusader against anti-social and criminal elements	Anti-establishment; rebelling against ineffective justice system	Victorious; resettles in life

(contd.)

Film	Portrayal	Social milieu	Dominant character	Genesis of character	Final manifestation of character
Akayla (1991)	Police officer	Urban	Upholder of law/vengeful crusader against evil forces	Anti-establishment; rebelling against ineffective justice system	Victorious
Khuda Gawah (1992)	Clan leader	Tribal area/urban	Upbeat romantic/disguised crusader for welfare of poor	People's hero	Victorious
Mrityudaata (1997)	Doctor	Urban	Sufferer due to wronged past/vengeful crusader against criminal elements	Dispenser of justice	Victorious
Major Saab (1998)	Army officer	Urban	Obstinate disciplinarian/crusader against anti-social forces	Upholder of law	Overcomes disabling attitudes through self-realization
Lal Badshah (1999) (double role)	1. Poor individual (father) 2. Community leader (son)	Urban	1. Wronged family man 2. Vengeful crusader against villainous forces	Anti-establishment; rebelling against ineffective justice system	Victorious
Bade Miyan Chhote Miyan (1999) (double role)	1. Small-time conman 2. Police officer	Urban	1. Romantic/humorous simpleton; inadvertently becomes crusader against criminal forces 2. Upright/dutiful	Upholder of law	Victorious
Kohram (1999)	Army officer-turned-community leader	Urban	Idealist pained by political decadence/simple-hearted community leader taking care of the people around him	Anti-establishment; rebelling against ineffective public institutions	Victorious

(contd.)

Film	Portrayal	Social milieu	Dominant character	Genesis of character	Final manifestation of character
Hindustan Ki Kasam (1999)	Former freedom fighter	Urban	Old-time nationalist pained by political decadence	People's hero	Victorious
Suryavansham (1999) (double role)	1. Landed aristocrat (father) 2. Entrepreneur (son)	Rural	1. Obstinate patriarch, suffering due to conflicting values/vengeful crusader against evil forces/ upholder of feudal pride 2. Humble sufferer due to lost family ties.	1. Anti-hero 2. Anti-establishment; rebelling against parental authority	Both overcome disabling attitudes through self-realization
Mohabbatein (2000)	Principal of *gurukul* (traditional school)	Urban ambience	Orthodox patriarch; fanatically against modern values and lifestyle	Anti-hero	Overcomes disabling attitudes through self-realization

2001 onwards

Film	Portrayal	Social milieu	Dominant character	Genesis of character	Final manifestation of character
Aks (2001)	Police inspector-turned-murderer	Urban	Psychedelic sadist suffering from compulsive behaviour syndrome caused by the spirit of the villain	Anti-hero	Regains normalcy
Ek Rishta (2001)	Business magnate	Urban	Upholder of management's and workers' dignity and rights through strong management-worker relations/ sufferer due to lost family ties	Protector of business ethics	Overcomes disabling attitudes through self-realization
Kabhi Khushi Kabhi Gham (2001)	Business magnate	Metropolis	Orthodox patriarch/ upholder of class values and family pride/sufferer due to lost family ties	Anti-hero	Overcomes disabling attitudes through self-realization

(contd.)

Film	Portrayal	Social milieu	Dominant character	Genesis of character	Final manifestation of character
Aankhen (2002)	Former banker-turned-bank robber	Metropolis	Self-possessed egoist with a criminal bent of mind	Anti-hero	Apparently murdered
Hum Kisi Se Kum Nahin (2002)	Doctor	Urban	Caring man, driven by sense of concern for others/humorous	Upholder of friendship	Overcomes misplaced approach
Kaante (2002)	Failed entrepreneur-turned-gangster	Metropolis	Desperate middle-aged man in search of quick money; gets sucked into a small-time crime syndicate; offers his managerial abilities for criminal activities	Anti-hero	Killed by fellow criminals
Armaan (2003)	Doctor	Country-side; upper middle class	Socially conscious idealist/sufferer due to lost love/ engaged in life-long two-fold mission of raising an orphan as his son and treating the sick	People's hero	Dies
Baghbaan (2003)	Retired man	Urban	Benevolent simple-hearted ordinary elder seeking comfort and care for his wife and himself in a joint family falling apart	Upholder of family ties	Resettles in life
Boom (2003)	Mafia don	Metropolis	Kinky character with dual personality	Anti-hero	Killed by fellow criminals

(contd.)

Film	Portrayal	Social milieu	Dominant character	Genesis of character	Final manifestation of character
Lakshya (2004)	Army officer	Urban	Disciplinarian and committed soldier presenting himself as the role model for today's directionless youth and yet often broods over ugliness of war	Upholder of army tradition and honour	Transforms young hero into a committed, brave soldier
Khakee (2004)	Police officer	Urban	Frustrated cop brooding over irresponsible and unethical law enforcers	People's hero	Victorious over renegades
Aetbaar (2004)	Rich man	Metropolis	Overprotective parent refusing to have faith in his daughter's yuppie love affair	Upholder of old views about love and matrimony	Adjusts to the times
Deewar (2004)	Army officer	Urban/ prisoner of war camp	Prisoner of war engineering freedom for fellow prisoners	People's hero	Victorious; hailed as army hero
Dev (2004)	Police officer	Metropolis	Upright individual, delegating his duty by rulebook and in the spirit of secularism	People's hero	Killed; murder engineered by fundamentalist colleague
Black (2005)	Therapist	Small town but affluent setting	Lonely, elderly and obsessive healer transcending his painful past by putting his professional expertise to rehabilitate and brighten the life of a deaf, dumb and blind girl; upholder of scientific and motivational approach to disability	People's hero	Disabled due to onset of Alzheimer's disease; cured symbolically by his own disciple

(contd.)

Film	Portrayal	Social milieu	Dominant character	Genesis of character	Final manifestation of character
Veer-Zaara (2004)	Visionary village leader	Rural	Symbol of Indian benevolence and big-heartedness	People's hero	Apparently dies of old age and pain of lost son (not shown in the film)
Waqt: The Race against Time (2005)	Industrialist	Metropolis	Cancer patient who wants to make his footloose son realize his family responsibilities	Upholder of family ties	Sees his son reformed before his death
Ek Ajnnabi (2005)	Retired army colonel	Metropolis	Bitter, unhappy alcoholic; discovers a new meaning to life when appointed bodyguard of a child	Dispenser of justice	Victorious in mission of avenging the murder of the child by kidnapper
Sarkar (2005)	Mafia don	Metropolis	All-powerful but cool-headed and kind man who negotiates his business acts with a sense of morality and dispenses justice to common people	Mass leader worshipped by people	Upholds his supremacy when his younger son kills the rebellious elder one
Bunti Aur Babli (2005)	Detective cop	Metropolis	Crazy and carefree	Upholder of the view that a humane approach is better than law to reform criminals	Lets criminal couple go after arrest to let them start an honest life
Viruddh (2005)	Elderly middle-class man	Metropolis	Peace-loving man turned-murderer when his son is killed by villain	Reluctant dispenser of justice	Shoots the villain dead

(contd.)

Film	Portrayal	Social milieu	Dominant character	Genesis of character	Final manifestation of character
Babul (2006)	Progressive man	Metropolis	Kind-hearted and true to his convictions; wants his widowed daughter-in-law to resettle in life	Upholder of new social values	Succeeds in getting daughter-in-law remarried
Kabhi Alvida Na Kehna (2006)	Business magnate	Metropolis	Nicknamed 'Sexy Sam'; fond of women but upholder of institution of marriage	Happy-go-lucky man	Dies of heart attack after advising his daughter-in-law to part ways with his son.
Family – The Ties of Blood (2006)	Mafia don	Urban	Ruthless perpetrator of crime and vengeance	Upholder of family ties	Repentant; finally dies
Nishabd (2007)	Elderly man	Metropolis	Faces dilemma: familial responsibilities versus love attention showered by an upbeat feisty teenager	Indulges in socially forbidden love	Returns to his family
Cheeni Kum (2007)	Chef; owner of Indian restaurant in London	Metropolis	Cynical bachelor; begins love affair with a girl 30 years younger; faces family and social embarrassment and rejection	Indulges in socially forbidden love	Brings about a change in attitude of others
Ram Gopal Verma Ki Aag (2007)	Mafia don	Urban	Sadistic villain	Ruthless by disposition	Killed by the two mercenaries hired by a vengeful police officer
Eklavya (2007)	Royal guard of palace	Royal; modern	Extremely loyal servant of princely family for decades	Upholder of feudalism-rooted values	Prepares to kill his illegitimate son accused of murdering the queen

(contd.)

Film	Portrayal	Social milieu	Dominant character	Genesis of character	Final manifestation of character
Bhoothnath (2008)	Ghost in limbo	Urban	Angry and cynical; undergoes transformation through pure love of a child	Upholder of human sentiments	Ghost finds deliverance
The Last Lear (2008)	Theatre thespian	Urban	Cynical; rages against the ways of modern world; reluctant to act in a film	Upholder of old acting tradition of high professionalism and commitment	Makes his mark as film actor
Zamaanat (2008)	Blind lawyer	Urban	Recluse; agrees to defend an innocent youth accused of murder	People's hero	Brings the real murderer to book
Sarkar Raj (2008)	Mafia don	Metropolis	All-powerful but cool-headed and kind man who negotiates his business acts with a sense of morality and dispenses justice to common people	Mass leader worshipped by people	Regains original position

The Repetition Syndrome

One of the most disquieting aspects of Bachchan's films belonging to the angry young man genre was the repetition syndrome as seen in the thematic thrust and in the design of the portrayals. The prolonged repetitions in this genre resulted in two stereotypes: one in which he was the perpetual angry young man with the typical anti-establishment stance (for example, *Trishul* and *Andha Kanoon*) and the second in which he combined his comic persona with that of the powerful dispenser of justice, taking his revenge against those who had wronged him and his dear ones either in childhood or in adulthood (for example, *Khoon Pasina*, *Mr Natwarlal* and *Naseeb*).

Dual Persona Syndrome

Another peculiar feature of Amitabh Bachchan's cinema is the 'portrayal changeover syndrome'. In a large number of films, the actor would either undergo a distinct transformation in characterization or play double roles representing two entirely different personalities. In a narrative, this duality is intended not only to establish the thematic premise of a film but also to depict the conflicting social positions being taken up by the protagonist. In this portrayal changeover, as the character makes a shift in his social milieu, he would undergo distinct personality changes and thus would take on a new identity. The three alternatives – (1) double role (one triple role in *Mahan*); (2) the obvious coincidental physical resemblance between two characters; and (3) the character making a changeover by discrete make-up – have been used as a narrative ploy by the film makers to derive many benefits. First, it helped in introducing, maintaining and finally resolving the main conflict in the narrative. Secondly, it enabled Amitabh Bachchan to achieve easily high portrayal diversity in a film by appearing in roles widely diverse in their respective personality traits, background and lifestyle. And thirdly, it helped in mounting the film on a big canvas, with the aura of Bachchan spread virtually over the whole footage.

Table 3.3 presents details regarding the portrayal changeover syndrome in Bachchan's cinema. The actor employed a dual persona in many of his films. In fifteen films 'impersonation' was a vital factor. This impersonation act depicted two identities: one as an explorer of opportunities for his selfish ends (*Faraar* and *Zameer*) and the other as a dispenser of natural justice or an extended arm of the law to pursue and punish the perpetrators of crime, social oppression or exploitation (*Do Anjaane, Don* and *Ajooba*). Double roles based on blood relations formed the basis of six films.

Bachchan's portrayals also witnessed a change in the socio-economic status of the protagonist as seen in a large number of films. In all these films, except *Sanjog*, in which there was a lowering of the status, this change invariably was from a lower class to a higher class.

Table 3.3
Use of Dual Persona in Amitabh Bachchan's Cinema

Dual persona	Films
Double role as blood relation	*Adalat, Desh Premi, Aakhri Raasta, Lal Badshah, Mahan (triple role), Suryavansham*
Impersonation by resemblance coincidence	*Bandhe Haath, Don, Kasme Vade, The Great Gambler, Satte Pe Satta, Bade Miyan Chhote Miyan*
Impersonation by design	*Zameer, Faraar, Don, Barsaat Ki Ek Raat, Do Anjaane, Ajooba, Shahenshah, Toofan, Aks*

Directorial Support

Amitabh Bachchan has worked with more than seventy directors (see Table 3.4) but unlike Dilip Kumar, his directorial support has been quite wide-based, particularly in the later half of his career. In his early years, he had preferred to work with a select group of directors (Hrishikesh Mukherjee, Manmohan Desai, Prakash Mehra, Yash Chopra, Ramesh Sippy, Rakesh Kumar and Tinnu Anand).

Table 3.4
Directors of Amitabh Bachchan's Films

Director	Film
1. Manmohan Desai	*Amar Akbar Anthony* (1977), *Parvarish* (1977), *Suhaag* (1979), *Naseeb* (1981), *Desh Premi* (1982), *Coolie* (1983), *Mard* (1985) and *Ganga Jamuna Saraswati* (1988)
2. Hrishikesh Mukherjee	*Anand* (1970), *Namak Haram* (1973), *Abhimaan* (1973), *Mili* (1975), *Chupke Chupke* (1975), *Alaap* (1977), *Jurmana* (1979) and *Bemisaal* (1982)
3. Prakash Mehra	*Zanjeer* (1973), *Hera Pheri* (1976), *Muqaddar Ka Sikandar* (1978), *Laawaris* (1981), *Namak Halal* (1982), *Sharabi* (1984) and *Jadugar* (1989)
4. Yash Chopra	*Deewar* (1975), *Kabhi Kabhie* (1976), *Trishul* (1978), *Kala Patthar* (1979), *Silsila*, (1981) and *Veer-Zaara* (2004)
5. Ramesh Sippy	*Sholay* (1975), *Shaan* (1980), *Shakti* (1982) and *Akalya* (1991)

(contd.)

Director	Film
6. Rakesh Kumar	*Khoon Pasina* (1977), *Mr Natwarlal* (1979), *Do Aur Do Paanch* (1980) and *Yaraana* (1981)
7. Tinnu Anand	*Kaalia* (1981), *Shahenshah* (1988), *Main Azaad Hoon* (1989) and *Major Saab* (1998)
8. Mukul S. Anand	*Agneepath* (1990), *Hum* (1991) and *Khuda Gawah* (1992)
9. S. Ramanathan	*Bombay to Goa* (1972), *Mahan* (1983) and *Zamaanat* (2008)
10. Narendra Bedi	*Benaam* (1974) and *Adalat* (1976)
11. Ramesh Behl	*Kasme Vade* (1978) and *Pukar* (1983)
12. Shakti Samanta	*The Great Gambler* (1979) and *Barsaat Ki Ek Raat* (1981)
13. T. Rama Rao	*Andha Kanoon* (1983) and *Inquilab* (1984)
14. Mehul Kumar	*Mrityudaata* (1997) and *Kohram* (1999)
15. David Dhawan	*Bade Miyan Chhote Miyan* (1999) and *Hum Kisi Se Kum Nahin* (2002)
16. K. A. Abbas	*Saat Hindustani* (1969)
17. Ravi Nagaich	*Pyar Ki Kahani* (1971)
18. Sunil Dutt	*Reshma Aur Shera* (1971)
19. Jyoti Swaroop	*Parvana* (1971)
20. Prakash Verma	*Bansi Birju* (1972)
21. B. R. Ishara	*Ek Nazar* (1972)
22. S. S. Balan	*Sanjog* (1972)

Director	Film
23. Mukul Dutt	*Raaste Ka Patthar* (1972)
24. C. V. Sridhar	*Gehri Chaal* (1973)
25. O. P. Ralhan	*Bandhe Haath* (1973)
26. Sudhendu Roy	*Saudagar* (1973)
27. Arvind Sen	*Kasauti* (1974)
28. Ravi Tandon	*Majboor* (1974) and *Khuddar* (1982)
29. Manoj Kumar	*Roti Kapda Aur Makan* (1974)
30. Ravi Chopra	*Zameer* (1975), *Baghbaan* (2003) and *Babul* (2006)
31. Shankar Mukherjee	*Faraar* (1975)
32. Dulal Guha	*Do Anjaane* (1976)
33. Desh Mukherjee	*Imaan Dharam* (1977)
34. Sultan Ahmed	*Ganga Ki Saugandh* (1978)
35. Devan Verma	*Besharam* (1978)
36. Chandra Barot	*Don* (1978)
37. Basu Chatterjee	*Manzil* (1979)
38. Vijay Anand	*Ram Balram* (1980)
39. Raj Khosla	*Dostana* (1980)
40. Raj N. Sippy	*Satte Pe Satta* (1982)
41. Pramod Chakravarty	*Nastik* (1983)
42. Prayag Raj	*Giraftaar* (1985)

Director	Film
43. K. Bhagyaraj	*Aakhri Raasta* (1986)
44. Ketan Desai	*Toofan* (1989)
45. K. C. Bokadia	*Aaj Ka Arjun* (1990) and *Lal Badshah* (1999)
46. Shashi Kapoor	*Ajooba* (1991)
47. K. V. Raju	*Indrajeet* (1991)
48. Suneel Darshan	*Ek Rishta* (2001)
49. Veeru Devgan	*Hindustan Ki Kasam* (1999)
50. E. V. V. Satyanarayana	*Suryavansham* (1999)
51. Aditya Chopra	*Mohabbatein* (2000)
52. Rakeysh Omprakash Mehra	*Aks* (2001)
53. Karan Johar	*Kabhi Kushi Kabhi Gham* (2001)
54. Vipul Shah	*Aankhen* (2002)
55. Sanjay Gupta	*Kaante* (2002)
56. Honey Irani	*Armaan* (2003)
57. Kazaid Gustad	*Boom* (2003)
58. Vikram Bhatt	*Aetbaar* (2004)
59. Farhan Akhtar	*Lakshya* (2004)
60. Rajkumar Santoshi	*Khakee* (2004) and *Family – The Ties of Blood* (2006)
61. Milan Luthria	*Deewar* (2004)

Director	Film
62. Govind Nihalani	*Dev* (2004)
63. Sanjay Leela Bhansali	*Black* (2005)
64. Mahesh Manjrekar	*Viruddh* (2005)
65. Shaad Ali	*Bunti Aur Babli* (2005) and *Jhoom Barabar Jhoom* (2007)
66. Ram Gopal Verma	*Sarkar* (2005), *Nishabd* (2007), *Ram Gopal Verma Ki Aag* (2007), *Darna Zaroori Hai* (2007), *Sarkar Raj* (2008)
67. Apoorva Lakhia	*Ek Ajnnabi* (2005) and *Shootout at Lokhandwala* (2007)
68. Vidhu Vinod Chopra	*Eklavya: The Royal Guard* (2007)
69. R. Balu	*Cheeni Kum* (2007)
70. Vivek Sharma	*Bhoothnath* (2008)
71. Rituparno Ghosh	*The Last Lear* (2008)
72. Anil Sharma	*Ab Tumhare Hawale Watan Sathiyo* (2004)
73. Rumi Jaffrey	*God Tussi Great Ho* (2008)

Chapter 4

The Influence of Dilip Kumar on Amitabh Bachchan

The making of Amitabh Bachchan's indigenous hero was largely influenced by the manner in which thematic elements, characterizations or situations from certain earlier films (including some foreign) were used, inadvertently or otherwise, by his scriptwriters and directors. But it was the influence of Dilip Kumar's films and portrayals that provided the essential building blocks for the creation of the second indigenous hero.

In *Parvana*, Bachchan's role as the obsessed seeker of childhood love seemed to be 'inspired' by the senior actor's portrayal in *Arzoo* (1950), except that the lover this time becomes a murderer. In *Muqaddar Ka Sikandar* also, the protagonist's obsession with his childhood love, set across the rich–poor divide, and the dedication of the second heroine to the hero, seems to be borrowed from Dilip Kumar's roles in *Hulchal* (1951) and *Deedar* (1951). In *Mili*, the melancholic recluse, addicted to the bottle and brooding over his past, had shades of Dilip Kumar's performance in *Devdas*. Also, Bachchan's antics, while inebriated, in films like *Amar Akbar Anthony* and *Sharabi* looked quite imitative in their spirit and style, the original being Dilip Kumar's *Kohinoor* (1960), *Daag* (1952) and *Leader* (1964). The Bachchan character in *Do Anjanne* seemed inspired by that in Dilip Kumar's *Dastaan*. In *Faraar* the friendship between the hero (hiding from the police in the house of the heroine, who was once his beloved but now married to someone else) and the heroine's child had a similar appeal as that between Dilip Kumar's character and the paralytic child of his former love in *Musafir* (1957).

Dilip Kumar's masterpiece *Ganga Jumna* (1961) had a far-ranging influence on Bachchan's cinema. This film provided the basis for *Deewar* and thus helped the then young actor in consolidating the image of the rebel hero. The classic was again imitated, rather slovenly, in *Ganga Ki Saugandh*. The depiction of the *kabbadi* match between two villages in this film was a poor imitation of the one in the original film. Another example of borrowing from *Ganga Jumna* was in *Khuddar*, in which the virtually illiterate elder brother (as a taxi driver) toils day in and day out to educate the younger brother. The scene in which the hero sees off his brother at a bus stop and with tears in his eyes assuring his brother of his love and support had a striking similarity with a similar scene in *Ganga Jumna*, the only difference being that the site of departure was a village-side railway station.

The famous mirror comedy scene in *Kohinoor* involving Dilip Kumar and Jeevan found a companion in *Amar Akbar Anthony*, with Bachchan talking to his image, and again in *Pukar*, in which Jeevan's place in front of the mirror is taken by Prem Chopra. Bachchan's comic role in *Satte Pe Satta* had touches of Shyam from *Ram Aur Shyam* (1967).

In Bachchan's *Main Azaad Hoon*, the ambitious political leader, who is scared of the growing political stature and popularity of Azaad among the people, is persecuted in the same way as the worker in Dilip Kumar's *Sagina* (1974). Incidentally, while Dilip Kumar's favourite screen name was Shankar, the god who drinks the poison of life so that others may live, Bachchan's preference was Vijay, meaning victory.

In senior roles, Bachchan's characters of an idealistic, but imposing, patriarch in *Suryavansham, Mohabbatein, Ek Rishta, Kabhi Khushi Kabhi Gham* and *Dev* had a similar disposition as that of Dilip Kumar's in *Shakti* and also that of Prithviraj Kapoor's in *Mughal-e-Azam* (1960). Bachchan's vengeful crusade against three villains in *Aakhri Raasta* was structured on the same lines as that of Dilip Kumar's *Duniya* (1984). The protagonist in *Ek Rishta* had similar views on labour–management relations as those of the mill owner in the senior's *Mazdoor* (1983).

***

Among the many disciples of Dilip Kumar, Bachchan emerged at the top. In developing his formidable acting style, he borrowed heavily from among many elements of the master. He himself had once said that the stars may not admit it, but most of them, at one time or the other, have been greatly influenced by Dilip Kumar's method acting. Unlike other students, Bachchan has been able to invoke tremendous energy in projecting his characters and in infusing his roles with great depth.

The exacting influence of the master on the acting style and the characterizations of the new indigenous hero manifested itself in many ways.

In serious roles, Bachchan has appeared to be governed by the master's style of portraying his agony. Keeping in mind Dilip Kumar's sense memory technique (formulated by the adherents of the Konstantin Stanislavsky school of method acting), Bachchan has developed his emotional personality on the basis of his certain recallable experiences. Such experiences encompassed a series of traumas and seemingly unending disillusionment with society in general. His characters have cogently depicted the anguish caused by the aforementioned experiences. In such instances, Dilip Kumar keeps his agony burning within him (as if his physical frame is being gradually melted by the grief). His facial expressions and his body language seem to set the screen aglow. His manner is generally subdued and melancholic. Amitabh Bachchan, on the other hand, looks restless in his agony, and attempts to focus it somewhere outside his physical frame. In contrast with the senior, Bachchan's aggression often gets ignited like gunpowder and explodes.

For the 'brooding hero' roles, Bachchan too developed his acting style on the 'principle of reluctance'. Like the master, his articulation of emotions is not free but controlled: he pauses for a few moments before he speaks. He then modulates his voice and tone, keeping in view the requirements of the situation. In a typical scene, he first builds up his 'visual personality' as if attempting to foresee events, and then suddenly ignites his 'verbal personality' as the complete response to a given situation. But the principle of reluctance soon becomes evident in the dialogue delivery and he appears to restrict himself after the rapid-fire volley.

Bachchan based the angry young man fulminations on the emotive mechanism set in place by Dilip Kumar, but more belligerently and forcefully. As the anti-hero suffers in his despair, a single-point trigger in a scene all of a sudden unleashes a spontaneous outburst fully charged with anger. This emotional response is so earth-shaking that it resounds in the whole environment. But unlike Dilip Kumar, such outbursts often do not signify the internal vulnerability of the protagonist but become an expression of his inner strength and conviction.

The foregoing attributes in his acting style took Bachchan far ahead of the master in executing larger-than-life portrayals, with the result that his highly melodramatic heroism stood out, dominating the overall film milieu and also the other characters and events. While Dilip Kumar appeared to overcome his adversaries by deploying his inner strength and powers of persuasion, Bachchan, like many of his contemporaries, greatly magnified his masculinity in order to physically dwarf his enemies.

In many films, Amitabh Bachchan also capitalized on the death scene. The enactment strategy of such a scene had been patented by Dilip Kumar for enhancing the appeal of his image as a 'grand finale' for his histrionics. For Bachchan too, death becomes the ritualized climax after a lifelong struggle to achieve his goal, irrespective of whether he is successful in his endeavour or not. Reminiscent of Dilip Kumar's execution of this scene, Bachchan's hero dies in the arms of his father, mother or brother, or a very close friend, signifying his return to the fold of tradition in death (for example, in *Shakti* and *Deewar*).

***

As far as comedy is concerned, Amitabh Bachchan has exhibited greater ingenuity in mastering this genre than Dilip Kumar. Comedy, in fact, seemed to come spontaneously to Bachchan and, in some films, even overshadowed his angry man persona. Inspired apparently by some of the most hilarious elements of Dilip Kumar's comic style (as in *Aan*, 1952, *Azaad*, 1955, *Kohinoor*, *Ram Aur Shyam* and *Sagina*), he instituted a new variety of humour in Hindi cinema. His brand of humour was woven into the script and did not appear extraneous as did some of the antics of the 'professional comedians'. His humour could be self-deprecatory or aimed at the villain and his cronies, with telling effect. At times, he would take a dig the social or political scenario, lampooning the status quo and highlighting its deficiencies.

Like Dilip Kumar, Bachchan did not depict humour through slapstick comedy but personified it through a comic interpretation of the situation on hand. In this sense, he took up the role of a *bhand*, the typical character in the *nautanki* (vaudeville theatre) tradition. The actor also successfully incorporated two remarkable features in his comedy style. First was the use of the eastern Uttar Pradesh dialect to express a sense of natural eccentricity, which lent an earthy humour to his characterizations. He also began to rely heavily on the archetype of an immigrant settled in the metropolis and on his typical Allahabadi/Poorabiya mix for dialogue delivery. Evidently, this genre seemed to be inspired by Dilip Kumar's Ganga in *Ganga Jumna*. Secondly, again taking a clue from the terrific performance by Dilip Kumar as a drunkard in *Daag*, the actor adopted inebriated stupor as a highly useful technique, particularly in his humorous scenes.

Although Dilip Kumar may not be facing the studio lights any more, the shadow he has cast makes its presence felt more often than not!

Chapter 5

Amitabh Bachchan's Contemporaries

Amitabh Bachchan's seemingly all-encompassing and towering presence was undeniably the dominant factor of the Bollywood films of the mid to late 1970s and a major portion of the 1980s. However, he was surrounded by a large number of his illustrious contemporaries, who, on the basis of their distinguished cinematic presence, helped Hindi cinema build upon the thematic concerns and the socio-politico-economic milieu of the times.

Dharmendra: The Original 'Angry' Hero

Dharmendra, macho and rugged, was a strong contender for the top slot in the 1970s, competing diligently with Amitabh Bachchan and Rajesh Khanna. Dharmendra represented the persona of a truly multifaceted hero. His image presented a strange combination of various elements: the Bengali literary stereotype as incorporated in Hindi cinema, the perpetual victim caught in a milieu of existential suffering, the slapstick, romantic-comic hero and, above all, the angry dyed-in-the-wool 'son of the soil', dedicated to his motherland and striving to uphold the honour of the country, family or community against all odds.

Dharmendra was born as Dharmendra Keval Kishan Singh Deol on 8 December 1935 in Sahnewal, Punjab. While working as a mechanic in a factory, he applied for the Talent Search

Programme launched by United Producers under the aegis of the highly popular magazine *Filmfare*, which was scouting for new faces. This naïve youth from Punjab was selected by a panel, which had luminaries such as Guru Dutt and Bimal Roy as judges. He appeared in a tiny role in Ramesh Sehgal's *Railway Platform* released in 1955

Dharmendra

(incidentally, this film also introduced Sunil Dutt). The young aspirant remained a struggler for some years till producer-director Arjun Hingorani signed him for *Dil Bhi Tera, Hum Bhi Tere* (1960). He appeared in the role of a street-smart youth who falls in love with a housemaid (Kum Kum) and struggles to make a living in the company of his senior, Balraj Sahni, who plays a toughie. This film was followed by Ramesh Sehgal's *Shola Aur Shabnam* (1961), in which he appeared as a distraught lover. (This film is remembered for its fabulous melodies composed by Khayyam.)

Dharmendra came to be noticed after the release of Bimal Roy's *Bandini* (1963). In this movie, he appears as a warm-hearted doctor (assigned to duties in a jail in the pre-independence period) who falls in love with a young woman prisoner (Nutan) convicted for murder. In Chetan Anand's *Haqeeqat* (1964), set against the backdrop of the 1962 Chinese aggression, he made his presence felt in the role of a valiant army captain who falls in love with an innocent Ladakhi belle (Priya Rajvansh). He also put in a spirited performance in Phani Majumdar's classic, *Akashdeep* (1965). In *Baaharen Phir Bhi Aayengi* (1966), Guru Dutt's venture completed by his brother Atma Ram after the master's death in October 1964, Dharmendra appeared as an upright editor who comes into conflict with the business interests of his employer, a woman, played by Mala Sinha. He played a villain in Mohan Kumar's *Aayee Milan Ki Bela* (1964) to Rajendra Kumar's hero, both of whom are contenders for the heroine's (Saira Banu's) love.

Like Amitabh Bachchan later, Dharmendra, too, in his formative years, found in Hrishikesh Mukherjee a powerful and reliable mentor. The young actor came up with highly sensitive performances in *Anupama* (1966), *Majhli Didi* (1967) and *Satyakam* (1969), all three movies directed by the stalwart.

In the first movie, he portrayed a struggling idealistic writer who loves the guilt-ridden heroine (Sharmila Tagore) who has been blamed by her domineering father for her mother's death during delivery. She becomes an introvert and recedes into a shell. He rescues her from her isolation by writing a novel on her life, which emboldens her to break her emotional shackles.

Majhli Didi was an adaptation of the Bengali writer Saratchandra Chatterjee's novel. The theme was about ill-treatment of children in a semi-feudal domestic set-up.

In *Satyakam*, set around the time of India's independence, Dharmendra excelled in the role of an idealistic engineer with strong nationalist feelings instilled in him by his grandfather (superbly portrayed by Ashok Kumar). He refuses to obey the orders of his feudal master (Manmohan), who wants him to sign a fake blueprint, and is forced to quit his job. He marries a rape victim (Sharmila Tagore, who is carrying Manmohan's seed), and in the face of his aged grandfather's refusal to accept a child born of sin, he refers to a mythological tale from the Upanishads: Rishi Gautama accepted Jabala's son named Satyakam under similar circumstances. The hero is compelled to change jobs frequently as he refuses to compromise with his principles and values. He eventually falls victim to cancer and dies. His grandfather allows the 'illegitimate' son to light the funeral pyre. In this film Dharmendra played the role of a lifetime. He had great company in the form of Sanjeev Kumar, his college mate, an honest but practical individual, who knows how to adjust to the changing times.

B. R. Chopra's *Aadmi Aur Insaan* (1969), a melodrama based on the age-old clash between good and evil, again portrayed Dharmendra in the role of an upright engineer.

In Hrishikesh Mukherjee's unique movie, *Guddi* (1971), Dharmendra played himself. His objective in this film is to dispel the illusions of an impressionable teenaged girl (Jaya Bhaduri, in her first Hindi film) about the film world. He takes the teenager to various shooting locations to show her the harsh realities behind the façade of glitz and glamour.

The actor also imbued his role in Rajender Singh Bedi's masterpiece, *Phagun* (1973), with varying shades. This movie narrates a tragic story about the vulnerability of well-nurtured love when confronted by a sudden momentary humiliation. He plays the role of a poor artist married to a rich girl (Waheeda Rehman), who ridicules him for spoiling her saree (not bought by him) during Holi celebration, which takes place in the month of Phagun. He feels deeply insulted and runs away. He now begins making money and for years keeps on buying sarees for his wife. When his collection of sarees catches fire, he becomes insane and is admitted to a mental asylum.

***

In the 1960s, Dharmendra emerged as a highly refreshing romantic hero, injecting a new charm into the light romances being churned out by Bollywood as seen in Mohan Kumar's *Aap Ki Parchhaiyan* (1964), Rajendra Bhatia's *Neela Akash* (1965), Raghunath Jhalani's *Aaye Din Bahar Ke* (1966), T. Prakash Rao's *Izzat* (1968) and Jhalani's *Aaya Sawan Jhoom Ke* (1969). He carried this image forward in the 1970s also, with films such as Ramesh Sehgal's *Ishq Par Zor Nahin* (1970), Hrishikesh Mukherjee's *Chaitali* (1975), Devendra Goel's *Ek Mahal Ho Sapnon Ka* (1975) and Pramod

Chakravarty's *Dream Girl* (1978). He also appeared as a conscientious male figure in several woman-oriented family dramas (mostly opposite tragedienne Meena Kumari), often rebelling against the social conventions to stand up for the suffering woman protagonist as seen in Mohan Kumar's *Anpadh* (1962), A. C. Trilogchandra's *Main Bhi Ladki Hoon* (1964), Krishnan-Panju's *Mera Kasur Kya Hai* (1964), Narendra Suri's *Purnima* (1965), Ram Maheshwari's *Kaajal* (1965), D. D. Kashyap's *Dulhan Ek Raat Ki* (1966), O. P. Ralhan's *Phool Aur Patthar* (1966) and later M. A. Thirumugham's *Maa* (1976).

Phool Aur Patthar brought about a sudden change in Dharmendra's screen persona. He was transformed into a formidable 'angry' hero figure in Bollywood, often blending his 'he-man' image with romantic-comic ingredients as well as simplicity and naïvete.

In this film, he appeared as a hardened criminal, who takes care of a widow (Meena Kumari) abandoned by her uncaring relatives when plague hits a town. The hero opts to set up home with her and thrashes the neighbours and former criminal associates who oppose what they view as an 'illicit relationship'. The actor further energized this image with Prakash Mehra's *Samadhi* (1972, in a double role as father and son) and Nasir Hussain's superhit *Yaadon Ki Baraat* (1973) in a role that was similar to Amitabh Bachchan's in *Zanjeer*, released the same year. In *Yaadon Ki Baraat*, a lost-and-found vendetta tale, he appears as the eldest of three brothers (the other two being Vijay Arora and Tariq) separated during childhood after their parents are killed. He turns into a professional robber with a heart of gold, who launches a desperate search for the murderer of his parents (Ajit) and for his lost brothers. It is the title song of the film that ultimately brings the brothers together.

With the box-office success of *Phool Aur Patthar* and *Yaadon Ki Baraat*, Dharmendra, from the late 1960s onwards, made a rather permanent shift to crime thrillers and vendetta-packed melodramas, marking his macho performance with his trademark yelling to challenge his enemies: '*Main tuje jeene nahi doonga!*' (I will not let you live) and '*Kutte, main tera khoon pi jaoonga!*' (you dog, I will drink your blood). In this phase, he became a hot favourite of film makers specializing in this genre. Some of the films in this category are: Ramanand Sagar's *Aankhen* (1968), Arjun and Anil Hingorani's *Kab? Kyon? Aur Kahan?* (1970), Raj Khosla's *Mera Gaon Mera Desh* (1971, a precursor to *Sholay*, 1975), Arjun Hingorani's *Kahani Kismat Ki* (1973), Vijay Anand's *Blackmail* (1973), Pachchi's *International Crook* (1974), Ramesh Lakhanpal's *Pocketmar* (1974), Dulal Guha's *Dost* (1974), Ramanand Sagar's *Charas* (1976), Arjun Hingorani's *Khel Khiladi Ka* (1977), Krishna Shah's *Shalimar* (1978, co-starring with the Hollywood star, Rex Harrison of *Cleopatra* and *My Fair Lady* fame) and B. R. Chopra's *The Burning Train* (1980, probably India's first 'disaster' movie).

In films like Pramod Chakravarty's *Jugnu* (1973) and *Azaad* (1978), Rama Rao Tatineni's *Main Inteqam Loonga* (1982), Sudarshan Nag's *Insaaf Kaun Karega* (1984), K. R. Reddy's *Paap Ko Jala Kar Rakh Kar Doonga* (1988) and *Veeru Dada* (1990) and Rajkumar Kohli's *Virodhi* (1992), Dharmendra's action hero turned into a lone avenger.

In J. P. Dutta's *Batwara* (1989), set in the context of land reforms and the threat posed to the zamindar class, he appeared as the farmers' leader waging a war against the tyranny of the thakurs (belonging to the upper castes) led by villain Vinod Khanna. In *Hathiyar* (1989), also directed by Dutta, he played a fearsome mafia don, who is the protector of the hero's (Sanjay Dutt) family.

Dharmendra had earlier successfully transported his vengeful hero to the constume drama genre as seen in Manmohan Desai's *Dharam Veer* (1977), as the lost prince fighting for his right to the throne. He was given company by Jeetendra, a loyal friend, who turns out be his long-lost brother. In Kamal Amrohi's historical *Razia Sultan* (1983), set in the medieval Muslim era, Dharmendra portrayed the slave-lover (Jamaluddin Yakut) of the lonely queen (played by Hema Malini) fighting for survival amidst a slew of court intrigues. In Mukul S. Anand's *Sultanat* (1986), he dons the mantle of a Muslim nobleman who prepares his sons to avenge the wrongs done to him.

***

Dharmendra also proved his mettle in down-to-earth comedy roles.

In Hrishikesh Mukherjee's *Chupke Chupke* (1975), he appeared as one of the participants (along with Amitabh Bachchan) in organizing a hilarious leg-pulling caper (so common in Indian families, especially against one's in-laws). He plays havoc with the life of his wife's (Sharmila Tagore) sanctimonious brother-in-law (Om Prakash), who would always insist on speaking chaste Hindi and on occupying the high moral ground. (See also Chapter 2.)

In Dulal Guha's *Pratigya* (1975), Dharmendra's slapstick comedy made a great impact. He appears as a runaway from the law who takes shelter in a remote village, where nobody knows his real identity. He dons the uniform of a cop and 'converts' a group of villagers (who look like buffoons) into 'policemen' in order to protect the village against the recurrent attacks of bandits. The romantic element is provided by the vivacious Hema Malini (whom he later married; she became his second wife). As in *Yaadon Ki Baraat*, he seeks revenge against the dacoit played by Ajit, who has killed his parents.

In Ramesh Sippy's blockbuster *Sholay* (1975), he was truly in his element in the role of the footloose, boisterous, but courageous, Veeru, constantly making fun of himself and others. At times, he proves to be a source of embarrassment for his saturnine buddy (Amitabh Bachchan). In the later part of the film, he turns serious, especially during his confrontations with the dacoit-villain Gabbar Singh, a role played to perfection by Amjad Khan. The actor again appeared in the company of Bachchan and Ajit in Vijay Anand's *Ram Balram* (1980), but without any noticeable impact.

Most of Dharmendra's films were packed with highly popular songs, which helped in bolstering his image – as an idealist or a romantic – on screen.

***

In the early 1980s, Dharmendra entered film production, launching his elder son Sunny Deol (real name Ajay Singh Deol) in *Betaab* (1983). As an actor, he reappeared in films after a gap of many years. In Anurag Basu's *Life in a Metro* (2007), he portrayed a septuagenarian non-resident Indian (NRI), who has returned to India to spend the last years of his life with his first love (Nafisa Ali), now staying in an old-age home.

Anil Sharma's *Apne* (2007) was a touching tale about down-to-earth family solidarity that is unaffected by personal goals. In this film, Dharmendra co-starred with both his sons (Sunny Deol and Bobby Deol) for the first time. He made his mark as an ex-boxer suffering from the lifelong guilt of losing a crucial match. He can never forget the person who ruined his chances of becoming the champion. His younger son (Bobby Deol) gives up his career in music and trains himself to be a boxer and wins many titles. But in the final match, he becomes a victim of a conspiracy hatched by his scheming opponents and gets seriously injured. It is the elder son (Sunny Deol) who now steps in to turn the tables on the villains and bring his father the happiness that he has been longing for.

It is unfortunate that despite being a highly accomplished and versatile artiste, Dharmendra's talent has not been fully tapped to create meaningful cinema except probably in the formative years of his long career. In 1997, Dharmendra was bestowed with the *Filmfare* Lifetime Achievement Award for his contribution to cinema. While accepting the award from Dilip Kumar and his wife Saira Banu, Dharmendra became emotional and remarked that he had never received any *Filmfare* award in the 'best actor' category despite having worked in so many successful films. Speaking on the occasion, Dilip Kumar, commenting on the legendary handsome facial features of Dharmendra, observed: 'Whenever I get to meet with God Almighty I will set before him my only complaint: why did You not make me as handsome as Dharmendra?' In fact, at the peak of his film career, Dharmendra was considered a matinee idol and was included among the ten most handsome men in the world at that time.

Dharmendra entered politics as a member of the Bharatiya Janata Party and won a parliamentary seat from Bikaner (Rajasthan) in 2004.

The Indigenous Hero in Waiting: Vinod Khanna

Vinod Khanna

Vinod Khanna, who had a commendable presence in the cinema of the late 1960s and 1970s (and even later), was the most powerful counterpoint to Amitabh Bachchan's persona, what perhaps Raaj Kumar was to Dilip Kumar in the 1950s. In contrast with Bachchan's rather over-expressive angry hero, Khanna's screen image was relatively far more down-to-earth and dignified, infused with simplicity and warmth. Yet, unlike Bachchan's, his persona – despite his macho presence, rugged physique and strong convictions – would appear rather detached and self-composed, seldom betraying the anguish and turmoil that he is undergoing. A film commentator observes that there is a kind of beautiful sadness connected with a Vinod Khanna performance. Khanna exudes an existential melancholy that one could mistake for quiet resignation if not for the very evident fire smouldering behind his smoky eyes. Introspection is a true part of his characters, the searching gaze, the million questions behind the face that barely conceals the pathos within. However, like Raaj Kumar, he looked rather uncomfortable in romantic and comic roles although he essayed quite a few of them.

Vinod Khanna was born on 6 October 1946 in Peshawar, now in Pakistan. After Partition, his family migrated to Punjab (on the Indian side) and then to Bombay. He did his schooling at Barnes School, Deolali (now in Maharashtra) and graduation from Sydenham College, Bombay. In the late 1960s, the by-then well-established Sunil Dutt, as part of his experiment of grooming new talent for films, took Vinod Khanna (along with his brother Som Dutt) as apprentices in the field of acting.

Khanna's film journey represents an amazing transformation of screen image, rarely seen in Indian cinema. He began his career with a villainous role, in his mentor Sunil Dutt's *Man Ka Meet* released in 1968, followed by Rajesh Nanda's *Nateeja* (1969) as hero. In Mukul Dutt's *Aan Milo Sajna* (1970) and Manmohan Desai's *Sachcha Jhootha* (1970), in both of which Rajesh Khanna was the hero, he went back to playing the villain. Vinod Khanna stole the show in the role of a dreaded dacoit in Raj Khosla's *Mera Gaon Mera Desh* (1971), in which Dharmendra was the hero. But he soon moved out of the shadow of his mentor Sunil Dutt's image (arched eyebrows, blood-shot eyes and harsh expressions) and found through his second mentor, Gulzar (real name Sampooran Singh), opportunities to discover his talent as a sensitive hero. It was this writer-director who finally prepared the young actor for the place he was soon to find in Indian cinema.

In Gulzar's *Mere Apne* (1971), a harsh depiction of criminal politics amidst gang warfare in the late 1960s, the young actor appeared in the role of a college student who is forced to become a gangster (basically due to rampant unemployment). He and his minions are constantly fighting with a rival gang (led by

Shatrughan Sinha, who was once Vinod Khanna's friend, but later turns into a bitter enemy) in the streets and bylanes of a small city. He gives refuge to a simple-hearted old widow (Meena Kumari), who has been brought to the city from her village by a working couple pretending to be her relatives so that she can look after their uncared-for child. The hardened hoodlums (of both the gangs) are deeply moved by the motherly affection and care the widow bestows on them. They begin to realize the futility of their violent actions that are driven by hatred and vengeance. Khanna very ably captured the gradual humane transformation of the criminal under the comforting shadow of the mother-like figure, propagating, in her simplicity and innocence, the warmth of love and friendship between the two warring gangs. The gangs decide to reconcile when Meena Kumari is killed as a result of their rivalry.

Gulzar utilized the talents of his young disciple in another landmark film, *Achanak*, released in 1973. *Achanak* was evidently 'inspired' by R. K. Nayyar's *Yeh Raaste Hai Pyar Ke* (1963), a film based on the true life story of K. M. Nanavati, a navy officer, who after murdering his adulterous wife, surrenders to the police (see also Chapter 10 of Volume 1 under Sunil Dutt). However, in *Achanak*, the hero (an army man), after killing his disloyal wife, uses several tactics to evade being arrested by the police.

Khanna also appeared in the lead in Vikas Desai and Aruna Raje's offbeat film *Shaque* (1976) opposite Shabana Azmi (who plays his wife). In this film, he gives evidence in a murder trial against the accused. However, a decade later, another criminal surfaces and creates suspicion (*shaque*) in his wife's mind that her husband is not all that innocent.

Vinod Khanna entered big-budget cinema in the 1970s with Prakash Mehra's *Haath Ki Safai* (1974) and Raj Khosla's *Main Tulsi Tere Aangan Ki* (1978), followed by action-packed hits: B. R. Chopra's *The Burning Train* and Feroz Khan's *Qurbani*, both released in 1980.

In the decade of the 1970s, he reached the zenith of his career in counterpoint to Amitabh Bachchan, with whom he appeared in a string of hit films. Juxtaposing their position with the anti-establishment stance of Bachchan, Khanna's characters reflected the conviction of a common upright individual driven by his conscience to help the wrathful hero in his battle against the unjust and cruel world. Khanna's characterizations, in fact, reflected the moral, emotional as well as physical support arising within the socio-political milieu for the realization of the vision of the angry renegade. This kind of a bonding between individuals from diverse social settings who come together to promote the causes of social justice and personal redemption reached its high point in Prakash Mehra's *Muqaddar Ka Sikandar* (1978). In this superhit film, Khanna gave a memorable performance as a lawyer with a conscience who fulfils the dreams and hopes (both socially and psychologically) that Amitabh Bachchan's hero is unable to due to his tainted past.

Other films starring these two heroes together were *Khoon Pasina* (1977, directed by Rakesh Kumar), *Parvarish* (1977) and *Amar Akbar Anthony* (1977), both directed by Manmohan Desai. In the last-mentioned film, a runaway hit with some riproaring scenes, Vinod Khanna (Amar) plays an honest police officer vis-à-vis Amitabh Bachchan's hooligan (Anthony) with a heart of gold. They eventually join hands to defeat the villain (Jeevan) and his henchmen. The third hero Akbar (Rishi Kapoor) also pitches in to thwart the designs of the bad guys.

At a time when Vinod Khanna had established himself as one of the most successful actors in Bollywood, vying with Amitabh Bachchan for the top slot, he suddenly left the film industry in 1979 to become a follower of the spiritual guru Rajneesh (Osho). After his return to the film world eight years later, he still managed to rediscover his status, appearing in several important films of his career such as Mukul Anand's *Insaaf* (1987), Raj N. Sippy's *Satyamev Jayate* (1987), Balraj Tah's *Jallianwala Bagh* (1987, in the role of the revolutionary Uddham Singh), Feroz Khan's *Dayavan* (1988), Rajiv Mehra's *Aakhri Adalat* (1988), Yash Chopra's *Chandni* (1989) in the second lead (the main hero being

Rishi Kapoor), Gulzar's *Lekin* (1991) and David Dhawan's *Eeena Meena Deeka* (1994).

In *Dayavan*, a remake of the Tamil film *Nayagan* that starred Kamalahasan, and one of the most memorable movies of Khanna, he portrayed a seemingly invincible Bombay underworld don. The don is an unconstitutional power figure, worshipped by the common people as a hero for his kindness and the sense of protection his very presence provides.

In *Lekin* , a 'ghost story', he posted an impressive performance as a museum curator determined to liberate an unhappy 'ghost', Rewa (Dimple Kapadia), who haunts a royal palace, even risking his own life. The film had a superb musical score by Lata Mangeshkar's brother Hridyanath Mangeshkar.

As a senior actor, Khanna chose to appear in very few films, which include Ashu Trikha's *Deewaanapan* (2001) and Vishram Sawant's *Risk* (2007). He won the *Filmfare* Lifetime Achievement Award in 1999.

He entered politics as a member of the Bharatiya Janata Party (BJP) and became a minister in Prime Minister Atal Behari Vajpayee's cabinet in 2002.

Shashi Kapoor: A Romantic Hero

Shashi Kapoor (born on 18 March 1938 as Balbir Raj Kapoor), with his ever-smiling face and suave mannerisms, made his mark as a romantic hero in the cinema of the 1960s and 1970s. He stands out among the very few Indian actors who had a strong foothold in British stage and cinema. Shashi Kapoor is the son of Prithviraj Kapoor and the younger brother of Raj Kapoor and Shammi Kapoor. He started his career in 1944 as a child artiste in his father's stage production of Shakuntala. He appeared as the young Raj Kapoor in *Aag* (1948) and *Awara* (1951). After working for Prithvi Theatres for a few years, he joined, in 1957, Geoffrey Kendal's touring theatrical group that enacted William Shakespeare's plays (in English).

Shashi Kapoor

Shashi made his debut in Hindi cinema in 1961 with Yash Chopra's *Dharmputra* based on the famous Hindi novel by Acharya Chatursen Shastri set in pre-independence period. The young actor perhaps came up with his career-best performance in the role of Dalip, the 'illegitimate' son of a Muslim couple raised by a liberal Hindu family. He becomes a staunch Hindu nationalist, advocating the virtues of Hindu thought and culture. As politics and religion begin to divide the Hindu and Muslim communities, Dalip adopts an anti-Muslim stance and becomes a powerful leader of the Hindus. He even leads a group of rioters to burn down the house of his real mother (Mala Sinha). When he comes to know the truth about his identity, he finally realizes the futility of his ideology, which incites people to violence and bloodshed.

In the 1960s, Shashi Kapoor appeared in a series of love stories and family dramas that largely failed to offer any challenging roles to the young actor. These included Krishan Chopra's *Char Diwari* (1961), Suraj Prakash's *Mehndi Lagi Mere Hath* (1962), Bimal Roy's *Prem Patra* (1962), B. R. Chopra's *Waqt* (1965), Akhtar Mirza's *Mohabbat Isko Kehte Hain* (1965), Shiv Sahni's *Neend Hamari Khwaab Tumhare* (1966), Suraj Prakash's *Juari* (1968), Mohan Sehgal's *Kanydaan* (1969) and Prakash Mehra's *Haseena Maan Jayegi* (1968, in a double role). A couple of Shashi Kapoor films that went on to hit the box-office bullseye were Suraj Prakash's 1965 venture *Jab Jab Phool Khile* (the predecessor of Dharmesh Darshan's *Raja Hindustani*, 1996) and Nasir Hussain's *Pyar Ka Mausam* (1969). The first film was set in the picturesque locales of Kashmir and was studded with several highly popular songs composed by Kalyanji Anandji.

Shashi Kapoor also featured in a few crime thrillers such as *Aamne Saamne* (1967, directed by Suraj Prakash) and *Chori Mera Kaam* (1975, directed by Brij Sadanah).

In the 1970s, Shashi Kapoor acted in a slew of films, many of which did not make much of an impact. However, some of the more noteworthy ventures of this decade include Subodh Mukerji's *Abhinetri* (1970), Samir Ganguli's *Sharmeeli* (1971), Manoj Kumar's *Roti, Kapda Aur Makan* (1974), Ashok Rao's *Chor Machaye Shor* (1974), Raj Tilak's *Mukti* (1977) and Ramesh Talwar's *Doosra Aadmi* (1978).

In his brother Raj Kapoor's highly erotic venture, *Satyam Shivam Sundaram* (1978) opposite Zeenat Aman, Shashi Kapoor appeared as a youth who cannot accept any form of ugliness as a reality of human existence. This film was basically heroine-oriented and it was Zeenat Aman who hogged the limelight, especially when she sported skimpy costumes.

Romesh Sharma's *New Delhi Times* (1986) was perhaps his last important film as hero. In this film, a political thriller examining the links between crime and politics, he gave an impressive performance as the editor of an English-language daily, who has to confront a politician in league with a powerful lobby of illicit liquor manufacturers.

Shashi Kapoor's other cultural achievements include the revival of the Prithvi Theatres in Bombay in honour of his father.

In the 1970s and early 1980s, Shashi Kapoor like Vinod Khanna, established himself as the formidable second lead actor in a string of Amitabh Bachchan films: *Deewar*, 1975, *Kabhi Kabhie*, 1976, *Trishul*, 1978, *Kala Patthar*, 1979 (all directed by Yash Chopra), *Imaan Dharam* (1977, directed by Desh Mukherjee), *Suhaag* (1979, directed by Manmohan Desai), *Do Aur Do Paanch* (1980, directed by Rakesh Kumar) and *Shaan* (1980, directed by Ramesh Sippy).

Apart from Hindi cinema, Shashi Kapoor also entered into a long-term association with internationally renowned film makers James Ivory and Ismail Merchant, making his mark in movies (some of which were bilingual, i.e., in English and Hindi) such as *The Householder* (1963), *Shakespeare Wallah* (1965), *Bombay Talkie* (1970) and *Heat and Dust* (1983). He also won wide acclaim for his role in Conrad Rooks's *Siddhartha* (1972), a tale set in ancient India.

In 1978, Shashi Kapoor launched a very innovative experiment in film production to promote hitherto absent links and sharing of talent between mainstream cinema and art cinema. For this experiment, he commissioned some of the famous names of art cinema to direct his commercial ventures. In Shyam Benegal's *Junoon* (1979), set at the time of the 1857 Mutiny, he appeared as Javed Khan, a Pathan passionately in love with a British girl, Ruth Labadoor (Nafisa Ali). He is so very obsessed with Ruth's beauty that he pays scant attention to the tumultuous events happening around him. Incidentally, his wife in real life (Jennifer Kendal) played the role of Ruth's mother in this film.

In *Kalyug* (1981), also directed by Benegal, characters from the epic Mahabharata were set in a contemporary industrial society. Shashi Kapoor played the role of the mythological Karan, the firstborn son of Kunti, whom she discards as she is then unmarried. Shashi Kapoor is killed while changing a car tyre (in the original epic, Karan was killed by Arjun when his chariot wheel got stuck in wet mud). Aparna Sen's masterpiece *36 Chowringhee Lane* (1981), Govind Nihalani's *Vijeta* (1983) and Girish Karnad's costume drama *Utsav* (1985) were other films commissioned under Shashi Kapoor's banner.

Shashi Kapoor donned the director's mantle for *Ajooba* (1991), an Indo–Soviet production starring Amitabh Bachchan, brother Shammi Kapoor and nephew Rishi Kapoor. In 1993 he played an aging Urdu poet in Ismail Merchant's *In Custody* and in 1994 he appeared in the same director's film *Muhafiz*.

Amitabh Bachchan (in the driver's seat) and Dharmendra in a happy-go-lucky mood in *Sholay* (1975).

Amitabh Bachchan as a dockyard worker in *Deewar* (1975).

Amitabh Bachchan and Parveen Babi in another scene from *Deewar*.

Raakhee and Shashi Kapoor in *Kabhi Kabhie* (1976).

Rishi Kapoor and Dimple Kapadia in a tense situation
in *Bobby* (1973).

Shatrughan Sinha alias 'Shotgun' Sinha:
A Formidable Presence

Shatrughan Sinha, one of the most stylized actors of Hindi cinema and famous for his forceful dialogue delivery, was born

on 9 December 1947 in Patna, Bihar, in a Kayastha family. An alumnus of the Film and Television Institute of India, Pune, he began his career by playing small, but effective, roles in films such as Mohan Sehgal's *Sajan* (1968) and Rajesh Nahata's *Raaton Ka Raja* (1970). In Chander Vohra's *Khilona* (1970), his role as the suave villain vis-à-vis Sanjeev Kumar's hero was applauded by the

Shatrughan Sinha

audiences. He came up with riveting performances in Amarjeet's *Gambler* (hero Dev Anand) in 1971 and Gulzar's *Mere Apne* (released the same year) in the villainous role of a gang leader pitted against Vinod Khanna. He continued playing the villain (who was slick and polished) in movies such as Manmohan Desai's *Rampur Ka Lakshman* (1972) and *Bhai Ho To Aisa* (1972) and S. Ramanathan's *Bombay to Goa* (1972, hero Amitabh Bachchan). In B. R. Ishara's *Milap* (1972), he appeared in a variety of roles.

Around the mid-1970s, Sinha switched tracks. He appeared as a hero in the 1976 venture *Kalicharan* (Subhash Ghai's directorial debut) in the double role of an honest inspector and a ferocious prisoner roped in by the police to trace certain criminals. This film, in fact, set the mould of his dominant screen persona in future – either as an honest go-gooder or as a worldly wise criminal, both waging a war against injustice.

In *Dost* (1974) directed by Dulal Guha, Sinha played a street-smart pickpocket who is reformed by his idealist friend (Dharmendra). In Samir Ganguli's *Jaggu* (1975), he appears as a criminal who rescues a widow's daughter abducted by his boss and eventually marries her, but his boss sends a former associate to bump him off. Devendra Goel's *Aadmi Sadak Ka* (1977) saw him in the role of Abdul, who home-delivers groceries and who helps a once-affluent family fallen on bad days. In Hrishikesh Mukherjee's *Kotwal Saab* (1977), he plays a police officer who takes on a villainous politician (played by the multifaceted Utpal Dutt).

In the late 1970s, Sinha appeared in two of Subhash Ghai's hit ventures. In *Vishwanath* (1978), he plays an honest lawyer-turned-vengeful criminal after he is implicated and imprisoned at the behest of a powerful underworld don, but finds out that it is virtually impossible to prove his innocence by following the law. In *Gautam Govinda* (1979) he plays a small-town hitman Govinda who is hired by the main villain to get rid of a dedicated police inspector Gautam (played by Shashi Kapoor).

In 1979, Sinha played the role of a lifetime in Yash Chopra's *Kala Patthar* (as already mentioned, a film inspired by the flooding of a coal mine in Chasnala, then in Bihar, in 1975). He appears as Mangal Singh, a hardened criminal, who hides amidst coal mine workers to evade the police. He gets involved in a clash with the hero (Amitabh Bachchan), which was a highlight of this film. But later they join hands to rescue a group of miners trapped deep in the bowels of the earth.

In 1980, he and Amitabh Bachchan came together again in Raj Khosla's *Dostana* and Ramesh Sippy's *Shaan*. *Dostana* presented the two friends in love with the same woman (Zeenat Aman), which leads to a chasm between them as each feels that the other has betrayed him. In the end they patch up and together take on the battery of villains. The movie was studded with some memorable scenes and song sequences. *Shaan* depicted Sinha as a marksman (in a circus) who teams up with Amitabh Bachchan and Shashi Kapoor to avenge the murder of their brother (Sunil Dutt, a police officer in the film) by the sophisticated villain Shakal (played to perfection by Kulbhushan Kharbanda).

In 1981, Sinha and Bachchan appeared together again in Manmohan Desai's *Naseeb*, a true potboiler with numerous characters and intricate twists and turns of plot!

Sinha acted in a long string of films in the 1980s and 1990s. For instance: Manoj Kumar's *Kranti* (1981), Ravi Tandon's *Waqt Ki Deewar* (1981), Hrishikesh Mukherjee's *Naram Garam* (1981), Surendra Mohan's *Hathkadi* (1982), Subodh Mukerji's *Teesri Aankh* (1982), Raj Sippy's *Qayamat* (1983), Amjad Khan's *Chor Police* (1983), Raj Khosla's *Maati Maange Khoon* (1984), H. Dinesh's *Bhavani Junction* (1984), R. K. Nayyar's *Qatl* (1986), Rakesh Roshan's *Khudgarz* (1987) and *Khoon Bhari Maang* (1988), Indrajit Singh's *Iraada* (1991), Talat Jani's *Taaqat* (1995) and K. C. Bokhadia's *Zulm-o-Sitam* (1999).

In *Chor Police* Shatrughan Sinha came up with an unforgettable performance. He portrayed an inspector who investigates a triple homicide within a family.

In the new millennium, Sinha made his presence felt in films such as Chitrarath's Punjabi venture *Shaheed Uddham Singh* (2000), Madhur Bhandarkar's *Aan: Men at Work* (2004) and Tinnu Verma's *Raja Thakur* (2006).

Shatrughan Sinha joined the BJP in the 1980s and later became a minister in Prime Minister Vajpayee's cabinet. As already mentioned, his fellow actor Vinod Khanna too was his ministerial colleague.

Feroz Khan: The First Truly Americanized 'Ranch Hero'

Feroz Khan, one of most the flamboyant actors comparable in looks and style with Dev Anand, contributed a great deal towards the development of the Hollywood action hero prototype in Hindi cinema. Such a hero, infused with dynamism, displayed suave mannersims and possessed the aura of a macho figure. However, the full potential of this sensitive actor was not tapped by film makers. Feroz Khan, the son of an Afghan father and Iranian mother, was born on 25 September 1939 in Bangalore. He made his film debut in 1960 as the second lead actor (the hero being Sunil Dutt) in Narayan Kale's *Didi*. As hero his first film was Roop K. Shorey's

Feroz Khan

Main Shadi Karne Chala (1963), with newcomer Sayeda Khan as his leading lady. He continued appearing in several small-budget costume dramas and crime thrillers, such as Dwarka Khosla's *Reporter Raju* (1962) opposite Chitra, Homi Wadia's *Char Darvesh* (1964) opposite Sayeda Khan, Mohammed Hussain's *Teesra Kaun* (1965) opposite Kalpana, Naresh Kumar's *Ek Sapera*
Ek Lootera (1965, studded with a superb musical score by Usha Khanna) and B. K. Dubey's *Sau Saal Baad* (1966) both opposite Kum Kum, J. B. H. Wadia's *Tasveer* (1967) opposite Kalpana, Mohammed Hussain's *CID 909* (1967), A. Shamsheer's *Woh Koi Aur Hoga* (1967) both opposite Mumtaz, Shiv Kumar's *Raat Andheri Thi* (1967) and *Anjaam* (1968), Babubhai Mistri's *Anjaan Hai Koi* (1969), Chandrakant's *Kisan Aur Bhagwan* (1974) and Ravikant Nagaich's *Rani Aur Lalpari* (1975, as Gulliver). He also appeared in an English-language film *Tarzan Goes to India* (1962) opposite Simi Grewal.

In *Aag* (1967, heroine Mumtaz), Feroz Khan's first film in the social genre as hero, he appeared as a rural youth who turns into a dreaded and vengeful bandit due the intense oppression perpetuated by a local moneylender and his goons. In this genre,

he again appeared as hero in Mohan's *Anjaan Rahen* (1974) opposite
Mumtaz and Yusuf Naqvi's *Aaja Sanam* (1975) opposite Tanuja.
On the basis of three films – T. Prakash Rao's *Bahurani*
(1963), K. S. Gopalakrishnan's *Suhagan* (1964) (both with Guru
Dutt as hero) and Phani Majumdar's *Oonche Log* (1965) in the
company of Ashok Kumar and Raaj Kumar – Feroz Khan
became one of the most sought-after actors for the second lead.
In fact, Feroz Khan came into the spotlight with *Oonche Log*
(based on K. Balachander's Tamil play Major Chandrakant),
with his subtle portrayal of the playboy son of the blind Chandrakant
(Ashok Kumar). Feroz Khan is eventually killed by his beloved's
brother for having violated her without marrying her. The young
actor appeared (mostly as a sacrificing lover) in Ramanand Sagar's
Arzoo (1965, hero Rajendra Kumar), Satyen Bose's *Raat Aur Din* (1967,
hero Pradeep Kumar), Yash Chopra's *Aadmi Aur Insaan* (1969, hero
Dharmendra), S. S. Vasan's *Aurat* (1967) and Asit Sen's *Safar* (1970),
both films in the company of Rajesh Khanna. For *Aadmi Aur Insaan*
he bagged his first *Filmfare* award for the best supporting actor.

Despite having won critical acclaim for his supporting roles,
Feroz Khan's talent as hero remained largely underutilized. In
Mela (1971, directed by Prakash Mehra), he portrayed a dreaded
bandit, who will not permit any daughter of his clan to get married
as his sweetheart, Santho, was sexually assaulted and killed by a
person belonging to a high caste. Neither will he allow anybody
to plough a certain piece of land in his village, which he thinks
has been taken away from him by his uncle through deceitful
means, nor will he utilize it. He is also afflicted by the grief of
being separated (as children) from his brother at a *mela* (fair).
Meanwhile, the long-lost brother (played by his real brother
Sanjay Khan) turns up at the village as a city-bred agriculturist
who is greatly interested in rural welfare.

In the 1970s and beyond, he became a specialist in fast-track,
slick crime thrillers, appearing in his own film *Apradh* (1972),
Feroz Chinoy's *Kashmakash* (1973), Narendra Bedi's *Khhote Sikkay*
(1974), Ravikant Nagaich's *Kala Sona* (1975), Bolu Khosla's *Kabeela*

(1976), Ravikant Nagaich's *Jadu Tona* (1977), Chand's *Khoon Aur Paani* (1981) and his own film *Janbaaz* (1986), some of which drew in the crowds.

Like Manoj Kumar, he too turned producer-director to expand his domain as hero. After *Apradh*, he came up with *Dharmatma* (1975), an Indian version of *The Godfather* and the first Indian film to be shot in the mountainous regions of Afghanistan.

His next venture and his best-known movie, *Qurbani* (1980), turned out be a great hit. This film, which had strands of love, friendship and sacrifice woven into it, was mounted on a lavish scale. Feroz Khan played a high-class thief Rajesh, who steals many precious stones to help his friend Amar (Vinod Khanna) to settle abroad. But Amar gets accused of murder and he frames Rajesh so that he can keep all the money as well as the woman (Zeenat Aman) both of them are in love with.

After that, in *Dayavan* (1988), Feroz Khan made his mark in the role of a dedicated friend and adviser of the patriarch (Vinod Khanna).

Yalgaar (1992) was another film directed by him, in which he appeared with Sanjay Dutt and Manisha Koirala.

Feroz Khan made a comeback to cinema in 2003 after 11 years with *Janasheen* (2003), which also starred his son Fardeen Khan. He appeared in a negative role as Saba Karim Khan who gets a businessman killed over a property dispute but when he finds that the businessman's son (Fardeen Khan) resembles his dead son, he wants him to be his heir.

He starred with his son again in *Ek Khiladi Ek Haseena* (2005). He came up with a breezy performance in Aneez Bazmee's *Welcome* (2007) in the rollicking company of Anil Kapoor, Nana Patekar and Akshay Kumar.

Feroz Khan passed away on 26 April 2009 after a prolonged battle with cancer. He was planning to remake his 1980 hit *Qurbani*.

Sanjay Khan: Committed to Secular Themes

Sanjay Khan (born as Abbas Khan on 3 January 1941), the younger brother of Feroz Khan, made his successful debut in the 1964 Rajshri film *Dosti*. With his image of a warm-hearted, sober and sensitive youth, he soon became a regular face in run-of-the-mill love stories and family dramas such as Devendra Goel's *Dus Lakh* (1966), Mohan's *Dil Ne Pukara* (1967), Amit Bose's *Abhilasha* (1968), R. K. Nayyar's *Inteqam* (1969), Devendra Goel's *Ek Phool Do Mali* (1969), Harmesh Malhotra's *Beti* (1969), Madhusudhan Rao's *Saas Bhi Kabhi Bahu Thi* (1971), Devendra Goel's *Dhadkan* (1971), S. D. Narang's *Babul Ki Galiyaan* (1972), Vinod Kumar's *Daman Aur Aag* (1973), Kundan Kumar's *Duniya Ka Mela* (1974) and Umesh Mathur's *Zindagi Aur Toofan* (1975).

Sanjay Khan

Sanjay came up with riveting performances in Chetan Anand's *Haqeeqat* (1964) as a daredevil soldier, in *Ek Phool Do Mali* as the suffering lover of the heroine and in B. R. Chopra's *Dhund* (1973) as the secret lover of the heroine accused of killing her husband.

Like his elder brother, Sanjay Khan also turned producer-director to promote himself as hero in films such as *Chandi Sona* (1977), *Abdullah* (1980) and *Kala Dhanda Goray Log* (1986). In the late 1980s, he started making television serials based on Indian history and mythology. His well-known serials are: *The Sword of Tipu Sultan* (1989, during the shooting, he got severely burnt as a result of a huge blaze on the sets in Premier Studios, Mysore); *Jai Hanuman* (1997–2000); and *Maha Kavya*

Mahabharat (in the early years of the new millennium). He also later made a movie *Maryada Purushottam* (2005), starring Jackie Shroff.

The Four Shammi Kapoor 'Camp Followers': Biswajit, Joy Mukerji, Jeetendra and Mithun Chakraborty

In the era when Shammi Kapoor was the reigning swinging star specializing in light romances, many other actors attempted to follow in his footsteps. Four such actors are worth mentioning.

Biswajit: The 'Cute Lover Boy'

Biswajit Chatterjee, the handsome actor from Calcutta, arrived

Biswajit

in the early 1960s in Bollywood to seek his own space as a new romantic hero in the lighthearted musical love tales, which were then in vogue.

He had entered the film world in 1960, making his debut with the Bengali film *Natun Fasal*. Despite family opposition, he followed up his debut film with a small role in another Bengali movie *Dak Harakara*. Soon he rose to stardom in the Calcutta film industry with movies such as *Mayamrigo* (1960) and *Dui Bhai* (1961).

Biswajit's entry into Bollywood in 1962 was facilitated by singer-composer-turned-producer Hemant Kumar, who cast him opposite Waheeda Rehman in *Bees Saal Baad* (directed by Biren Nag). Based loosely on Arthur Conan Doyle's classic *The Hound of the Baskervilles*, this superhit film soon became a cult horror film. The eerie atmosphere and the haunting music made a powerful impact on the viewers. Biswajit appeared in the role of a foreign-returned zamindar who is frequently lured into a marsh by a vengeful 'spirit'. *Kohraa* (1964), also the creation of the Hemant Kumar–Biren Nag team, was another 'ghost story' in which the hero (Biswajit) and his newly wed wife (Waheeda Rehman) are pervaded by the spirit of his first wife killed under mysterious circumstances. Hemant Kumar's compositions in both movies were outstanding.

Riding on the success of these two horror films, Biswajit announced his arrival in Bollywood. He soon emerged as the 'cute lover boy' joyfully playing pranks and singing songs to capture the heroine's heart as seen in S. D. Narang's *Shehnai* (1964, heroine Rajshri), Subodh Mukerji's *April Fool* (1964, heroine Saira Banu), Amar Kumar's *Mere Sanam* (1965, heroine Asha Parekh), Brij Sadanah's *Yeh Raat Phir Naa Aayegi* (1966, heroine Sharmila Tagore), S. D. Narang's *Sagaai* (1966, heroine Rajshri), Kishore Sahu's *Hare Kanch Ki Choodiyan* (1967, opposite Naina Sahu), Brij Sadanah's *Night in London* (1967), Moni Bhattacharjee's *Jaal* (1967) and R. Krishnan and S. Panju's *Do Kaliyan* (1968), all three opposite Mala Sinha. He was the hero in heroine Rekha's debut film *Anjana Safar*. Though *Anjana Safar* was blocked by the censors, a scene from the film, which shows Biswajit kissing Rekha, appeared in *Life* magazine. The film was later released in 1979 with the new title *Do Shikari*. His most memorable performance during this period was in Tarun Majumdar's *Rahgir* (1969) in the role of a restless youth searching for the meaning of life.

His other movies include Sridhar's *Nai Roshni* (1967), Darshan's *Kahin Din Kahin Raat* (1968), T. Prakash Rao's *Vaasna* (1968), Manmohan Desai's *Kismat* (1968), Kotayya Pratyagatma's *Tamanna*, Hrishikesh Mukherjee's *Pyar Ka Sapna* (1969), Kundan Kumar's *Pardesi* (1970), Ramesh Sehgal's *Ishq Par Zor Nahin* (1970), Manmohan Desai's *Shararat* (1972) and Hrishikesh Mukherjee's *Phir Kab Milogi* (1974).

Biswajit turned producer-director with *Kehte Hain Mujkho Raja* (1975), which had an impressive star cast including Dharmendra, Shatrughan Sinha, Hema Malini and Rekha, apart from Biswajit himself.

Biswajit kept his links with Bengali cinema intact, appearing in the superhit *Chowringhee* (1968, with the eminent Uttam Kumar), *Srimaan Prithviraj* (1973) and *Baba Taraknath* (1977). His son Prasenjit is currently a superstar in the Bengali film world.

With the passage of time, Biswajit has been seen rather infrequently. Some of his later movies are Chandrakant's *Krishna Krishna* (1986), Ketan Desai's *Allah Rakha* (1986), Swaroop Singh's *Jigarwala* (1991) and Mithu Singh's *Inth Ka Jawab Patthar* (2002).

Joy Mukerji: In Shammi Kapoor's Shadow

Joy Mukerji, the son of Shasdhar Mukerji, the founder of the famous Filmistan studio, was launched by his father in the film *Love in Simla* (1960, directed by R. K. Nayyar). This film, in which the heroine Sadhana also made her debut, was filled with songs (penned by Rajinder Kishen and composed by Iqbal Qureshi). Joy Mukerji's paternal uncle was the well-known film maker Subodh Mukerji and veterans Ashok Kumar and Kishore Kumar were his maternal uncles.

Joy Mukerji

Joy Mukerji, tall and sturdily built, essayed several roles that were cast in the Shammi Kapoor mould. The films that come to mind include his first film (*Love in Simla*), Raj Khosla's *Ek Musafir Ek Hasina* (1962), Nasir Hussain's *Phir Wohi Dil Laaya Hoon* (1963), Pramod Chakravarty's *Ziddi* (1964) and *Love in Tokyo* (1966) and Samir Ganguli's *Shagird* (1967). In all these films, songs played the dominant role; the characters, the plot and the storyline were incidental. Somehow, despite all his efforts and despite lyp-synching some of Mohammed Rafi's most popular songs on screen, Joy Mukerji could not quite match the original.

Joy Mukerji's other major films include Ram Mukherjee's *Hum Hindustani* (1960; hero Sunil Dutt), B. Mitra's *Ji Chahta Hai* (1964), K. Amarnath's *Ishara* (1964), R. K. Nayyar's *Aao Pyar Karen* (1964), Devendra Goel's *Door Ki Awaaz* (1964), T. Prakash Rao's *Bahu Beti* (1965), Subodh Mukerji's *Saaz Aur Awaaz* (1966), R. K. Nayyar's *Yeh Zindagi Kitni Haseen Hai* (1966) and Ram Mukherjee's *Ek Baar Muskura Do* (1972).

In 1968, to boost his career, he produced and directed the film *Humsaya*, which, despite some fabulous music by O. P. Nayyar, was not a box-office success.

In the late 1970s and beyond, Joy Mukerji just faded away and was briefly seen in the 1985 film *Insaaf Main Karoonga*, directed by Shibu Mitra. He is currently planning to produce and appear in a TV serial.

Jeetendra: The Jumping Jack

Jeetendra, a major star whose career spanned almost a quarter of a century and who has appeared in more than 200 films, represented a continuity with Shammi Kapoor's swinging hero. As his career progressed, he devised his own dance style, integrating it with the image of a lighthearted charming seducer.

Jeetendra

Jeetendra was born as Ravi Kapoor on 7 April 1942. He spent his childhood in Bombay. A discovery of none other than veteran film maker V. Shantaram, he first appeared as the heroine Sandhya's double in *Navrang* (1959), in the Holi song *Ja Re Hat Natkhat ...*, and then as hero in *Geet Gaya Pattharon Ne* (1964), opposite Shantaram's daughter Rajshri. In the second film he plays the role of a sculptor in pursuit of a perfect female figure as an inspiration to fulfil his creative urge.

Soon after his entry into films, Jeetendra, however, brought about a sea change in the image built up by his mentor. The makeover was made possible by Ravikant Nagaich's runaway hit *Farz*, released in 1967, that marked his arrival as the new dancing hero of Hindi cinema. The costume (T-shirt and tight pants) and patent leather white shoes that he picked up from a retail outlet for the song *Mast Baharon Ka Main Aashiq* ... in *Farz* (sung by Mohammed Rafi) became his trademark. His rambunctious dancing style in films such as L. V. Prasad's *Jeene Ki Raah* (1969), Ravikant Nagaich's *Jigri Dost* (1969), Ramanna's *Waris* (1969) and *Humjoli* (1970), Nasir Hussain's *Caravan* (1971) and S. M. Abbas's *Ek Bechara* (1972) earned him the epithet 'Jumping Jack'. Soon, he sought to change his image again and did so successfully, thanks to the sensitive director Gulzar's three films: *Parichay* (1972), *Khushboo* (1975) and *Kinara* (1977).

In *Parichay*, an adaptation of the English musical *The Sound of Music* (1965) and perhaps also inspired by Satyen Bose's *Jagriti* (1954, featuring Abhi Bhattacharya as an idealistic school teacher), he appeared as the tutor who arrives at a household (which follows a strict, regimented lifestyle) to reform some orphaned children. In *Khushboo*, Jeetendra convincingly portrayed a doctor who is committed to helping his fellow human beings, irrespective of the odds stacked against him (such as epidemics). He even keeps away from the heroine (Hema Malini) for as long as possible because he is dedicated to his profession. In *Kinara*, he appeared as a considerate and understanding person who helps the heroine (Hema Malini), a classical dancer, to overcome her trauma and despair. He is trying to atone for the fact that he was in a way responsible for the death of the heroine's husband (Dharmendra), who is killed in an accident when his car collides with Jeetendra's. All the three films had remarkable musical scores by Rahul Dev Burman.

Jeetendra was paired with almost all the top heroines of that period such as Rajshri, Sharmila Tagore (*Mere Humsafar*, 1970), Saira Banu (*Aakhri Daao*, 1975), Nanda (*Dharti Kahe Pukar Ke*, 1969), Asha Parekh (*Caravan*, 1971), Babita (*Banphool*, 1971), Hema Malini (*Waris*, 1969), Tanuja (*Jeene Ki Raah*, 1969), Leena Chandavarkar (*Humjoli*, 1970), Raakhee (*Yaar Mera*, 1972), Rekha (*Anokhi Ada*, 1973), Mumtaz (*Roop Tera Mastana*, 1972) and Reena Roy (*Pyaasa Sawan*, 1981).

While it is not possible to list all his movies here, some of his major ventures are: Vinod Kumar's *Mere Huzoor* (1968), Dulal Guha's *Dharti Kahe Pukar* Ke (1969), Khalid Akhtar's *Naya Raasta* (1970), Sridhar's *Gehri Chaal* (1973, co-starring Amitabh Bachchan), C. V. Rajendra's *Dulhan* (1974), Rajkumar Kohli's *Nagin* (1976, a real multistarrer), J. Om Prakash's *Apnapan* (1977), Manmohan Desai's *Dharam Veer* (1977, co-starring Dharmendra), Dasari Narayan Rao's *Swarg Narak* (1978), Raghunath Jhalani's *Badaltey Rishte* (1978), Rajkumar Kohli's *Jaani Dushman* (1979, which had a huge star cast), J. Om Prakash's *Aasha* (1980), B. R. Chopra's *The Burning Train* (1980, co-starring Dharmendra, Vinod Khanna and Vinod Mehra) and Narayan Rao's *Pyaasa Sawan* (1981).

In the early 1980s, Jeetendra's brand of 'quickie' cinema pioneered the development of a highly improvised form of 'shop-floor' film production in South India. This assembly-line mode of producing several formula films simultaneously with improvised scripts, elaborate colourful sets, long dance sequences featuring hundreds of extras, fast electronic music (mostly provided by Bappi Lahiri) and lyrics full of double entendres established a fairly strong commerical viability. This viability was seen in the huge success of Raghavendra Rao's *Himmatwala* (1983), *Justice Choudhury* (1983), *Jaani Dost* (1983) and *Tohfa* (1984), K. Bapaiah's *Mawaali* (1983) and *Maqsad* (1984) and Dasari Narayana Rao's *Prem Tapasya* (1983). In these films, he made a popular pair with either or both the South Indian heroines Sridevi and Jayapradha.

Jeetendra's output in the 1990s was consistent. He acted, on an average, in two movies per year. His daughter, Ekta Kapoor is famous a film and TV producer. Jeetendra made a brief appearance in one of his daughter's films *Kucch To Hai* (2002), where he appeared alongside his son Tusshar Kapoor. He recently played the role of an old man in his daughter's long-running TV serial *Kyunki Saas Bhi Kabhi Bahu Thi.*

Mithun Chakraborty: From Art Films to Disco Dancing

Mithun Chakraborty, the 'other Amitabh Bachchan', adored especially by the urban poor and rural masses, is one of the few actors from the mainstream film world who also had a worthwhile presence in art cinema. This attribute reflects two entirely contradictory dimensions of his film persona – a top-notch artiste with pathbreaking roles in films made by stalwarts such as Mrinal Sen and Buddhadev Dasgupta and the first-ever hero who pioneered the cult of disco dancing in Hindi cinema.

Mithun was born Gouranga Chakraborty on 16 June 1950 in Barisal (now in Bangladesh). An alumnus of the Scottish Church College, Calcutta (from where he obtained his Bachelors degree in chemistry), he later joined the Film and Television Institute of India, Pune. He made a fabulous debut in

Mithun Chakraborty

1976 in Mrinal Sen's *Mrigaya* for which he won the National Award for the best actor. He also acted in a realistic political film, K. A. Abbas's *The Naxalites* (1980).

His early films include Dulal Guha's *Do Anjaane* (1976; hero Amitabh Bachchan), Deepak Bahry's *Tarana* (1979), Shakti Samanta's *Khwab* (1980), Swaroop Kumar's *Unees Bees* (1980), Deepak Bahry's *Humse Badkar Kaun* (1981), Basu Chatterjee's *Shaukeen* (1981) and Umesh Mehra's *Ashanti* (1982).

With B. Subhash's *Disco Dancer* released in 1983, which immensely popularized the trend of disco songs in Indian films, Mithun emerged suddenly as a dancing star, gaining a huge following in India and abroad, especially in the erstwhile Soviet Union. The story of *Disco Dancer* revolves around a struggling roadside performer who becomes a highly successful disco dancer on the basis of his innate talent and dedication. He is supported by his sister (Kalpana Iyer) and girlfriend (Kim). The music composed by Bappi Lahiri took the nation by storm, especially the number *I Am a Disco Dancer* ..., sung by Vijay Benedict. Mithun consolidated this image with the same director's *Kasam Paida Karne Wale Ki* (1984) and *Dance Dance* (1987).

Mithun also became a cult figure, thanks to low-budget gangster/vendetta films (a kind of rehash of Bachchan's angry cinema). Such films include Ravikant Nagaich's *Suraksha* (1979), Bapu's *Hum Paanch* (1980), Ravikant Nagaich's *Wardaat* (1981) (a sequel to *Suraksha*), Ambrish Sangal's *Wanted* (1983), Raj N. Sippy's *Boxer* (1984), Pramod Chakravarty's *Jagir* (1984), Umesh Mehra's *Jaal* (1986), Rama Rao Tatineni's *Watan Ke Rakhwale* (1987), B. Subhash's *Commando* (1988), K. Bapaiah's *Waqt Ki Awaaz* (1988) and Shakti Samanta's *Dushman* (1990). He also starred in many successful romantic films and family dramas such as Rama Rao Tatineni's *Mujhe Insaaf Chahiye* (1983), Vijay Sadanah's *Pyar Jhukta Nahin* (1985) and K. Bapaiah's *Swarg Se Sunder* (1986) and *Pyar Ka Mandir* (1988). Among these films, in *Hum Paanch* (1980), a remake of Puttanna Kanagal's *Paduvarahalli Pandavaru* (1978; in Kannada) and derived from a popular Mahabharata fable set in a feudal heartland, he made his mark in a role based on the character of Bhima. He plays an army officer who decides to use his military skills to defend his community from the rapacious thakurs who control the village.

Mithun, like Vinod Khanna, earlier played a very impressive second lead to Amitabh Bachchan in movies such as Manmohan Desai's *Ganga Jamuna Saraswati* (1988) and Mukul Anand's *Agneepath* (1990). Mithun won the *Filmfare* Best Supporting Actor Award for his performance in *Agneepath*. He also bagged the *Filmfare* Best Villain Award for his performance in T. L. V. Prasad's *Jallad* (1995). By the mid-1990s Mithun started acting in low-budget movies, mainly in the Bhojpuri dialect. He has a large cult following even today in eastern Uttar Pradesh and Bihar.

Meanwhile, Mithun made a short shift to art cinema. He was very impressive in Buddhadev Dasgupta's Bengali film *Tahader Katha* (1992), for which he won the National Award for the best actor. He also played a noteworthy role in G. V. Iyer's *Swami Vivekananda* (1996), for which he bagged the National Award for the best supporting actor. He made a comeback to the mainstream film Hindi film industry in 2005 with the film *Elaan* (directed by Umed Jain) followed by Radhika Rao and Vinay Sapru's *Lucky: No Time for Love* (2005) and Mani Ratnam's *Guru* (2007). In the lastmentioned movie, his role as a media baron was quite impressive.

In Samir Karnik's *Heroes* (2008), Mithun appeared as Dr Naqvi whose son Sahil (Dino Morea) has died for his country (see also Chapter 8 under Salman Khan). In Soham Shah's *Luck* (under production), he played Major Jabbar Singh in need of money so that surgery can be performed on his wife, who is in the terminal stage. He gets the money by winning a shooting game. He pitches in as Salman Khan's father in Anil Sharma's *Veer* (under production).

Mithun was a staunch follower of the Maoist ideology and had even left his family to become a political activist. But after his only brother died in a freak accident, he returned to his family and left the Naxalite fold. Mithun has also been active in promoting football in West Bengal and is the founder of the Bengal Football Academy. In 1999, he travelled by bus all over West Bengal to raise Rs 37 lakh by playing in exhibition matches.

Raj Babbar: A Multifaceted Artiste

Raj Babbar (born on 23 June 1952 at Agra), an exponent of meaningful cinema, is known for his contemplative style and distinct dialogue delivery, like his senior Raaj Kumar. He is an alumnus of the National School of Drama, New Delhi. He made his debut in films in 1977 with Amrit Nahata's *Qissa Kursi Ka*, a political satire on the Emergency imposed by Prime Minister Indira Gandhi in June 1975 and lifted in March 1977.

Raj Babbar

Raj Babbar made his presence felt in B. R. Chopra's *Insaaf Ka Tarazu* (1980) in the negative role of an obsessive rapist who is finally killed by one of his victims (Zeenat Aman). He remained a favourite in the Chopra camp, appearing in *Nikaah* (1982), *Mazdoor* (1983) and *Aaj Ki Awaaz* (1984).

His other well-known films include Sudesh Issar's *Prem Geet* (1981), T. Rama Rao's *Jeevan Dhara* (1982), Rajkumar Kohli's *Naukar Biwi Ka* (1983), Lekh Tandon's *Agar Tum Na Hote* (1983), Hrishikesh Mukherjee's *Jhoothi* (1985) and Rama Rao Tatineni's *Sansar* (1987). With his second wife, Smita Patil (a highly talented actress who died when she was just 31), he appeared in several films: Sisir Misra's *Bheegi Palkein* (1982), K. Prasad's *Kanoon Meri Muthi Mein* (1984), Durai's *Pet, Pyar Aur Paap* (1984), Ravikant Nagaich's *Shapath* (1984), Chander Vohra's *Mera Ghar Mere Bachche* (1985) and Krishna Kant's *Teesra Kinara* (1986).

Apart from *Insaaf Ka Tarazu*, he also appeared in several women-oriented films like Muzaffar Ali's *Umrao Jaan* (1981), B. R. Chopra's *Nikaah* (1982), Anwar Pasha's *Dulha Bikta Hai* (1982), Ramanand Sagar's *Salma* (1985), Avtar Bhogal's *Zakhmi Aurat* (1988) and Kalpana Lajmi's *Rudaali* (1993).

Two of his films, Bapu's *Hum Paanch* (1980) and Shyam Benegal's *Kalyug* (1981), were based on episodes from the Mahabharata epic set in modern times.

Raj Babbar also achieved success in Punjabi cinema with remarkable performances in Chitrarath's *Chan Pardesi* (1980) and Surinder Singh's *Marhi Da Deeva* (1989). In *Chan Pardesi*, set against the backdrop of feudal oppression, he played the son of a woman raped by a landlord, who falls in love with his half-sister. *Marhi Da Deeva*, based on the famous novel by Gurdial Singh, also sought to capture the ills of feudalism in the agrarian Punjab society. Babbar appeared as the son of a deceased sharecropper, who faces the village community's ridicule because of his love affair with the newly wed wife of an impotent barber. He finally dies due to physical and mental deterioration when the new breed of landlords takes away his sharecropping rights and opts instead for mechanized farming. In Chitrarath's *Shaheed Uddham Singh* (2000), he made his mark by portraying the life of the legendary patriot from Punjab, who goes to Great Britain to kill General Reginald Dyer, the man responsible for the 1919 Jallianwala Bagh massacre. In the process, he becomes a martyr. In Manmohan Singh's *Yaraan Naal Baharaan* (2005), he played role of the upcoming youngster Jimmy Shergill's father. Raj Babbar has also produced *Karamyodha*, released in 1992.

Amol Palekar: The Next-Door Urban Middle Class Hero

In the 1970s, despite all the social and political turmoil and upheaval being witnessed by society at large, Amol Palekar's hero stood out, probably for the first time in Indian cinema, as a symbol of middle-class simplicity and ordinariness. Even his depiction of a love affair and its consequences, as if they were routine events, without the usual melodramatic tensions normally seen in our cinema, really impressed the audiences. In view of his middle-class tag, some film distributors often described him as 'an actor with too narrow capabilities, with boundaries that ended at Virar', the last local train station on Western Railway in Bombay. But soon he proved his detractrors wrong.

Amol Palekar

Born on 24 November 1944 in Bombay, Amol Palekar is an alumnus of the Sir J. J. School of Art, located in the city of his birth. He started working as a bank clerk, and later joined the Marathi experimental theatre along with the well-known dramatist Satyadev Dubey. In 1972, he set up his own street theatre-inspired group, Aniket. He introduced the 'theatre of the absurd' on the Marathi stage. He made his debut in Bollywood with Basu Chatterjee's *Rajnigandha* (1974), playing a small-time clerk with convincing ease. He falls in love with the heroine (Vidya Sinha) but is too timorous to admit his feelings for her. He went on to act in the same director's *Chhoti Si Baat* (1975), *Chitchor* (1976), *Do Ladke Dono Kadke* (1978) and *Baaton Baaton Mein* (1979). All these movies were lighthearted musical romances with the hero depicted as an unassuming character who later emerges as a strong-willed individual.

Veteran Hrishikesh Mukherjee cast him as a middle-class youth in *Golmaal* (1979), *Naram Garam* (1981) and *Rang Birangi* (1983). In all these three movies, studded with comical scenes, Amol Palekar was truly in his element. *Golmaal*, a spoof on the 'double roles' in numerous films, stands out as one of the all-time great comedies of Hindi cinema.

He also appeared in a serious role in Bhim Sen's *Gharonda* (1977). In this film he and the heroine (Zarina Wahab) lose all their life's savings, which they have invested in building a 'dream house', a project that falls through. The hero then asks the heroine to marry a rich older man (Dr Shreeram Lagoo) in the hope that he will die soon and they can acquire his wealth and property. But that does not happen. The film's highlight was a fabulous musical score by stalwart Jaidev.

In Shyam Benegal's sublime creation *Bhumika* (1977), Amol Palekar's contolled but seething performance as the jealous husband of a famous actress (Smita Patil) was spellbinding.

Amol made his debut as director in 1981, with the Marathi film *Akriet*, set against the backdrop of the trbial ritual of human sacrifice. He himself played the role of a cunning high-caste trader. His other directoral ventures include *Ankahi* (1985), *Thodasa Rumani Ho Jaye* (1990), *Bangarwadi* (1995), *Daayraa* (1996), *Kairee* (2001), *Dhyaas Parva* (*Kal Ka Aadmi in Hindi*) (2001) and *Thaang* (2006) based on Raghunath Karve's (a pioneer in the fields of family planning and childbirth) life, which won the National Award for the best film on family welfare. He has also been connected with TV serials such as *Kachchi Dhoop* (1987), *Naqab* (1988), *Paoolkhuna* (1993), *Mrignayanee* (1991) and *Kareena Kareena* (2004).

Paheli (2005), a film directed by him, was India's official entry in the race for the best foreign film at the 2006 Oscars. This film (starring Shahrukh Khan and Rani Mukherji) depicted rural Rajasthan in all its colourful splendour.

Rishi Kapoor: The First Teenage Hero Prototype

Rishi Kapoor, the second son of Raj Kapoor, stamped the persona of Bollywood's first teenage 'lover boy' hero on the silver screen. Born on 4 September 1952 in Bombay, he made his famous debut in 1970 in his father's magnum opus *Mera Naam Joker*. In this film, he played his father's childhood role. He is infatuated with his lady teacher (Simi Grewal) who gets married to Manoj Kumar, leaving the youngster heartbroken.

His trendsetting movie was his father's breezy, teenage romantic venure *Bobby* (1973), which introduced Dimple Kapadia as a heroine. This movie, studded with catchy songs and sensuous scenes, took the nation by storm, especially the youngsters. Rishi Kapoor's performance was rewarded with a *Filmfare* Best Actor Award. After appearing in several teen love stories such as Narendra Bedi's *Raffu Chakkar* (1975), Sikandar Khanna's *Zinda Dil* (1975) and Ravi Tandon's *Khel Khel Mein* (1975), he went on to act in yet another version of the immortal love tale: H. S. Rawail's *Laila Majnu* (released in 1976). In this costume drama, he plays Qais (who is later given the name Majnu) with rare panache. The film was packed with songs, some of which were composed by the musical genius Madan Mohan.

Rishi Kapoor

After his untimely death in July 1975, another talented musician, Jaidev, completed the musical score.

In Yash Chopra's music- and poetry-oriented 1976 masterpiece *Kabhi Kabhie*, he pitched in as the second-generation hero. He plays the son of Shashi Kapoor and Raakhee, who unlike his mother, wants to choose his own life partner.

In Nasir Hussain's 1977 musical blockbuster *Hum Kisi Se Kam Nahin*, he infuses tremendous energy and verve into his character, who wins the hand of one of the heroines (Kajal Kiran), only to deceive her. He is actually in love with the other heroine, Zeenat Aman.

The other movies of Rishi Kapoor in the late 1970s and 1980s include: Manmohan Desai's *Amar Akbar Anthony* (1977), Ramesh Talwar's *Doosra Aadmi* (1977), Sikandar Khanna's *Phool Khile Hai Gulshan Gulshan* (1978), Raghunath Jhalani's *Badaltey*

Rishtey (1978), Tinnu Anand's *Duniya Meri Jeb Mein* (1979), Surendra Mohan's *Aap Ke Deewane* (1980), Subhash Ghai's *Karz* (1980), Raj Khosla's *Do Premee* (1980), Manmohan Desai's *Naseeb* (1981), Nasir Hussain's *Zamane Ko Dikhana Hai* (1981), Raj Kapoor's *Prem Rog* (1982), Manmohan Desai's *Coolie* (1983), Tinnu Anand's *Yeh Ishq Nahi Aasaan* (1984), Ramesh Talwar's *Duniya* (1984, co-starring Dilip Kumar), B. R. Chopra's *Tawaif* (1985), Ramesh Sippy's *Saagar* (1985), Harmesh Malhotra's *Nagina* (1986), Sukhwant Dadda's *Ek Chadar Maili Si* (1986) and Yash Chopra's *Chandni* (1989).

There were three films in which Amitabh Bachchan was his co-star. In *Amar Akbar Anthony* he appeared as Akbar, the ultra-romantic qawwali-singer, raised by a Muslim tailor; in *Naseeb* as the Chaplinseque brother of Bachchan; and in *Coolie* as a tipsy journalist and a buddy of Big B.

In *Ek Chadar Maili Si* (1986), Rishi appeared as the youngster forced to marry his widowed sister-in-law (Hema Malini).

In the blockbuster *Karz*, he portrayed with élan and poise the role of a highly popular singer (Monty) who recalls his previous birth (as Ravi Verma), in which he was killed by a scheming woman (Simi Grewal). Monty and his troupe then enact on stage the murder of Ravi Verma to trap the real culprit (à la *Asha*, 1957, and *Dastaan*, 1972). Fabulous songs (especially *Om Shanti Om* and *Dard-e-Dil, Dard-e-Jigar* ...) enabled this film to zoom towards box-office success. In 2007, a tribute was paid to *Karz* by Farah Khan in the form of the film *Om Shanti Om* (starring Shahrukh Khan and newcomer Deepika Padukone), in which the reincarnation theme has been repeated.

Rishi Kapoor made a great impression in *Prem Rog*, directed by his father, while portraying an orphan, who is brought up by his uncle, an orthodox priest. He decides to marry his childhood sweetheart, who, unfortunately, has been widowed. This move creates havoc in the highly traditional community, which fordbids widow remarriage.

Chandni, a tale about man's infatuation with a female visage, had Rishi (opposite Sridevi) in the role of a lover who keeps clicking her photographs almost interminably. He is seriously injured when showering flowers on her from a helicopter. In order not to burden her, he moves out of her life. The heroine then comes close to another man (Vinod Khanna) and just as they are on the verge of getting married, Rishi Kapoor (now totally cured) re-enters her life.

In the 1990s, Rishi Kapoor continued playing hero, but with diminishing success. *Henna* (1991), directed by his elder brother Randhir Kapoor and produced under the Raj Kapoor banner, used a tragic love tale as its theme to highlight the futility of the seemingly unending enmity between India and Pakistan. Rishi portrayed an Indian youth, who falls into the stormy Jhelum river (on the Indian side) after a road accident and is swept across the border (into Pakistan) in an unconscious condition. He is rescued by a local tribal community, but he has lost his memory due to the accident. He soon falls in love with Henna (played by Zeba Bakhtiar, a Pakistani actress), who has nurtured him back to health. He is not aware of the fact that was earlier in love with an Indian girl (Chandni, played by Ashwini Bhave). Just before his marriage to Henna, Rishi regains his memory but is arrested on suspicion of being an Indian spy. Finally, the tribal people rescue him and take him to the Indian border, where Henna dies while saving the life of her lover in a shootout involving the Pakistani police. The beautiful locales and the moving songs were other plus points of this film, apart from splendid performances by the entire cast, especially by the veteran Saeed Jaffrey as the tribal chief. *Henna* was released much before Yash Chopra's 2004 venture *Veer-Zaara*, based on a similar theme.

Rishi also appeared in David Dhawan's *Bol Radha Bol* (1992), Vinod Mehra's *Gurudev* (1993), Rajkumar Santoshi's *Damini* (1993), David Dhawan's *Eena Meena Deeka* (1994), Raj Malhotra's *Daraar* (1996), younger brother Rajiv Kapoor's *Prem Granth* (1996),

Partho Ghosh's *Kaun Sachcha Kaun Jhootha* (1997) and Manoj Kumar's *Jai Hind* (1999). However, in these films he somehow failed to capture his earlier charisma and joie de vivre.

In 1999, Rishi donned the director's cap for RK Films' *Aa Ab Laut Chalen*, with Akshaye Khanna (Vinod Khanna's son) and Aishwarya Rai in the lead roles. Rajesh Khanna also played an important part in this film as the estranged father of Akshaye Khanna.

In the new millennium, Rishi has switched over to playing character roles in films like Rahul Rawail's *Kuch Khatti Kuch Meethi* (2001), David Dhawan's *Yeh Hai Jalwa* (2002), Dev Anand's *Love at Times Square* (2003), Kunal Kohli's *Hum Tum* (2004), Hriday Shetty's *Pyar Mein Twist* (2005), Kunal Kohli's *Fanaa* (2006), Vipul Amrutlal Shah's *Namastey London* (2007), Aditya Raj's *Don't Stop Dreaming* (2007, an English film) and Kunal Kohli's *Thoda Pyaar Thoda Magic* (2008).

Vinod Mehra: The Ever-smiling, Chocolate-faced Hero

Vinod Mehra, born on 13 February 1945, made his debut in the 1958 film *Raagni* as a child artiste. He played the young Kishore Kumar. He appeared as a junior in a few more films such as I. S. Johar's *Bewaqoof* (1960) and Vijay Bhatt's *Angulimal* (1960).

Roop K. Shorey, the famous maker of classics like *Ek Thi Ladki* (1949) and *Dholak* (1951), was once sitting at Gaylord, a popular restaurant at Churchgate, Bombay, which film folks regularly patronized. He spotted Vinod Mehra there and was impressed by his demeanour. He gave the youngster his first break in *Ek Thi Rita* (1971) opposite Tanuja. The same

Vinod Mehra

year saw him appear in other movies such as K. Ramanlal's
Elaan and Sushil Majumdar's *Lal Patthar*. In the latter movie,
Vinod Mehra was rather subdued in the presence of the
towering, gravelly voiced Raaj Kumar, who dominated the
film.

Vinod Mehra shot into prominence with Shakti Samanta's
family drama *Anurag* (1972) opposite Moushumi Chatterjee. In
this movie, highly idealistic in its theme, he played a Good
Samaritan who is willing to marry the blind heroine despite his
father's objections. In this film, Rajesh Khanna's cameo was truly
touching.

Vinod Mehra's other important films in the 1970s were
Atma Ram's *Aarop* (1973), R. Krishnan and S. Panju's *Shandaar*
(1974), Nisar Ahmed Ansari's *Jurm Aur Sazaa* (1974), Basu
Chatterjee's *Us Paar* (1974), S. Ramanathan's *Do Phool* (1974.
along with Mehmood), Dinesh Ramanesh's *Raftaar* (1975), Jitu
Thakur's *Do Jhoot* (1975), S. Ramanathan's *Sabse Bada Rupaiyya*
(1976, again along with Mehmood), Sawan Kumar Tak's *Saajan
Bina Suhagan* (1978), Manik Chatterjee's *Ghar* (1978) and Jugal
Kishore's *Dada* (1979).

He also became an important actor in the second lead in
films such as *Lal Patthar* (already mentioned), Hrishikesh
Mukherjee's *Arjun Pandit* (1976, with Sanjeev Kumar), Shakti
Samanta's *Anurodh* (1977, along with Rajesh Khanna), Dasari
Narayana Rao's *Swarg Narak* (1978, along with Jeetendra),
Hrishikesh Mukherjee's *Jurmana* (1979, with Amitabh
Bachchan), and R. Krishnamurthy and K. Vijayan's *Amar Deep*
(1979, with Rajesh Khanna). He also appeared in a negative
character role in Mohan Sehgal's *Kartavya* (1979, hero
Dharmendra).

In the 1980s also, Vinod Mehra made his presence felt in a
wide range of movies. Some of them are as follows: B. R.
Chopra's *The Burning Train* (1980), Dasari Narayana Rao's
Pyaasa Sawan (1981), Hrishikesh Mukherjee's *Bemisaal* (1982),
Ravi Tandon's *Khuddar* (1982), Amjad Khan's *Chor Police* (1983),

Zaheer D. Lari's *Sweekar Kiya Maine* (1983), Dasari Narayana Rao's *Zakhmi Sher* (1984), Raj N. Sippy's *Satyamev Jayate* (1987) and Naresh Saigal's *Mahaveera* (1988). A few of his films were released posthumously such as Lawrence D'Souza's *Prateeksha* (1993), Sikander Bharti's *Police Wala* (1993) and Tony Juneja's *Insaniyat* (1994).

Vinod Mehra became a director with *Gurudev*, starring Rishi Kapoor, Anil Kapoor and Sridevi. After his untimely death on 30 October 1990 due to a heart attack, the film was completed by Raj Sippy and released in 1993.

Other Heroes in the Fray

Some of the other heroes of this era were only occasionally successful; in other words, their career graphs formed a zigzag pattern.

***

Vijay Anand (22 January 1934 to 23 February 2004), the younger brother of Dev Anand was more successful as a director than as an actor. Among his well-known films as hero are Anil Ganguly's *Kora Kagaz* (1974), Prem Prakash's *Chor Chor* (1974) and Raj Khosla's *Mein Tulsi Tere Angan Ki* (1978).

***

Randhir Kapoor (born 15 February 1947), the eldest son of Raj Kapoor, had some noteworthy films to his credit: his own directed venture *Kal Aaj Aur Kal* (1971, featuring three generations of Kapoors: Prithviraj, Raj and himself); Manmohan Desai's *Rampur Ka Lakshman* (1972); Narendra Bedi's *Jawani Diwani* (1973); Prakash Mehra's *Haath Ki Safai* (1974); his own directed movie *Dharam Karam* (1975); Prayag Raj's *Ponga Pandit* (1975); Bhappie Soni's *Bhanwar* (1976); Vijay Sadanah's *Chor Ke Ghar Chor* (1978); Rahul Rawail's *Biwi-O-Biwi* (1981); and Ramesh Behl's *Harjaee* (1981).

Randhir also played the second lead in many hit movies such as: Manmohan Desai's *Chacha Bhatija* (1977, in the company of

Dharmendra); Ramesh Behl's *Kasme Vade* (1978, in the company of Amitabh Bachchan in a double role); Ashok Roy's *Heeralal Pannalal* (1978, in the company of paternal uncle Shashi Kapoor); and Ramesh Behl's *Pukar* (1983, in the company of Amitabh Bachchan). He did very few films later such as Harmesh Malhotra's *Khazana* (1984) and Honey Irani's *Armaan* (2003; co-starring Amitabh

Randhir Kapoor

Bachchan and Anil Kapoor). Randhir Kapoor tried his hand at direction and fairly effectively at that in movies such as *Kal Aaj Aur Kal*, *Dharam Karam* and *Henna*. His two daughters, Karisma and Kareena, have also made their presence felt in Bollywood.

***

Rakesh Roshan (born 6 September 1949), is the son of the melodious composer Roshan and the father of Hrithik Roshan. His notable films include T. Prakash Rao's *Ghar Ghar Ki Kahani* (1970), Surendra Mohan's *Seema* (1971), Rajendra Bhatia's *Paraya Dhan* (1971), J. Om Prakash's *Aankhon Aankhon Mein* (1972), Raja Thakur's *Zakhmee* (1975), Ravi Tandon's *Khel Khel Mein* (1975), J. Om Prakash's *Akraman* (1975, a war film), Basu Chatterjee's *Khatta Meetha* (1978), Hrishikesh Mukherjee's *Khoobsurat* (1980), Surendra Mohan's *Aap Ke Deewane* (1980), Swaroop Kumar's *Unees Bees* (1980), Basu Chatterjee's *Hamari Bahu Alka* (1982), K. Vishwanath's *Kaamchor* (1982) and J. Om Prakash's *Bhagwan Dada* (1986). He emerged as a successful producer-director, thanks to films such as *Khudgarz* (1987), *Khoon Bhari Maang* (1988), *Karan Arjun* (1995), *Kaho Naa ... Pyaar Hai* (2000, in which he launched his son Hrithik as hero), *Koi ... Mil Gaya* (2003) and *Krrish* (2006).

***

Deb Mukerji, the younger brother of Joy Mukerji, appeared as a promising 'angry' hero in Rono Mukerji's 1965 movie *Tu Hi Meri Zindagi*. In this movie, his role as a firebrand freedom fighter (for the liberation of Goa, which was under Portuguese rule) was greatly appreciated. After that, he switched over to family dramas and socials such as Satyen Bose's *Aansoo Ban Gaye Phool* (1969), Ajoy Biswas's *Sambandh* (1969, with some fabulous O. P. Nayyar songs), S. M. Sagar's *Adhikar* (1971), Tapan Sinha's *Zindagi Zindagi* (1972) and Ram Mukherjee's *Ek Baar Muskura Do* (1972, in which Joy Mukerji also appeared). In senior roles, Deb Mukerji's films include Mansoor Khan's *Jo Jeeta Wohi Sikandar* (1992), V. Menon and Memon Roy's *Rock Dancer* (1995) and Basu Chatterjee's *Gudgudee* (1997).

***

Parikshat (aka Ajay) Sahni, the son of Balraj Sahni, made an entry as a sensitive and caring hero, but could not attain the degree of sophistication and depth that his father did. His important movies (as hero) include Asit Sen's *Anokhi Raat* (1968), Rajendra Bhatia's *Pavitra Paapi* (1970, in which he co-starred with his illustrious father), V. Madhusudhana Rao's *Samaj Ko Badal Dalo* (1970), Anil Ganguly's *Tapasya*

Parikshat Sahni

(1976), Bimal Dutta's *Kasturi* (1980) and Ved Rahi's *Nadaniyan* (1984). He later emerged as a reliable character actor and went on to act in a slew of films apart from TV serials.

***

Dilip Raj, the son of actor Jairaj, performed well in K. A. Abbas's *Shehar Aur Sapna* (1963) and *Aasmaan Mahal* (1965, co-starring the formidable Prithviraj Kapoor), but could not establish himself as a hero after that. He then became a character actor.

***

Farooque Sheikh, whose small but impressive role in M. S. Satyu's 1973 masterpiece *Garam Hawa* earned him a great deal of critical acclaim, soon went on to make his mark in Hindi cinema. His much-appreciated films include Muzaffar Ali's *Gaman* (1978), Manmohan Krishna's *Noorie* (1979), Muzaffar Ali's *Umrao Jaan* (1981), Sai Paranjpye's *Chashme Buddoor* (1981, a laugh riot), Raman Kumar's *Saath Saath* (1982), Sagar Sarhadi's *Bazaar* (1982), Sai Paranjpye's *Katha* (1983), Hrishikesh Mukherjee's *Rang Birangi* (1983), Pankaj Parashar's *Ab Aayega Mazaa* (1984), Kalpana Lajmi's *Ek Pal* (1986), Muzaffar Ali's *Anjuman* (1986) and J. K. Bihari's *Biwi Ho To Aisi* (1988). He also anchored a well-researched and well-made TV series titled *Jeena Isika Naam Hai* in the new millennium.

***

Anil Dhawan, a tall and well-groomed figure, appeared in films such as B. R. Ishara's *Chetna* (1970), B. O. Shenoy's *Do Raha* (1971), Asit Sen's *Annadata* (1972), Basu Chatterjee's *Piya Ka Ghar* (1972, a hilarious film highlighting the lack of privacy in Bombay's housing clusters), Ajoy Biswas's *Samjhauta* (1973), Hiren Nag's *Honeymoon* (1973), Sawan Kumar Tak's *Hawas* (1974), Rajkumar Kohli's *Nagin* (1976), Sawan Kumar Tak's *O Bewafaa* (1980) and Amar Kumar's *Mahfil* (1981). He continued to appear in several films and TV serials with the passage of time.

Anil Dhawan

***

Navin Nischal's first film, *Sawan Bhadon* (directed by Mohan Sehgal), released in 1970, announced his arrival on the Bollywood scene. He featured in a series of films (some of which

Navin Nischal

were hits) such as Jyoti Swaroop's *Parvana* (1971, the villain being Amitabh Bachchan), Hrishikesh Mukherjee's *Buddha Mil Gaya* (1971), Brij Sadanah's *Victoria No. 203* (1972, in which stalwarts Ashok Kumar and Pran stole the show), Chetan Anand's *Hanste Zakhm* (1973, with an exquisite musical score by Madan Mohan), Chand's *Dharma* (1973), B. R. Chopra's *Dhund* (1973), Mohan Sehgal's *Woh Mein Nahin* (1974), Brij Sadanah's *Paise Ki Gudiya* (1974), Prakash Mehra's *Desh Drohi* (1980) and Manmohan Desai's *Desh Premi* (1982), in which Amitabh Bachchan was the hero. He continued to appear in various films, apart from TV serials, in the 1980s and beyond. He played a worthwhile role in Dibakar Bannerjee's 2006 movie *Khosla Ka Ghosla*, in which Anupam Kher played the title role.

***

Deepak Prashar, a debonair looking individual, appeared in films such as B. R. Chopra's *Insaaf Ka Tarazu* (1980), Ambrish Sangal's *Aap To Aise Na The* (1980), Sham Ramsay and Tulsi Ramsay's *Sannata* (1981), Anand Sagar's *Armaan* (1981), Kukoo Kapoor's *Waqt Ke Shehzade* (1982), B. R. Chopra's *Nikaah* (1982) and *Tawaif* (1985), Mohinder's *Meetha Zehar* (1985) and Sham Ramsay and Tulsi Ramsay's *Purani Haveli* (1989).

Deepak Prashar

***

Sudesh Kumar (hero of Dhirubhai Desai's 1960 musical *Saranga*) and Dheeraj Kumar (hero in Rajesh Nahata's *Raaton Ka Raja*, 1970, and Jugal Kishore's *Deedar*, 1970) could not make it to the big league and opted for playing character roles.

***

Sachin (full name Sachin Pilgaonkar) began as a child artiste and emerged as a hero in Rajshri Productions *Geet Gaata Chal* (1975, directed by Hiren Nag). His other films as hero include Vijay's *Zid* (1976), Shantilal Soni's *Raksha Bandhan* (1976), Tarun Majumdar's *Balika Badhu* (1976), Hiren Nag's *Ankhiyon Ke Jharokhon Se* (1978), Shantilal Soni's *Aankh Ka Tara* (1977) and *College Girl* (1978) and Govind Moonis's *Nadiya Ke Paar* (1982). Sachin continued to act in Hindi and Marathi films and also made his presence felt in some TV serials.

***

Vijayendra Ghatge first caught the public eye in Basu Chatterjee's *Chitchor* (1976), in which he and Amol Palekar were vying for the heroine's hand. He went on to appear in other films (in major roles) such as Esmayeel Shroff's *Agar* (1977), Madan Bawaria's *Shaayad* (1979), S. M. Sagar's *Nazrana Pyar Ka* (1980) and Kalidas's *Aakhri Insaaf* (1980). Later on, as a character actor, in both films and TV serials, his performances were greatly applauded.

***

Mohnish Behl, the son of the famous actress Nutan, acted in a few films as hero such as Umesh Mehra's *Teri Baahon Mein* (1984) and Madan Sinha's *Yeh Kaisa Farz* (1985), before switching over to villainous and character roles.

***

Kiran Kumar, son of character actor and villain Jeevan, appeared as as hero (or side hero) in movies such as Chand's *Inspector* (1970), Rajendra Bhatia's *Jangal Mein Mangal* (1972), R. K. Bannerjee and T. N. Sharma's *Chalaak* (1973), Ramanand Sagar's *Jalte Badan*

(1973), Rajendra Bhatia's *Aaj Ki Taaza Khabar* (1973, a comedy), Jugal Kishore's *Apradhi* (1974), Kaushalraj Batra's *Free Love* (1974), Ashwini Kumar's *Bhula Bhatka* (1976), Joginder's *Yari Zindabad* (1976), Krishankant's *Kulvadhu* (1977) and Dinesh Rawal's *Ashaati Beej* (1979). He has also come up with a prolific output as a villain or character actor in numerous films and TV serials.

***

Vijay Arora (1946–2007), a promising actor, kicked off with B. R. Ishara's *Zaroorat* (1972; also heroine Reena Roy's first film). He then came up with fairly good performances in films such as Hrishikesh Mukherjee's *Sabse Bada Sukh* (1972), Virendra Sinha's *Ek Mutthi Aasman* (1973), Sohanlal Kanwar's *Naatak* (1975), H. K. Verma's *Kadambari* (1976) and Murugan Kumaran's *Jeevan Jyoti* (1976). The highlight of his career

Vijay Arora

was his starring in Nasir Hussain's 1973 blockbuster *Yaadon Ki Baraat*. In this film, he along with the heroine Zeenat Aman got the opportunity to lyp-sync (in the voices of Mohammed Rafi and Asha Bhosle) one of the most melodious compositions ever: *Chura Liya Hai Tumne Jo Dil Ko* .... He played noteworthy cameos in movies such as Manmohan Desai's *Roti* (1974), Subhash Ghai's *Gautam Govinda* (1979), K. Vishwanath's *Sargam* (1979) and Manmohan Desai's *Naseeb* (1981). His role as Indrajit (the son of Ravana), in Ramanand Sagar's immensely popular TV serial *Ramayana* (1987–88), earned him a lot of kudos.

***

Ashok, the son of film maker Kidar Sharma, appeared in his father's ventures *Hamaari Yaad Aayegi* (1961) and *Fariyad* (1964) but faded away after that.

***

Raj Kiran, a robustly built actor, began with a lot of promise but somehow could not make it to the top league. His notable films include B. R. Ishara's *Kaagaz Ki Naao* (1975), S. Ramanathan's *Shikshaa* (1979), Hiren Nag's *Saajan Mere Main Saajan Ki* and *Maan Abhimaan* (both 1980), Subhash Ghai's *Karz* (1980), Dilip Naik's *Nakhuda* (1981), Ramesh Talwar's *Basera* (1981), Mahesh Bhatt's *Arth* (1982), Chander Bahl's *Sun Meri Laila* (1983), Ravi Chopra's *Mazdoor* (1983), V. Ravindra's *Chatpati* (1983), Prakash Jha's *Hip Hip Hurray* (1984) and K. Bapaiah's *Ghar Ek Mandir* (1984). In *Arth*, he 'sang' some fabulous melodies in the baritone voice of Jagjit Singh.

***

Kumar Gaurav, the son of Rajendra Kumar, made a very impressive beginning with *Love Story* (1981, produced by his father and directed by Rahul Rawail). This film was a huge box-office success. Some of his other major films are Vinod Pande's *Star* (1982), A. C. Trilogchandra's *Teri Kasam* (1982), Ramanand Sagar's *Romance* (1983), Bharathi Raja's *Lovers* (1983), Mohan Sehgal's *Hum Hain Lajawab* (1984) and Mahesh Bhatt's *Janam* (1985)

Kumar Gaurav

and *Naam* (1986, in which he co-starred with his brother-in-law Sanjay Dutt). Kumar Gaurav's films in the late 1980s and 1990s did not quite make it big. In Sanjay Gupta's 2002 venture *Kaante*, he managed to hold his own in the company of Amitabh Bachchan and Sanjay Dutt, among others. He is currently acting in a silent movie *My Daddy Strongest*, being directed by Rahul Kapoor.

Chapter 6

The 'Modern' Hindi Film and the Search for the 'Modern' Hero

The Impact of Liberalization and Globalization

As discussed in Chapter 2, by the late 1980s, the celebrated cinema of violence led by the lonely angry young man began to lose its charm. Hindi films once again began moving towards a new cinematic expression in response to the noticeable changes in India, basically on the socio-economic and political fronts, which started taking place in the early 1990s. The country was now entering the era of liberalization and globalization of the economy in the hope of creating widespread growth and prosperity. As a precursor to this scenario of great promise, the new economic environment began to promote lifestyles studded with modern-day gadgets, apart from exotic luxuries and glamorous appurtenances: for instance, electronic items (mainly swanky colour TV sets and home theatres, mobile phones and personal computers), cars, furnishings, sanitaryware or garments. (Nowadays, most of these items have become commonplace, but in the 1990s, they were considered 'status symbols'.) Such a trend led to a buying frenzy among the burgeoning middle class, the main potential beneficiaries of the market-sponsored consumerism.

The people belonging to the lower strata of society also began dreaming big. They too sought more comforts and a more fulfilling life. They soon started aspiring to be a part of the new affluent lifestyles either by going in for cheaper substitutes or by trying to imitate the upper crust. (Unfortunately, large segments of society living just above or below the poverty line did not benefit much from liberalization and globalization.) As a consequence, the new market-driven environment demanded the distancing of the new consumers from the earlier concerns about social welfare and development of society. This change in priorities transformed, virtually overnight, the seemingly perpetual disillusionment of the majority of the middle class into tantalizing urges for self-gratification. The motto became: 'grab, utilize/consume and forget.'

The new ambience was governed by the values and lifestyles associated with the rich and the powerful in the globalized world. The onslaught of the Western media, chiefly through television networks, radically changed the common Indian perceptions. The new-age mantra appeared to be the least complicated: 'I, me and myself.' This mantra provided a new 'worldview' to the people for self-discovery, ascendancy and, thus, identity. The IT revolution was taking place. The main driving force was to become technology-savvy and thus make it big in the worlds of business and glamour in one shot. There was hardly any time for patient contemplation of social issues and very little, if any, commitment to any activity outside one's professional sphere.

As a result, in the highly glitzy world of quick success and quicker riches, the Indian mindset became extremely competitive. Irrespective of his or her aptitude, capabilities and talents, virtually every youngster was now caught up in a rat race to come first at any cost. This state of affairs resulted in an entirely new kind of upwardly mobile aspirants, further pampered by a blitzkrieg of enticingly glossy advertisements in hoardings, newspapers, magazines and over television. Rapid Westernization and the accompanying lure of consumerism resulted in an extreme narrowing down of the perspectives of the people, particularly the youth. Indiscriminate urbanization also contributed its bit in this context.

Reflecting such a dramatic socio-economic transformation, Hindi films and film music, along with the proliferating television channels and the powerful ever-growing advertising regime, became the mainstay of the extremely alluring consumerist culture. There was now a new class of audience, 'blessed' with the privilege of considerable spending power. The astute film makers, ever ready to seize opportunities, made an unprecedented shift in their audience base. The first segment of the new audience comprised mainly the rich city youth (or yuppies).

The second segment of the new audience was made up of the supersuccessful, but largely self-centred, NRI (non-resident Indian) diaspora. The members of this huge community, in the post-liberalization period, all of sudden started, zealously at that, rediscovering their long-lost homeland as it provided them a sense of importance among their less-privileged compatriots who were slogging in India amidst the heat and the dust, not to mention power and water shortages. Behind the new, fashionable façade of 'Mera Bharat Mahan' (My Great India) and the widely proclaimed cultural inferiority of the Western culture (marked by a high degree of materialism), which, ironically, nurtured their very success, the diaspora began to showcase their love for their home country and its culture at various fora, both in India and other countries.

The third segment was the high school and college crowd, mostly from the middle and upper classes, which started flocking to the cinema halls in increasing numbers. The modern Hindi film became the focus of attention and even a fashionable preoccupation among the 'elitist' English-speaking students. They now found the new form of film music as fascinating as Western pop – their regular music trip. The new-age stars in cinema became their role models.

The end result of this reaching out to these three segments was a version of the Hindi film that mainly belonged to the 'India exclusive' thronging the multiplexes (located mainly in urban India) and not to the rural and native Bharat. Certain top-notch film makers like Yash Chopra, Sanjay Leela Bhansali, Karan Johar and Subhash Ghai have openly asserted that their films have been designed primarily for the neo-rich and the Indians living abroad.

In praise of the Indian globalized film, the perceptive writer and journalist Suketu Mehta notes (*National Geographic*, February 2005):

> Bollywood has become a globally recognized brand; like Darjeeling tea or the Taj Mahal, it has become an emblem of India. Its films are popular in the Middle East, Central Asia, Africa, Latin America – and now the US and Europe, where immigrants from Bollywood-loving countries make up most of the audiences and provide more than 60 per cent of overseas revenues .... The newer Bollywood films are aimed at Indian's urban consumers and the overseas market – some 20 million Indian expatriates around the world – who love Hindi films even after they have forgotten Hindi. Bollywood has even changed the wedding rituals of overseas Indians. Young brides in the Indian diaspora now hire choreographers, costume themselves in chiffon sarees and perform dances at their weddings – an act [once] unthinkable in much of India .... With its easy mixture of old and new India, the films soothe the insecurities many Indians felt in the mid-nineties, when economic reforms ushered in satellite television along with Coca Cola and Levis. The movies suggested it was possible to remain true to Indian culture while embracing globalization ...

There have been movies set in rural areas, but few and far between. One somewhat anomalous feature has been that even the villages appeared to be 'decked up' in many such films.

The Making of the Present-day Indian Film

The design of the neo-modernist Indian film can be attributed to three key influences: Raj Kapoor's 1973 venture *Bobby*; certain aspects of Amitabh Bachchan's angry young man image; and the MTV-motivated choreography and music.

For developing the globalized image of the Indian film, the film makers chose the urban youth as their core audience. *Bobby* was selected as the reference point for neo-youth films. This film, according to *The Times of India* (11 May 1973), 'was intended, as claimed to "project the teenagers of today, their hopes and aspirations, their conflicts and their frustrations and, above all, their attitude to love and life", but it could not become more than a skilfully packed dream merchandising – a handsome boy and an innocent-looking nymphet traipsing through picturesque scenery to the accompaniment of chocolate music with seductive escapism making way for the formula rough track-fights get-aways and chases'.

In spite of its shallowness, the *Bobby* model was employed to trap the younger audience, film after film, through the fantasies of highly glamourized teenage romantic extravaganzas. Again, the vast expanse of glossy decor and fancy costumes added to the sense of gratification. Thus, entertainment was now reduced merely to a childish caricature of a boy–girl romance without the intensity seen in the films of the classical era and even a few years thereafter. The teenage viewers were fed a diet of whims and fancies as embodied by a new crowd of yuppie stars, looking like aliens in the context of the Indian ambience and Indian sensibilities. In contrast, K. Balachander's *Ek Duje Ke Liye* (1981) starring Kamalahasan and Rati Agnihotri was a remarkably credible film with a sound social and cultural setting.

In the format of the some of the new-age films, Bachchan's angry young man image was employed but without the original authenticity, intensity or even its larger-than-life projection. This drawback can be ascribed to the fact that none of the new-age heroes could quite match Bachchan's stature or histrionics. Amidst the environment of sensuous and, at times, steamy romances, extraneous features such as the underworld and its nexus with corrupt politicians and law enforcers were crudely incorporated in the narrative. In some movies, the moppet-like hero, half-lover and half-he-man, was now projected as the new-age angry young man in the making. Somehow, the hero, despite his vigorous efforts, seemed to fall short of expectations, except in rare cases.

The influence of MTV threw up a radical transformation in music and choreography in Indian films and helped them acquire their ultra-modern and neo-youth image. The melodious musical notes and the exquisite and aesthetic dance movements and expressions, so very central to the Indian film, began to be interpreted in a completely Westernized idiom, marked by split-second tempo music and visual cutting. The choreographers, particularly in South Indian cinema, introduced many innovations (evidently inspired by the dancing sensation Prabhu Deva) to magnify the glamour and the sensuality through rapid changes in the attires of the lead pair and the accompanying dancers, not to mention technological gimmickry. The effect was felt on Hindi cinema as well. The elaborate dance compositions involving group performers looked more like an aerobic exercise rather than an aesthetic creation. With the storylines largely becoming irrelevant and without much substance in the plot, the main relief was sought through mounting song-and-dance sequences, many shot in foreign locations. These sequences look so similar that they no longer carry the individualistic signature of their creators. In this context, the well-known writer, Partho Chatterjee, observes:

> Today's urban Indian boy and girl, as exemplified by the lead pair in any Bombay film, know all about sex and the "kick" it gives but do they know anything about its psychological,

spiritual implications? It seems not, judging by the animal-like grunts coming out of lax, hanging jaws in a face out [of] which stare glassy eyes as the body threatens to collapse under the wanton animal energy summoned by the song (why not call it dance data?) on the sound track .... The songs have reached a nadir from where it will take a long time to come back. A hammering, insistent beat with raucous vocals given some shape and form by the miraculous forces of modern electronics during recording has resulted in a sound that is accepted as music in the absence of the genuine article – and to it is added doggerel of the worst kind. The final product for some inexplicable reasons is called a song – a film song. Its musical qualities are of no consequence either to the director of the film or its viewer; it is a sound to which the oversexed young hero and heroine will dance – or it is gyrate?[1]

In a similar vein, journalist and film critic Iqbal Masood (1995) writes:

Dances in today's cinema are choreographed differently projecting the group as a force with aggressive intent. The dances now have less of folk [or] classical pretension and the emphasis is more on aerobics .... The group is not conceived as "extras" providing a background to the hero/heroine who is set off against it. The group now represents a volume, a mass of force that has to be reckoned with and the hero/heroine forms part of this aggressive mass. An aggressive sexuality is also in vogue.[2]

The foregoing influences have been highly disturbing for, and detrimental to, latter-day Indian cinema. It seems to have lost its links with the classical traditions except for 'borrowing' characters, themes, events or even complete scenes, whenever the new-era writers run out of original themes and ideas. Hollywood also provides ample grist for these writers' mills. In their efforts to go global and attain parity with Hollywood, thematically as well as commercially (particularly in terms of access to overseas markets), the present-day film makers have engineered a complete 'liberation' of Indian cinema from its creative roots. The outcome has been an unending celebration of the new format whose basic ingredients, in most cases, are mindless violence, base sensuality and overwhelming glitz and glitter. Of course, there are a few exceptions, for which one has to be thankful.

The new-age cinema, as the dominant expression of our country's 'feel-good' factor and quite in keeping with the global Americanized culture, has been evolved by the film fraternity as a business entity than a piece of art. Cinema now has become a trans-national enterprise designed to boost upmarket lifestyles, attitudes, appearances and mannerisms besides serving as an avenue for promoting tourism and even brands and products.

Thus, the 'global' Indian film, focusing on the fast-paced lifestyle and weird inspirations of the footlose Generation X, and the following generation, a product of globalized consumerism, showcases the idiosyncracies of the yuppie – suave, but directionless, donning imported clothes, sporting designer hairdos, enjoying foreign trips and driving luxury cars, besides gallivanting. Although the hero vaguely adheres to Indian values, he is too keen to imbibe the material trappings of affluence and the Western lifestyle without a twinge of guilt. And in his carefree attitude and ease of a life of abundance (seeking identity in fashion statements and associated preoccupations), he becomes a model for imitation for millions of improvised poor youth, thus waylaying them into the enticing trap of *apparent* affluence and opulence.

Present-day cinema has also begun to reflect, in an utterly 'honest way', the growing hypocrisy of the privileged category of Indians living in the country and abroad. An Indian of this category can give his Western counterpart a run for his money as far as an opulent lifestyle goes. However, such an Indian camouflages his modernity with the mantle of tradition. He respects family, kinship and chooses the traditional docile Indian girl as his wife. In other words, he does not or cannot shed the baggage of the past. As Rachel Dwyer (a professor from the University of London, who has keenly studied Indian culture and cinema) points out, 'the key features are not those of the modern or post-modern world, but those of a world that is almost feudal: family *(khaandaan)*, honour *(izzat)*, modesty *(laaj)* and, increasingly, religion *(dharma)*, as opposed to work, companionate marriage, self-knowledge, or the pursuit of happiness'.[3] And within the framework of an aggressive portrayal of outward modernity, associated glamour and yuppie culture, most films seek to project women as the traditional archetype (at least post-marriage): submissive, obedient and subservient. The men are often swaggering, stylish and urbane jet-setters (or aspiring to be so), but they want the women they seek to be docile, dedicated to serve other family members and to perform all domestic chores, apart from procreating and raising children, irrespective of the lifestyle these women followed before marriage.

The modern film thus represents the growing neurosis in society, adroitly concealed by the self-confident, flamboyant trendy lead pair, both of whom have become the archetypes of the positive looking, modern and upbeat new MTV generation. Internally, however, they appear to be highly susceptible to mood swings and their attention span seems to be narrow, despite being tech-savvy. Morevoer, their commitment to relationships seems to be shallow. The parental figures too in these films are often shown as ultra-rich or aping the ultra-rich. They also appear modern and global in their outlook, eager to partake in the celebrations with the young crowd in psychedelic discotheques, ritzy restaurants, five-star hotels and opulent mansions. These films project most of the youngsters as modern-day votaries of materialism who cannot or will not comprehend the wider social realities. They acquire the objects of their desire with an almost mercenary-like approach, without any remorse for trampling upon others.

The modernization of the Indian film has also led to a redefinition of the aesthetics involved. The new-age 'designer' films appear to be carefully packed and branded products, in which due attention has been paid to every little visual and physical detail. These films, in fact, look more like lifestyle and fashion statements than mere narratives. The advertising industry could learn a thing or two from the present-day films. The imagery is mostly elaborate and extravagant, with saturated colour effects, stylized sets, trendy costumes, fairy-tale locales made up of misty mountainsides, snow-capped peaks, fabulous beaches, exquisite lakes (or rivers) and lush gardens with a proliferation of multihued flowers.

For the festival-related song-and-dance sequences or on special celebratory occasions, the women are decked up in opulent attires, as if they were brides. The men, for the traditional ceremonies, shed their Western dresses and flaunt their Indianness by donning an exquisite silken kurta–pyjama ensemble or the sherwani/achkan–tight pyjama combination. The costume show is nothing short of ostentatious; some critics have even termed it 'a vulgar display of prosperity'.

The younger heroines nowadays appear in designer jeans, mini-skirts, skimpy tops and sportswear. Veteran Yash Chopra admitted in an interview: 'We copy fashion from English magazines or the designers go to London to look at fabric, design and cut. Previously only *bad girls* [italics added] wore Western clothes, now they all can. It's part of our life. What's the harm in Western clothes? We have to show what's happening. The fashion for faces has changed too, so have hairdos and makeup. If we give an Indian hairdo, they'll say the girl looks 'verny' (vernacular), so we can't do that.'[4]

Thus, the basic elements of wonder, involvement with the characters and narrative and the attainment of joy and satisfaction, which define the appeal of a film, are being

overridden by technological razzle-dazzle (which film historian
B. D. Garga calls 'braver flourishes of technique'[5]) in today's
cinema. Although traditional values of love, devotion and chastity
are still upheld, the new-age showmen seem to lack the social
concern, commitment and dedication of their formidable
counterparts of the formative and classical periods of Hindi
cinema. The entire persona of a film in terms of cohesion appears
amiss. Also, other drawbacks include the fact that the talents of
many of the artistes have not been fully utilized and *creative* use
of the audio and visual has been lacking.

***

In view of the foregoing changes, the modern-day Indian films
can be broadly slotted into six genres: teenage/yuppie romances-
cum-family dramas; the diasporic cinema; nationalist
melodramas; remakes of classics; cinema of vengeance in the
shadow of Amitabh Bachchan; and comical escapades.

Teenage/yuppie romances-cum-family dramas, like most
modern films, are opulently mounted love stories often built
around the upper-class family structures. The sets and the decor
are snazzy, studded with the latest gizmos, and, at times, have
an Oriental touch. With the new-age music and the group dance
form as their basic ingredients, most such movies seek to
legitimize the hyperactive teenager/yuppie infatuations. The
conflicts are often not between the hero and the villain, but
between Western and Indian cultures or the traditional rich and
poor. Sometimes, the plot simply seems to be the handiwork of
destiny.

These romances project the ritzy consumerist lifestyle as the
new model for the 'global Indian love affair'. The strange ways in
which the lead pair simulates the love act, often shot in choice
foreign locations, in fact, leave the local spectators watching the
shooting amazed and, sometimes, appalled.

Yet the lovers, in their 'rebellion', adhere (somewhat
uncharacteristically) to the traditional values such as respect for

elders, obedience to the patriarchal order and conformity to the wishes of the larger family and community. The protagonist either possesses, or strives to imbibe, all the qualities of seduction of the rich and powerful. He does not wish to oppose his own or his sweetheart's family, even if they are against his plans; he only seeks their blessings and bides his time. In this kind of cinema, the suffering itself appears 'glamorous' and becomes a mere corollary to one's persona, failing to articulate the purity, the pathos and the profundity of soulful love depicted during the classical era.

These new-age romances and family dramas are mere hi-tech extensions of numerous similar films churned out by AVM in the 1950s and 1960s and later by the house of Barjatiyas. This cinema of the middle and upper classes championed the cause of family kinship, importance of the joint family system and the amenability among various generations; any deviant behaviour from the traditional set-up was appropriately corrected within this perspective. They are now made in the modern yuppie style and using yuppie lingo but without the emotional core of the originals. The representative films of this genre are: *Maine Pyar Kiya* (1989), *Love* (1990), *Dil Hai Ke Maanta Nahin* (1991), *Hum Aapke Hain Kaun?* (1994), *Dil To Pagal Hai* (1997), *Kuchh Kuchh Hota Hai* (1998), *Jab Pyar Kisi Se Hota Hai* (1998), *Janam Samjha Karo* (1999), *Kaho Na ... Pyar Hai* (2000), *Kabhi Khushi Kabhi Gham* (2001), *Aap Mujhe Achche Lagne Lage* (2002), *Na Tum Jano Na Hum* (2002), *Dil Chahta Hai* (2003) and *Namaste London* (2007).

Rajshri Films' blockbuster *Hum Aapke Hain Kaun?* (*HAHK*), an urban version of *Nadiya Ke Paar* (1982) made under the same banner, was the archetype of the new version of the family drama. The cast included Madhuri Dixit, Salman Khan, Alok Nath, Anupam Kher, Reema Lagoo, Renuka Shahane and Mohnish Behl. The film presented a heady mix of unbridled modern-day consumerism and age-old religiosity. A celebration of a fantasy focusing on the multifarious, if somewhat extravagant, preoccupations of the country's neo-rich class, the film serialized the array of festivities and rituals involved in a typical North Indian wedding. Later, the childbirth ceremonies were also depicted with a grand flourish. What resulted was a seemingly never-ending carnival of song and dance and an enormous consumption of numerous delicacies, besides exchanges of mountains of gifts. The pranks played upon each other by the youngsters, which were laden with sexual and voyeuristic undertones, were also thrown in for good measure. The older generation too seemed to be caught up in the bonhomie and excitement and attempted to revive their youthful passions by belting out rambunctious songs.

Amidst such an atmosphere, the bride (Renuka Shahane), the heroine's (Madhuri Dixit) elder sister, who is pious and devout, is the key motif for projecting the glory of the traditional Indian woman. She is portrayed as the ideal daughter-in-law who is blessed by divine grace. Lord Krishna and Lord Rama bestow happiness on the two families, as they become the instruments for revealing the love affair between the hero (Salman Khan) and the heroine. As Ashish Rajadhyaksha and Paul Willemen point out, 'the fantasy of a feudal elite that has successfully negotiated its transition of capitalism while retaining its alleged "traditional" religiosity underpins an appeal to the audience's voyeurism as well as to a devotional fervour hitherto reserved for explicitly religious themes.'[6]

Fareed Kazmi, a well-known writer, describes how HAHK focuses on one single 'idyllic' sphere to the exclusion of the realities outside it: 'The film ... "colonizes" all people, all spaces. It makes invisible "other" people, "other" places, "other" lives. The world of HAHK is people only by "us". The "others" are simply blanked out. Likewise, by locating almost the entire film in a single space (the house of the protagonist), all other spaces are made invisible.'[7]

Another disturbing trend of this cinema is the subtle (but perverted) packaging of immorality as heroism, showing that all means are fair for achieving material success and love. An adventurous youth, often a *tapori* (vagabond) or even a literary person (as in *Shabd*, 2004) seeks to conquer the world of riches and fame by hook or by crook, with scant respect for well-accepted legal, moral and ethical codes. *Dhoom* (2004), *Garam Masala* (2005), *Golmaal* (2006), *Dhoom 2* (2006), *Jhoom Barabar Jhoom* (2007), *Bluffmaster* (2007) and *Cash* (2007) are some of the films that have set this trend.

***

The diasporic cinema of the 1990s and later tapped the overseas market (and lucratively at that) by reawakening memories of India among the NRIs, many of whom had virtually lost touch with their homeland in their obsessive pursuits to make it big in the West or the Gulf countries. This cinema sought to depict a cultural transformation of the alienated NRI youth often through a 'chance' discovery of 'Indianness'. But this transformation appeared superficial because the films of this genre intended to legitimize Indianness, as seen by the NRIs. Such films also provided them a fig leaf to try and cover their guilty conscience caused by their constantly ignoring their 'impoverished' homeland for so long, while they enjoyed a very luxurious lifestyle. These films thus represent colonalism in a new form – appeasement of the NRIs and creating the myth of their Indianness, ostensibly far more profound and genuine than that of the Indian rich living in India. The Indianness is worn by the NRIs like a badge but most of them lay negligible emphasis on nationalist concerns and duties towards the nation and society.

The diasporic cinema, therefore, presents India, to the NRI audiences, as a 'cultural commodification', which encompasses the portrayal of its religions, traditions, ceremonies and rituals on a grand scale. This variety of cinema shows that although many of the modern urban Indian women appear to be 'Westernized', and in spite of their outward appearance, they are still ethnic to the core and continue to be the guardians of tradition and family values. The return of the NRI male to his homeland (often to find a traditional bride for his and his family's cultural gratification) kindles in the diasporic audience a nostalgic relationship with 'home'. However, this viewing of India is from a superior position. The NRI is projected as an ideal individual who earnestly upholds the Indian values despite his Western gloss and despite the larger hegemonizing impact of the Western lifestyle and values at the global level. And the Indianness, considered sacred, is expressed through a number of clichés reminiscent of those employed by Manoj Kumar in *Purab Aur Paschim* (1970) and by Dev Anand in *Hare Rama Hare Krishna* (1971), although these two films tried to establish the superiority of Indian culture over the Western variety without any compromise on lifestyle and values. Even a lesser-known film, the Kishore Kumar–Anita Guha starrer *Chacha Zindabad* (1959), handled the clash of the two cultures in a realistic manner (represented by a highly Westernized male and a traditional girl refusing to accept each other due to widely differing lifestyles and outlooks).

The diasporic cinema has also performed the function of an advertising agency to market overseas 'Heritage India': the exotica, the ethnic people (including the tribals) and cultures, the folk music and dance, and monuments and palaces. It has depicted an India in which the five-star culture co-exists happily with the indigenous folk culture, largely ignoring once for all the hackneyed images of poverty and filth shown earlier to the West by our realist and new-wave cinemas.

Also significant has been the timing of the arrival of this genre of cinema. With liberalization and globalization making a dramatic impact on India's economic policies from the early 1990s onwards, the prosperity and skills of the NRI became very tempting and even crucial for solving the problems of India's economic development, which appeared insurmountable by the country's elite. The members of the diaspora, who were earlier accused of 'brain drain', have been idolized and appeased as the 'brain bank' by both policy makers and the middle classes.

Yash Chopra's *Lamhe* (released in late 1991) was the first of a string of 'diasporic' films. This venture served as the grand inspirational model for the wealthy sections of the British Asian community, which was then trying to create its own space as a separate transnational class. Their benchmark of success is, as Rachel Dwyer observes, 'the international "five-star" look of their homes'.[8] This genre sought to represent the NRIs' links with their homeland, in particular their obsession with beautiful Indian women. In *Lamhe*, the hero's (Anil Kapoor, who is on a visit to India from the UK) first love (Sridevi) represented the 'ethnic model' of the Indian woman, while her daughter (also Sridevi), despite her outward Western lifestyle, is the inheritor of her mother's ethnicity through her knowledge of traditional customs and rituals apart from folk songs and folk tales. The elder Sridevi marries someone else and gives birth to a female child, who grows up to be her look-alike. The mother dies in the film. The hero returns to India and falls in love with the daughter. Thus when the younger Sridevi discovers that the hero loves her, she, without hesitation, discards her Western attire and switches over to the traditional saree and other typical ethnic symbols (such as the bindi and bangles). The film, therefore, reassured the audience that however much a woman may change on the surface, deep down she is still the ideal 'modern yet conservative Indian woman', the protector of traditions and family values. *Lamhe* was followed by other diasporic films such as Yash Chopra's *Dilwale Dulhaniya Le Jayenge* (shortened to *DDLJ*, 1995), Subhash Ghai's *Pardes* (1997), Satish Kaushik's *Hum Aap Ke Dil Mein Rahte Hain* (1999), Subhash Ghai's *Yaadein* (2001), Karan Johar's *Kabhi Khushi Kabhi Gham* (2001), Kunal Kohli's *Mujhse Dosti Karoge* (2002) and Nikhil Advani's *Kal Ho Na Ho* (2003). Each of these movies had a different approach towards the NRIs and their associations with the home country. Among these movies, the most successful venture was *DDLJ*, with Shahrukh Khan and Kajol in the lead, which went on to create box-office history: the film has been running continuously for about *thirteen* years at a theatre in Bombay.

***

The modern period also saw the release of a number of 'pygmy versions' of Amitbah Bachchan's angry young man cinema. While some films like *Tezaab* (1988), *Phool Aur Kante* (1991, Ajay Devgan's first film), *Koyla* (1997) and *Hathiyaar* (2002) followed the conventional 'revenge' format, others worked out an entirely new persona of the protagonist: for instance, *Khalnayak* (1993), *Kaante* (2002), *Aankhen* (2002) and *Plan* (2004). In the latter category, the 'hero' is invariably a criminal, or a member of the underground or a terrorist group without any ethical and moral concerns.

***

Amidst the simmering thematic crisis and the worrying pattern of commercial failures of soft as well as vengeful cinema in the 1990s and later, certain film makers have sought to revive the patriotic film. This quest has resulted in a variety of cinema that has, with a few exceptions, failed to impress the discerning viewer. This cinema sought to cash in on the nationalist sentiments of the people propelled by the events of the 1990s and the new millennium, especially the upsurge of terrorism and the 1999 Kargil war. (A neighbouring country was invariably depicted as the 'villain of the piece'.) Bachchan's angry young man variations were transformed overnight into aggressive nationalists, who strived to achieve twin objectives: to infuse a spirit of patriotism among the people and also to reverse the sagging interest in cinema, leading to losses in the film market. The films in this category include *Indian* (1996), *Border* (1997), *Mission Kashmir* (2000), *Maa Tujhe Salaam* (2001), *LOC Kargil* (2003), *Deewar* (2004), *Ab Tumhare Hawale Watan Saathiyo* (2004), *Lakshya* (2004), *1971* and *Sarhad Paar*, both released in 2007.

However, while the earlier great sagas of patriotism on celluloid (the 1948 *Shaheed*, *Jagriti*, *Pehla Aadmi*, *Samadhi*, the 1965 *Shaheed* and *Haqeeqat* among others) emotionally linked the viewers with the nation, in the present-day patriotic cinema, the jingoistic elements, apart from the glitz and glamour, tend to dominate the nationalistic perspectives. Even Manoj Kumar, who pioneered the brand of 'masala patriotism', considers these aggressive crusaders of nationalism Rambos who show people belonging to other countries or following a different culture in a demeaning light.[9] Some films also carry derogatory statements against certain religions. Kamalahasan too has been critical of this trend in cinema: 'Such characters are half-baked terrorists who kill individuals and forget bigger problems. So there is a need for models, which uphold and promote democratic forms of protest and governance. Indian cinema is increasingly becoming obsessed with pop patriotism and the dangerous ideology of vigilantism.'[10]

***

Some film makers have attempted to 'reinvent' the past in order to resurrect the lost glory of the medium. They have reworked old film classics, but in an entirely different framework as far as aesthetics, sets, music, emotional appeal and presentation are concerned. The whole approach seems to be to 'liberate' these classics from their original purpose of entertaining and enlightening the viewers on the basis of their characterizations, depth and seriousness. This trend was set in motion by the spate of films made on Shaheed Bhagat Singh in 2002. Others soon followed, such as Sanjay Leela Bhansali's *Devdas* (2002), J. P. Dutta's *Umrao Jaan* (2006), Anant Mahadevan's *Victoria No. 203* (2007) and *Ram Gopal Verma Ki Aag* (2007, a remake of *Sholay*). Some other films, like a remake of *Sahib Bibi Aur Ghulam* (with Salman Khan in the lead role, performed in the original by Guru Dutt!), are on the anvil.

The Bhagat Singh character played by Bobby Deol and Ajay Devgan, in their respective films, were passable, but nowhere near Manoj Kumar's role in the 1965 film.

The 2002 *Devdas* (with Shahrukh Khan in the title role) seemed to focus more on the dazzling sets and costumes rather than on the characters or the storyline. In fact, Bhansali took a few liberties with the original story. One amazing aspect of the film was that a *kotha* (brothel) supposed to be located in the dingy bylanes of Calcutta was decked like a five-star hotel!

The new *Umrao Jaan* (based on the life and times of a nineteenth-century courtesan) seemed to portray Aishwarya Rai as Aishwarya Rai. She somehow could not infuse the same depth and authenticity into the character of Umrao Jaan that Rekha did so very convincingly in the 1981 film. Despite Anu Malik's laudable efforts at composing *ghazals*, his score was a far cry from Khayyam's masterpieces (in the earlier version of the movie), rendered ever so poignantly by Asha Bhonsle and Talat Aziz (a talented *ghazal* singer).

The latest version of *Victoria No. 203* failed to enthuse the audiences, whereas the 1972 original was a rip-roaring success, thanks to some great slapstick comedy by veterans Ashok Kumar and Pran.

Ram Gopal Verma Ki Aag sank without a trace, despite the formidable Amitabh Bachchan appearing as a dreaded dacoit (originally played with admirable panache by Amjad Khan)!

***

The aforementioned trends have been further supplemented by a new genre of escapades where a small-town trickster reaches a metropolis propelled by the dream of 'striking gold'. (Such films project ruthlessly the so-called virtues of urban migration against the ills of moffusil/rural existence.) This pattern has been seen in films like *Raju Ban Gaya Gentleman* (1992), *Ram Jane* (1995), *Yes Boss* (1997), *Ishq* (1997), *Bas Itna Sa Khwab Hai* (2002) and *Bunti Aur Babli* (2005).

The Search for the New Indigenous Hero

While K. L. Saigal and Dilip Kumar represented our cinema's first- and second-generation indigenous heroes, and Amitabh Bachchan's towering persona commanded the status of third-generation hero, the somewhat alien identity of today's average Hindi film has underscored the crucial need for a fourth-generation indigenous hero who can represent the aspirations of the people in the present times. Although extremely popular and greatly admired by the largely impressionable masses, the present dominant hero persona of Hindi cinema seems to be out of tune with the rapidly changing political, economic and social milieu. This hero's image is reflective of only a small section of society, mainly the upper crust. The modern hero no longer seems to understand and articulate his social context; he rationalizes his existence through an inane exercise in image building and an extraneous self-promotion. The macho protagonists in the new crowd are not worshipped for their larger convictions but for their ad-model looks. In most movies, the heroines too have been largely made part of the décor and appear like beautiful ramp models on display in fashion shows. In other words, they are mostly reduced to objects of desire. And as these fourth-generation actors are part of the new era that thrives on materialism and are also representatives of the prevailing yuppie culture, most of them are not equipped to evoke the awe, the dignity and the grandeur of Hindi cinema's earlier legendary artistes.

***

From the mid-1980s onwards, the domain of the Hindi film hero can be broadly divided into four dominant categories: the 'durable heroes' (represented by Anil Kapoor, Sanjay Dutt, Sunny Deol and Jackie Shroff), who made their presence felt during the beginning of the 'modern era'; the 'new-age heroes' represented by the Khan troika (Shahrukh, Aamir and Salman), as also Ajay

Devgan, Govinda, Akshay Kumar, Aksaye Khanna, Bobby Deol, Saif Ali Khan and Fardeen Khan among others; a host of the 'new-millennium' heroes (Hrithik Roshan, Abhishek Bachchan, Viveik Oberoi and John Abraham among others); and 'the non-conformists' represented by Naseeruddin Shah, Om Puri, Kamalahasan, Nana Patekar, and later by Manoj Bajpai, Kay Kay Menon, Arshad Warsi, Rahul Bose and Irfan Khan. All of them have been vying to occupy the top slot after Amitabh Bachchan, but none could attain his iconic status nor match his powerful presence. Significantly, except for Jackie Shroff, Shahrukh Khan, Govinda, Akshay Kumar, John Abraham, Kamalahasan, Nana Patekar, Manoj Bajpai, Kay Kay Menon, Arshad Warsi and Irfan Khan, the rest have reached the film world through their family contacts.

The personas of these actors and their films are discussed in the chapters that follow.

Notes and References

1. Partho Chatterjee, 'A Bit of Song and Dance', in Aruna Vasudev (ed.), *Frames of Mind: Reflections on Indian Cinema*, New Delhi: UBSPD, 1995.
2. Iqbal Masood, 'The Great Four of the Golden Age', in Aruna Vasudev, op. cit.
3. Rachel Dwyer, *Yash Chopra: Fifty Years in Indian Cinema*, New Delhi: Roli Books, 2002.
4. Ibid.
5. B. D. Garga, *So Many Cinemas: The Motion Picture in India*, Bombay: Eminence Designs, 1996.
6. Ashish Rajadhyaksha and Paul Willemen, *Encyclopedia of Indian Cinema*, London: British Film Institute and New Delhi: Oxford University Press, 1994.
7. Fareed Kazmi, *The Politics of India's Conventional Cinema: Imaging a Universe Subverting a Multiverse*, New Delhi: Sage, 1999.
8. Rachel Dwyer, op. cit.
9. Manoj Kumar, 'Today's "Indians" Are Not Mr Bharat but Rambos', *The Times of India*, 10 November 2002.
10. Kamalahasan, 'Cinema at the Crossroads' (an interview with Subhash K. Jha), *The Times of India*, 29 March 2002.

Chapter 7

The 'Durable' Heroes

Anil Kapoor

Anil Kapoor (born on 24 December 1959), who started off in the late 1970s, eventually *arrived* in the film world in 1983. He diligently worked to establish a durable alternative to the angry persona of Amitabh Bachchan. His debut film was a light-hearted comedy, but after that, he appeared in a series of films as a romantic but disillusioned hero, who seeks revenge against the perpetrators of evil, either individually or in collaboration with others. Another variation he attempted was moulding his character on Raj Kapoor's delightful Chaplinesque image (such as in *Eeshwar*, 1989) as if to prove that innocence and endearing bonhomie can co-exist with vengeance and violence. Like his junior Shahrukh Khan and some other contemporaries, Anil Kapoor apparently nurtures an ambition of finding a place among the immortal artistes in cinema.

Anil Kapoor began his career with small roles in films like *Hamare Tumhare* (1979), *Ek Baar Phir* (1980) and *Hum Paanch* (1981). He also acted in a few Kannada and Telugu films. In Bollywood, he made his debut as hero in his home production, *Woh Saat Din* (1983, produced by his father Surinder Kapoor and directed by Bapu), as a small-town musician who moves to Bombay and aspires to become a music director in films. The movie was packed with several hilarious episodes. Next, in Yash Chopra's *Mashaal* (1984), he played a small-time Bombay goon who turns into a principled young journalist – thanks to the guidance of his mentor (none other than Dilip Kumar) – who gets caught in the morass of the underworld.

Anil Kapoor caught the popular imagination as the jovial lover but yet vigilante youth in films such as Subhash Ghai's *Meri Jung* (1985), *Karma* (1986) and *Ram Lakhan* (1989), Rajiv Rai's *Yudh* (1985), Shekhar Kapur's *Mr India* (1987), Vidhu Vinod Chopra's *Parinda* (1989) and *1942 – A Love Story* (1994), N. Chandra's *Tezaab* (1988) and Shankar's offbeat *Nayak* (2001).

In *Meri Jung*, he came up with a scintillating performance as a budding lawyer pitted against veteran Amrish Puri (the public prosecutor), who takes immense pride in sending convicts to the gallows, whether they are guilty or not. In this category falls Anil Kapoor's father (Girish Karnad). Despite Anil Kapoor's mother's (Nutan) plead-

Anil Kapoor

ings (which Anil Kapoor watches as a boy), Puri does not relent and Karnad is hanged. Nutan then loses touch with reality and is sent to an asylum. Eventually, after a string of action-packed episodes and high-voltage courtroom dramas, Anil Kapoor outwits the senior advocate, extracts his revenge and brings his mother back home, where she regains her mental balance. Amrish Puri, in the end, turns insane and lands up in a mental asylum.

Rajiv Rai's *Yudh* saw Anil Kapoor in a double role: as an advocate and also as a slick gangster. The gangster manages to lay the blame for his crimes on the advocate, but, as expected, in the end good triumphs over evil. In this movie, he was in the company of Jackie Shroff, another hero who hit big time with Subhash Ghai's *Hero* (1983). These two went on to act in many films together as ideal foils for each other.

Subhash Ghai's *Ram Lakhan* (yet another vengeance drama) brought together Jackie Shroff and Anil Kapoor as brothers, one as a police officer and the other as a rakish vagabond who takes to crime to earn quick money (somewhat like Shashi Kapoor and Amitabh Bachchan in *Deewar*). Eventually, he reforms himself and the two brothers seek their revenge on ace villain Amrish Puri. Anil Kapoor virtually 'lived' the role of Lakhan on screen with his characteristic vivacity and boisterousness.

Shekhar Kapur's *Mr India* is like a sci-fi film, which moves along at a frolicsome pace, thanks to a well-crafted plot and some breezy songs composed by Laxmikant Pyarelal and brought to life very effectively by the hero, heroine and a band of children. Anil Kapoor takes care of many orphans (like Shammi Kapoor did in the 1968 movie *Brahmachari*). He keeps them entertained and happy despite facing a perpetual shortage of money. To be able to pay the rent, he sublets a part of the residence to a journalist (Sridevi). However, many sinister forces (led by Amrish Puri as Mogambo) combine in an attempt to evict him and the children from their house. Mogambo wants to take over India and establish his own rule. He has his own fortress, which is a self-contained township in itself. Anil Kapoor's father, before he died, had fabricated a watch that makes people disappear (they can be seen only in red light), which is given to the hero by his father's friend (Ashok Kumar). Mogambo wants to lay hands on this watch. Eventually, Anil Kapoor (as the invisible Mr India), with the help of the children and the heroine, takes on the villain and his minions and destroys his fortress. Anil Kapoor, Sridevi, the children and the members of the cast came up with creditable performances, but it was Amrish Puri who stole the show with his extremely popular catch phrase: '*Mogambo khush hua!*'

N. Chandra's blockbuster *Tezaab* boosted Anil Kapoor's career tremendously. In fact, it was the role of a lifetime for this actor. He initially appears as a patriot who wants to serve his country. He falls in love with Madhuri Dixit, a dancer, who is forced to perform on stage by her dad (Anupam Kher), an alcoholic, so that he can get his daily dose of liquor from her earnings. However, the hero is framed on a crime charge and convicted. He undergoes a metamorphosis and becomes a dreaded gangster, who has many scores to settle. In the end, he manages to wipe out the blemishes on his character and is united with the heroine. Anil Kapoor's riveting performance (especially his brooding scenes) won him many plaudits. The highlight of *Tezaab* was the racy number *Ek, Do Teen...*, picturized on Madhuri Dixit, who announced her arrival on the scene with this film.

Vidhu Vinod Chopra's *Parinda* again paired Anil Kapoor (as Karan) and Jackie Shroff (as Kishen) as brothers. Kishen is the henchman of an underworld don (Nana Patekar) and to keep his brother out of the crime world, Kishen sends Karan abroad. But Karan returns to Bombay to seek his earlier love in the form of Madhuri Dixit (Paro), whose brother (Anupam Kher, an honest policeman) is Karan's friend. The policeman is shot dead in front of Karan by Nana Patekar's gang members. Attempts by Karan to track the killers turn out to be futile. Next, Karan and Paro are killed by the same gang soon after their wedding. When Kishen comes to know of this development, he turns against his mentor and burns him alive (Nana Patekar suffers from a deep-seated phobia against fire). This film was packed with powerful undercurrents and memorable performances by the entire cast, especially Nana Patekar.

1942 – A Love Story (again directed by Vidhu Vinod Chopra) brought on screen a touching tale of romance set against the backdrop of India's freedom movement. Anil Kapoor played the son of an affluent man who is a British loyalist. He falls in love with Manisha Koirala, the daughter of a freedom fighter. They face many obstacles due to the diametrically opposing stances of their respective fathers. Anyway, the hero becomes inspired enough to join the freedom movement and to hold the Indian flag aloft. Jackie Shroff played an impressive cameo as a freedom fighter assigned to assassinate a visiting British military official. The outstanding feature of this movie was the enchanting music by Rahul Dev Burman.

In Shankar's *Nayak* (2001), Anil Kapoor came up with a riveting performance as an ordinary TV reporter who accepts a challenge to become the chief minister of a state for 24 hours after exposing the wrongdoings of the present occupant of the post (Amrish Puri). He acts swiftly and ruthlessly (rushing from one trouble spot of Bombay to another with his officials) to tackle numerous problems and provide instant solutions (mainly, he suspends all the errant officials). He soon emerges as the peope's hero and wins over the heroine (Rani Mukherji) as well.

Unlike some of his contemporaries, Anil Kapoor is quite comfortable in slipping into traditional family dramas set in a modern milieu. For instance: in Indra Kumar's *Beta* (1992), he was the all-trusting simpleton, à la Guru Dutt in *Bahurani* (1963); he played the two-timing husband in David Dhawan's *Gharwali Baharwali* (1998) who perpetuates a male worldview; in K. Vishwanath's *Eeshwar* (1989), he was projected as a dullard who choses to marry a widow despite social rejection; and he appeared as the caring lover of a rape victim (Aishwarya Rai) in Satish Kaushik's *Hamara Dil Aap Ke Paas Hain* (2000).

Anil Kapoor tried his hand as a 'tough guy with a tender heart' in Indra Kumar's *Rishtey* (2002). Here he portrayed a boxer who supports his son after being separated from his wife (Karisma Kapoor) as a result of his extremely wealthy father-in-law refusing to accept him as a son-in-law (due to his low status).

Apart from those in the aforementioned films, Anil Kapoor has played a variety of other roles.

In *Bulandi* (2000) Anil was a benevolent but diehard feudal lord whose worldview is shattered by a haughty city-bred girl (Raveena Tandon) married to his younger brother (also played by Anil Kapoor). In Satish Kaushik's *Badhaai Ho Badhaai* (2002),

Anil Kapoor appeared in the role of delightful 'saviour' who, like Rajesh Khanna in *Bawarchi* (1972) (see Chapter 9 of Vol. 1), becomes the focal point in making the environment tension free and happy. He exhibited an amazing felicity as the overwrought eldest brother (the younger ones being Abhishek Bachchan and Fardeen Khan) in Anupam Kher's *Om Jai Jagdish* (2002) and in Honey Irani's *Armaan* (2003), he was a disgruntled doctor troubled by a possessive and jealous wife.

In Subhash Ghai's *Taal* (1999), a new-age musical about soulful love and sacrifice, Anil Kapoor played a music director/ orchestra conductor seeking to discover soul in his music through his love for the upcoming dancer (Aishwarya Rai). Yash Chopra's *Lamhe* (1991) (discussed earlier) and Satish Kaushik's *Hum Aap Ke Dil Mein Rahte Hain* (1999) marked his foray into diasporic cinema. In the latter film, he portrayed a suave NRI brought up in the USA who comes to India to reconstruct his lost love. However, it was in Priyadarshan's *Virasat* (1997) that he was in full command. In this movie, in contrast with the popular trends in diasopric films, he realistically portrayed the final return of an NRI to his roots.He appears as a youth who returns to his village, along with his girlfriend (Pooja Batra), after completing his education abroad. As he realizes the misery caused by underdevelopment in the region and the unending conflicts in the village's divided community, he decides to don the feudal robe and becomes a respected leader of the people. He marries a local girl (Tabu), who proves to be an ideal companion in his mission for rural uplift.

In Vivek Agnihotri's *Chocolate* (2005), Anil made his mark as advocate Krishan Pundit, who fights the case of two innocent Indian youth PP (Irfan Khan) and Sim (Tanushree Dutta), who have been arrested by the British police after an explosion on Christmas eve in London for their alleged links with Al Qaeda.

In Dharmesh Darshan's *Bewafaa* (2005), a film about changing morals and values in a fast changing world, Anil appeared as a business tycoon who gets married to the heroine Kareena Kapoor, much younger to him, after his wife, her elder sister (Sushmita Sen), dies after giving birth to twins (girls). But lack of compatibility with her husband and the growing frustrations within her force Kareena to have an extramarital affair with her ex-lover. In the end, Kareena chooses to forsake her lover for the sake of her nieces and her husband. The story had a striking resemblance to B. R. Chopra's *Gumrah* (1963).

Anil Kapoor's recent films, such as Nikhil Advani's *Salaam-e-Ishq* (2007), Anees Bazmee's *No Entry* (2007) and *Welcome* (2007), Vijay Krishna Acharya's *Tashan* (2008) and Abbas-Mustan's *Race* (2008), somewhat undermined the image of this artiste.

In *No Entry*, a nonsensical comedy about a lecherous man's obscene obsession with his masculinity and fulfilling sexual urges through any means, he even becomes a disciple of a 'love guru' (Salman Khan) specializing in training desperate men in the art of luring young girls and deceiving their wives.

In *Welcome* (2007), a comedy, Anil Kapoor and his elder brothers Nana Patekar and Feroz Khan are Hong Kong-based comic mobsters, who want their sister (Katrina Kaif) to marry a handsome bachelor, Rajiv (Akshay Kumar). When Rajiv's uncle (Paresh Rawal) does not approve of his nephew's association with a dubious family, the lopsided trio use their smart and engagingly comic stunts to get the uncle to agree to the alliance.

Tashan (2008), like several other contemporary films, glorified the criminal way of life. Anil Kapoor is a maverick goon, Bhaiyyaji, who steals the heroine Pooja's (Kareena Kapoor) father's money. Pooja and her boyfriend (Saif Ali Khan), in turn, steal Bhaiyyaji's money and run away. Bhaiyyaji hires Bachchan Pande (Akshay Kumar), a gangster, to catch them. In the end, Pooja kills Bhaiyyaji and marries Pande, who turns out to be her childhood friend.

In *Race* (2008), Anil Kapoor appeared as a lopsided cop (with a penchant for fruits) who investigates the criminal antecedents of two high-flying brothers (Saif Ali Khan and Akshaye Khanna) who are out to kill each other.

In Subhash Ghai's *Black and White* (2008), based on a plot borrowed from the Harrison Ford–Brad Pitt-starrer *Devil's Own* (1997), Anil once again made a foray into serious cinema, coming up with one of his most toned-up performances. He appeared as Rajan Mathur, a benevolent professor of Urdu literature. Professor Mathur shelters a terrorist Numair Qazi (Anurag Sinha), commissioned by a Muslim fundamentalist group to blast a bomb near the Red Fort on 15 August. He not only takes the boy on an enlightening journey of a communally harmonious life in Chandni Chowk in old Delhi but also arranges an entry pass for 15 August celebrations at the Red Fort. Yet the professor's affection and worldview fail to alter the terrorist's prefocused perceptions, which are steeped deep in his faith and his designated task. India's stage legend, Habib Tanvir in the cameo of an old-time Urdu poet in this film, made a great impression.

In Subhash Ghai's *Yuvraaj* (2008), Anil Kapoor portrayed an autistic individual who inherits a huge fortune, much to the chagrin of one of his brothers (played by Salman Khan). (See also Chapter 8, under Salman Khan.)

In Danny Boyle's 2008 runaway hit, *Slumdog Millionaire* (which bagged several Oscars), Anil Kapoor was very impressive as the quiz master who conducts the show in which a boy from the slums of Bombay wins a huge amount of money.

Sanjay Dutt

Sanjay Dutt (born on 29 July 1959), the son of Sunil Dutt and Nargis, seemed to represent a continuity with Amitabh Bachchan's cinema exemplifying the present-day youth's alienation and anger. Some of Sanjay's films, as less intense versions of the Bachchan genre, sought to capture the despair and anxieties of the urban poor. After his none-to-inspiring debut in *Rocky* (1981), directed by father Dutt, and a somewhat amateurish performance in *Vidhata* (1982), in the company of a legend like Dilip Kumar, he reached the top rungs of popularity

Dilip Kumar, Waheeda Rehman and Anil Kapoor in *Mashaal* (1984).

Manisha Koirala, Anil Kapoor and Jackie Shroff in *1942 – A Love Story* (1994).

Sunny Deol and Tabu in *Himmat* (1996).

Shahrukh Khan in *Pardes* (1997).

Gracy Singh and Aamir Khan in *Lagaan* (2001).

Salman Khan, Sanjay Dutt and Karisma Kapoor in *Chal Mere Bhai* (2000).

with three noteworthy films – Mahesh Bhat's *Naam* (1986) and *Sadak* (1991) and Lawrence D'souza and Som Haksar's *Saajan* (1991, a love triangle inspired by Raj Kapoor's 1964 venture *Sangam*).

Sanjay's cine persona and his real-life story make for fascinating reading. From a teen romantic hero (like Rishi Kapoor in *Bobby*), he adorned the garb of a criminal, often reflecting, in

Sanjay Dutt

some sense, the respectability being given to deviant individuals in political and public life by equally corrupt people. He also portrayed the stereotypical vigilante people's hero for a while and then shifted to playing a comic underworld don who – despite his evil presence and crude mannerisms – strives to be share space with ordinary people. And like Dev Anand and Amitabh Bachchan in their younger days, he has not appeared in any typical long-drawn-out family dramas.

Sanjay's 'angry' cinema is represented by films like *Hathiyaar* (1989), *Aatish* (1994), *Dushman* (1998), *Vaastav* (1999), *Mission Kashmir* (2000), *Kurukeshtra* (2000), *Pitaah* (2002), *Thatastu* (2006), *Shootout at Lokhandwala* (2007) and *Sarhad Paar* (2007).

In J. P. Dutta's *Hathiyaar*, he depicted an innocent youth-turned-revengeful gangster. Sanjay Gupta's *Aatish* presented him as the usual wronged man waging a war against his tormenters. Interestingly, the film highlighted the Hindu–Muslim camaraderie that transcended the moral and legal boundaries of society. Tanuja Chandra's crime thriller, *Dushman* (1998), a film that had the touch of Vijay Anand's handling of this genre, presented Sanjay in a down-to-earth role of a blind major trying to build up courage in the heroine (Kajol) who is being harassed by a serial killer.

In Mahesh Manjrekar's *Vaastav*, a befitting document on the underworld, Sanjay poignantly displayed his cutting edge in negotiating the role of an upright crusader with an engrossing display of surging passion and seething anger.

In the lacklustre *Kurukeshtra*, again directed by Mahesh Manjrekar, Sanjay, in a role borrowed heavily from Bachchan's cinema, was the upright cop trapped in a web of political corruption.

In Vidhu Vinod Chopra's *Mission Kashmir*, the actor depicted, with rare acumen, the trauma of a secular Kashmiri Muslim police officer trying to retrieve his foster son (Hrithik Roshan) from the trap of fundamentalist ideology.

Mahesh Manjrekar's *Pitaah* portrayed Sanjay as 'Father India', an utterly simplistic gender reversal of his mother Nargis's immortal role in *Mother India*. True to the times, the film sought to capture the brutality of feudal exploitation pitted against the rage of a tormented father whose daughter has been raped. He now takes a vow to wipe out the evil forces single-handedly. Unfortunately, the sequences were haphazard and failed to impress.

Anubhav Sinha's *Thatastu*, with Sanjay in the lead role, was about a poor man's desperate struggle in the face of the country's inhuman and at times corrupt medical system to arrange for a heart transplant for his dying son. Unable to pay the huge sum demanded for the operation, he holds 30 people hostage in a hospital. His stand is that he will release the hostages only after his son has been operated upon. The doctors agree and he decides to release the hostages. However, he later finds out that a surgery is being done – not on his son, but on a politician's son.

In Apoorva Lakhia's *Shootout at Lokhandwala*, his role was that of a police officer, who along with his team, is involved in a fierce gun battle with a dreaded gangster (played by Viveik Oberoi) and his minions. The film was inspired by the killing of the Maya Dolas gang in 1991 by a police force.

In Raman Kumar's *Sarhad Paar*, a film celebrating the warmth and goodwill of the mutual confidence building between India and Pakistan, Sanjay appeared as an army major who loses his memory when he is held captive by a dreaded terrorist in Pakistan and mercilessly tortured. On his return to India with the help of a Pakistani captain, he regains his memory after he happens to see the terrorist and his men sneaking around a gurdwara.

Sanjay Gupta's 'Rise and Fall' (one of the episodes of *Dus Kahaniyan*, 2007) has Sanjay Dutt in the role of a gang leader whose relations between him and his old friend and second-in-command (Suniel Shetty) are marked by tension and distrust. The senior gangster thinks that he will be murdered soon. The focus then now shifts to two teenagers, who are great friends, and are hoping to gain respect and position in the gang by killing another gang's leader. In the end, the duo takes on many gangsters before eventually being killed.

Sanjay experimented with villainous roles as well. He started off with Subhash Ghai's *Khalnayak* (1993). In Sanjay Gupta's *Kaante* (2002), in the august company of Big B, he appears as one of the social misfits dreaming of robbing a New York bank.

David Dhawan's *Ek Aur Ek Gyarah: By Hook or by Crook* (2003) presented Sanjay as a petty thief, who, along with his friend (Govinda), employs all the tricks of the trade to settle scores with two wanted criminals (Gulshan Grover and Ashish Vidyarthi, respectively). The film was filled with zany comic sequences.

Hriday Shetty's *Plan* (2004), a kidnap drama, presented Sanjay again in the stereotypical role of a powerful underworld don who is abducted by some youth (who think he is a wealthy businessman) so that they can get a huge ransom.

He appeared as a new-age guru in Mani Shankar's fantasy film *Rudraksh* (2004), a venture designed to impress the upmarket and foreign audience with a rudimentary touch of mystic India.

In *Shabd* (2005, directed by Leena Yadav), Sanjay appeared in a shoddily conceived role of a once-successful author in search of a real story to regain his fame. This writer-with-a-block makes his beloved wife enter into a relationship with a younger man so that he can feel the true spirit of pain and suffering to stimulate his mind.

In Ajay Chandok's *Nehle Pe Dehla* (2006), a brazen copy of Hollywood's *Weekend at Bernie's* (1989), Sanjay played a small-time charlatan, who, in collaboration with his buddy Saif Ali Khan, lays hands on Rs 30 crore embezzled by a dishonest hotelier (Shakti Kapoor). The other villain (Mukesh Rishi) plans to kill the hotelier and lay the blame on the duo, but they outsmart him.

In *Anthony Kaun Hai?* (2006) directed by Raj Kaushal, Sanjay was a contract killer hired to assassinate a conman named 'Anthony'.

In Afzal Khan's *Mehbooba* (2008), an uninspiring tribute to the beauty of true love, Sanjay essayed the character of an arrogant, indulgent and debauched NRI, who stands to be reformed by a virtuous Indian girl (Manisha Koirala). The dashing seducer manages to get engaged to Manisha Koirala. He then tells her that his love for her was merely a pretence so that he could sleep with her. In the end, he realizes his fault of considering a woman merely as a commodity after he gets counselling from his younger brother (Ajay Devgan), a warm-hearted NRI devoted to love.

In contrast with the above roles, Sanjay also appeared as the brave man either defending his country or taking on the criminals.

In J. P. Dutta's *LOC Kargil* (2003), which staged on celluloid a battle and the impact it had on the lives of sacrificing soldiers and their respective families, he was Lieutenant Colonel Y. K. Joshi, a daredevil soldier honoured with the Vir Chakra.

Milan Luthria's *Deewaar: Let's Bring Our Heroes Home* (2004) cast him as a goodhearted, valiant man engaged in cross-border arms and drug trafficking who sacrifices his life while freeing some Indian prisoners of war from a Pakistani jail.

Anubhav Sinha's *Dus* (2005) portrayed Sanjay as the head of the Anti-Terrorist Cell who uncovers a proposed terrorist attack by a group based in Canada. Although he is deceived by his girlfriend (Shilpa Shetty) who works as a double agent, he manages to save thousands of lives at a stadium where a special exhibition soccer match is to be played between India and Canada in the presence of the prime minister of India.

Sanjay Gadhvi's *Kidnap* (2008) was about an NRI father's (Sanjay Dutt) nerve-wracking struggle to retrieve his daughter from a sadist kidnapper's clutches. The child has been living with her mother, after the divorce of her parents. The search helps the father in coming closer to his offspring.

Although the depiction of uncouth violence has been his forte, Sanjay is quite adept at handling comedy. Ram Gopal Verma's *Daud* (1997) laid the foundation of his comic persona. He played a footloose burglar who happens to lay hands on a box containing a neutron bomb, which is also being sought by international gangs.

His comic persona found perfect expression in three of David Dhawan's films: *Chal Mere Bhai* (2000), *Jodi No. 1* (2001) and *Hum Kisi Se Kum Nahin* (2002). In the first film, he and Salman Khan provided the laughs. In the second, he and Govinda regaled the audiences with numerous antics and, in the third, he and Amitabh Bachchan did likewise.

His career-best movie, Rajkumar Hirani's *Munnabhai MBBS* (2003), had everyone in splits and clamouring for more. This film, a rib-tickling parody of modern medical science and the healthcare system, in fact, highlighted the possibilities of our cinema venturing into novel, meaningful contemporary themes. Munnabhai is an underworld don, who, in order to please his parents, pretends that he is a doctor running a charitable clinic in Bombay. When his parents come to know that he is a fake, they are shattered. He now decides to become a real doctor, and using all the tricks up his sleeve, he gains admission to a medical college where his uncorrupted innocence and humaneness lead him to expose the mechanistic and inhuman medical system.

Munnabhai MBBS:
Review in the *British Medical Journal*

Beneath the surface humour in this film there is a hidden –
or perhaps not so hidden – message throughout. As if
inspired by *Patch Adams* [1998], the Robin Williams film
about a doctor who believes in laughter as the best medicine,
Munnabhai MBBS exhorts doctors to be more humane towards
patients. There are references to senior staff regarding
patients as exhibits, which is most humiliating for the
patients as I know from my own experience as a patient
when a classmate saw me as an 'interesting case'. While some
scenes stretch credibility – for example, when the medical
school dean (played by Boman Irani) states that empathy is
unnecessary and patients must be seen purely from a
scientific perspective – surely we all know doctors who
could do with a little more humanity.

Some of the funny episodes are based on real-life incidents,
which, of course, are not that funny but instead rather
worrying. For example, Munnabhai uses his cellular phone
(among other creative methods) to cheat in examinations.
Such activity has been reported in India recently. There is also
a scene where gangsters enter the hospital in the middle of
the night, which is obviously based on an incident that took
place about 10 years ago. There is also a takeoff [on] laughter
therapy as an alternative medicine.

As one who firmly believes that physicians must read outside
their profession to become better doctors, I found myself
strongly recommending *Munnabhai MBBS* to all my colleagues.

Source: Dr Sanjai Pai, *British Medical Journal*, No. 12, 2004.

In another comedy, Mahesh Manjrekar's *Vaah! Life Ho To Aisi*
(2005), Sanjay appeared as Yamraj, the god of death in Hindu

mythology. He accepts the request of a young man (Shahid Kapoor), who has died in an accident, to bring him back to life again, as the latter has to attend to a lot of unfinished business. The large-hearted Yamraj not only gives him powers to defeat his evil uncle bent upon destroying his family but also allows him to stay alive. The film carried shades of the Rajendra Kumar starrer *Jhuk Gaya Aasman* (1968).

Lage Raho Munnabhai (2006), the sequel to *Munnabhai MBBS*, also directed by Rajkumar Hirani, can be adjudged as one the most curious pacifist films ever made. This time Sanjay's *tapori* undergoes a weird personality transformation through learning the virtues of goodness and non-violence. This transformation, in fact, edifies a rediscovery of Mahatma Gandhi and his relevance in today's world marred by hate, suspicion and brutal violence in every walk of life. Munna (Sanjay Dutt) falls in love with a feisty radio jockey (Vidya Balan). He poses as a history teacher, and, in the process, he rediscovers the Mahatma and learns the almost-forgotten concept that truthfulness is next to godliness. Like a true social experimentalist, he puts into practice his newly acquired enlightenment when a builder and his goons want to throw out a group of senior citizens who live in the heroine's house and take possession of it. In this way, a *tapori* puts to shame the hordes of our khadi-clad politicians who have been making a mockery of Gandhi's name by using it to promote their own political ends. As one reviewer on the Internet writes: '*Lage Raho* ... holds up a mirror to each of one us, showing us how we think that deceit, lies and shortcuts are the pathways to success.' Sanjay, once again showed his excellence in this comic role. The site www.gandhigiri.org is dedicated to the Mahatma and has become a huge hit among the public just like the movie.

With *Munnabhai MBBS* and *Lage Raho Munnabhai*, the new iconic figure generated by cinema seemed to have brought about a reassessment of the contemporary dehumanized social milieu through a process of self-discovery. This is despite the fact that the comic treatment to the serious issues raised had slightly undermined their critical importance in today's insensitive world. Munnabhai's next avatar, in *Munnabhai Chale America*, is eagerly awaited.

After the huge success of the Munnabhai films, Sanjay has been being cast in several comedies. David Dhawan's *Shadi No. 1* (2006), a jaded comedy about man's insatiable libido, cast Sanjay in the role of Lucky Bhaiya. He creates chaos in the lives of couples, and, in the process, makes the wives suspicious and paranoid. Three husbands (Fardeen Khan, Zayed Khan and Sharman Joshi) want to have a fling with three highly desirable women (Riya Sen, Sophie Chaudhary and Arti Chabaria), but Lucky Bhaiya informs the respective wives about their spouses' predilections.

In *Dhamaal* (2007), a comedy directed by Indra Kumar, Sanjay appeared as an eccentric police inspector, who catches hold of a group of four suspicious looking buddies. He finds them in the vicinity of a dying criminal (whose car has fallen off a cliff) for whom he has been searching for years. The criminal has just told the quartet that he has hidden crores of rupees at a particular place in Goa and gives them the clues to get there. Then begins the crazy race to get to the money! (This movie was loosely based on the 1963 Hollywood rip-roaring comedy *It's a Mad Mad Mad Mad World*.)

Saurav Kabra's 2008 film, *EMI* (easy monthly instalment), was an offbeat attempt to highlight the havoc being played by the credit economy in the lives of so many ambitious upmarket residents. While Satar Bhai (Sanjay Dutt) is a good-hearted creditor serving people in need of money, his clients opt for EMI schemes. A newly wed couple opt for the EMI scheme for buying a house, a car and other gadgetry and also for honeymooning abroad. But as they are unable to pay up the EMIs, their love withers and they finally file for a divorce. Other characters in the narrative also part with their happiness in their compulsions to go in for the EMI. For instance: A DJ is taken for a ride by a spendthrift girl friend; a father financing his son's expensive education; and a wife unable to get her husband's insurance money after he is killed in an accident.

As the title implies, *Luck* (2009), an action thriller directed by Soham Shah, is about the role of luck in the making of one's destiny and fortune. Sanjay Dutt plays Mossa Bhai, a remarkably lucky man who has, incredibly, escaped alive despite a mosque collapsing around him and despite jumping from a four-storied building. In the end, he survives a tricky pistol shooting game in which the other player is Ram Mehra (Irfan Khan), another lucky man.

Chatur Singh Two Star (under production), an action comedy film being directed by Ajay Chandhok and inspired by the Hollywood classic *The Pink Panther*, cast Sanjay in the title role of an goofy member of the Mumbai police who, in his career, has been botching up cases and making an ass of himself. When he is assigned a very difficult case, his idiotic mannerisms, clumsiness and his obsession with his 'superintelligence' set off a string of hilarious events, leading to a lot of chaos and confusion all around.

Anthony D'Souza's *Blue* (under production) is about the daredevil search by Sanjay Dutt and Akshay Kumar for treasure that lies at the bottom of an ocean and is guarded by sharks. The script was written by American writers Joshua Lurie and Bryan M. Sullivan. Kylie Minogue (an Australia-born singer and actress) makes a guest appearance in the film.

In *Aladin* (under production), directed by Sujoy Ghosh, Sanjay Dutt appears as a cool and villainous ringmaster. Sanjay's third Munnabhai movie, *Munnabhai Chale Amerika*, also directed by Rajkumar Hirani, is shortly being released. *Padosan Remake*, a new version of 1968 laugh riot *Padosan*, directed by Neeraj Vora, is under production.

In real life, when the Bombay blasts took place in 1993, Sanjay was said to be involved with underworld dons and he was believed to be in possession of an AK-56 rifle. He spent some 18 months as an undertrial in a Bombay jail from April 1993 onwards, before being released on bail. He was eventually convicted by the Bombay High Court in November 2006 and spent some more time in jail before being released again on bail in November 2007. His plea to contest in the general elections in April-May 2009 from Lucknow (as a Samajwadi Party candidate) was rejected by the Supreme Court of India.

Sunny Deol

Sunny Deol (born as Ajay Singh Deol on 19 October 1961), like Sanjay Dutt, consolidated further the film hero's image of the urban, Rambo-type vigilante. He soon became a master of well-timed and calculated melodrama, and brought into his roles – like his illustrious father Dharmendra – the 'son of the soil' ruggedness and a self-inspired dignity. He also exhibited an innate sense of resilience and uprightness.

Sunny Deol

Among the present-day big stars, Sunny is one who has consistently refused to be swayed by the pop-disco soft romance genre of today's cinema. As the archetype of the idealist macho hero and like the fiery Nana Patekar (who appears in Chapter 10), he continues to present himself as a messianic figure for the wronged victims and as a sturdy pillar of the nation-state.

Sunny's first film as hero was Rahul Rawail's *Betaab* (1983), which was also the heroine Amrita Singh's debut movie. Sunny and his mother (Nirupa Roy) stay in a small town. They begin looking for a place to run a poultry farm. Sunny finds a place but it is a mess. He wants to clear the area and set up the infrastructure. He meets a young woman (Amrita Singh), who initially tries to thwart his efforts, but later discovers that they were childhood friends. She decides to help him. They soon fall in

love, but have to face stiff resistance from Sunny's mother and
Amrita's father (Shammi Kapoor). Anyway, after some thrilling
sequences, the hero and heroine are united.

Sunny then appeared in several movies such as *Manzil Manzil*
(1984), *Arjun* (1985), *Sultanat* (1986) and *Dacait* (1987). But he really
rose to fame with two films: Rajiv Rai's *Tridev* (1989) as the
courageous but disgruntled cop commissioned by the state to
bring to book a dreaded criminal and *Ghayal* (1990), a powerful
vigilante drama produced by Dharmendra and directed by
Rajkumar Santoshi. He then expanded his persona with an
imposing role as a beleaguered lawyer in *Damini* (1993), who
provides professional help to a harassed woman (a witness to a
rape).

In N. Chandra's *Narsimha* (1991) Sunny, as a lone crusader,
took up the 'repair work' of the crumbling law and order
machinery. Raj Kanwar's *Farz* (2001) presented Sunny as the
tough, no-nonsense police officer (moulded on the former Punjab
police chief K. P. S. Gill's image) who outsmarts Mumbai's local
police in cleaning up the city by driving out the crooks and the
anti-national mafia lords. In Guddu Dhanoa's *Ziddi* (1997), he
portrayed an ill-tempered youth who becomes a dreaded gangster
after he is jailed for brutally beating a man as he attempts to
molest his sister. In films like R. Maharajan's *Indian* (2001) and
Tinu Verma's *Maa Tujhe Salaam* (2002), Sunny's persona sought
to edify the Bharat image of his predecessor Manoj Kumar with
resounding jingoism and high-pitched rhetoric.

Sunny reached the peak of his career with a powerful
performance in Anil Sharma's *Gadar – Ek Prem Katha* (2001), set
against the backdrop of the agonizing period of Partition. Sunny
played a Sikh truck driver who rescues a Muslim girl (Ameesha
Patel) from a rapacious mob. He marries her and they have a child.
He effectively brought alive on celluloid the trauma of a victim of
forbidden love. He somehow develops the strength and courage
that empower him to transcend the conflicting spaces
represented by the two newly formed nation-states (India and

Pakistan). The film posed the question of national identity in the context of an individual's freedom to choose his/her citizenship without offending the constraints imposed by the state. The protagonist becomes the vehicle in which his child rides to become a symbol of extended goodwill and harmony, thus erasing the borders not only in the minds of the people but in the physical space also. *Gadar*, in spite of being a formulaic melodrama, captured very ably the anguish of Partition, and is comparable with the memorable film, Filmistan's *Nastik* (1954), scripted and directed by I. S. Johar.

Sunny's participation in soft romantic roles has been limited. Suneel Darshan's insipid tale of love *Ajay* (1996), which depicted the conflict between traditional and modern ways of life, cast him in the role of a cowherd who falls for a modern girl (Karisma Kapoor) and eventually makes her shed her minis and dress up as a traditional Indian woman. Thus, the film seemed to contend that the restless elements of modernity can find peace only by a return to traditional methods. Sunil Sharma's *Himmat* (1996) was perhaps one of the few films in which Sunny sought to transcend his cine persona to acquire a global image. He appeared to be the Indian version of James Bond. This macho hero (a secret agent), who leads a luxurious life in the company of girls amidst the Swiss Alps, suddenly turns patriotic (when one of his colleagues is believed to have been killed) and takes on a bunch of mercenaries trying to steal nuclear technology secrets from India. However, he seemed rather unconvincing in this role when compared to the original Bond.

Anil Sharma's *The Hero: Love Story of a Spy* (2003) presented Sunny in the role of an army officer (Major Arun Khanna) who sets up an espionage network with the objective of getting information regarding terrorist activities across the border. He recruits Reshma (Preity Zinta) to work for his network. When terrorists attack the ship they are on, Reshma goes missing and Major Khanna is presumed dead. He fakes his own death, and plans to infiltrate the terrorist network. He follows the terrorists to Canada, where it is revealed that they are planning to build a nuclear bomb. Khanna changes his identity to a nuclear scientist Wahid, working at a well-known Canadian nuclear research organization. After many thrilling sequences, the hero emerges victorious and also finds his lost love.

In Arindam Chowdhuri's *Rok Sako To Rok Lo* (2004), set against the backdrop of sports rivalry between two schools, Sunny played the legendary Kabir 'Phantom' Mukherjee, the sportsman who has won many coveted awards for many years at annual sports fests. As a coach, he prepares the students of his old school for continuing its winning tradition.

In Rahul Rawail's *Jo Bole So Nihaal* (2005), Sunny Deol portrayed Nihaal Singh, an honest constable from Punjab, who unwittingly aids a dreaded terrorist Romeo in his escape. Labelled as a traitor, he is suspended from his job. Also, he is ridiculed and humiliated and his family is ostracized by the other villagers. Meanwhile, Romeo enters the US and hatches a plot to kill the president. The FBI, desperate to find him, recruits Nihaal and asks him to come to New York so as to help in capturing Romeo. Sunny lays down a condition for his help: he would like to take the villain to his hometown in Punjab, thereby clearing his name and restoring his former glory.

In Sachin Bajaj's *Naksha: Unlock the Mystery* (2006), Sunny, the son of an archaeologist, appeared as a brave investigator who carries out a desperate search for a mysterious map that holds the key to finding the armour of the legendary warrior Arjun of the epic Mahabharata. This armour can destroy all life if it were to fall into the wrong hands. Unfortunately, the film turned out to be lacklustre.

Teesri Aankh (2006), directed by Harry Baweja, was an offbeat work about the inhuman misuse of modern technology. This film projected Sunny as a cop desperately hunting for a gang, which runs a racket all over India, by trapping innocent, vulnerable women who have been photographed by a hidden camera. The film symbolized the hero's sharp focused hunt for the criminals in the form of the omnipotent Lord Shiva's 'third eye' in Hindu mythology.

In Anil Sharma's *Apne* (2007) Sunny virtually re-created his father's trademark 'vendetta hero'. He appeared as one of the sons who enters the boxing arena as a formidable player, putting to shame his treacherous competitors. In this movie, the father (Dharmendra) and both the sons (Sunny Deol and Bobby Deol) performed creditably.

In *Fool n Final* (2007), directed by Ahmed Khan, Sunny essayed his stereotype role of a boxer of international repute, who, with the help of a criminal (Shahid Kapoor), his girl friend (Ayesha Takia) and her uncle (Paresh Rawal), takes on three international gangsters in pursuit of a priceless diamond.

Guddu Dhanoa's *Big Brother* (2007) portrayed Sunny as the loving brother who avenges the rape of his step-sister by the home minister's son. He kills the culprit, and abducts a number of men who have raped and those who have burned their daughters-in-law. He soon launches a mass movement to work for the suffering people with the support of women and thus becomes their 'big brother'.

In Ammtoje Mann's *Kaafila* (2007), Sunny portrayed a mysterious man, who, in return for a huge fee, acts as a guide to a group of people who have lost their way in Eastern Europe while traveling illegally to the UK. The *kaafila* (caravan) goes through difficult times as it winds its way through various countries and eventually lands up in Pakistan. There, left to fend for themselves, they discover each other and forge new relationships.

In Samir Karnik's *Heroes* (2008), Sunny appeared as the wheelchair-bound former Indian Air Force pilot, whom two film academy students, Vatsal Sheth and Sohail Khan, rope in as part of their project to make a documentary highlighting reasons *not* to join the Indian armed forces. They find that he is very proud of his brother's (an army officer played by his real-life brother Bobby Deol) sacrifice for his country. The script of the film has been acquired by the Academy of Motion Picture Arts and Sciences, USA.

Neeraj Pathak's *Right Ya Wrong* (2008) featured Sunny as an honest cop who becomes the prime suspect in the murder of his own wife (Isha Koppikar), a case being investigated by his closest friend and colleague (Irfan Khan).

Sunny has also directed *Dillagi* (1999); he appeared in this film as the elder brother of the hero (Bobby Deol) who helps him to discover the real meaning of life.

Jackie Shroff

Jakie Shroff, who announced his arrival with Subhash Ghai's *Hero* (1983), was also a formidable representative of vendetta cinema.

Jackie Shroff

Known for his down-to-earth yet larger-than-life persona, he, like his senior Shatrughan Sinha, specialized in portraying the roles of an upright cop and also an over-the-board criminal, often starting off as a street urchin waging a lonely battle against the villains. In his mannerisms and style, he reflected the go-getter confidence of Hollywood's action heroes like Harrison Ford. No wonder, he often laments that if he had made his career in the USA, he would have been among the top stars of Hollywood.

Jackie Shroff was born as Jaikishan Kakubhai Shroff in Bombay on 1 February 1957 into a Gujarati family. He was introduced in films by Dev Anand in 1973 in *Heera Panna* in a small role; the veteran cast him again in *Swami Dada* (1982) where he was in the company of Mithun Chakraborty and Naseeruddin Shah. He played his first leading role in 1983 in *Hero*, in which he appeared as a kidnapper, who undergoes a change of heart in the company of the heroine, his hostage.

Jackie soon emerged as a cult figure in a number of successful vendetta films, often pairing with Anil Kapoor.

In Raj N. Sippy's *Shiva Ka Insaaf* (1985), he appeared as an orphan, raised by his Muslim and Christian mentors who teach him to destroy evil as well as help him to seek out the killers of his parents and end their tyranny.

In Rajiv Rai's *Yudh* (1985), he played an upright police officer who launches a crusade to bring to book the villain, the murderer of his cop father, who is planning to get his foster mother killed. In this movie he has Anil Kapoor for company.

In Subhash Ghai's *Karma* (1986), he appeared as one of the three dreaded convicts roped in by Dilip Kumar to destroy the sadistic villain; the other two were Anil Kapoor and Naseeruddin Shah.

Ketan Desai's *Allah Rakha* (1986) featured him as the kidnapped son of a cop who ends up growing on the streets as an orphan and in Anil Ganguly's *Sadak Chhap* (1987) he played an orphaned urchin who grows up to become instrumental in exposing a closely guarded conspiracy involving people known to him.

Jackie's vengeful image reached its zenith in the late 1980s and early 1990s with a slew of releases in a row. In Subhash Ghai's *Ram Lakhan* (1989), he was an honest cop and the son of a distraught widow (Raakhee) who wants her two sons (the other being Anil Kapoor) to avenge the murder of their father.

As already mentioned, Vidhu Vinod Chopra's *Parinda* (1989) cast him as the henchman of a psychotic don (Nana Patekar) who insists that his (Jackie's) younger brother (Anil Kapoor) stay away from the world of crime. When Anil Kapoor and his bride are brutally killed on their wedding night by the don's goons, Jackie avenges himself by setting the don ablaze. He won the *Filmfare* Best Actor Award for his performance in this film.

In *Tridev* (1989), he pitched in as one of the three protagonists who take on a powerful crime lord, the other two being Sunny Deol and Naseeruddin Shah.

Apart from *Parinda*, Shashilal K. Nair's *Angaar* (1992), Priyadarshan's *Gardish* (1993), Mukul Anand's *Trimurti* (1995) and Mazhar Khan's *Gang* (2000) are considered the actor's best works. In *Angaar*, he portrayed a youth, frustrated with crime and corruption, who launches a violent campaign against the system. *Gardish* was about a common man taking on the criminal elements in society. In *Trimurti*, he was the eldest son of a suffering mother who along with his brothers (Anil Kapoor and Shahrukh Khan) avenges the havoc played by a notorious goon with the life of their mother. In *Gang* he appeared as Gangu, one of the four friends from different cultural and religious backgrounds, who join hands to start their career in crime and extortion. However, Jackie compels them to begin an honest life.

In Rajkumar Santoshi' *Lajja* (2001), one of the most important works in our cinema on the plight of women in Indian society and their urge for liberation, Jackie essayed the negative role of a morally loose NRI husband of the film's main female protagonist Vaidehi (Manisha Koirala) chasing her to get possession of their would-be child. On the run, she is exposed to the gory existence of three other women, all victims of male chauvinism and social oppression. In the end, the repentant husband realizes his mistake (that is, he has caused much misery for his wife).

In Shashi Ranjan's *Dobara* (2004), our hero appeared as a successful writer, whose married life with a psychiatrist (Mahima Chaudhary) goes haywire after his former sweetheart, a schizophrenic (Raveena Tandon), reveals that he has a son borne by her.

Divorce: Not Between Husband and Wife (2005) directed by M. J. Ramanan, an offbeat film addressing a complex family issue, had Jackie in the role of a socially conscious lawyer, who agrees to take up the case on behalf of a child for his parents' separation as the two are unable to build up and lead a happy family life. (Both the father and the mother are preoccupied with boosting their respective careers.) Jackie wins the case and the judge directs the Indian Government to amend the law to permit a child to seek divorce of his/her parents on the ground of their unbearable mutual incompatibility or neglect of the child.

Bhoot Unkle (2006), a children's film by Krishan Choudhry and Aneesh Arjun Dev, and directed by Mukesh Saigal, had Jackie playing the spirit of a dreaded pirate, which has been lying dormant in an abandoned lighthouse for a long time. An orphaned kid stumbles upon this spirit. The ghost then shares his magical powers to help the boy in saving the town from the evil designs of the villain.

Apart from the foregoing roles, Jackie has also exhibited his acumen in negotiating a wide variety of characterizations. For instance, Subhash Ghai's *Saudagar* (1991) cast him as the son of Dilip Kumar who dies in his pursuit to bring about peace between two feuding families. In the same director's *Khalnayak* (1993) Jackie played a cop in pursuit of a criminal (Sanjay Dutt). As already mentioned, he played a freedom fighter in *1942 – A Love Story* (1994). He impressed as a famous cinestar in Ram Gopal Verma's *Rangeela* (1995; the hero was Aamir Khan). In J. P. Dutta's war movie *Border* (1997), Jackie chipped in as an Indian Air Force wing commander. His role as a brooding terrorist in Vidhu Vinod Chopra's *Mission Kashmir* (2000) was memorable. He played the character of Chhunilal in Sanjay Leela Bhansali's *Devdas* (2002). He was a major (retired) who is on the lookout for two criminals in David Dhawan's *Ek Aur Ek Gyarah: By Hook or by Crook* (2003). He appeared as Chhote Mia in Kazaid Gustad's *Boom* (2003), who wants to outwit Medium Mia (Gulshan Grover) to get hold of the jewellery taken away by three models. The role of Bade Mia was played by Amitabh Bachchan.

Jackie's other notable supporting roles were in Goldie Behl's *Bas Intna Sa Khwab Hai* (2001), Madhur Bhandarkar's *Aan: Men At Work* (2004), Sangeeth Sivan's *Apna Sapna Money Money* (2006), Priyadarshan's *Bhagam Bhag* (2006), Sachin Bajaj's *Naksha: Unlock* the Mystery (2006), Vidhu Vinod Chopra's Eklavya (2006), Ahmed Khan's Fool n Final (2007), Mani Shankar's Mukhbir (2008) and Lucky Kohli and Rajesh Bajaj's Hari Puttar: A Comedy of Terrors (2008). He was appreciated for his performance in the Bengali film Antar Mahal (2005). He has also appeared in Maryada Purushottam (2006), a TV production by Sanjay Khan.

In Deepak Balraj Vij's Malik Ek (under production), Jackie appears as Sai Baba of Shirdi. He plays an important role in Partho Ghosh's Ek Second ... Jo Zindagi Badal De? (under production), a thriller. In Chargesheet (under production), directed by Dev Anand, Jackie appears along with the senior. In this film, the politician Amar Singh is to play the home minister. Jackie don's the villian's mantle in Veer (under production), a period film directed by Anil Sharma, in which Salman Khan is the hero. Jackie Shroff is due to make his debut in Tamil cinema with Aaranya Kaandam directed by Thiagarajan Kumararaja.

Jackie is one of the few film stars known for his exemplary philanthropic efforts for helping the poor and needy, particularly children. Amazingly, he is also a very well-known snake charmer.

Chapter 8

The New-Age Heroes

In the late 1980s and 1990s, a bunch of young heroes – peppy, energetic and buoyant – emerged on the scene. They put in place the persona of the new-age hero as per the 'prescriptions' of the modern Indian film.

Shahrukh Khan

Among the young aspirants to the top slot, Shahrukh Khan made his presence felt in the early 1990s. He went on to become the main architect for moulding the new-age hero. He became the frontal figure not only of the much celebrated diaspora cinema but also of the soft romances of the 1990s. He represents the delightful romantic for whom suffering in love or otherwise is incidental and not part of one's social predicament or disillusionment. His hero, despite his largely Westernized demeanour and outlook, would yet claim *'phir bhi dil hai Hindustani'* (even then the heart is Indian). Apart from aforementioned genres, this actor's cinema also reflects four other manifestations of the protagonist in tune with modern times: anti-hero obsessions, an anti-establishment stance, get-rich-quick aspirations and vigilantism.

Born in Delhi on 2 November 1965, Shahrukh Khan started off as an amateur stage and television actor. He came into prominence with his role in the TV serials *Fauji* and *Circus* that were telecast in the late 1980s. He made his debut in an art film,

Shahrukh Khan

Mani Kaul's *Idiot* (1991), and announced his entry into commercial cinema with Raj Kanwar's *Deewana* (1992). In a relatively short span his career zoomed to dizzying heights. He has also emerged as the brand ambassador for many highly priced products including upmarket cars and watches.

In his formative phase itself, he established his place as a top-rung actor with two anti-hero roles, the forte of his two iconic predecessors: Dilip Kumar and Amitabh Bachchan. *Baazigar* and *Darr*, both released in 1993, depicted the inhuman commodification of women; they are treated as objects to be possessed by the predatory male.

In *Baazigar* (directed by Abbas Burmawalla and Mustan Burmawalla), inspired by Dilip Kumar's *Duniya* (1984) and Amitabh Bachchan's *Aakhri Raasta* (1986) but far more savage and morbid, Shahrukh played an unusually vicious type of sadist. He becomes a gambler in order to win over the heroine, but eventually engineers the complete ruin of her family. The depiction of the cold-blooded murder of the heroine's sister became controversial. Although the film intended to capture the sadistic undercurrents in the human psyche, it was eventually reduced to a horrifying murder drama.

Yash Chopra's *Darr* presented the young actor as a pathologically sick man: a stalker who shadows and harasses the heroine Juhi Chawla (the object of his love) and makes her life miserable. In contrast with Dilip Kumar in *Insaniyat* (1955), Amitabh Bachchan in *Jurmana* (1979) and Kamalahasan in *Sagar* (1985) – in which ungratified love inspired the rejected lover to sacrifice his own life, thus transforming the relationship into a platonic one – here the psychotic lover, in his obsession, forces the woman to become a part of his suffering, leading to an all-around emotional destruction. He is ultimately clobbered mercilessly by the heroine's husband (Sunny Deol), when the latter comes to know about his identity. The film failed to offer psychoanalytical insights into the weird behaviour of the obsessed stalker. It thus evoked a disturbing sense of loss of dignity to the celebrated model of love patented by Indian cinema over so many decades. *Baazigar* and *Darr*, as Dinesh Raheja and Jitender Kothari observe, 'redefined the motivations and the morality behind violence in the post-Bachchan period'.[1]

In depicting the get-rich-quick aspirations of the new-age protagonist, Shahrukh's cinema also came to promote the yuppie culture of the modern age. This trend was seen in a number of films like *Deewana* (1992), *Raju Ban Gaya Gentleman* (1992), *Kabhi Ha Kabhi Na* (1993), *Ram Jaane* (1995), *Chahat* (1996), *Yes Boss* (1997) and *Phir Bhi Dil Hai Hindustani* (2000).

In Raj Kanwar's *Deewana*, Shahrukh plays a small-town commoner who stalks a rich widow to gain access to a prosperous lifestyle. Aziz Mirza's *Raju Ban Gaya Gentleman* portrayed him as a small-town youth who reaches Bombay, seeking a job in an industrial house. He covertly acquires a gentleman's look to impress the lady owner so that he can climb the social ladder and become part of the city's well-to-do strata. Kundan Mehta's *Kabhi Ha Kabhi Na* further exemplified the defiant, self-gratifying attitudes of today's upmarket youth. The protagonist is an upbeat collegian who wants to become a pop singer against the wishes of his orthodox father. He also stalks a girl who loves another man and vigorously schemes to break their relationship.

Rajiv Mehra's *Ram Jaane* showcased, in an entirely reprehensible way, the growing aspirations of the urban poor to lead a life of prosperity and luxury by any means. Shahrukh portrayed the transformation of a simple-hearted city orphan to a trigger-happy goon. Mahesh Bhatt's *Chahat* turned out to be a caricature of the Indian folk tradition. In this film, Shahrukh initially appears as a folk singer who later becomes an entertainer in a five-star hotel and seeks s a sybaritic lifestyle by indulging in a love affair with a girl from an affluent family. The theme of this film was somewhat similar to that of Amitabh Bachchan's *Yaraana* (1981).

One true marker of the downfall of modern cinema was Aziz Mirza's *Yes Boss*. This venture highlighted, without a twinge of remorse, the 'gain-instant-wealth' syndrome and the associated element of immorality as making up the ideology of the country's middle class. Designed as a comedy, the film was about a middle-class boy and girl struggling to make it big in a metropolis. They are enamoured of the prevalent glitz-and-glamour culture. They constantly scheme and con others with no concern for ethics and values. The hero, employed as a junior partner in an advertising agency, entices young girls for his boss (who is married), while the heroine (Juhi Chawla) starts an affair with the same boss. While spurning the hero, her contention is that two unsuccessful people cannot lead a successful life. Absolutely moronic in its conception, the film seriously undermined the image of Shahrukh Khan.

In the same director's *Phir Bhi Dil Hai Hindustani*, Shahrukh and Juhi Chawla played television reporters, representing a whole new breed of ambitious, aggressive, confident and upwardly mobile young Indians. Each of them shouts from the rooftops: 'I'm the best, I'm the best.' Modesty, evidently, is no longer a virtue. They start off as rivals, but they eventually team up and use the power of TV to rescue an innocent man, branded as a terrorist, from the gallows.

In Mahesh Bhatt's *Duplicate* (1998), Shahrukh, in a double role, sought to invent a brand new image of a comic hero, perhaps suddenly inspired by Jim Carrey's mind-blowing role in *The Mask* (1994). In the first role he is an overgrown child (à la Kishore Kumar in *Half Ticket* who was far more convincing) who does not leave his mother's lap. In the other role, he is the villainous character who finds sadistic pleasure by indulging in facial contortions. However, in both roles, Shahrukh Khan presented an extremely untidy act, which lacked both depth and finesse.

***

Shahrukh's engagement with diasporic cinema began with *Dilwale Dulhania Le Jayenge* (1995), produced by Yash Chopra and directed by Aditya Chopra. The film went on to become a tremendous success. The actor portrayed an upbeat NRI Punjabi youth who discovers his authentic Indian identity through the ethnicity of native women. Unlike Dilip Kumar or Amitabh Bachchan's hero, Shahrukh, as the protagonist, does not have to struggle against a dominant and cruel social order. Instead, he smoothly assimilates, despite his outward display of modernity, the virtues of feudal patriarchy and dons the mantle of 'Indianness' with incredible felicity. In *DDLJ*, the hero and heroine (Kajol) meet while they are on a trip around Europe. After a few spats, they fall in love. The heroine's father (Amrish Puri), though settled in the West, strictly follows Indian traditions. He decides to get his daughter married in his native village in Punjab to a local lad. When the hero comes to know of this development, he lands up in the village. Under the pretext of helping with the wedding preparations, he works his way into the heroine's household. He also befriends many of the local people. He ultimately succeeds in winning over the heroine's father and manages to marry his true love. The film was embellished with some fabulous photography and catchy songs.

In *English Babu Desi Mem* (1996, directed by Praveen Nischol), Shahrukh portrays an NRI who comes to India to take custody of the child of his dead brother being brought up by his foster mother. That is the essence of an otherwise convoluted plot.

Pardes (1997), directed by Subhash Ghai, was designed virtually in the same format as that of *DDLJ* except that it featured people from Uttar Pradesh living in the USA. Shahrukh played the foster son of an NRI (Amrish Puri), who is on a visit to India to arrange the marriage of his excessively Americanized real son.

In the ensuing contest between these two suitors for the heroine – an NRI woman who upholds Indianness despite her modernity – the film sought to establish the superiority of the Indian way of life over the American. Film critic Nikhat Kazmi writes: 'I can only marvel at Ghai's attempt to supply complicated bonds. Is it really possible to transmute my idea of India into adolescent musings that declare India-Indian are the best?' (*The Times of India*, 10 August 1997.) Shahrukh pitched in with a restrained performance as the adopted son who is overwhelmed by the depth of gratitude to his foster father. He looked more at ease in this film compared to his earlier roles.

Swades (2004), directed by Ashutosh Gowarikar, was about the 'patriotic awakening' within a successful NRI (a high-profile engineer working with NASA), played by Shahrukh Khan, after seeing the plight of the rural poor in his home country. The film depicted the first-hand experiences of the alien protagonist, a specialist in global water mapping, about the grassroot realities of rural India and his transformation into a rural development expert and activist. This high priest of the modern world, empowered with top-class technical knowhow, solves the problem of water shortage in the village through social mobilization. Also, virtually in one fell swoop, he convinces the village community about the perils of a caste-ridden society.

The film, unfortunately, suggested rather contrived and superficial solutions to the complexities of rural development. Looking through the perspective of an outsider (belonging to the upper class) who could never get really assimilated with the ethos of the targeted community, the film failed to dissect convincingly the castiest, feudalistic and cultural impediments to the modernization it sought to propose.

Despite these limitations, the film was able to capture, with some degree of realism, two contradictory aspects of the Indian rural reality. The first is the strong caste-based differentiation as seen in the case of the poor tenant farmer who is not allowed to cultivate land by the farmers' lobby because he is a weaver by caste. The other is the bubbling inspiration on the part of the roadside *dhaba* owner who dreams of opening an eatery in the USA in partnership with the NRI hero. Shahrukh Khan, with his trademark overstylization, is unable to capture, in the true spirit, the dilemma of a man caught at the interface of two worlds. On the other hand, K. L. Saigal's *Dharti Mata* (1938), Dilip Kumar's *Shikast* (1953) and Dev Anand–Suraiya's *Vidya* (1948) were far more authentic works in portraying the painful transition from orthodoxy to modernity in a rural setting.

***

Apart from the foregoing diasporic films, Shahrukh Khan's hero also became a trendsetter for the silkily soft romances of the 1990s. He became a hot favourite of the youngsters, especially the teenagers.

In Yash Chopra's *Dil To Pagal Hai* (1997), he essayed the role of a 'visionary' stage director (for dance-based musical shows). He possesses all the ingredients of an ideal man: he is caring, inspired, vivacious and, above all, highly creative. Shahrukh and his team perform on stage with great gusto. His leading dancer is Karisma Kapoor, who invariably prances around in hot pants. Unfortunately, she fractures her leg during a rehearsal and has to be hospitalized. He begins a desperate search for a replacement and 'discovers' Madhuri Dixit. She, after some initial reluctance, decides to join his troupe. She appears as the 'Indian' woman, who wears chiffon saris and Punjabi suits. Karisma is secretly in love with Shahrukh, but he treats her only as a friend. Madhuri is due to marry the macho Akshay Kumar, but finally she and Shahrukh find true love in each other. In this film, while Western attires and attitudes are hailed as symbols of modernity, the outward pretence of being Indian is idolized. The superb choreography by Shamik Davar and the melodious musical score by Uttam Singh played significant roles in ensuring the success of the movie.

Karan Johar's *Kuchh Kuchh Hota Hai* (1997) projected yet another new-age love triangle, just like in *Dil To Pagal Hai*, except that the hero's arena here is a college campus. The hero falls in love with the first heroine (Kajol, named Anjali in the film), an extrovert tomboyish basketball player, only when she appears before him in a saree. In a college ragging scene, when the second heroine (Rani Mukherji who has just returned from the UK after a long time) is asked to sing a song, she disarms her seniors by singing the traditional bhajan *Om Jai Jagdish Hare*. The hero falls for her and they soon get married. Kajol then leaves town. A daughter is born to them whom they name Anjali. Rani dies after childbirth, but leaves behind a series of letters for her daughter to be opened on each successive birthday. The daughter comes to know about her namesake (the older Anjali) and makes sincere efforts to unite Kajol and Shahrukh. Unforuntately, the treatment of the subject was superficial and maudlin. Film critic Nikhat Kazmi notes that *KKHH* was seared to strike instant chords with the young and the romantic who have two main addictions: MTV and Mill & Boons. The film had a generous sprinkling of both – an MTV ambience with everyone cat walking in GAP and Tommy Hilfiger (two internationally famous brands) apparels and a preponderance of Valentine Day flavours.

Nikhil Advani's *Kal Ho Na Ho* (2003), reminiscent of Raj Kapoor's *Aah* (1953), Sridhar's *Dil Ek Mandir* (1963) and the Rajesh Khanna starrer *Safar* (1970, directed by Asit Sen), presented Shahrukh in a love triangle in which the virtues of sublime affection and supreme sacrifice are highlighted. After the upbeat hero, a suave NRI, discovers that he is a heart patient, he pretends aloofness towards his beloved (Preity Zinta) and asks her to marry the man (Saif Ali Khan) who really loves her. Before he dies, Shahrukh manages to unite Saif and Preity. The film is set in New York and is replete with fabulous outdoor shots and ritzy party scenes.

Karan Johar's *Kabhi Alvida Na Kahna* (2007), an indictment of growing marital discord among today's young couples, had Shahrukh as the simple-hearted introvert married to an ambitious high-profile fashion designer (Preity Zinta). He eventually finds solace in the company of a down-to-earth girl (Rani Mukherji) of similiar disposition but married to a man (Abhishek Bachchan) who likes partying and merry making.

In view of his dominant position as the new-age hero, Shahrukh's association with outright vigilante cinema has only been marginal. He appeared as a vengeful youth (with Salman Khan for company) in Rakesh Roshan's *Karan Arjun* (1995) and *Koyla* (1997). In the second venture, set in a feudal milieu and a designed on a typical Dilip Kumar film format, he appears as a mute worker in a zamindar's farm who stages a revolt against the latter's tyranny. He was again seen as an upright cop battling a drug syndicate in Shashilal Nair's *One 2 Ka 4* (2001).

In the domain of realist cinema, he came up with a credible performance in Ketan Mehta's *O Darling Yeh Hai India* (1995) and Mani Ratnam's *Dil Se* (1998), perhaps his most outstanding role. In this film, he played a sensitive journalist who seeks to deindoctrinate a young woman terrorist (Manisha Koirala) but eventually fails.

In Farah Khan's *Main Hoon Naa* (2004), Shahrukh appeared in the role of a do-gooder army man who becomes a college student in order to trace his lost stepbrother (Zayed Khan), apart from taking on a gang of terrorists who are out to foil any attempts at friendship by India and Pakistan. The film, despite its slick photography and technical finesse, was somewhat sloppy in its overall approach.

Shahrukh, in one phase of his career, sought to refurbish his image as a sufferer in love in films such as Karan Johar's *Kabhi Khushi Kabhi Gham* (2001), Sanjay Leela Bhansali's *Devdas* (2002), Yash Chopra's *Veer-Zaara* (2004), Amol Palekar's *Paheli* (2005) and Farah Khan's *Om Shanti Om* (2007).

In *Kabhi Khushi Kabhi Gham*, he appeared as the foster son of a egotistical business magnate (Amitabh Bachchan), who defies his father and marries a peppy middle-class girl and moves to London with her and her younger sister.

In Sanjay Leela Bhansali's *Devdas* (2002), Shahrukh took up the challenge of portraying this immortal role played earlier by many stalwarts including K. L. Saigal and Dilip Kumar. However, Bhansali's attempt to reproduce a film faithful to this immortal literary work was found wanting. (He took a few liberties vis-à-vis the original. It is the director's good fortune that the author is no longer alive.) Bhansali seemed to be totally engrossed in presenting the character and his milieu in the disoriented framework of the new-age cinema. In the present times of consumerist display, the spirit of the novel *Devdas* was completely lost and Shahrukh appeared uncertain about his moorings. In fact, the film maker sought to bring in the 'feel-good factor' and insert certain scenes that would have an overseas appeal. For instance, he sends Devdas off to Oxford, instead of Calcutta (as in the original), for his education. And to 'authenicate' his UK-returned look, the hero is made to wear vintage suits from London. Moreover, the two lovers (Shahrukh and Aishwarya Rai as Paro) look like the yuppy lovers of the modern era. According to *Jansatta* (15 September 2002) Aishwarya Rai in this version 'looks more [like] Miss Universe [actually she was Miss World] than Paro and Madhuri Dikshit could not capture even one per cent of the personality of Chandramukhi. Shahrukh Khan for all his popularity has too hyper and restless an image with his energy ... spilling on [to] the screen. The film thus will be remembered more for big sets, the heavy silken attire and ornaments than acting.'

The 2002 version of *Devdas* also destroyed the writer Saratchandra's deep concerns for the women suffering in a male-dominated orthodox society and their unending search for identity. Devender Bir Kaur (*The Tribune*, 8 June 2002) comes down heavily on some aspects of the movie: 'The anguish of the old film lovers ... that arose every time Devdas Dilip Kumar spoke, the hopelessness of Chandramukhi's [Vyjayanthimala] plight in having to face unrequited love and the stoic acceptance and helplessness of the deeply-in-love Paro [Suchitra Sen] cannot be conveyed in the opulence and extravaganza of the film created by the present director. To dress up a tragedy in frills is surely making a mockery of it. Cinema as a visual medium is supposed to fill in the blanks present in the piece of fiction on which it is based. To do a complete take-off is criminal. Perhaps, the right thing could have been for the director to be inspired by the novel and make a film on similar lines and name it, maybe, *Ramdas* ...'

Among Shahrukh's romances, Yash Chopra's *Veer-Zaara* (2004) stands out. This movie marked a surprising turnaround towards resurrecting the classical Indian film but in the modern lingo, thanks to the efforts of the veteran director. A love story set across the divide between India and Pakistan, this film, very much like Raj Kapoor's *Henna* (1991), highlighted the destructive quality of mutual suspicion and also the futility of the unending enmity between the two countries. The film advocated a lasting peace in the subcontinent. The haunting music by composer Madan Mohan (taken posthumously from his unused collection of tunes; he passed away on 14 July 1975), one of the architects of classical film melody of the 1950s, greatly added to the appeal of the narrative.

Veer Pratap Singh (Shahrukh) is an Indian Air Force pilot who rescues a Pakistani girl Zaara Hayat Khan (Preity Zinta) stranded (after a bus accident) in a village in Punjab (on the Indian side). They fall in love. He next takes her back to Pakistan, but cannot marry her as she is already engaged to another man (played by Manoj Bajpai). Meanwhile, Veer is wrongly arrested on the charge of being an Indian spy. He languishes in prison for more than two decades, when his case is taken up by a Pakistani human rights lawyer (Rani Mukherji), who tries to reunite Veer and Zaara.

Yet, as per the dictates of the 'glamorous realism' of Yash Chopra, the lovers represented the stereotypes of the new age. They stand unquestionably for family honour and prestige, respect for the elders and family togetherness. Thus, it is not only the lovers who have changed their responses but also the families and the communities to ensure perfect harmony. The platonic love was portrayed as a celebration, while Pakistan was cleverly represented by the claustrophobic prison, full of violence and violation of human rights by the Pakistani army. Shahrukh was in his element in this film.

In contrast to *Veer-Zaara*, in the love legends filmed during the formative and classical periods of our cinema, it was the individual lost deeply in the spirituality of the separation from the beloved that challenged and destabilized the ideological dominance of tradition, family, community and even the nation. The ultimate victory of this emancipated self was metaphorized in complete freedom, often in the meeting of the souls in death. Even a less known but well-made film, *Shaheed-e-Mohabbat Buta Singh* (released in 1999) presented an authentic depiction of classical love. It was based on a true love story of Buta Singh, a Sikh, and a Muslim girl Zainum, still remembered with much reverence on both sides of the Punjab border between India and Pakistan. In sharp contrast with *Gadar – Ek Prem Katha* and *Veer-Zaara* (both star-studded ventures and designed in a large-scale format), this low-budget film, made in Punjabi and Hindi, was far more realistic and horrifying in laying bare the tragic consequences of Partition.

Veer-Zaara and *Gadar* were perhaps inspired by the Pakistani film maker Raza Mir's *Lakhon Mein Ek*, made in 1967. This film also presented a humane unbiased view of the love affair between a Hindu girl, left behind in Pakistan during the communal disturbances and brought up with her own religious identity by a Muslim family friend, and his lost son, who becomes her benefactor. The writer was the famous film maker Zia Sarhadi, who had moved to Pakistan in the 1960s.

Paheli, which cast Shahrukh in a double role, was based on a short story 'Duvidha' written by the renowned Rajasthani writer Vijaydan Detha. The film highlighted the ethical dilemma of a girl who has to choose between a ghost's (a look-alike of her husband) eternal love and the insensitive monotony of her husband, who is only interested in making money, and leaves her on the wedding night. The picturesque scenes and the dialogues captured authentically the essence of rural Rajasthan.

Om Shanti Om was a somewhat weird movie that used rebirth as a ploy to define soulful love and to draw up a comparison (rather flimsy at that) between Bollywood's past with its present. Om (Shahrukh Khan) works as a film extra in the 1970s' cinema and dreams of becoming a star. He silently loves the top heroine of that era Shanti (Deepika Padukone), who is lured by a famous but lecherous film director (Arjun Rampal). During the shooting of a film also titled *Om Shanti Om*, the set catches fire and Om dies as he tries to save the heroine (à la *Mother India*) but in vain. He takes birth again as a star-son and starts remembering the experiences of his previous life. He now wants to complete Shanti's film. As he sets the set ablaze, the soul of Shanti (as in *Madhumati*) arrives to reveal that his death was engineered by the director in love with her. The film drew its inspiration from Subhash Ghai's 1980 hit *Karz*.

Shahrukh rose above his usual performances in a truly inspirational role in Shimit Amin's nationalist drama *Chak De India* (2007). He played a Muslim coach, Kabir Khan, who takes on a challenge and coaches the Indian women's hockey team for the Hockey World Cup. His character was based on the former goalkeeper of the Indian men's hockey team Mir Ranjan Negi, who couldn't stop a penalty stroke in the final minutes of the match that caused the Indian team to lose to arch-rivals Pakistan. He faced utter humiliation and the shame of being labelled a traitor. Despite Kabir's life being torn apart by conflicts of region, class and ethnicity, he inculcates in his players a sense of team spirit and asks them to put the country first. The team finally defeats the defending champions. The Academy of Motion Picture Arts and Sciences (California, USA) also requested a copy of the film script for the Margaret Herrick Library located at Beverly Hills, California.

Shahrukh portrayed 'an ordinary man' who goes in for an image makeover in Aditya Chopra's 2008 venture *Rab Ne Bana Di*

Jodi. As Surinder Sahni (Suri), a run-of-the-mill office worker, he falls in love with his former professor's daughter Tania (Anushka Sharma), whom he meets when she is about to get married. Tania's father has a heart attack when the news is revealed that her fiancé and his family have been in killed in an accident. The professor then asks Suri to marry her as he feels that Tania would be left alone in the world. Suri agrees; Tania too agrees to marry Suri only to keep her father happy. After a quick wedding, Suri asks Tania to accompany him to his ancestral house in Amritsar (Punjab). Tania tells him that she can never love him because she has no love left within her. Suri, nevertheless, tries his best to keep her happy by fulfilling her desires. She wants to see many films and has fantasies about romance and also a passion for dancing. With Suri's permission, she joins an expensive dance class so that she can get out of her usual rut. Suri feels inadequate in comparison to the strong, masculine images of heroes that Tania admires. Upon the advice of a friend, he undergoes a complete makeover and emerges as 'Raj Kapoor', a jaunty and happy-go-lucky individual, and joins the same dance class as Tania. He becomes Tania's partner in a competition. With the passage of time, Raj professes his love for her. Tania is torn apart by an internal conflict: she desperately wants to flee from her despair-filled life and find a new existence, but cannot do so because of a promise that she has made to her father. As Raj, he offers to elope with her, to which she agrees to tearfully. They plan to do so on the night of a competition. On the day of the competition, Suri takes Tania to the Golden Temple. For the first time she reflects on her husband (Suri) and realizes the integrity and power of his character. Tania then tells Raj that she cannot elope. During the competition, Tania is amazed to see Suri, rather than Raj, join her on the stage.

In Priyadarshan's *Billu* (2009), Shahrukh played a Bollywood superstar (Sahir Khan) who comes to the village (where he grew up) for a shoot. In this village, lives Billu the barber (played by Irfan Khan), who tells his family that he knows Sahir without giving any details. His children spread rumours that their father and Sahir are friends. Virtually overnight, Billu, who had earlier been derided due to his penury, becomes the focus of attention. People who had neglected him now begin cosying up to him in the hope that they can meet Sahir. Billu refuses to oblige them and downplays his friendship with the star. A moneylender (played by veteran Om Puri) demands that Billu introduce him to Sahir and is even willing to give costly presents to the barber. When Billu fails to introduce the people of the village to Sahir, he is subjected to ridicule. He is accused of lying about his friendship to the star and everyone, including his wife and children, starts casting aspersions on his character and integrity. Through all this, Billu remains quiet about the nature of his friendship with Sahir. On his last day in the village, Sahir speaks at a local school. He recalls his own impoverished childhood when he had nothing but a very special friend named Billu. It was Billu, he point outs, who took care of him and who eventually helped him travel to Mumbai where he became a famous star. Billu, who is standing at the back among the audience, slips away, without revealing his presence to Sahir. But Sahir manages to trace Billu and he visits his house to express his gratitude. Billu and his family are overwhelmed with joy.

Shahrukh's forthcoming films are *Dulha Mil Gaya* and *My Name Is Khan*.

Shahrukh made a foray into the historical genre in Santosh Sivan's *Asoka* (2001). In this film, his interpretation of the benevolent king (one of the finest and most respected emblematic historical figures of our country), through a make-believe love tale, was found to be rudimentary and even vulgar by some historians as well as the common viewers. The modern-day filmic approach to the theme was somewhat incongruous.

In his style, Shahrukh tends to depend, as if desperately, on his remarkable verve and flippancy with a surge of self-displayed vitality and agility to portray a character on hand. Like Rajendra Kumar and Rajesh Khanna in the earlier periods, his acquired stylization also tends to undermine his potential as an actor. In her review of *Veer-Zaara*, film critic Nikhat Kazmi has written that temperance and the art of underplay were obviously not his style but his intensity, sincerity and refreshing zeal made him stand out.

In serious roles, Shahrukh Khan's screen persona is built around the standard suffering lover model of Dilip Kumar. In such roles, the actor makes earnest attempts at evoking the necessary histrionics but often is able to depict only the outer layers of the characterizations on hand. He seeks to release his inner self in a frenzied burst of energy, but often displays an excess of emotions. Comedy seems to come more naturally to him due to good timing and also because he can exhibit a wide range of comical expressions and use his body flexibly. Nowadays, every hero ought to be able to dance and proficiently at that, quite in contrast to the older heroes. Shahrukh has mastered the art of dancing and skilfully at that. In an era in which the outward appearance of a film is considered more important than capturing the deep complexities of the characters, his in-built talent has not been fully exploited by today's film makers in creating for him a series of meaningful roles set in a definite socio-cultural milieu.

Aamir Khan

Among the new-age heroes, Aamir Hussain Khan (born on 14 March 1965) has progressively refurbished his cine image from an upper-class teen hero to a street-smart *tapori* (vagabond or ruffian) and then to an important representative of realist cinema. He has also donned the director's mantle.

Aamir, who made his debut way back in 1973 as child artiste in his uncle Nasir Hussain's *Yaadon Ki Baraat*, went on to become an assistant to his uncle during the production of *Manzil Manzil* (1984) and *Zabardast* (1985). He then went on to essay a wide variety of roles. He appeared as part of a college group in *Holi* (1984) directed by Ketan Mehta. As hero, his first film was Mansoor Khan's *Qayamat Se Qayamat Tak* (1988), followed by a slew of films such as Indra Kumar's *Dil* (1990), Mahesh Bhatt's *Dil Hai Ke Maanta Nahin* (1991), M. Shahjehan's *Afsana Pyar Ka* (1991), Mansoor Khan's *Jo Jeeta Wohi Sikandar* (1992), Mahesh Bhatt's *Hum Hain Rahi Pyar Ke* (1993), Rajkumar Santoshi's *Andaz Apna Apna* (1994), Ram Gopal Verma's *Rangeela* (1995), Indra Kumar's *Ishq* (1997), Dharmesh Darshan's *Raja Hindustani* (1996), Mukesh Bhatt and Vikram Bhatt's *Ghulam* (1998) and Farhan Akhtar's *Dil Chahta Hai* (2001). In these films he adeptly carved out his persona as the modern prototype of a debonair Dev Anand and a jaunty Shammi Kapoor of the 1950s and 1960s.

Aamir Khan

With *Qayamat Se Qayamat Tak*, Aamir brought the teenage hero centrestage much as Rishi Kapoor did in *Bobby* (1973). He became the idol of the 1990s' teenagers who found the rebellious heroes of the past redundant in the changed socio-cultural ethos. The film, essentially a musical (with an excellent score by youngsters Anand and Milind, the sons of veteran composer Chitragupta), was a tragic love story on the lines of *Romeo and Juliet*. This runaway hit lent Aamir the image of the boy-next-door with the enigmatic smile and squeaky-clean earnestness.

Dil, a musical romance, was a story about runaway lovers (Aamir Khan and Madhuri Dixit) from wealthy families estranged by interfamilial tensions. The hero becomes a labourer to support his beloved but finally the young couple is pardoned by the seniors and get back all the luxuries. A lot of melodramatic dialogue was built into the film's script.

Aamir reinforced his teen hero image in *Jo Jeeta Wohi Sikandar* – by and large an Indian version of Randal Kleiser's *Grease* (1978). Using the motif of sports rivalry, the film sought to convey among the impressionable youth the need for aggressive upmanship in today's highly competitive world despite the class differences and lack of resources faced by certain sections of society. Aamir, a middle-class college student, pretends to be rich in order to woo an ultra-modern girl. When she ditches him, he deploys all his energies to win the annual cycle race against stiff competition offered by a villainous student leader who comes from a wealthy family. (Aamir's adversary's tactics to defeat him in the race by dubious means seem to be inspired by the famous chariot race in the 1959 Hollywood classic *Ben-Hur*.)

In *Dil Hai Ke Maanta Nahin*, Aamir played the romantic role earlier done with élan by Clark Gable in *It Happened One Night* (1934), Raj Kapoor in *Chori Chori* (1956) and Dev Anand in *Nau Do Gyarah* (1957). He appears as an upbeat reporter who falls in love with a rich girl who has run away from home.

Aamir appeared as a jovial well-to-do collegian in pursuit of his love interest in *Afsana Pyar Ka*; as a hard working entrepreneur in *Hum Hai Rahi Pyar Ke*; and as a small-time conman and ambitious son of a barber, seeking to get rich quickly by conquering the heart of a rich NRI girl on a visit to India to find a 'true Indian man' in Rajkumar Santoshi's *Andaz Apna Apna*, which was set in a comedy mould. He had Salman Khan for company in this film.

Ishq presented the young actor as one of the four representatives of Gen-X: spunky, naughty and reckless, for whom making merry is the driving motive of existence without any regard for responsible behaviour, virtually an Indian updated version of the American youth. He is an ordinary but ambitious garage mechanic who aspires to climb the social ladder by stalking a rich girl. Another important hit of Aamir Khan in the same vein was *Raja Hindustani*. This film brought on screen the love story of a poor lad from the hills chasing the dream of winning the heart of a rich girl. It was virtually a remake of *Jab Jab Phool Khile* (1965), starring Shashi Kapoor and Nanda.

In *Rangeela* (1995) and in *Ghulam* (1998), the young actor transcended his usual romantic image: he appeared as a street-smart commoner typified by loud gestures, gaudy clothes and the use of the local Bombay slang.

In *Rangeela*, he was a small-time black marketeer in love with a neighbourhood girl (Urmila Matondkar) who dreams of making it big as a film actress. The encouragement from her lover and finally talent scouting by a film star (Jackie Shroff) help her to achieve stardom. The hero is left in the cold, away from the colourful and glamorous world of cinema.

In *Ghulam*, Aamir played an amateur boxer who gets involved with an underworld gang. After meeting the heroine (Rani Mukherji) he decides to give up his shady activities. The highlight of this film was a song that he himself sang.

Dil Chahta Hai, a comparative study on the attitudes of today's youth towards love, presented Aamir in the role of a misogynist who undergoes a change in attitude when he falls in love. Critically acclaimed by the Anglicized classes as the true 'realistic global Indian film', *Dil Chahta Hai* further legitimized the aura of the new-age cinema. Focusing on the glitzy lifestyle and zany obsessions of Gen-X, caught in the web of globalized consumerism, the film showcased the idiosyncracies of the yuppies. It portrayed them as suave but directionless. They are shown donning designer clothes, with designer hairdos, apart from enjoying foreign trips and driving luxury cars. Although Aamir vaguely adheres to Indian values, he is very keen to acquire the material trappings of affluence and the Western lifestyle without a twinge of guilt. And by projecting such an image, he becomes a model for millions of youngsters (including those from the lower strata of society). Many of them are enticed into committing criminal acts in order to achieve the lifestyle depicted on the silver screen. Saif Ali Khan and Akshaye Khanna provided company to Aamir Khan in this film.

***

With eight films in a row – Mansoor Khan's *Akele Hum Akele Tum* (1995), Deepa Mehta's *1947 – Earth* (1997), John Mathew

Matthan's *Sarfarosh* (1999), Ashutosh Gowarikar's *Lagaan* (2001), Ketan Mehta's *Mangal Pandey* (2005), Kunal Kohli's *Fanaa* (2006), Rakeysh Omprakash Mehra's *Rang De Basanti* (2006) and his own directoral debut *Taare Zameen Par* (2007) – Aamir has undergone a complete transformation, indicating perhaps his permanent shift to serious and meaningful cinema.

Akele Hum Akele Tum shows how a strong script and credible characterization help an actor to rediscover his/her hidden resources of talent. Aamir, in this soulful rendition of marital discord, gave a performance marked with grace and sobriety. The film, inspired by the 1979 Hollywood classic, *Kramer vs. Kramer*, and by Jaya Bhaduri and Amitabh Bachchan's *Abhimaan* (1973), sought to capture the tensions and misunderstandings engulfing the lives of the modernized upper class. It depicted the contest for independence between a hotel crooner (Aamir Khan) and his wife (Manisha Koirala), an ambitious singer, who goes on to become a famous film star. As the wife refuses to get 'domesticated' by the insensitive and selfish husband, she walks out of the marriage, leaving him to take care of their child, which he does stoically despite facing many difficulties.

1947 – Earth, set in the pre-Partition days in Lahore, presented Aamir in a powerful negative role of a Muslim ice candy seller, who, unable to win over the Hindu girl he aggressively loves, becomes a rioter. It is his unsatisfied libido that turns him into a fundamentalist bent upon avenging the loss of his love through violence. The film, by taking the Partition of India as a tragic example, sought to show that the division of the earth and devastation of its innocent inhabitants have been perpetuated by mankind's own perverted mind.

Sarfarosh, inspired by the persona of a real-life deputy commissioner of police from Delhi,* established Aamir in the

---

* The DCP was Mohan Kudesiya, one of the most upright, academically inclined and professional officers of Delhi Police. He was a close friend of the author. He died an untimely death in 1996.

domain of realist cinema. He plays a simple-hearted policeman, fond of literature and poetry, who unearths the links of terrorists with his poet friend (Naseeruddin Shah). Shah's activities are a cover-up for anti-national operations. Aamir's down-to-earth portrayal and some powerful scenes made *Sarfarosh* a memorable film, despite its run-of-the-mill storyline.

In *Lagaan* (meaning land tax), his home production, Aamir discovered for himself a new genre and a new cine persona. Set in the colonial era, the film centred on the age-old instrument used by the British imperialists to oppress Indian peasantry, namely, *lagaan*. The film depicts the clash of the impoverished farmers with the new rulers, but cleverly links it with the most obvious arena of nationalist feelings and identity, namely, cricket. Given that cricket matches between nations are played virtually like proxy wars with the 'patriotic spectators' running wild and even violent as the games proceed, the makers of this film hit gold by transporting this patriotic display into the time of the Raj. The crux of the movie is that the colonial rulers promise to exempt the peasants from paying *lagaan* (for three years) if their team could beat the British in a cricket match. Aamir Khan leads the farmers' team (made up of a motley band) and he has a very limited period in which to bring them to a stage where they can compete with the professional Brits. Despite their initial clumsiness and goof-ups, the farmers manage to pull off a spectacular win!

Lagaan, after a long time, vividly unravelled, on celluloid, India as a community on the move. The film showed how, irrespective of differences of caste, class and religion, the people had mobilized themselves to rise to the immediate historic challenge. Presented more like an IPTA (Indian People's Theatre Association)-inspired community films of the late 1940s and 1950s (*Neecha Nagar* 1946, *Boot Polish* 1954, *Naya Daur* 1957 and *Char Dil Char Raahein* 1959, for instance), the film attempted to reconstruct an idealized community, which has rectified its social and religious aberrations and concentrated hidden energies to come together for a common cause. In this crusade, the low castes, high castes and the Muslims join hands to rediscover their hidden ingenuity and talents to master an alien game as a weapon to fight the apparently superior people. Even an enthused nationalist Sikh youth from Punjab joins the 'community's cricket club'.

However, some discerning critics found the drama in *Lagaan* rather contrived in which the main political conflict was crudely externalized in the form of a 'club activity' between the two alienated cultures of the rulers and the ruled. Though it looked innovative and refreshing in the present-day cinema context, it lacked the vision and treatment, which make great cinema. As writer Mitu Sengupta observes: 'If Bollywood is all that's available to the average Indian consumer; the fluff movies it churns out will end up being taken much too seriously and, like *Lagaan*, be celebrated as the pinnacle of achievement for Indian cinema and culture. That would be a grand shame.'[2] About the box-office success of *Dil Chahta Hai* and *Lagaan*, the well-known writer Saibal Chatterjee observes: 'While a section of Hindi film watchers, especially in the big metropolitan cities, related instinctively to the worldview propounded by *Dil Chahta Hai*, audiences in the smaller towns remained cold to its style and panache, as they did, perhaps to a lesser extent, to the flair and precision of *Lagaan*.'[3]

Lagaan: Excerpts from a Review

... India begins to live in its village once again in popular Hindi cinema. Champaner, 1893, is a throbbing picture of life. Longing, love and legionnaires. Brave little Aamir ...

Again, he defines a whole new formula for film-making. One where integrity of approach is more important than mirch-masala stuff. The village is stark, barren, impoverished instead of being a designer one, with every pot in place, every bushel of hay pruned, every village wall plastered with folksy art work. The people are small, simple, non-heroic winners instead of being larger-than-life heroes of run-of-the-mill cinema. The song (Javed Akhtar–A. R. Rahman) and dance [have] been carefully created and orchestrated as a harmonious blend to the story and setting. The film is redolent with a pristine honesty that stands out in this preponderance of kitsch and compromise ...

And finally, he paves the way for a whole new brand of cinema. One where the venturesome can fly free in an unlimited expanse. Where the film-maker can actually play Ulysses – striving, seeking and not too yielding to formula, fashion and box office diktat ...

Of course, the success of *Lagaan* lies both in its non-compromising approach and its eat-cricket-sleep-cricket-dream-cricket orientation. In a masterstroke, the film blends India's two strongest passions – cricket and patriotism – and whips up a heady potion which manages to thrill, despite the odds ...

Source: *The Times of India*, 17 June 2001.

In *Rang De Basanti*, Aamir Khan articulated with tremendous energy the politicization of the contemporary, confused and seemingly aimless Indian youth through an intimate political training built on the ideals of nationalism as enshrined in the country's freedom struggle. The story was about a British film maker Sue (Alice Patten) who has come to India to make a short film about some revolutionary heroes (Bhagat Singh and his associates) of the country's freedom movement. She casts four footlose friends – a Sikh, a Hindu, a Muslim and a Parsi – in the film. As these extremely reluctant boys learn more about the history of the Independence movement and the sacrifices made by ordinary people, they lose their cynicism and start thinking what contribution they can make to society. Meanwhile, an

Indian Air Force pilot is killed in air crash because the corrupt defence minister (Mohan Agashe) had received a large kickback in a contract for the supply of spurious aircraft spare parts. The protagonists decide that they must emulate the early freedom fighters. They kill the minister and as they reveal the true story to the public through a radio station, they are all killed in a combined attack by the police and the commandos. (This incident was inspired by the death of Flight Lieutenant Abhijit Gadgil who died in a MiG-21 training exercise in 2001.) But, after investigations, it was concluded that the problem lay in the low quality of aircraft maintenance.

Rang De Basanti aroused interest among today's Indian youth to know about the country's freedom struggle and inspired some real-life protests, such as the protest against the acquittal of the alleged culprits in the Jessica Lall murder case in 2006 and the anti-reservation protests the same year. Even the line, 'there are only two ways to lead your life – either, let things happen in their own way, keep tolerating it, or, take responsibility to change it,' spoken by the character Daljeet, was adopted by Indian students protesting against the increase in university seats for Other Backward Castes announced by the Central Government.

The film was India's entry for the Oscars in the best foreign film category, but it did not make to the short list. It won a nomination for the 'best film not in the English language' at the BAFTA (British Academy of Film and Television Arts) Awards in 2006.

Fanaa, a tragic tale about the inevitable eclipsing of intrinsically beautiful love by utterly wrongful convictions, presented Aamir in the powerful role of a dreaded Kashmiri terrorist. During his mission to blow up the Indian Parliament, he falls in love with a blind Kashmiri girl (Kajol) who is visiting Delhi as a tourist with her friends. In the end, his own woman shoots him dead as she comes to know about his plans of acquiring biological weapons technology to be used by the terrorists against the Indian armed forces.

Taare Zameen Par, directed by Aamir himself, is a truly remarkable piece of work in the annals of meaningful cinema. This film, which brought back the freshness of earlier masterpieces like *Jagriti* (1954), *Jaldeep* (1956) and *Masoom* (1983), is an important contribution to the largely forgotten genre of children's cinema. It presented the actor as the sensitive art teacher, who defies the child-unfriendly autocratic schooling milieu and irresponsible parenthood, and very effectively comes to the rescue of a miserable child (played so elegantly and convincingly by Darsheel Safary) suffering from dyslexia. This teacher-hero virtually exemplified the deep sensitivity towards the least understood kid, as seen in reality among those social activists working diligently with handicapped children. Aamir exhibited his acumen in several scenes like when he establishes a rapport with the isolated misfit child and when he bargains with the school principal to allow the child one more chance before expulsion.

Taare Zameen Par and *Black* (2005) reflect a renewed concern of some of our film makers for the disadvantaged in society not only to lend an emotional appeal to their works, but also to arouse deep empathy among the audience that at present is constantly subjected to violent movies and superficial love tales with large dollops of sex thrown in.

For A. R. Murugadoss's *Ghajini* (2008), Aamir physically underwent a total transformation. He undertook a rigorous body-building regimen and emerged as a muscular and brawny he-man. In this movie (a remake of the 2005 Tamil original with the same title), he appeared as Sanjay Singhania, a businessman afflicted by a peculiar form of amnesia: his memory is wiped out every 15 minutes. Consequently, he relies on notes, photographs and tattoos on his body to regain his memory after each memory loss. When he reads the tattoo 'Kalpana was killed', he seeks to avenge her death. Kalpana was a kind-hearted girl and a promising model, whom he proposed to marry. He then begins killing the people he thinks are responsible for Kalpana's death. His main target is

'Ghajini', who turns out to be a prominent socialite involved in many nefarious activities.

Three Idiots (under production), directed by Rajkumar Hirani, is rumoured to be loosely based on the famous novel, *Five Point Someone* by the Indian writer Chetan Bhagat. Aamir Khan and Kareena Kapoor play the lead roles.

In his acting style, Aamir Khan at times looks premeditative, caught up in a deep thought process, as if seeking to transcend his own personality in order to assimilate the overall persona of the character he is playing. A thinking actor, he looks far more earnest than his contemporaries. Yet he seems to hold back his full potential due to undue constraints. The artiste now needs more classical roles and visionary directors to enable him to create a cinema responsible towards society and thus enable him to make a place among the great acting icons of our cinema.

Salman Khan

Salman Khan (born on 27 December 1965), the true poster boy of modern cinema, rose to fame as yet another new-age hero with Sooraj Barjatya's *Maine Pyar Kiya* (1989). (His first film was *Biwi Ho To Aisi*, 1988.) He zealously buttressed this lover-boy image with films like *Love* (1991), *Dil Tera Aashiq* (1993), *Andaz Apna Apna* (1994), *Jab Pyar Kisi Se Hota Hai* (1998), *Pyar Kiya To Darna Kya* (1998), *Janam Samjha Karo* (1999), *Hum Saath Saath Hain* (1999), *Hum Dil De Chuke Sanam* (1999), *Hello Brother* (1999), *Har Dil Jo Pyar Karega* (2000), *Kahin Pyar Na Ho Jaaye* (2000) and *Yeh Hai Jalwa* (2002).

Salman Khan

These films were 'designer romances' in which the ambience and mood are set up through Indipop and packed with fluorescent colours and picturesque locales. The mandatory song sequences are replete with Salman Khan's macho physique and the heroines' gyrations (not to mention their skimpy attire) along with the inevitable accompanying troupes of dancers.

Maine Pyar Kiya, a typical rich-boy-poor-girl romance, sought to redefine the content and imagery of the new-age film and its hero. Salman initially wafts around as a leather-jacketed hero who is obsessed with motorbikes, pop music and posters of American and other pop icons (including a poster of himself). He undergoes a transformation after the arrival of the heroine (Bhagyashree) in his house. He becomes more responsible, caring and understanding. The sound track uses an 'I-love-you' refrain throughout the film.

In Suresh Krishna's *Love*, Salman was a modern, guitar-playing, footloose youth seeking the attention of a rich Christian girl. Rajkumar Santoshi's *Andaz Apna Apna* featured him in the role of a charlatan son of a tailor who competes with his rival, also a conman (Aamir Khan), to acquire wealth by winning the heart of a rich heiress.

In Deepak Sareen's *Jab Pyar Kisi Se Hota Hai*, Salman again presented a true manifestation of the new-age hero – a debonair dandy who has a penchant for high life, is obsessed with fast cars and enjoys merry making in the company of wine and women.

In Sooraj Barjatya's *Hum Saath Saath Hain*, he appeared as the foreign-educated younger son in a rich business family. He was the sacrificing 'Bharat' who seeks the return of his elder brother 'Ram' to the family's fold. The film was a shoddy adaptation of the epic Ramayana to the modern times.

Pyar Kiya To Darna Kya featured Salman as belonging to a wealthy background, who falls in love with the heroine (Kajol) during their college days. However, Kajol's brother wants her to marry another man and takes her back to their village. The hero follows, but is rejected by the heroine's brother. The hero then manages to save the heroine's uncle from getting killed and he offers him refuge. Eventually, after the usual twists and turns, the lovers are united.

Sanjay Leela Bhansali's *Hum Dil De Chuke Sanam*, a fanciful and exotic package of ethnic architecture, textiles and folk music for the NRIs and foreign tourists, attempted to put in place a transnational image of classical love. Salman is an Indian-Italian who has come to Kathiawad (Gujarat) in search of real classical music and meets an old-time maestro. He falls in love with the maestro's daughter, and she finds this vivacious hero far more desirable than the local men around her. Her authoritarian father forces her to marry a local youth, Ajay Devgan. But this big-hearted man helps the lovers as he hands over his wife to the man she loves. However, the film tends to overwhelm viewers with its splendour of ethnic India as if rural life were only about festivities and cultural displays.

In Raj Kanwar's *Har Dil Jo Pyar Karega*, a soft, candyfloss romance filled to the brim with Valentine Day sentiments, Salman was a bubbling, lovable youngster who reaches Bombay with a guitar, striving to become a pop star. He gets involved with two heroines: Rani Mukherji (whom he saves from being killed, but who slips into a coma) and Preity Zinta.

K. Murali Mohana Rao's *Kahin Pyar Na Ho Jaaye*, a sloppy copy of Adam Sandler's *Wedding Singer* (1998), presented Salman as an aspiring singer who is rejected by his fiancée on his wedding day. He falls with in love with another girl in the neighbourhood, but she too rejects him. The actor's efforts at expressing his grief left much to be desired. Overall, the movie would qualify for the adjective 'awful'.

In David Dhawan's *Yeh Hai Jalwa*, a sordid rehash of Yash Chopra's *Trishul* (1978) and Michael Schultz's *Carbon Copy* (1981), Salman appeared as an industrialist in search of his real father, a renowned business tycoon played by Rishi Kapoor.

Salman's link with 'sentimental' cinema is represented by few films and include Deepak Shivdasani's *Baaghi* (1990), Sawan Kumar Tak's *Sanam Bewafa* (1991), Satish Kaushik's

Tere Naam (2003), Puneet Issar's *Garv: Pride and Honour* (2004), Revathi's *Phir Milenge* (2004) and William Carroll's *Marigold* (2007).

In *Baaghi*, a fairly realistic film, the hero (à la Sunil Dutt in *Sadhana*, 1958, and Amitabh Bachchan in *Ek Nazar*, 1972, and *Muqaddar Ka Sikandar*, 1978) rebels against his family and society to free a dancing girl from the stigma attached to her profession.

Sanam Bewafa was a traditional love story set against the backdrop of enmity between two Muslim aristocratic families. Salman Khan somehow managed to fit into the role of a maudlin lover.

In *Tere Naam* (attempted to be set in the classical mould), perhaps the most outstanding film of his career so far, Salman depicted the suffering caused by ungratified love. The film sought to highlight the clash between the 'ultramaterialistic and soulless' Western lifestyle and the caring soulfulness of the traditional Indian ethos. The hero is a debonair college student, a hot favourite of the yuppie crowd for his phenomenal disco dancing. He is brash and arrogant in his ways. He falls in love with a simple, sober girl from a higher caste. Her folks want to get her married to a person from their own caste. After he is hit on the head (by one of the girl's relatives), he becomes insane and is eventually sent to a mental asylum. Finally, when the heroine realizes the heart-rending intensity of the hero's love, she commits suicide.

In *Garv*, he appeared as an honest police inspector waging a relentless war against a politician having underworld connections with the support of his buddy (Arbaaz Khan).

In *Phir Milenge*, he played a deceitful lover who holds his AIDS infection a secret from his partner (Shilpa Shetty). When she too gets infected and, consequently, loses her job, he flees to a foreign country.

In *Marigold*, Salman appeared again in a designer role, this time as a film choreographer who becomes the love interest of the American actress Marigold Lexton (Alison Elizabeth Larter). She has come to India to shoot a low-budget Hollywood movie but as the project fails to take off, she takes up a small role in a Bollywood musical. In the end she marries the choreographer, while his fiancée (Nandana Sen) opts for Marigold's boyfriend (Ian Bohen).

In David Dhawan's 2007 film *Partner*, Salman Khan donned the mantle of a love guru who solves the problems of his clients. He meets Govinda who seeks his help to win the hand of Katrina Kaif, who is his (Govinda's) boss' daughter. Salman himself falls in love with Lara Dutta, a photojournalist whom he rescues from the clutches of gangsters.

God Tussi Great Ho (2008), directed by Rumi Jaffrey, presented him in a cut-out prankish role. The film was an amateurish attempt to take a dig at those social rejects who are failures in life in today's competitive world, but who look for miracles to transform their helplessness into success. The hero, a brattish but ambitious new-age youth, is a struggling TV host unable to get enough work or find love. As he curses God for his miseries, the Almighty (a modern version donning a pale-white suit enacted by Amitabh Bachchan) decides to play a game with him. He allocates to him His power for 10 days to grant every wish he chooses to. With his newly found power, he ushers an ambience of abundance around him, but soon realizes the illogicality of the 'virtual reality' embarked upon by him. In the end, God Himself addresses the audience to accept the highs and lows of life and be a part of hopeful humanity. This venture was inspired by Hollywood's *Bruce Almighty* (2003, starring Jim Carrey and Morgan Freeman).

In Samir Karnik's *Heroes* (2008), he appeared as a youth whose father (an army officer) has been killed in action. A couple of students (who are making a documentary on why one should *not* join the armed forces) find that the entire village is greatly proud of the heroic officer and his sacrifice for the country. The students meet some other families whose members have laid down their lives for their country. They ultimately realize that a soldier is true patriot who loves his motherland very much and is willing to sacrifice everything to protect his country. Years later Salman Khan becomes a soldier himself and visits the two former students who have joined the military academy.

In Subhash Ghai's *Yuvraaj* (2008), supposedly a musical, Salman Khan played an aspiring singer who enters into an agreement with his girlfriend's (Katrina Kaif, also a musician) father (Boman Irani) that in forty days he would emerge as a billionaire. He is under the impression that his affluent father would have left this amount for him in his will, but he is in for a shock. When he returns home to claim his share, he discovers that, as per his father's will, only one of his two brothers (the one who is autistic, played by Anil Kapoor) will inherit the entire property.

Veer (under production), a period film directed by Anil Sharma, presents Salman Khan in a Robin Hood kind of a role. The film has been written by the actor himself.

Wanted (under production), a remake of the blockbuster Telugu film *Pokiri* (directed by the noted dancer and choreographer Prabhu Deva), is set against the backdrop of Bombay's bloody gang wars. The film cast Salman as a police officer masquerading as a hardcore gangster in order to infiltrate the underworld. Prabhu Deva has directed the Hindi version too.

Prem Soni's *Main Aur Mrs Khanna* (under production) is a movie about an extramarital affair affecting the congenial life of Samir Khanna (Salman Khan) and Raina Khanna (Kareena Kapoor).

London Dreams (under production), directed by Vipul Shah, is about the struggle of two childhood friends (Salman Khan and Ajay Devgan) who want to make it big in the music industry. 'London Dreams' is the name of their band and the heroine (Asin Thottumkal), the dancer for the band, is the love interest of both friends.

Salman, like Rajendra Kumar and Jeetendra earlier, has exhibited remarkable durability as a hero, thanks largely to a hyper image building of male sexuality, despite his limited portrayal diversity and association with meaningful cinema.

Ajay Devgan

In sharp contrast with his numerous contemporaries, Ajay Devgan represents largely the persona of a deglamorized, down-to-earth film hero, the archetype of disillusioned urban youth. Born on 2 April 1969 in Bombay as Vishal Devgan in a Punjabi

Ajay Devgan

family, he studied at Silver Beach High School and Mithibai College. His father is Veeru Devgan, a well-known fight composer and stuntman, who also tried his hand at film direction. Ajay began his career as a director of video films based on his own storylines but soon found fame as hero with his famous debut in Kuku Kohli's *Phool Aur Kante* (1991), followed by a slew of films such as Farouq Siddiqui's *Vijaypath* (1994), *Jaan* (1996, directed by Anil Devgan, Raj Kanwar and Manish Sharma), Harry Baweja's *Diljale* (1996), Govind Nihalani's *Thakshak* (1999), Rajkumar Santoshi's *Lajja* (2001), Anees Bazmee's *Deewangee* (2002), Ram Gopal Verma's *Company* (2002) and Harry Baweja's *Deewane* (2000) and *Qayamat* (2003).

Ajay's cinema has been primarily dominated by two trends: a prototype of Amitabh Bachchan's vigilantism (wherein the hero upholds the law, despite the odds being heavily stacked against him) and a brand of post-modern realism. Like in some of Bachchan's films, in Ajay's films too, often there is virtually no romantic subplot and the scenes and dialogues have pronounced political overtones.

In *Phool Aur Kante*, he portrayed an orphaned college youth who wages a lone war against the drug-peddling son of his college trustee. In *Jaan*, Ajay appeared in the role of a mercenary who has to carry out the dual task of protecting and killing a rich heiress, who eventually falls in love with him. In *Deewane* Ajay appeared in a double role and like in numerous similar roles played by Big B, he was a small-time conman impersonating an upright cop. In *Qayamat*, he was a reformed terrorist helping the state machinery to track down a mercenary gang planning to blast important Indian cities with nuclear bombs.

In *Lajja*, he appeared as a bandit, a follower of the Mother Goddess Kali and a protector of womanhood. He eventually avenges the rape and death of the village mid-wife Ramdulaari (Rekha) by two feudal landlord brothers.

In *Deewangee*, Ajay attempted to play Edward Norton's role in *Primal Fears* (1996): that of a psychologically tortured maniac (who is a murderer) appearing to be a nice person. This film showed a killer getting away with murder.

Company sought to capture the ambitions, greed and grit of a section of wayward city youth led by anti-hero Ajay Devgan and his protégé Viveik (Anand) Oberoi (whose films are discussed later in this chapter). They want to grab and hold onto the power centre of the mafia underworld (à la Dawood Ibrahim and Chhota Shakeel, real-life gangsters and extortionists). Eventually, the film highlights their downfall due to intergang rivalry. However, the high point of the film was Mohan Lal's (the legendary actor from South India) realistic portrayal of a diehard police officer, a phenomenon rarely witnessed in Hindi cinema. He is cynical, weary and yet is passionately driven by an unwavering sense of duty. Amitabh Bachchan pitched in later with a similar superb performance in *Dev* (2004).

Ajay's went on to feature in a variety of films, some of which are now discussed.

Ram Gopal Verma's *Bhoot* (2003), a murder mystery, saw Ajay in the role of a helpless man whose wife starts behaving strangely after the couple moves into a new house. She claims to have seen the ghost of the earlier occupant: a young woman who had committed suicide.

In Anil Devgan's *Blackmail* (2005), a lacklustre cops-and-robbers thriller, Ajay featured as the criminal hired by the mafia to kidnap an honest police officer's son. Ajay looked jaded and insipid in this movie.

In Rohit Shetty's *Golmaal* (2006), he appeared in a badly conceived role of a trickster who, along with his friends, hatches a plan to con a blind couple. Anubhav Sinha's *Cash* (2007) cast him as one of the three burglars hired to steal a legendary diamond belonging to the British times and in John Mathew Matthan's *Shikhar* (2005), he played a negative role as an industrialist who is a land grabber.

Raju Chacha (2000, directed by Anil Devgan) was an interesting diversion as far as Ajay's overserious and consciously held image was concerned. He attempted an extremely delightful role (à la Julie Andrews in the 1964 masterpiece *The Sound of Music*) in the company of a group naughty children living up their fantasies in a castle.

In the domain of realist cinema, Ajay Devgan made his presence felt in ventures such as Mahesh Bhatt's *Zakhm* (1998), Mahesh Manjrekar's *Tera Mera Sath Rahe* (2001), Rajkumar Santoshi's *The Legend of Bhagat Singh* (2002), Prakash Jha's *Gangajal* (2003), J. P. Dutta's *LOC Kargil* (2003), Mani Ratnam's *Yuva* (2004), Rituparno Ghosh's *Raincoat* (2004), Soham Shah's *Kaal* (2005), Prakash Jha's *Apaharan* (2005), Farouque Kabir's *The Awakening* (2006) and Vishal Bharadwaj's *Omkara* (2006).

In *Zakhm*, Mahesh Bhatt's semi-autobiographical film, he portrayed the seemingly endless trauma of an illegitimate son who has to live through the suffering of his parents (a Hindu–Muslim couple) unable to find peace in a society deeply fractured due to widespread communal acrimony. Ajay's role, however, was at times marred by very superficial and melodramatic handling of the communal situation. However, it was the junior artiste (Kunal Khemu as the young Ajay) who gave a memorable performance in the first half by his ability to capture the anguish, pain and love of a child trapped in the maze of his parents' guilt.

In *Tera Mera Sath Rahe*, a less inspiring predecessor of *Black*,

Ajay plays a tender-hearted man who joyfully takes care of his mentally retarded younger brother.

In *The Legend of Bhagat Singh*, Ajay's fiery revolutionary tended, in tune with the present times, to lapse into inane rhetoric and had a rather glamourized image compared to that of Manoj Kumar, who (in *Shaheed*, 1965) depicted the martyred freedom fighter with remarkable sincerity and depth.

Gangajal was based on the gruesome Bhagalpur (in Bihar) blindings, which stunned the nation in the early 1980s. (In this shocking incident, the police poured acid into the eyes of many inmates in a Bhagalpur jail.) This down-to-earth movie projected Ajay as the police officer (based upon the exploits of a real-life individual) who investigated and exposed the perpetrators of the crime.

In *LOC Kargil*, a movie inspired by the 1999 Kargil war, Ajay portrayed Lieutenant Manoj Pandey, a courageous and dedicated army officer. The huge star cast included Sanjay Dutt, Abhishek Bachchan, Akshaye Khanna, Saif Ali Khan and Manoj Bajpai.

Yuva, set in Calcutta (now Kolkata), a city dominated by Leftist politics, presented the actor in the role of a committed radical student leader who bravely attempts to break up the local politician—mafia nexus. In this film, Ajay had, for company, Abhishek Bachchan and Viveik Oberoi. All the three protagonists pitched in with spirited performances.

Raincoat, one of the most offbeat films in recent years, sought to highlight the overwhelming preoccupations of ordinary people with material success in today's world and how they try to project a false lifestyle based on such success. In a well-articulated role, Ajay is a small-town youth aspiring desperately to acquire wealth because his lover (Aishwarya Rai) has married a city-based man. When he meets her later, he poses as a media tycoon, while the lady, although living in a penurious condition, boasts about her life of comfort and abundance. In the end, the film very remarkably juxtaposes her posturing with the protagonist's heroic surrender to compassion and goodwill. The film seemed to be inspired by O. Henry's classic short story, *The Gift of the Magi*.

In *Kaal*, Ajay appeared as Kaali, a guide in a forest famous for its wildlife, where many persons are mysteriously killed.

Apaharan depicted how a poor but honest youth switches over to the lucrative kidnapping profession after he is denied a job in the police despite having paid a huge bribe.

The Awakening cast Ajay in an offbeat role of a man who offers solace to a distraught child rendered an orphan during floods that ravaged Bombay in 2005 by narrating to him his own experiences.

In *Omkara*, a modern-day adaptation of William Shakespeare's masterpiece *Othello*, Ajay sets in motion a drama of revenge set in the heartland of Uttar Pradesh, which is marked by sordid violence. The trio Omkara (Ajay Devgan), Langda Tyagi (Saif Ali Khan) and Kesu Firangi (Viveik Oberoi) showcase a world where lawlessness and strong-arm tactics are not only the way of life and but also a means of survival. When jealousy rears its ugly head, Omkara, who suspects his wife (Kareena Kapoor) of being involved with Kesu, vehmently reacts and kills her without realizing he is being played for a fool. The film was replete with pithy dialogues, sexy dances and mind-boggling violence.

Ajay's romantic ventures have been very few. The film that comes to mind in this context is Indra Kumar's *Ishq* (1997). Here, he and Aamir Khan are paired with Kajol and Juhi Chawla, respectively. (In real life, Ajay later married his heroine.) The film was marked by some hilarious episodes and mix-ups.

Ajay Devgan's other ventures include Rohit Shetty's *Sunday* (2008), Rajkumar Santoshi's *Halla Bol* (2008), *U, Me Aur Hum* (2008, which he himself directed), Afzal Khan's *Mehbooba* (2008) and Rohit Shetty's *Golmaal Returns* (2008).

In *Sunday*, based on a plot borrowed from the Telugu hit *Anukokunda Oka Roju*, Ajay appeared as a cop, who, while investigating the amnesia of the heroine (Ayesha Takia), stumbles upon a murder mystery and the involvement of some goons in her life.

Halla Bol (2008) focuses upon the troubled journey of self-discovery of a small-town youth (Ajay Devgan). He becomes a famous film star after his initiation into acting by a street theatre group. However, he is soon alienated from the life of glamour, showmanship and adulation as a result of a murder he witnesses (committed by a top politician's son), in which nobody is willing to testify against the accused. He decides to tell the truth. He finally returns to grassroots political activism as a true-life hero.

U, Me Aur Hum (2008) featured Ajay's real-life wife Kajol. In the first part, Ajay (Ajay Devgan) woos Piya (Kajol). The second half reveals that marriage is not merely enjoying happy times together but also each partner should be willing to help out the other when one of them strikes a bad patch. Marriage also involves fulfilling commitments and trusting each other. During a cruise, Ajay falls in love with Piya at first sight. However, he happens to be sozzled at that time and Piya is hardly impressed. Not one to give up, Ajay resorts to every trick in the book to win Piya over. The bond between them grows strong. However, deception and mistrust put an end to their relationship. But love unites them again and they get married, and everything appears hunky-dory. But soon many problems crop up and their realationship again becomes strained.

In *Mehbooba*, Ajay plays Sanjay Dutt's brother. The latter ill-treats his wife (Manisha Koirala), whom he considers a 'sexual conquest'. She flees from him and gets married to Ajay!

In *Golmaal Returns*, he has to concoct a story to prove to his wife (Kareena Kapoor) that he was not cheating on her since he has had to spend a night in a yacht with Celina Jaitley after he saves her from her a bunch of goons. He calls upon his friend (Shreyas Talpade) to provide him with an alibi and act as 'Anthony Gonsalves'. Next, a dead body turns up at Anthony Gonsalves's address (given by Ajay to Kareena!). Anyway, after a series of twists and turns, things are ultimately sorted out.

Ajay stars in *London Dreams* (under production) (for details, see under Salman Khan).

Ajay's acting style is punctuated by intense underplay as well as powerful melodrama. Like Amitabh Bachchan in his earlier films (*Anand* and *Namak Haram*), he displays an uneasy sense of withdrawal, keeping his own autonomous space in the narrative. However, his portrayals are marked by an unnatural posturing and overconfident self-display in order to appear to be profound and intense. His ability in comedy has not been fully explored.

Govinda

Govinda (born as Govinda Arun Ahuja on 21 December 1963), who made a low-profile debut in Esmayeel Shroff's *Love 86* (1986), later rose to fame as the foremost comedy hero. Like Amitabh Bachchan in his younger days, Govinda helped Hindi cinema to reinvent its trademark comedy genre. His persona of an innocent and big-hearted yokel evokes the jester image of Raj Kapoor in a bid to

Govinda

link this original tramp with the contemporary milieu. Like Kapoor in *Awara*, *Shri 420*, *Jagte Raho* and *Anari*, this modern-day yokel seeks to juxtapose his emotional and ethical innocence with the decadent and materialistic urban India. And in caricaturing the rural simpleton, Govinda also seemed be influenced rather discreetly by a few elements from Dilip Kumar comic roles in *Gopi*, *Sagina* and *Bairaag*, especially the rapid-fire dialogue delivery and rustic mannerisms. He acted in numerous movies in the 1980s and 1990s.

Govinda discovered his comic self in the company of his mentor David Dhawan as the duo sought to redefine the art of comedy with a series of 'quickies' in the 1990s: *Shola Aur Shabnam* (1992), *Aankhen* (1993), *Coolie No.1* (1995), *Sajna Gaye Sasural* (1996),

Hero No. 1 (1997) and *Biwi No. 1* (1999). These films were accompanied by *Bade Miyan Chhote Miyan* (1998) and *Jodi No.1* (2001), with Govinda in the humorous company of Amitabh Bachchan and Sanjay Dutt, respectively.

In the same director's *Deewana Mastana* (1997), Govinda was Kishore Kumar reincarnate from *Half Ticket*, the overgrown mama's boy who suffers from strange phobias, walks in baby steps and yet is shrewd and worldly wise. The focus of the comedy was his zealous pursuit of the girl in competition with the street-smart Anil Kapoor and the way they try to outwit each other.

In Manoj Agarwal's *Pardesi Babu* (1998), Govinda appeared as a rural simpleton on a trip to the corrupt and ugly metropolis. He gives lessons highlighting the ethics and purity of rural life. His delivery of the expression 'India is cow' was truly hilarious.

In Harmesh Malhotra's *Dulhe Raja* (1998), the comedy antics of Govinda juxtaposed the survival instincts of the urban poor with the idiosyncracies of the filthy rich. He played a self-respecting and carefree *dhaba* owner who falls in love with the haughty daughter of a hotelier who keeps on scheming to evacuate him from the hotel premises.

However, in subsequent films, Govinda's comedy began to lose its earthy flavour. Unlike Raj Kapoor whose clowning had strong undercurrents of seriousness and realism, Govinda's buffoonery looked more like hamming than the slickness of cutting-edge humour. *Aunty No. 1* (1998) was marked with bawdy stuff, trying desperately to evoke Dada Khondke's salacious brand of humour. Unlike Kamalahasan's authentic feminine aunty (in *Chachi 420*, released in the same year), Govinda's comic attire was just a stereotypical man–woman changeover.

Govinda virtually drew a blank in some films: as a carefree, rich boy in love with a girl from the hills in Naresh Malhotra's *Achanak* (1998); as a villager making fun of urban life and values in Mahesh Manjrekar's *Jis Desh Mein Ganga Rahta Hai* (2000); and as a zany *tapori* guide in love with a foreign tourist in Deepak Sareen's *Albela* (2001).

His buoyancy and effervescence also looked contrived in some of his roles: as a small-town man driven by get-rich-quick ambition through deceit and impersonation in David Dhawan's *Kyon Ki Main Jhooth Nahi Bolta* (2001) (a rehash of the 1997 Hollywood movie *Liar Liar* starring Jim Carrey); as a hen-pecked husband in K. Raghavendra Rao's *Aamdani Atthani Kharcha Rupaiya* (2001); and as an unloved orphan in Kirti Kumar's *Pyar Diwana Hota Hai* (2002), who (by posing as a disabled person) gains the sympathy and later love of a rich benevolent NRI girl on a visit to India.

In Harmesh Malhotra's *Akhiyon Se Goli Maare* (2002) he failed to impress as a rich man chasing his love interest who is to be married to a criminal by her scheming father.

Kirti Kumar's *Sukh* (2005) featured him as a clever schemer, who introduces a divorced woman as his wife to appear in a poster campaign being launched by the milk product company where he is employed. He then desperately wants to stop the posters from going public and keep his real wife from finding out the truth.

In Priyadarshan's *Bagham Bhag* (2006), an Indian theatre group that performs shows within the country is offered a chance to display its talents in London. The leader of the group, Paresh Rawal, is ready to go abroad but the heroine suddenly disappears. Paresh Rawal gives an ultimatum to the two heroes, Govinda and Akshay Kumar, to find the heroine. He also stipulates that whoever finds the heroine will be the hero. Then, after a complex series of twists and turns, things are eventually resolved.

In Nikhil Advani's multistarrer *Salaam-e-Ishq* (2007), he was a warm-hearted taxi driver who wins over a foreign girl on a visit to India to meet her boyfriend (who has deceived her).

In David Dhawan's *Partner* (2007), he appeared in a shoddily crafted role as a love-starved male seeking the guidance of a professional love expert (played, as already mentioned, by Salman Khan).

Yet another Govinda 'comedy', *Money Hai To Honey Hai* (2008, directed by Ganesh Acharya), was a clumsy depiction of a man's greed for making oodles of quick money, which is considered the barometer of success in the contemporary world of virtually instant self-gratification. A group of vulnerable persons – our jester-hero, who runs away from home to prove himself, a lottery winner-turned-loser, an unemployed copywriter, a struggling model, a TV star desperate to become a film heroine and a struggling dress designer – are trapped by an unscrupulous SMS to part with money for obtaining ownership of a shady Rs 1000-crore company.

In Neeraj Vora's *Run Bhola Run* (under production), two convicts (Govinda and Tusshar Kapoor) try to escape from jail to find the heroine Ameesha Patel.

In *Do Knot Disturb* (under production), a comedy directed by David Dhawan, Govinda essays the role of a rich businessman who wants to hide his extramarital affair with a supermodel through his trademark use of mistaken identities and misunderstandings.

In Rumi Jaffrey's *Life Partner* (under production), a comedy about the differing perceptions about the institution of marriage in today's society, Govinda appears again as a philanderer: he is a divorce lawyer who doesn't believe in marriage and has affairs with many women.

Akshay Kumar

Akshay Kumar's screen persona represents the genesis of today's cinema of globalized romance, designer bodies and perfect action sequences, apart from the mandatory presence of conmen and wheeler-dealers. In his style and mannerisms, he appears to be Clint Eastwood and Bruce Lee rolled into one, considering his commendable skills in performing his stunts all by himself.

Akshay Kumar was born as Rajiv Hari Om Bhatia on 9 September 1967 at Amritsar. His family then moved to Delhi and later to Bombay, where he attended school and college. Before joining films, he worked as a chef in Bangkok and also

Akshay Kumar

took up martial art training in Hong Kong. He entered films with *Saugandh* (directed by Akash Mehra, Nadir Irani and Raj Sippy) released in 1991. However, it was *Khiladi* (directed by Abbas Burmawalla and Mustan Burmawalla), released in 1992, that catapulted Akshay to stardom. He appeared as a fun-loving college student, who, along with his friends, is compelled to solve the murder of a fellow girl student. As they try to get rid of any clue that may lead to their involvement, they discover an even bigger conspiracy surrounding the death and eventually find the real killer. The success of this film led to a seies of 'khiladi' films, which established him as a top-notch action hero comparable only with Dharmendra in his heydays: Sameer Malkan's *Main Khiladi Tu Anari* (1994), Umesh Mehra's *Sabse Bada Khiladi* (1995) and *Khiladiyon Ka Khiladi* (1996), David Dhawan's *Mr and Mrs Khiladi* (1997) and Umesh Mehra's *International Khiladi* (1999).

Rajiv Rai's *Mohra* (1994), in which he 'sang' *Tu Cheez Badi Hai Mast Mast* ... (and also gyrated to its rhythm in the company of heroine Raveena Tandon), also reinforced his image as a daredevil hero. In Sunil Agnihotri's *Jai Kishan* (1994), Akshay appeared in a double role as two brothers separated in childhood after their father is killed by three mafia dons. One of the sons, Kishan, goes missing, and the other, Jai, becomes blind but emerges as a master sword fighter, while his brother grows up as conman. Both finally avenge the killing of their father. This film had shades of Manmohan Desai's 1979 venture *Suhaag* (see Chapter 2).

Apart from his action films, Akshay has also acted in love stories and sentimental melodramas. In Yash Raj Films' *Yeh Dillagi* (1994, directed by Naresh Malhotra), he played the upright son of a business family and the dream man of the ambitious daughter of his car driver who becomes a successful model. In Dharmesh Darshan's *Dhadkan* (2000), he portrayed a distraught husband who upholds his love for his wife despite the tirade of her former villainous lover. In the same director's *Bewafaa* (2005) he appeared as the musician-lover of the heroine who is forced to marry her widower brother-in-law (Anil Kapoor).

Akshay has also played negative roles in a few films. He depicted a scheming playboy in Abbas-Mustan's *Ajnabee* (2001) and a corrupt cop in Rajkumar Santoshi's *Khakhee* (2004).

Priyadarshan's *Hera Pheri* released in 2000 became a major turning point in Akshay's career, opening the door for a series of comedy roles. The film presented a ham-fisted Akshay in the company of Suniel Shetty and Paresh Rawal, where they plot to make quick money but get involved with real gangsters. The trio come to know that Kabira (Gulshan Grover) has kidnapped a girl from a very rich family as Paresh Rawal receives the call from Kabira on his telephone. They then demand double the amount that Kabira wants from the family. They plan to give Kabira his ransom and keep the rest for themselves! In the sequel, *Phir Hera Pheri* (2006), directed by Neeraj Vora, the trio who had made a neat pile in the last film now tries to double it but get conned and lose it all. The trio then decides to steal drugs and sell them for a huge sum but their plan goes haywire.

In Priyadarshan's *Garam Masala* (2005), Akshay portrayed an upstart photographer who flirts around with many girls simultaneously but finally stands exposed.

The same director's *Bhagam Bhag* (2006) presented a hilarious peep into the working of amateur theatre, with all its ego clashes and petty squabbling.

In Sajid Khan's *Heyy Babyy* (2007), the footloose Akshay in the company of his equally disoriented fun-loving friends (Fardeen Khan and Riteish Deshmukh) discovers a sudden change in his worldview when all of them have to bring up an eight-month-old baby they find at their doorstep.

In *Welcome* (2007), directed by Anees Bazmee, he appeared as a bridegroom from a respectable family chosen by an underworld don for his sister (Katrina Kaif). (See also Chapter 7 under Anil Kapoor.)

In Priyadarshan's *Bhool Bhulaiyan* (2007), a horror thriller with comical elements, Akshay played a psychiatrist who is commissioned by his royal friend, an erstwhile raja living in England, to resolve the mystery of a ghost dwelling in his ancestral *haveli*. The spirit has taken possession of a young girl (Vidya Balan). It is finally revealed that the impressionable village girl (a là Madhubala in *Mahal*, 1949) has been carried away by the numerous ghost stories that she has been listening to since her childhood and starts behaving as if she were the dead maharani.

Vipul Shah's *Namastey London* (2007) cast Akshay in the role of a simple Punjabi rural youth who gets married to a reluctant NRI girl (Katrina Kaif). She has adpoted a Western lifestyle and hates whatsoever is Indian. As the girl still flirts with her British boyfriend and intends to marry him, the hero slowly and steadily makes her fall in love with him.

Anees Bazmee's *Singh Is Kinng* (2008), a uncanny mix of Frank Capra's films *Lady for a Day* (1934) and *Pocketful of Miracles* (1961) and Jackie Chan's *Miracles* (1989), was a weird caricature of simple-heartedness and willingness to help associated with a Punjabi persona. Akhsay appeared as Happy Singh, a Sikh youth from rural Punjab, who promises to bring Lucky or Lakhan Singh (Sonu Sood), the 'king' of the Australian underworld, back to his village. In Australia, he encounters a series of adventures. He also saves the life of Lucky, who is paralysed. Happy then becomes the new 'king'. He meets a kind elderly lady (Kirron Kher) and her daughter Sonia (Katrina Kaif) and becomes the victim of the plot hatched by Sonia's fiancé (Ranvir Shorey) to get him killed by Mika Singh (Javed Jaffrey), Lucky's evil-minded brother. The high point of this tardy narrative was the message that a true

Suniel Shetty, Naseeruddin Shah and Akshay Kumar in *Mohra* (1994).

Abhishek Bachchan and Aishwarya Rai in *Dhai Akshar Prem Ke* (2000).

Aishwarya Rai and Ajay Devgan in *Hum Dil De Chuke Sanam* (1999).

Hrithik Roshan in *Koi Mil Gaya* (2004).

Naseeruddin Shah and Sonam in *Tridev* (1989).

Nana Patekar in *Hu Tu Tu* (1996).

king does not fight for his own fortunes but for the well-being of others.

In Vijay Krishna Acharya's *Tashan* (2008), Akshay Kumar played a gangster who happens to be the childhood friend of the heroine (for more details, see Chapter 7 under Anil Kapoor).

In Sabir Khan's *Kambakht Ishq* (2009), Akshay appeared as a daring stuntman who treats women as objects of desire. He meets his match in the heroine (Kareena Kapoor), a defiant, no-nonsense feminist with an acerbic tongue.

In Anthony D'Souza's *Blue* (under production), he appears as a daredevil diver taking up the search of treasure that is buried at the bottom of an ocean and is guarded by sharks. Akshay Kumar, a certified deep-sea diver, was injured while shooting for the film.

Akshay's foray into 'serious' cinema is represented by a handful of films: Tanuja Chandra's *Sangharsh* (1999), Suneel Darshan's *Ek Rishtaa: The Bond of Love* (2001), Madhur Bhandarkar's *Aan: Men at Work* (2004), Vipul Shah's *Waqt: The Race against Time* (2005), Shirish Kunder's *Jaan-e-mann* (2006), Nikhil Advani's *Chandni Chowk to China* (2009) and Nagesh Kukunoor's *8x10 Tasveer* (2009).

In *Sangharsh*, an offbeat film, he was seen in an unusual role as a professor researching on occult practices who helps the police track down a dreaded sadhu engaged in child sacrifice.

Ek Rishtaa presented him as a new-age entrepreneur who refuses to accept his industrialist father's (Amitabh Bachchan) obsolete business management practices.

In *Aan: Men at Work*, Akshay appeared as an honest and diligent cop who, with the help of his colleague, Shatrughan Sinha, brings about reforms in the police system and brings to justice three dreaded mafia dons.

In *Waqt: The Race against Time*, again with Bachchan in the role of his father, he made his mark as an irresponsible lad eventually transforming himself into dutiful son who takes care of his ailing father.

In *Jaan-e-mann*, he played a shy scientist in love with a girl left in the lurch by her actor-husband.

Chandni Chowk to China, the first Indian film to be shot in China, can be considered a semi-autobiographical work with regard to Akshay Kumar. He played a simple-hearted cook from Chandni Chowk (the famous area of old Delhi known for its numerous lanes and bylanes, crowded markets and a variety of cuisines), who is mistaken for the reincarnation of an ancient peasant warrior by two visitors from China. They take him to their country to free an oppressed village from a tyrant. The heroine (Deepika Padukone) featured in a double role as a Chinese woman and also an Indian woman. The Chinese superstar Gordon Liu made his Bollywood debut in this film.

In *8x10 Tasveer*, Akshay possesses the supernatural ability to enter a photograph and recollect the events just before the photograph has been taken. However, he can stay in the photograph only for a minute and, after that, he is subject to some harrowing experiences that drain him of energy. He uses this ability for good causes and it helps him solve the murder of his father.

Akshaye Khanna

Akshaye Khanna is one of the most sensitive artistes of today's cinema, cut in the mould of a classical hero. Devoid of the usual aggressive and melodramatic punch, he displays a naturalist style often marked by grace and precision. He has often portrayed the agonized sufferer unable to come with terms with his life's predicaments and the alienating surroundings.

Akshaye, the youngest son of actor Vinod Khanna, was born on 28 March 1975 in Bombay. He made his debut in 1997 in his father's production *Himalaya Putra*. He came into the limelight with J. P. Dutta's multistarrer *Border*, also released in 1997, in the role of an army officer considered to be timid by his fellow soldiers and who finally proves his courage by holding back a Pakistani and, in his vengeful protest, starts indulging in alcoholism and debauchery. He even undergoes a brief conversion to Islam. Akshaye in this challenging role looked absolutely inspired, particularly in those scenes that showed him deteriorating morally and physically.

Akshaye's roles have been diverse in nature as revealed by the following ventures.

In Anees Bazmee's *Deewangee* (2002), he appeared as a sympathetic lawyer who takes up the murder case of an individual (Ajay Devgan) pretending to be suffering from schizophrenia.

In Abbas-Mustan's *36 China Town* (2006), a murder mystery, he played an investigating police officer. Shahid Kapoor and Kareena Kapoor were his co-stars in this movie, which was a bit of a disappointment.

In *Shaadi Se Pehle* (2006), directed by Satish Kaushik, he first appeared as an unemployed youth who wants to marry an affluent girl (Ayesha Takia) but her folks reject him. He then finds a job and earns enough money to ask for her hand again. But then he comes to know that he is suffering from cancer and breaks off his relationship with Ayesha (not wanting her to suffer due to his illness). In reality, he is not a victim of cancer but has only overheard a conversation between a patient and doctor and started believing about his illness. He then turns his attention towards Mallika Sherawat but is forced into an extortion racket by her brother (Suniel Shetty).

Dharmesh Darshan's *Aap Ki Khatir* (2006), a rip-off of Hollywood's *The Wedding Date* (2005), depicted Akshaye as a simple-hearted lad who is picked up by a haughty rich girl (Priyanka Chopra) and brought to London to pose as her lover in order to antagonize her ex-boyfriend (Dino Morea).

Akshaye has also appeared in run-of-the-mill love stories like Reema Rakesh Nath's *Mohabbat* (1997), Priyadarshan's *Doli Saja Ke Rakhna* (1998), Kailash Surendranath's *Love You Hamesha* (1999) and Rajat Rawail's *Deewana Tere Naam Ka* (2002).

Abbas-Mustan's *Humraaz* (2002) had him in a negative role as the scheming musician hired by a ship owner (Bobby Deol). Akhsaye compels his girl friend (Amisha Patel) to marry his boss so that he can get hold of his wealth. But his plan misfires.

In *Naqaab* (2007), also directed by Abbas-Mustan, the heroine, who is engaged to Bobby Deol, is attracted to him. But all of them have past secrets to conceal.

Anil Mehta's *Aaja Nachle* (2007), cast him as a politician (a Member of Parliament) from a small town who opposes the NRI dancer (Madhuri Dixit) when she wants to revive the dance institution set up by her now-deceased guru.

In Abbas-Mustan's *Race* (2008), a film packed with thrills, intrigue and sibling rivalry, Akshaye portrayed a debonair individual who lives life on the edge. He and his stepbrother (Saif Ali Khan) are in the business of horse racing. Saif sacrifices his love for Bipasha Basu as Akshaye wants to marry her, but he plans to kill him (Akshaye) for the insurance money (a whopping sum).

Akshaye has also displayed some ingenuity in comedies such as *Hungama* (2003) and *Hulchul* (2004), both directed by Priyadarshan.

In Priyadarshan's *Mere Baap Pehle Aap* (2008), Akshaye played the son of a widower (Paresh Rawal). Akshaye decides to take care of his father as the latter grows older. Akshaye gets crank calls from a girl, who later turns out be his friend from college. She is staying with her guardian (Shobana), a lady who happens to be Paresh Rawal's old flame! Akhsaye tries to arrange the marriage of his father with Shobana. He also finds true love from his college mate.

Neeraj Vora's *Short Kut: The Con Is On* (2009) depicted Akshaye Khanna as a talented and aspiring assistant director struggling to make it big in the film industry. When a junior artiste (Arshad Warsi) steals his prized script and is catapulted to stardom, he goes into depression but soon plans his revenge against the upstart.

Bobby Deol

Bobby Deol, the younger son of Dharmendra, was born as Vijay Singh Deol on 27 January 1967 in Bombay. As a child he made a very brief appearance in the 1977 movie *Dharam Veer* where he appeared as the young Dharmendra. He made his debut as hero in 1995 in Rajkumar Santoshi's *Barsaat*, for which he bagged the *Filmfare* Best Debut Award.

Bobby Deol

Soon, Bobby, following his elder brother Sunny's style, began to achieve fame as yet another vengeful hero in the making.

In Rajiv Rai's *Gupt: The Hidden Truth* (1997), he made his mark as the distraught youth accused of murdering his father (Raj Babbar), with whom he did not get along well. He wants to marry Manisha Koirala but his father has other ideas; he announces that Bobby would marry another girl (Kajol). But Bobby sticks to his guns and seeks out Manisha. However, he underestimates the overpossessive nature of Kajol, who turns out to have homicidal tendencies.

In Abbas-Mustan's *Soldier* (1998), he was the idealist youth who kills a man whom he believes to be his father (a corrupt character who is involved in illegal arms dealing), but his real father was a patriot who sacrificed his life for his motherland, but was wrongly accused of betraying the nation. He also gathers evidence to clear his real father's name.

In yet another Abbas-Mustan venture, *Ajnabee* (2001), Bobby becomes the victim of a playboyish but villainous neighbour (Akshay Kumar), who frames him for murder.

In Raj Kanwar's *Badal* (2000), he was a victim of the 1984 riots* who has been brought up by a terrorist. The latter wants to eliminate a policeman responsible for the murder of innocent people in the villages of Punjab including his whole family.

Bichhoo (meaning scorpion), directed by Guddu Dhanoa, also released in 2000, presented him in the role of a ruthless contract murderer who sacrifices his life to save a helpless girl (Rani Mukherji), the witness to the excesses committed by unscrupulous cops. In the end, the scorpion, the pet of the vengeful hero, which he always kept on his forearm, was to remain a reminder of his sacrifice for the girl.

The film *23rd March 1931: Shaheed* (2002), produced by his father and directed by Guddu Dhanoa, offered him the challenging role of the revolutionary Bhagat Singh.

Anil Sharma's *Apne* (2007) saw him, his brother and father starring together for the first time. He was the younger brother of Sunny who takes up boxing in order to save the honour of his humiliated father.

In Suneel Darshan's *Shakalaka Boom Boom* (2006) and Abbas-Mustan's *Naqaab* (2007), he played negative roles.

In Rahul Rawail's *Aur Pyaar Ho Gaya* (1997), Bobby went in for a smart changeover to a flamboyant romantic hero with a touch of comedy. He appeared as the lover of a strong-headed girl (Aishwarya Rai; this was her first Hindi film) who mistakes him for the prospective groom selected by her parents. The music of this film was composed by the famous Pakistani *qawwal*, Nusrat Fateh Ali Khan.

In 1999, he starred in his brother Sunny Deol's directorial debut film *Dillagi* as a spoilt lad being helped by his sibling in matters of heart and family togetherness.

---

*In the wake of Prime Minister Indira Gandhi's assassination by her Sikh bodyguards (on 31 October 1984), large-scale riots broke out in some parts of India, in which thousands of Sikhs were killed. Also, there was large-scale destruction of their possessions and properties.

In the comedy *Chor Machaaye Shor* (2002), a film by David Dhawan, he played a top-notch thief who steals a diamond and hides it in a building under construction, which is soon converted into the police headquarters. He now has to devise a plan to extricate the diamond!

In Shaad Ali's *Jhoom Barabar Jhoom* (2007), the actor won appreciation for his role as a rock star. The other hero in this film was Abhishek Bachchan.

Samir Karnik's *Heroes* (2008) projected Bobby as a courageous soldier who has laid down his life for his motherland.

In Sangeeth Sivan's *Ek – The Power of One* (2009), Bobby was projected as an assassin with a heart of gold. To create sympathy for himself, a politician asks Bobby to make a fake assassination attempt on him at a rally. However, the politician is really killed by someone else and the police begin chasing Bobby as the prime suspect.

His other films include Vidhu Vinod Chopra's *Kareeb* (1997), Kundan Shah's *Hum To Mohabbat Karega* (2000), Indra Kumar's *Aashiq* (2001), Abbas-Mustan's *Humraaz* (2002), Anil Sharma's *Ab Tumhare Hawale Watan Saathiyo* (2004), Suneel Darshan's *Barsaat* (2005) and *Dosti: Friends Forever* (2005) and Bunty Soorma's *Humko Tumse Pyaar Hai* (2006).

In *Ab Tumhare Hawale Watan Saathiyo*, Bobby essayed a double role: first as an army officer who loses his life in action during the 1971 Indo–Pak war and second his son, also an army officer, who lacks the commitment to serve the nation.

Three films that stand out in Bobby's filmography till date are Mani Shankar's *Tango Charlie* (2005), Samir Karnik's *Nanhe Jaisalmer* (2007) and Kabeer Kaushik's *Chamku* (2008), each belonging to a different genre.

The first film, told through the pages of a diary, written by a soldier (Bobby) code-named Tango brings out the sacrifices that Indian soldiers have to make to protect the nation's integrity and how little recognition they get from society at large. The film highlights Bobby's daredevil actions in army operations against separatist groups in Manipur, Maoists in Andhra Pradesh, the communal rioters in Gujarat and the Mujahideen in Kashmir.

Nanhe Jaisalmer, a landmark children's film, brought Bobby to the interface between show biz and tourism. The film was about the actor Bobby Deol's friendship with a ten-year-old boy Nanhe, a tourist guide in Jaisalmer (Rajasthan), who arranges camel safaris. As a baby, Nanhe had appeared briefly in a shot with Bobby for a film. As he grows up, Bobby influences his thoughts and actions. When the actor visits Jaisalmer for a film shooting, he meets the boy and his words of wisdom and encouragement finally help Nanhe in overcoming the obstacles he faces in his daily life.

Kabeer Kaushik's *Chamku* (2008), a vendetta on the lines of Amitabh Bachchan's *Zanjeer* (1973), presented Bobby as a vengeful lad in search of the murderer of his family. An orphan, raised by a Naxalite leader (Danny Denzongpa) in the interiors of Bihar, he becomes part of a covert governmental programme launched by the country's intelligence agencies to carry out political assassinations. He decides to lead a reformed life after he falls in love with a kindergarten teacher (Priyanka Chopra), but a chance encounter with the murderer brings him back to the world of crime again.

Saif Ali Khan

Saif Ali Khan

Saif Ali Khan, the son of Mansoor Ali Khan Pataudi (a former cricket captain of India) and actress Sharmila Tagore, was born on 16 August 1970 in New Delhi. After finishing schooling, he studied at the Winchester College in the UK, just as his father had done a few decades ago. He entered Bollywood in 1992 with Yash Chopra's *Parampara* (a complex tale marked by vengeance and bloodshed), starring Sunil Dutt, Vinod Khanna and Aamir Khan, among others. He won the *Filmfare* Best Debut Award for the film *Aashiq Awara* (1992, directed by Umesh Mehra). Soon he made his way through several multistarrer hits like Sameer Malkan's *Main Khiladi Tu Anari* (1994), Naresh Malhotra's *Yeh Dillagi* (1994), Milan Luthria's *Kachche Dhaage* (1998), Sooraj Barjatya's *Hum Saath-Saath Hain* (1999) and Kundan Shah's *Kya Kehna* (2000).

Saif's career soared in the new millennium, thanks to a series of films released in quick succession: Farhan Akhtar's *Dil Chahta Hai* (2001), Nikhil Advani's *Kal Ho Naa Ho* (2003), J. P. Dutta's *LOC Kargil* (2003), Ram Gopal Verma's *Darna Mana Hai* (2003), Kunal Kohli's *Hum Tum* (2004), Siddharth Anand's *Salaam Namaste* (2005), Pradeep Sarkar's *Parineeta* (2005), Vishal Bharadwaj's *Omkara* (2006), Vidhu Vinod Chopra's *Eklavya: The Royal Guard* (2007) and Siddharth Anand's *Ta Ra Rum Pum* (2007).

In *Dil Chahta Hai* he appeared as a light-hearted and carefree romantic who is always dreaming about falling in love.

LOC Kargil cast him in the role of the daredevil Captain Anuj Nayyar who is awarded the Mahavir Chakra.

In *Darna Mana Hai* (a film with six stories woven into it), he appeared as a photographer addicted to smoking, who gets involved in some bizarre activities.

In *Hum Tum*, he portrayed the transformation of a spoilt youth into a mature adult. He has an on–off relationship with the heroine (Rani Mukherji), which eventually stabilizes. For this film, he won the National Award for the Best Actor.

Salaam Namaste, a movie about discord between lovers opting for a live-in-relationship, presented Saif as a lazy, irresponsible but ambitous NRI youth who ditches his partner (Preity Zinta) when she becomes pregnant.

Parineeta (a remake of Bimal Roy's 1953 Ashok Kumar–Meena Kumari starrer of the same name and based on the famous work of the Bengali writer Saratchandra) portrayed Saif as the romantic involved in a neighbourhood love affair with the heroine (played by Vidya Balan).

In *Omkara* (described earlier in this chapter under Ajay Devgan), Saif won critical acclaim for portraying the treacherous Langda Tyagi, with tobacco-stained teeth and foul-mouthed coarseness. In fact, there was a bit of a controversy with regard to his dialogues, which some people considered to be vulgar.

Vidhu Vinod Chopra's *Eklavya: The Royal Guard* (2007) saw him and his mother together for the second time after *Aashiq Awara*. He appeared as an Indian prince settled in the UK, but is forced to return to India so that he can claim his kingdom. (See also Chapter 2.)

Ta Ra Rum Pum (2007) brought on screen the highly spirited struggle of a racing car driver for survival, given the murky business of fixing in many races. He starts off as a petrol station worker, who wins a race, marries his girlfriend (Rani Mukherji) and builds a house by taking loans. He meets with an accident, which pushes the family into an acute financial crisis. But soon he re-emerges as the top-seeded competitor.

Saif appeared in a negative role in Sriram Raghavan's *Ek Hasina Thi* (2004). In 2006, Saif played very effectively the lead role (a negative one) in Homi Adajania's offbeat English-language film *Being Cyrus*, in which his co-stars were Naseeruddin Shah, Dimple Kapadia and Boman Irani.

In Kunal Kohli's *Thoda Pyar Thoda Magic* (2008), Saif portrayed the reformation of an arrogant, cold and unfriendly man who becomes a compassionate and caring guardian when a court order makes him raise four orphaned children. He had killed their parents in a rash accident. The story had several elements borrowed from Hollywood movies like *Mary Poppins* (1964), *The Sound of Music* (1965), *Rent a Kid* (1995) and *Nanny McPhee* (2005).

Race (2008) has already been described earlier in this chapter under Akshaye Khanna.

In Vijay Krishna Acharya's *Tashan* (2008), Saif appeared as Jimmy Cliff, a call centre worker who helps the heroine to settle scores with the villainous Anil Kapoor. In the end, Jimmy opens his own call centre, where only girls work. (See also Chapter 7 under Anil Kapoor.)

In *Love Aajkal* (2009, directed by Imtiaz Ali), he portrayed a modern-day individual who looks at love from a practical viewpoint in contrast to his older version (in a double role) that treated love as something precious and almost divine.

Fardeen Khan

Fardeen Khan has inherited the suave, debonair and flamboyant image of his father Feroz Khan. And like his father, he has also emerged as one of the most important actors in the second lead in recent Bollywood films. Born on 8 March 1974, he did schooling in Bombay and his business management from the University of Massachusetts (USA). He

Fardeen Khan

was launched by his father in 1998 with *Prem Aggan*, which failed at the box office. He made his mark with Ram Gopal Verma's *Jungle* (2000) in the role of an adventurous youth who enters a scary forest to save his woman kidnapped by forest bandits. The young actor soon became a major romantic hero figure with a slew of breezy love stories: Rajat Mukherjee's *Pyaar Tune Kya Kiya* (2001), E. Nivas's *Love Ke Liye Kuch Bhi Karega* (2001), Ahathian's *Hum Ho Gaye Aapke* (2001), Ravi Sharma Shankar's *Kuch Tum Kahon Kuch Hum Kahein* (2002) and S. J. Suryah's *Khushi* (2003).

Apart from the foregoing films, Fardeen has essayed a variety of roles through which he has exhibited his talent and ability.

In *Janasheen* (2003), the ambitious project of his father, Fardeen appeared as an Australia-based youth who is caught on the horns of a dilemma as to whether or not to punish his long-lost biological father, the murderer of his foster father.

In Supam Verma's *Ek Khiladi Ek Haseena* (2005), Fardeen played a conman who becomes a victim of his own game when things go horribly wrong.

Indra Kumar's *Pyare Mohan* (2006) attempted to strike a humane note. The film was about the friendship between two former Bollywood stunt artistes, the visually challenged Pyare (Fardeen Khan) and the aurally challenged Mohan (Viveik Oberoi). The duo intervenes to save two innocent sisters who are to be murdered as they have come to know by default the identity of a dreaded criminal who is believed to be dead.

In *Shadi No. 1* (2006), Fardeen Khan, Zayed Khan (his cousin in real life) and Sharman Joshi want hassle-free enjoyment with other girls despite being married. Fardeen's wife (Ayesha Takia) is deeply religious (obsessed with god) and has no itme for her husband.

In Rumi Jaffrey's *Life Partner* (under production), Fardeen plays a character for whom being in love is paramount as opposed to Govinda's gallivanting.

In Suparn Verma's *Acid Factory* (under production), he is one of the five men who find themselves locked inside a factory and who have lost memories of their past.

Fardeen has also tried his hand at comedy in two multistarrers: Anees Bazmee's *No Entry* (2005) and the already-mentioned Sajid Khan's *Heyy Babyy* (2007).

In two films, Fardeen rose above the ordinary in terms of content and presentation of his screen persona.

In *Om Jai Jagdish* (2002), he made his mark as the tech-savvy car designer who (along with Abhishek Bachchan) saves the honour of his family by earning money abroad and preventing their house from being auctioned.

In Govind Nihalani's *Dev* (2004), in which the actor posted perhaps his career-best performance, he was a disillusioned Muslim youth, who becomes the focus of conflict between two opposite ideologies to define his identity: between the upright police officer (Amitabh Bachchan) and his senior and close buddy

(Om Puri), a zealous representative of Hindutva in the law-enforcement apparatus of the state. (See Chapter 2 for more details.)

Other Heroes in the Field

Apart from the top-rung heroes currently dominating the Indian screen, there are many others in the running, who entered the fray in the 1990s. For instance, Suniel Shetty (*Mohra*, 1994, *Border*, 1997, *Hera Pheri*, 2000, *Dhadkan*, 2000, *Phir Hera Pheri*, 2006 and *Cash*, 2007), Arbaaz Khan, Salman Khan's brother (*Daraar*, 1996, *Hello Brother*, 1999, *Maa Tujhe Salaam*, 2002, *Tumko Na Bhool Paayenge*, 2002, *Hulchul*, 2004, and *Maine Pyar Kyun Kiya*, 2005) and Chandrachur Singh (*Maachis*, 1996, *Silsila Hai Pyar Ka*, 1999, *Josh*, 2000, *Aamdani Atthanni Kharcha Rupaiya*, 2001, *Bharat Bhagya Vidhata*, 2002 and *Sarhad Par*, 2007) have also developed their own screen personas.

Notes and References

1. Dinesh Rajeha and Jitender Kothari, *The Hundred Luminaries of Hindi Cinema*, Bombay: India Book House, 1996.
2. Mitu Sengupta, '*Lagaan*'s Men', *The Hindustan Times*, 29 March 2002.
3. Saibal Chatterjee, '1990–2001: Designer Cinema' in Gulzar et al (eds.), *Encyclopedia of Indian Cinema*, New Delhi: Encyclopedia Britannica, 2004.

Chapter 9

The New-Millennium Heroes

The new millennium has thrown up its share of heroes, some of whom have sustained themselves creditably and some of whom have just managed to survive in the highly competitive world of Bollywood. Even as this book goes to press, newer and newer heroes keep cropping up on a regular basis.

Hrithik Roshan

Hrithik Roshan (born on 10 January 1974) entered the film world as a child artiste in his maternal grandfather's (J. Om Prakash) *Aasha* (1980). He also appeared in Surendra Mohan's *Aap Ke Deewane*, released the same year. In this film, his father, Rakesh Roshan, was one of the heroes. In the year 2000, Hrithik emerged as the ultimate manifestation of the new-age hero. He appeared as a carefully designed and manufactured cine figure for firmly establishing the hold of the globalized Indian film over the teen audience. This perfectly moulded macho hero – muscular, exceedingly handsome, with Grecian features and who danced brilliantly – in his screen image came to represent a highly successful Indian prototype of the Hollywood bodybuilder hero. Fortunately, despite such an image, the young actor proved that he could come up with a credible performance as required by a particular role.

Hrithik Roshan

Launched by his mentor, none other than his father, Hrithik made his debut in *Kaho Na Pyar Hai*, which was released in January 2000. Presenting the young actor in a double role, the film sought to juxtapose, and also bring together, the two Indias: first the ordinary people trying to reach out to the globalized world and second the prosperous and 'superior' India symbolized by the NRI diaspora, celebrated for its acumen for success in the highly demanding Western world. Hrithik, given his aforementioned image and scintillating dancing, became an instant hit especially among impressionable upper- and middle-class teens. The film went on to bag a record number of *Filmfare* awards, including the best actor trophy for Hrithik. The film was studded with some hit songs (composed by Rajesh Roshan, the younger brother of Rakesh Roshan). This film offered an enticing mix of dance, romance, music, thrills, murder, suspense and, above all, the brand-new hero twice over!

Vikram Bhatt's *Aap Mujhe Achche Lagne Lage* (2002), a follow-up of *Kaho Na Pyar Hai*, presented Hrithik as a middle-class tough boy with a tender heart who seeks to win over an upmarket girl. With this film, the actor reasserted himself as the ultimate teen icon with his impressive floor dancing.

In Arjun Sablok's *Na Tum Jano Na Hum* (2002), he played a photographer from the 'high seat of glamour' (Bombay) who casts a spell over a small-town girl (Esha Deol) and her family. But they remain merely friends as both of them are in love with their respective pen pals.

In Subhash Ghai's *Yaadein* (2001), Hrithik appeaed as a vivacious NRI whose dramatic visit to India destabilizes the worldview of a middle-class family with three daughters of marriageable age.

Hrithik again plays a suave NRI youngster in Kunal Kohli's *Mujhse Dosti Karoge?* (2002), a rehash of Hollywood's *When Harry Met Sally* (1989) and *You've Got Mail* (1998). This film firmly anchored Hrithik in the new-age lifestyle through an Internet and cyber-driven upper-class teen love affair. This NRI sends e-mails from London to his childhood friend (Kareena Kapoor). As the girl does not return his cyber epistles, self-obsessed as she is with her world of high fashion, the affable other girl (Rani Mukherji), the cyber mate of the hero, falls in love with him.

In Karan Johar's multistarrer *Kabhi Khushi Kabhi Gham* (2001), Hrithik, who played Shahrukh Khan's younger brother (both sons of Amitabh Bachchan; SRK being a foster son), performed his role capably, especially the dance sequences. However, overall, his presence in the movie was incidental since the main theme was the clash between Big B and Shahrukh Khan.

Hrithik has, however, also exhibited his remarkable ability to convincingly portray highly sensitive characterizations as in Vidhu Vinod Chopra's *Mission Kashmir* and Khalid Mohammed's *Fiza*, both released in late 2000. As the sufferer, not at peace with himself and trapped as he is in the duality of the beauty and ugliness of the world around him, he captured the anguish and the painful identity crisis being faced by the Muslim youth in contemporary India.

In *Mission Kashmir*, a hard-hitting movie, Hrithik portrayed the disillusionment and the growing alienation of a Kashmiri youth named Altaf. (Altaf was symbolic of Kashmiri society.) The film sought to dissect the factors (such as alienation of the people and injustices against them, leading to bitterness and acrimony) that lead to the making of a Kashmiri terrorist: what Gulzar sought to project in the backdrop of the Punjab militancy in *Machchis* (1996). Like Tinu Verma's *Maa Tujhe Salaam* (2002) and Kamalahasan's *Hey Ram* (2000), *Mission Kashmir* was about how a terrorist is born and how painful is his return to the nationalist fold. As a child, Altaf had witnessed the massacre of his entire family during a counter-insurgency operation carried out by a Muslim police officer (Sanjay Dutt). He grows up but is unable to forget his childhood trauma (as was seen in *Zanjeer*, 1973; Amitabh Bachchan's first portrayal of the angry young man). He becomes a terrorist but is brought back to the mainstream by none other than Sanjay Dutt himself.

In *Fiza*, Hrithik effectively brought alive on screen a simple-hearted, ordinary urban Muslim youth, who, as a victim of circumstances, is drawn into a vortex of intrigue and terrorism. He is unable to come to terms with certain nerve-racking experiences and finds himself in a state of helplessness and anger. He thus takes refuge in fundamentalist ideology and runs away from home to join a bunch of terrorists. Set against the backdrop of the Hindu–Muslim riots that rocked Bombay in 1993, *Fiza* was a laudable film in that it projected the complexities of communalism from the point of view of the minority community. It also sought to capture the dislocations faced by a lower-middle-class Muslim family caught inadvertently in the whirl of the riots in its neighbourhood. The hero, virtually in the firebrand terrorist mode, seeks a transformation of his community's alienation to a larger cause of social justice and a radical change towards a reorganization of society.

Interestingly, as the protagonist decides to wipe out communal politicians, he expresses his emotions through the *tandav* dance. In this sequence, the film maker weaves the dance of destruction of the Hindu god Shiva into the Muslim martial ritual of self-flagellation as a tribute to the martyr, Husain, the grandson of Prophet Mohammed.

Fiza (played by Karisma Kapoor) pleads with her brother (Hrithik, whom she tracks down with great difficulty after he runs away from home) to give up his violent and self-destructive path and seek redress through peaceful means. But Hrithik refuses to return to the fold of his family and friends. She is finally compelled to kill him. This climax seems to be inspired by *Mother India, Ganga Jumna, Deewar* and *Shakti*, in which social morality is metaphorically upheld by the desperate killing of the social renegade by his own kin (mother, brother or father).

In *Koi Mil Gaya* (2004), a sci fi film directed by Rakesh Roshan, Hrithik gave a convincing performance as a mentally challenged youth, who very bravely seeks to overcome his disability and his loneliness. Designed in the classic Steven Spielberg mould, the film sought to enlighten the mind of the hero through the ET (extraterrestrial) fantasy. The highlight of the film was the character of the space alien named Jadoo (magic).

In *Krrish* (2006, again directed by Rakesh Roshan), a sequel to *Koi Mil Gaya*, Hrithik was endowed with superhuman powers, thanks to Jadoo passing them onto the hero in the earlier movie, who happens to be his father. (His father is killed under mysterious circumstances.) He lives amidst nature, abounding with snow-clad mountains, fast-flowing rivers and a variety of flora and fauna. The birds and animals are his 'friends'. He can 'walk over' rivers, swing from one tree to another and climb mountains with absolute ease. He is kept away from the big cities by his grandmother (played by Rekha) who fears that the evil urban forces would exploit his abilities. But our hero follows the heroine (Priyanka Chopra) to Singapore after he saves her life when she is stuck high on a very tall tree and they fall in love with each other. (She is a part of a mountaineering expedition.) In Singapore, he dons a mask (like Zorro) and uses his talents for noble purposes. He performs many good deeds and saves many lives when a circus tent catches fire. He literally flies across the streets of Singapore in his daredevil missions (thanks to the special effects wizards). He also takes on the slick and smooth-talking villain (played by Naseeruddin Shah) and foils his attempts at using technological advances for achieving sinister objectives.

Farhan Akhtar's *Lakshya* (2004) depicted Hrithik as a lethargic youth who shakes off his torpor and joins the Indian Army. He is posted to Kargil, high in the Himalayas, where he displays immense courage and resilience while confronting the enemy. He had Big B for company in this movie besides the heroine (Preity Zinta).

In Sanjay Gadhvi's fast-paced *Dhoom 2* (2006), Hrithik (in a negative role) shared the screen space with Abhishek Bachchan among others. He appeared as a professional thief who is very much tech-savvy. He teams up with his female version (played by Aishwarya Rai), both of whom pull off some spectacular heists and are pursued by Abhishek (who played a cop) and his force.

Hrithik portrayed the Mughal Emperor Akbar in Ashutosh Gowarikar's *Jodha Akbar* (2008). As the title suggests, the film brought on screen the romance between Akbar and the Rajput princess Jodha (played by Aishwarya Rai). Hrithik came up with an impressive performance as also Aishwarya. There were some unique scenes in *Jodha Akbar*, such as Hrithik taming a wild elephant and the sword fight between him and the heroine. The movie was embroiled in controversy as some historians held the view that Jodha was, in fact, the wife of Akbar's son Salim, who later took on the title Jehangir.

In Zoya Akhtar's *Luck by Chance* (2009), Hrithik appeared as an actor who walks out of the sets of a film being produced by his friend (Rishi Kapoor). The film attempted to portray the behind-the-scenes events that take place in Bollywood. The star cast included Farhan Akhtar, Konkona Sen Sharma, Isha Sharvani, Dimple Kapadia and Juhi Chawla. Many top-notch actors (such as Aamir Khan, Shahrukh Khan and Abhishek Bachchan) put in brief appearances.

Abhishek Bachchan

Abhishek Bachchan (born on 5 February 1976) arrived on the scene as a promising new-age hero apparently after hectic grooming by none other than his father Amitabh Bachchan and mother Jaya Bachchan.

In his debut film *Refugee* (2000, directed by J. P. Dutta), a cross-border love affair between an Indian Muslim youth and a Pakistani girl, he reflected the sensitivity, the sadness and the vulnerability of the young Amitabh as in *Anand, Nanak Haram* and *Abhimaan.* However, his depiction of his internal anger and fury looked far less intense. Anyway, he was recognized for his screen presence and talent that have taken him far over the years.

Abhishek's films till date reflect his ability to pull off diverse roles ranging from portraying the distraught lover, vigilante hero, family drama participant, new-age yuppie, anti-hero and, above all, the small-town lad dreaming of making it big in a metropolis.

Raj Kanwar's *Dhai Akshar Prem Ke* (2000) did not do much

Abhishek Bachchan

for Abhishek's career because of an amateurish script and sloppy direction. He portrayed an army man on a holiday who becomes the saviour of the runaway heroine (Aishwarya Rai), who is witness to a murder.

In *Tera Jadoo Chal Gayaa* (2000), the director (A. Muthu) sought to transfer, albeit unconvincingly, the sombre lover image of Abhishek into the larger-than-life presence of Amitabh. The young actor played the role of a simple-hearted artist from Agra who reaches Bombay and wages a lone war against the corrupt rich.

In Goldie Behl's *Bas Itna Sa Khwab Hai* (2003), Abhishek portrayed an ambitious small-town boy who wants to make it big in the glitzy world of business. He becomes a media tycoon and fulfils his dream of becoming the subject of a classy TV show. The actor won accolades for his convincing and sensitive portrayal marked by restraint and refinement.

In Shaad Ali's runaway hit *Bunti Aur Babli* (2005), Abhishek easily slid into the role of a conman in the zany company of the heroine, Rani Mukherji, also cast in the same mould. Both of them have run away from their respective homes and soon team up to try out their schemes or rather scams, which are ingenious, to bring in quick money. They take on the names Bunty (Abhishek) and Babli (Rani) and manage to dupe quite a few persons into parting with their money. In fact, they even 'sell' the Taj Mahal to a gullible foreigner! They keep on moving from one place to another to evade the law. However, they are assiduously pursued by a dedicated cop (none other that Amitabh Bachchan). They decide to get married, but do not give up their illegal activities. However, when a child is born to them they decide to reform themselves and lead an honest life. The highlight of the movie was the song-and-dance sequence (*Kajrare, Kajrare ...*) featuring Aishwarya Rai and the two Bachchans. In fact, it was the senior Bachchan who appeared more energetic and peppy! This movie was loosely based on the 1967 Hollywood classic *Bonnie and Clyde* starring Warren Beatty and Faye Dunaway.

In Rohan Sippy's *Bluff Master* (2005), Abhishek was again a conman, whose victims were many. He falls in love with Priyanka Chopra, but she rejects him when she comes to know of his shady activities. He then meets a youngster (Riteish Deshmukh) who wants to become his disciple and learn the tricks of the trade. Abhishek takes him under his wing. Ultimately, it turns out that Riteish has conned the senior in order to settle scores. (Riteish's father had earlier been ripped off by Abhishek.)

In Shaad Ali's *Jhoom Barabar Jhoom* (2007), Abhishek once again portrayed a confidence trickster (who hails from a small city in Punjab) who meets a Pakistani girl (played by Preity Zinta) at a railway station in London. He claims that he could sell the Buckingham Palace to the Queen! They are apparently waiting for their respective partners, who do not turn up. Anyway, after many mix-ups and a lot of scheming, the hero and heroine fall in love with each other.

In other romantic roles, the young hero played a wayward husband in Dharmesh Darshan's's *Haan ... Maine Bhi Pyaar Kiya* (2002, heroine Karisma Kapoor) and a suave NRI who falls in love with a local girl (Kareena Kapoor) in Sooraj Barjatya's *Main Prem Ki Diwani Hoon* (2003). In the first film, his wife (Karisma Kapoor) divorces him as she suspects him of having an extra-marital affair. She walks out of his life and, after a while, plans to marry another man (Akshay Kumar), but, at that stage, Abhishek re-enters her life. In *Main Prem Ki Diwani Hoon*, he is the victim of a mix-up. He is supposed to marry the girl whom the other hero (Hrithik Roshan) falls in love with. The theme of this film was somewhat similar to that of Basu Chatterjee's *Chitchor* (1976).

Kunal Kohli's *Hum Tum* and Ram Gopal Verma's *Naach*, both realeased in 2004, failed to create a definite niche for the young aspirant.

In *Hum Tum* he appeared as the heroine's (Rani Mukherji's) husband who dies in a car accident. (He puts in a special appearance in this film; the hero was Saif Ali Khan.)

In *Naach*, he and the heroine (Antara Mali) initially struggle in their respective fields. He wants to be a successful film actor and she a successful choreographer. He achieves his goal and wants to help the heroine, but she wants to make it big on her own.

In Jeeva's *Run* (2004), a simple tale about forbidden love, he was again a small-town student in a metropolis whose girlfriend's overpossessive and highly conservative brother, a powerful don, would punish anyone flirting with his sister.

In Sanjay Gadhvi's *Dhoom* (2004) and *Dhoom 2* (2006), however, Abhishek appeared in a different role: a straightforward detective cop (like his father in *Bunti Aur Babli*) in pursuit of the supersmart tricksters and tech-savvy robbers.

Abhishek's foray into meaningful cinema reflects the interesting thematic concerns of some of the present-day directors.

Gurudev Bhalla's *Shararat* (2002) depicted the evolution of a directionless and thoroughly spoilt brat into a responsible man with a social purpose. The protagonist (Abhishek) is obsessed with speeding in his car, but one day, he gets involved in an accident, with serious repercussions. Instead of sending him to jail, the judge asks him to serve in an old-age home where initially he is unable to develop a rapport with the inmates, but eventually undergoes a change of heart.

In Anupam Kher's *Om Jai Jagdish* (2002), reminiscent of Raj Khosla's *Do Raaste* (1969), he portrayed the transformation of brattish lad (a hacker) into a software wizard who uses his exceptional skills to save his family's house from being auctioned. Anil Kapoor and Fardeen Khan, among others, shared the screen space with Abhishek.

In Apoorva Lakhia's *Mumbai Se Aaya Mere Dost* (2003), the city-bred protagonist becomes an agent of social change in rural India (by installing satellite dishes and TV sets), despite the fact that the film could present only a convoluted view of rural development.

In J. P. Dutta's *LOC Kargil* (2003), he was a daredevil soldier who is awarded the Param Vir Chakra (India's highest military decoration) for his bravery.

In Revathi's *Phir Milenge* (2004), Abhishek posted a riveting performance as a lawyer fighting successfully the case of a distressed woman who has been infected by AIDS after an affair with a man. (See also Chapter 8 under Salman Khan.) Meanwhile, the Supreme Court of India has proclaimed that in AIDS infection precipitated through marriage, the onus of the care and rehabilitation of the sufferer would fall on the other partner if he/she has not declared his/her state of health before marriage.

Mani Ratnam's *Yuva* (2004) presented the young actor in a

realistic political drama (set in Calcutta). He pitched in with an impressive performance in the negative role of a contract killer hired by a local politician to eliminate a firebrand radical student leader. Ajay Devgan and Viveik Oberoi were the other two heroes in this fast-paced film.

In Ram Gopal Verma's *Sarkar* (2005), Abhishek, in a role modelled on the suave Michael Corleone (played by Al Pacino) in the original *Godfather* (1972), very ably captured the transition of a detached son into a cold-blooded avenger. According to a reviewer, the father–son combination of Amitabh (as the senior don with high political and business connections) and Abhishek in this film brought a kind of bridled intensity that was felt when Dilip Kumar and Amitabh played father and son in Ramesh Sippy's *Shakti* (1982).

Mani Ratnam's *Guru* (2007) marked the high point of Abhishek's career. His role as Gurukant Desai (inspired by the saga of Dhirubhai Ambani of Reliance fame) seemed to be tailor-made for him. As the noted film critic Khalid Mohammed writes (*Hindustan Times*, 13 January 2007): '... the [film] belongs to Abhishek Bachchan – he is astonishingly nuanced and unwaveringly forceful in his career-best performance after *Yuva*. The work presents very vividly the mind-boggling economic consolidation of the neo-rich brand of India's business class, notorious for manipulating all the means to appropriate the nation's wealth (unlike Mahatma Gandhi's celebrated view that the business people are mere trustees of the wealth generated by them for the nation and therefore are accountable to society). In the rags-to-riches story, the protagonist is an absolutely focused calculating young man determined to capture ... centre stage in business by adopting an entirely new methodology for generating wealth. After a long struggle he finally emerges as a textile tycoon and [is] hailed as the "visionary", spearheading the country's rapid economic development and also the role model for the success-hungry neo-rich class.' Abhsihek was truly in his element as also were other members of the cast, including Aishwarya Rai (who played his wife) and Mithun Chakraborty (who played a media magnate).

Laaga Chunari Mein Daag (2007), directed by Pradeep Sarkar, was a powerful depiction of women's plight in today's harsh competitive world. Badki (Rani Mukherji), the eldest daughter of a family from Varanasi, had come to Bombay to find work so that she could support her family back home and also fund her younger sister's education. But as she struggles to earn a living in the lecherous metropolis and runs out of options, she ends up becoming a high-class call girl. Abhishek essayed the role of an enlightened young man, a lawyer by profession, who knowingly falls in love with Badki. Although she leaves her suitor, thinking that he would be disgusted by her profession, the hero in the end marries her.

In Anubhav Sinha's *Dus* (2008), Abhishek featured as the younger brother of the head of the Anti-Terrorist Cell (played by Sanjay Dutt) sent to bust a terrorist set-up in Canada, keeping the mission unofficial and secret from the Canadian authorities. He dies while taking away a bomb to be planted at a football stadium, meant to kill thousands of people.

Drona (2008, directed by Goldie Behl), a fantasy action adventure film designed in the format of the Harry Potter and Indiana Jones movies, cast Abhishek in the role of a lone crusader, who has to guard a cosmic secret that has remained unrevealed for millennia. According to the legend, if this precious secret is revealed, it will lead to the destruction of the entire cosmos and the annihilation of mankind. The narrative was built around numerous special-effect shots engineered by EyeQube (a company specializing in computer animation).

Tarun Mansukhani's *Dostana* (2008), a youthful comedy, featured Abhishek as a light-hearted seducer in love with a girl (Priyanka Chopra) who is also being sought by his buddy John Abraham. He and John pretend to be gays in order to get accommodation in an apartment in Miami, Florida (USA).

The landlady wants to ensure that no male makes any overtures towards her niece.

In *Sarkar Raj* (2008, directed by Ram Gopal Verma), the sequel to *Sarkar*, Abhishek tries to convince his father (played by his real father Amitabh Bachchan) to grant his approval for a power project in rural Maharashtra, which is to be financed by a foreign company (represented by Aishwarya Rai). The senior is worried about the large-scale displacement of people that such a project would lead to. Behind the scenes, however, many sinister forces are working to eliminate both Abhishek and his father.

In Mani Ratnam's latest venture, *Raavan* (under production), Abhishek plays a role based on the eponymous demon king of Lanka, the main villain in the epic Ramayana. When the hero's sister is humiliated publicly by a character played by Vikram (a well-known South Indian actor), Abhishek kidnaps Vikram's wife (played by Aishwarya Rai) as revenge. They seek shelter in a jungle after being chased by the police. Soon, they fall in love. *Raavan* is also being made in simultaneously in Tamil with the title *Ashokavanam*.

Despite his fairly impressive track record, Abhishek is yet to attain the status of the foremost hero figure in Hindi cinema as his father did in his younger days. Although he does possess some of the characteristics of the classical era hero, he apparently seeks to build his screen presence as the new-age hero comparable with his more flamboyant and upmarket contemporaries. This sensitive actor holds much promise in that he can push forward the legacy of his illustrious father. His cine image and acting acumen may even inspire film makers to venture into more meaningful and purposeful cinema. For instance, he could emerge as the ideal protagonist for movies focused on the present social, cultural and political issues.

Viveik (Anand) Oberoi

At an actors' workshop in London in the early 1990s, a director from one of the faculties of New York University spotted a young talented participant from India and took him to his university to study in a course leading to a Masters in film acting. On his return to India, this formally trained young actor, Viveik Oberoi, was cast by Ram Gopal Verma's in *Company* (released in 2002) in the role of an ambitious don who defies his own mentor (Ajay Devgan). (For more details, see Chapter 8 under Ajay Devgan.)

Viveik Oberoi

Viveik's performance in this film was greatly appreciated and he bagged two awards: best actor in a supporting role and best debut.

Viveik, one of the sons of actor Suresh Oberoi, was born on 3 September 1976 in Bombay. He attended Mayo College, Ajmer (Rajasthan), before going to New York.

Company was soon followed by Rajat Mukherjee's *Road* (2002), in which he (along with his girlfriend, Antara Mali) appeared as the harassed victim of a serial killer (Manoj Bajpai) who has taken refuge in his vehicle. Viveik and Antara have eloped and are travelling in a car, and offer a lift to a hitchhiker who turns out to be a killer.

Viveik then expanded his repertoire to portray an assortment of interesting characters.

In Shaad Ali's *Saathiya* (2002), he appeared as a commonplace husband in frantic search of his wife, a medical student, who has left him due to unbearable marital discord.

He donned the mantle of a self-proclaimed dispenser of justice under the shadow of the police system in E. Nivas's *Dum* (2003).

In Ram Gopal Verma's *Darna Mana Hai* (2003, a film with six stories woven into it), he appeared as a 'ghost'!

He depicted an aggressive student leader in Mani Ratnam's *Yuva* (2004), in which Ajay Devgan and Abhishek Bachchan too played important roles.

In Vishal Bharadwaj's *Omkara* (2006), Viveik delineated the character of Kesu Firangi effectively. (See also Chapter 8 under Ajay Devgan.)

He pitched in as a daredevil youth who joins his stepbrother to trace the mysterious map in Sachin Bajaj's *Naksha* (2006). (For more details, see Chapter 7 under Sunny Deol.)

In Apoorva Lakhia's thriller, *Shootout at Lokhandwala* (2007), inspired by the massacre of the Maya Dolas gang by a police task force in 1991, Viveik appeared in the role of this dreaded gangster. The huge star cast included Amitabh Bachchan and Sanjay Dutt.

In the same director's *Mission Istaanbul* (2008), Viveik appeared as Rizwan Khan, a Turkish commando who assists an Indian TV journalist, Vikas Sagar (played by Zayed Khan), in carrying out a mission against an Istaanbul-based TV channel, which is a cover organization for certain international terrorist groups.

Apart from the aforementioned genres, Viveik has also ventured into comedy.

In Indra Kumar's *Masti* (2004), he appeared as one of the irresponsible husbands (the others were Riteish Deshmukh and Aftab Shivdasani) who defy societal norms and try to allure young girls. However, one of the girls they are involved with is killed and this development leads to all sorts of complications.

Sujoy Ghosh's *Home Delivery* (2005) featured Viveik as a young energetic newspaper columnist (a workaholic) who is also a screenplay writer and has deadlines to meet. One day, he realizes that he has no food in the house and decides to order a pizza, which is home-delivered by Boman Irani. Irani's entry into Viveik's life changes his world forever. He loses his job at at the newspaper; he breaks up with his fiancée (Ayesha Takia); and begins dating a popular film star (Mahima Chaudhary). Also, he is forced to make excuses to Karan Johar (a well-known producer and director, who plays himself in the movie), whose script he is yet to complete. To top it all, he leaves himself open to attack by a crazed killer!

In Soham Shah's *Kaal* (2005), he played a fun-loving adventurer (see also Chapter 8 under Ajay Devgan).

As already mentioned in Chapter 8, in Indra Kumar's *Pyare Mohan* (2006), he portrayed the aurally challenged Mohan.

Ahmed Khan's *Fool n Final* (2007) cast Viveik as a small-time crook who promotes new fighters wanting to take part in illegal boxing matches in Dubai. He has a priceless diamond in his possession, which is being sought by three gangsters.

John Abraham

In the new millennium, the arrival of John Abraham – with a truly macho physique – marked the definite modernization of the Hindi film hero's image both in looks and in the delineation of lifestyle. A model-turned-actor, he was born on 17 December 1972 in Bombay. After obtaining his MBA, he started his career as a media planner. He emerged as the winner in 1999 Gladrags Manhunt Contest and bagged many assignments as a model. He then entered Bollywood.

John's first two films (both released in 2003 and both controversial) – Amit Saxena's *Jism* and Pooja Bhatt's *Paap* – dealt with the impact of a hyperactive libido on an individual's life.

John Abraham

In *Jism*, he appeared in the role of a young lawyer seduced by an ambitious and scheming married woman (Bipasha Basu). She wants John to finish off her husband so that she can inherit his property. The film made waves because of its steamy sex scenes.

In *Paap*, an interesting film about the man–woman relationship in the context of one's spiritual search for innner peace, John portrayed a police officer charged with investigating the murder of another cop witnessed by a young female Buddhist nun (Udita Goswami) and a young child thought to be reborn as the revered Buddhist teacher, the Rinpoche. He is forced to make an escape to Spiti (a place high in the snow-clad mountains of Himachal Pradesh) along with the nun and the young boy, where the nun falls in love with him. He helps her in coming to terms with the dilemma of her spiritual search within and satisfying her long subdued natural instincts for intimate love.

Anurag Basu's *Saaya*, a movie dealing with a paranormal subject and also released in 2003, was about the hero's (John Abraham) links with the spirit of his dead wife, a doctor engaged in providing health services in a rural area who has died in an accident.

In Sanjay Gadhvi's *Dhoom* (2004), John's hero ushered into Indian cinema the prototype of the ultramodern and tech-savvy youth driven by an obsession for superspeed bikes and for amassing wealth quickly. He is the leader of a group of bikers who plan to steal money to upgrade their lifestyle. He is pursued by a diligent cop (Abhishek Bachchan) who manages to trap him as he is about to rob a casino. In the end, his obsession with speed leads him to his death as he drives his bike over a cliff.

In Priyadarshan's *Garam Masala* (2005), he was a struggling fashion photographer who steals the work of his fellow photographer (Akshay Kumar).

In Kabir Khan's *Kabul Express* (2006), a story set in war-torn Afghanistan post the 9/11 attacks on the USA, John appeared as an Indian TV journalist Suhel Khan, who along with three others – a TV journalist Jai Kapoor (Arshad Warsi), a photo journalist Jessica Beckham (Linda Arsenio) and their Afghan guide – is taken hostage by a Pakistani soldier on his way back to his country's border. He herds them into a jeep labelled 'Kabul Express', and they travel towards Pakistan hiding their identity from the soldiers of the Northern Alliance (an Afghani group fighting the Taliban) and the Hazara militants operating along the route. During their 48-hour journey, faced with inevitable danger at virtually every stage, the hostages develop a strong bond among themselves.

In Nikhil Advani's multistarrer *Salaam-e-Ishq: A Tribute to Love* (2007), John was featured as a caring husband who helps his wife recover her memory, which she has lost in an accident.

Vivek Agnihotri's *Dhan Dhana Dhan Goal* (2007), a low-key version of Shimit Amin's *Chak De India* (released earlier the same year), presented John in the role of a UK-settled ace football player, who is caught in the murky squabbling prevalent among various club teams. After he is discriminated against (as he is of Indian origin) by a whites-only team, he goes over to another team made up of players from South Asia. He ensures that his team emerges victorious in the matches it plays.

John's association with 'serious' cinema till date is represented by the following films.

In Deepa Mehta's *Water* (2005), set in the colonial India of the late 1930s, John underwent a complete change of image and appeared for the first time in a culture-specific role. He got rid of the 'hunk' label. He portrayed an upper-class idealistic Gandhian youth, who is moved by the plight of the Hindu widows in Varanasi living under miserable conditions as victims of a cruel and oppressive system. They are forced to lead lives marked by extreme penitence and deprivation. As he seeks the love and attention of a young widow (Lisa Ray), he starts convincing the women to question both their faith and their future. He gets ample support from a feisty child widow, who, with her innocence, brings in an air of freshness and warmth among the dejected and despondent dwellers of an ashram. The film was nominated for the Best Foreign Language Film at the 79th Oscar Awards.

Ravi Chopra's *Baabul* (2005) presented John as a progressive NRI youth, ready to marry Rani Mukherji, who has lost her husband (Salman Khan).

In Milan Luthria's *Taxi No. 9211* (2006), John portrayed the inner transformation of today's rich, carefree and, at times, arrogant youth into a responsible individual. He is the son of a very affluent business magnate who is forced to take a taxi (because he is unable to use his car, which has developed some defects) driven by Nana Patekar as he has to produce a document in court (his father's will) so that he can win his case against another person who claims his (John's) father's property. He constantly urges Nana Patekar to drive faster and, eventually, the taxi gets involved in an accident. John then rushes on foot towards the place where the will is kept (in a locker). He then realizes that has lost the key to the locker, which he surmises must have fallen in the taxi. Patekar finds the key and steals the will from the locker after John (who manages to get the taxi driver's address and reaches his house, where he meets Patekar's wife) informs her that her husband is a taxi driver and not an insurance agent as she been led to believe. She leaves the house in a huff. John finds the torn will. He soon realizes the fulility of unearned money. He then sets out to reunite Patekar and his wife.

In Anurag Kashyap's film *No Smoking* (2007), designed as a powerful anti-tobacco statement, John appeared as a chain smoker, who opts for unconventional treatment to shake off the habit after his wife (Ayesha Takia) leaves him.

In *Dostana* (2008), John appeared along with Abhishek Bachchan. (This film has already been discussed earlier in this chapter.)

Nagesh Kukunoor's *Aashayein* (2009) was about a fun-loving, self-obsessed youth (played by John) who has only 90 days to live. He moves into a calm hospice where he discovers a new meaning to life and a rekindling of courage to face his inevitable death through his interactions with the inmates.

John has also starred in Sooni Taraporevala's *Little Zizou* (2009), a movie about a Parsi boy's obsession with football and his desire to meet the famous player Zinedine Zidane.

In Deepa Mehta's film *Luna* (2009), he portrays an environmentalist. This film is based on the true story of an American who protested against the felling of trees.

In Kabir Khan's *New York* (2009) John's character as a suspected terrorist was greatly appreciated. This film was set against the 9/11 backdrop.

David Dhawan's *Hook Ya Crook* (under production), a comic thriller based on cricket, presents John Abraham, Kay Kay Menon, Shreyas Talpade and Genelia D'Souza in key roles.

Other Heroes in the Fray

In the new millennium, a host of new heroes have come up in Bollywood in quick sucession, contending vigorously to carve a niche for themselves. Those with family connections include

- Javed Jaffrey (*Jajantrum Mamantrum*, 2003), the son the comedian Jagdeep,
- Tusshar Kapoor (*Mujhe Kucch Kehna Hai*, 2001, *Kyaa Dil Ne Kahaa*, 2002, *Jeena Sirf Merre Liye*, 2002, *Gayab*, 2004, *Kyaa Kool Hai Hum*, 2005, and *Aggar*, 2007, among other films), the son of Jeetendra,
- Ranbir Kapoor (*Sawariya*, 2007, and *Bachna Ae Haseenon*, 2008, *Wake Up Sid*, 2009), the son of Rishi Kapoor,
- Shahid Kapoor (*Ishq Vishk*, 2003, *Fida*, 2004, *Dil Maange More*, 2004, *Vaah! Life Ho To Aisi!*, 2005, *Chup Chup Ke*, 2006, *Vivah*, 2006, *Jab We Met*, 2007, *Kismat Konnection*, 2008, *Kaminey*, 2009 and, *Dil Bole Hadipa* (2009), among other films), the son of character actor Pankaj Kapoor (who also featured in several TV serials),
- Sanjay Kapoor (*Prem*, 1995, *Raja*, 1995, *Auzar*, 1997, and *LOC Kargil*, 2003, among other films), the younger brother of Anil Kapoor,
- Riteish Deshmukh (*Tujhe Meri Kasam*, 2003, *Masti*, 2004, *Kyaa Kool Hai Hum*, 2005, *Bluffmaster*, 2005, *Cash*, 2007, *Heyy Babyy*,

2007, and *Dhamaal*, 2007, among other films), the son of
Vilasrao Deshmukh, the former chief minister of Maharashtra
and later a Union minister;

- Imran Khan (*Jaane Tu Ya Jaane Na*, 2008, *Kidnap*, 2008, and *Luck*,
  2008), the nephew of Aamir Khan;
- Neil Nitin Mukesh (*Johnny Gaddaar*, 2007, and *New York*, 2009),
  the grandson of the famous playback singer Mukesh;
- Zayed Khan (*Chura Liya Hai Tumne*, 2003, *Main Hoon Na*, 2004,
  Dus, 2005, *Cash*, 2007, *Mission Istaanbul*, 2008 and *Yuvraaj*, 2008),
  the son of Sanjay Khan and Fardeen Khan's cousin, and
- Abhay Deol (*Socha Na Tha*, 2005, *Ahista Ahista*, 2006, *Ek Chalis
  Ki Last Local*, 2007, *Oye Lucky! Lucky Oye!*, 2008, and *Dev D*,
  2009), the nephew of Dharmendra and the cousin of Sunny
  Deol and Bobby Deol. (*Dev D*, an unconventional presentation
  of the classic *Devdas*, got rave reviews.)

These heroes are facing competition from a flock of other
promising entrants who have largely made it on their own in the
film world. For example,

- Roshan (Shiney) Ahuja (*Hazaaron Khwaishen Aisi*, 2003, *Life in
  a Metro*, 2007, and *Khoya Khoya Chand*, 2007, among other
  films),
- Shreyas Talpade (*Iqbal*, 2005,* *Dor*, 2006, *Aggar*, 2006, *Om
  Shanti Om*, 2007, and *Welcome to Sajjanpur*, 2008),
- Arjun Rampal (*Dewanapan*, 2001, and *I See You*, 2006, among
  other films),
- Emraan Hashmi (*Footpath*, 2003, *Murder*, 2004, *Zeher*, 2005,
  and *Raaz – The Mystery Continues*, 2009, among other films),
- Himesh Reshammiya** (*Aap Ka Saroor*, 2007, and *Karzzzz*,
  2008),

---

* Nagesh Kukunoor's *Iqbal* was a highly inspiring movie that showed how a
small-town boy, despite being unable to hear or speak, makes it to the Indian
cricket team through perseverance and commitment.
** Himesh Reshammiya is basically a composer and a singer.

- Kunal Khemu (*Kalyug*, 2005, *Traffic Signal*, 2007, and *Superstar*, 2008),
- Jimmy Shergill (*Machchis*, 1996, *Mohabbatein*, 2000, *Silsilay*, 2005, and *Dus Kahaniyaan*, 2007, among other films)
- Ranvir Shorey (*Ek Chhotisi Love Story*, 2002, *Khosla Ka Ghosla*, 2006, and *Mithya*, 2008, among other films) and
- Anurag Sinha, who made an impressive debut in Subhash Ghai's *Black & White* (2008).

The New-Age Heroes as Victims

As evident from the cinema of the new-age protagonists, these actors (and other new faces arriving regularly on the scene) are becoming victims of the continuing downfall of HIndi cinema and the resulting changes in the persona of the film hero. The talents and energies of these actors are being dissipated in endless films depicting a crude mixture of superficial teen romances, sensational politics, underworld operations, uncouth violence, ghastly murders and sexual innuendo, apart from raunchy songs and titillating 'dances'. They often look overwhelmed and bewildered amidst the excess of everything in their films: characters, subplots, spectacular chases and fights, guns, big cars and other gizmos. It would make a little difference to the quality and content of a film if one hero were replaced with another.

Apart from a few exceptions (like Aamir Khan), these actors, in fact, are flowing with the tide, unable to stand on their own as the frontal figure to give any direction or focus to Hindi cinema. Unable to lend new meaning and purpose to the social context of cinema, their characterizations are not reflective of the socio-economic inequalities plaguing present-day society, but are a crude justification of the status quo. Even their films of the serious genre are in general simplistic and patchy, largely failing to evoke a passionate interpretation of social reality. Their histrionics too do not possess an innate power or intensity to become part of the viewers' memory, as was the case with their illustrious predecessors.

None of these actors, at least for the time being, could become the truly emblematic hero of the present times. They are in search of identity in a cinema that has lost its roots and where utter confusion prevails. Equally unfortunate is their inability to garner worthwhile opportunities by inspiring the film makers to venture wholeheartedly into a new sphere of meaningful cinema.

As Hindi cinema is increasingly moving beyond the domain of committed indigenous directors with a well-defined vision guiding their creative pursuits, the film stars are required merely to create a fanciful rapport with their upmarket viewers. This state of affairs has simplified not only the task of the artistes but also that of scriptwriters and the directors. In fact, none of the present-day performances compare favourably with those of artistes who were considered 'average' in the earlier times. The seemingly unending 'modernization' of the Hindi film has indeed scuttled the basic process of selecting new talents, irrespective of the source. Nowadays, elite family connections largely provide the new breed of actors and actresses.

Barring a few exceptions, it seems as if good cine artistes are no more born, scouted for or created. In the absence of the earlier studio system for training of young artistes, film schools and theatre could have been the main source of new talent. However, the contribution of the Film and Television Training Institute of India (FTTII), Pune, and the National School of Drama, New Delhi, and other such institutions (mostly private) over the past many decades has been only marginal. In contrast, some of the best artistes in Western cinema continue to have their origins in theatre before their introduction to celluloid.

Thus, as the offspring or relatives of established film personalities in various fields crowd the film sets, openings are no more readily available for the people from the ordinary world: like the street singer from Jalandhar. the gatekeeper of a theatre, the son of a fruit merchant, a runway youth from a moffusil town or a tubewell mechanic from Punjab. In present times, legends are no more in the making and the contribution of the earlier ones is seen as redundant; they are revered sometimes but do not inspire any more.

Chapter 10

The 'Misfits'

Amidst the top-notch actors and the ever-growing population of the new-age hero, the 'misfits' – Kamalahasan, Naseeruddin Shah, Om Puri, Nana Patekar, Manoj Bajpai, Kay Kay Menon, Arshad Warsi, Rahul Bose and Irfan Khan – represent a different category altogether. All of them possess amazing proficiency and precision in the cinematic art, blending their powerful cine persona with the context and content of a definitive and meaningful cinema. While the first four are relatively senior actors, the others reached the film world in the 1990s and made their presence felt in the new millennium as well.

Kamalahasan

Kamalahasan (born on 7 November 1954 in Paramakudi, Tamil Nadu), perhaps the most versatile third-generation actor of Indian cinema after Amitabh Bachchan, could have proved an ideal contender for the indigenous hero. Unfortunately, his success rate in Hindi films remains questionable as compared to that in his South Indian films (mainly in Tamil). With a screen persona rooted in the cultural traditions of the country as well as reflecting a genuine sense of Indian modernity, he brought into his acting style a rare blending of simplicity, naturalism and intensive underplay. Starting off as a child artiste in *Kallathur Kannamma* in 1960, he made his debut as hero in K. Balachander's

Arangetram (1973). He then featured in a string of films by the same director during the 1970s. Kamalahasan hit big time with the Telugu hit *Maro Charithra* (1978) and in its equally successful Hindi remake, *Ek Duje Ke Liye* (1981), both directed by the aforementioned Balachander. He then appeared in some Hindi films such as Narendra Bedi's *Sanam Teri Kasam* (1982), Rama Rao Tatineni's *Yeh To Kamaal Ho Gaya* (1982), K. Balachander's *Zara Si Zindagi* (1983), Balu

Kamalahasan

Mahendru's *Sadma* (1983), Ramesh Sippy's *Sagar* (1985) and Prayag Raj's *Giraftar* (1985). In *Sagar*, he essayed a role similar to that played by Dilip Kumar in the classic *Insaniyat* (1955).

An innovative experimenter in the art of cinema, Kamalahasan has continuously worked on remodelling his persona in one film after another. In the early 1980s, he broke away from his established image by appearing as a Bharatanatyam dancer-cum-teacher in K. Vishwanath's Telugu movie *Sagara Sangamam* (1983). He held the viewers spellbound with his phenomenal dancing skills. This film was followed by terrific comedy in the silent film *Pushpak* (1988, directed by Srinivasa Rao Singeetham). In Mani Ratnam's *Nayakan* (1987, in Tamil), he won tremendous critical acclaim for his role as a benevolent mafia lord, worshipped by the people (à la Godfather). In Srinivasa Rao Singeetham's *Apoorva Sahodarargal* (1989, in Tamil), as a dwarf, and in *Chachi 420* (1998, directed by himself, and inspired by *Mrs Doubtfire*, 1993) as a young urbanite who disguises himself as an elderly woman, Kamalahasan exhibited his immense skills in depicting physical transformations (inspired by such efforts by Hollywood actors such as Robert De Niro, Robin Williams and Dustin Hoffman).

Thevar Magan (1993, directed by Bharathan) focused on undercurrents of feudalism in Tamil Nadu. Here, Kamalahasan was facing his formidable predecessor Sivaji Ganesan in what turned out to be a stupendous show of comparative acting (à la Dilip Kumar pitted against Amitabh Bachchan in *Shakti*, 1982).

In *Indian* (1996, directed by S. Shankar), he portrayed a disillusioned commoner turned vigilante hero.

Hey Ram (2000), his magnum opus, further validated his histrionics as an actor as well as producer-director. This film (which featured Shahrukh Khan as well) provided a different interpretation of communalism in the background of Partition.

In 2005, he featured in the thriller *Mumbai Express* (directed by Srinivasa Rao Singeetham).

In a unique experimental movie, in K. S. Ravikumar's *Dasavatram* (2008, in Tamil), he appeared in ten different roles, including one as the former US president, George W. Bush. The Hindi version of this film was released in early 2009.

However, the inability of this great artiste to reach the heights of stardom in Hindi cinema is unfortunate as well as intriguing.

Naseeruddin Shah

Naseeruddin Shah's name evokes the heydays of India's new-wave or parallel cinema of the 1970s and 1980s. He is one of the few Bollywood actors who has negotiated new-wave, mainstream and international cinema, not to mention the theatre and TV, with remarkable finesse and felicity.

Naseeruddin Shah

Like his illustrious predecessor Balraj Sahni (see Chapter 10, Volume 1), Shah is a thinker-actor, and with his seemingly casual but yet intense bearing coupled with a slightly hesitant speech pattern, he has lent (and continues to lend) an impressive aura to the wide range of his realist characterizations.

Shah was born on 20 March 1950* in Barabanki, Uttar Pradesh. He did his schooling at St Anselm's, Ajmer (Rajasthan),

---

*Some sources give his date of birth as 20 July 1950.

and his graduation from the Aligarh Muslim University. He then joined the National School of Drama in Delhi and later the Film and Television Institute of India (FTII), Pune. He soon emerged as a professional actor.

Shah became the reigning 'king' of India's new-wave cinema immediately after his debut in 1975 in Shyam Benegal's highly acclaimed *Nishant*. He appeared in a negative role as the younger brother of a tyrant landlord family, who, along with his brothers, rape a school master's wife (Shabana Azmi). Eventually, he keeps her as his mistress. The vengeful teacher, with the help of a priest, leads an uprising against the seemingly never-ending feudal oppression, resulting in the killing of the landlord brothers.

After *Nishant*, Shah became the hot favourite of several new-wave film makers, appearing in at least 20 films in quick succession.

In *Bhumika* (1977), also directed by Benegal, he again portrayed a negative character – a nihilistic and self-centred film director who has an affair with a desperately unhappy married film actress, played by Smita Patil, but disappears when they decide to end their lives together.

In yet another Benegal film, *Junoon* (1979, based on Ruskin Bond's story 'The Flight of Pigeons'), set at the time of the 1857 Mutiny, he appeared as Sarfaraz Khan, a fanatic freedom fighter who has a pathological hatred for the British. The intensity of his performance was one of the highlights of the film. (See Chapter 5 under Shashi Kapoor for more details.)

In Sai Paranjpye's *Sparsh* (1980), Shah won critical acclaim for portraying the commitment of a blind teacher to demonstrate that visually challenged children are no less talented and no less self-sufficient than the others. When a singer-turned-committed social worker (Shabana Azmi) joins his mission and wants to marry him, he thinks her love for him is out of pity, which puts him in a quandary. Shah won the National Award for Best Actor for this film.

Aakrosh (1980), cinematographer Govind Nihalani's directorial debut and written by the renowned Marathi playwright Vijay Tendulkar, was based on an actual incident in Bhiwandi, a small town outside Bombay. Shah appeared as a committed lawyer who is appointed to defend a tribal (Om Puri) accused of murdering his wife. But the accused, stunned by excessive oppression and violation of his humanity, does not utter a single word. After a long investigation, during which his own life comes under threat, the lawyer reveals in court that the man's wife had been raped and killed by a group of evil men. Shah received the *Filmfare* Best Actor Award for this role.

Saeed Akhtar Mirza's *Albert Pinto Ko Gussa Kyon Aata Hai* (1980) was Shah's first lead role. The film was about the radical transformation into a responsible adult of a garage mechanic (Shah) who wants to own expensive cars but is troubled by his girlfriend Stella's (Shabana Azmi) flirting with his colleagues and also by the fact that his lecherous boss wants to 'possess' her. He becomes a politically aware youth when his father joins the textile workers' strike. The film depicted quite realistically the turmoils of urban life in the late 1970s.

Chakra (1980), directed by Rabindra Dharmaraj, brought on screen the desperate struggle for survival amid oppression in Bombay's slums. This film portrayed Shah as a petty crook and pimp (and a drug addict to boot) who gives shelter to Amma (Smita Patil) and her son when they flee from their village to seek shelter in Bombay's slums after her husband has killed a lascivious moneylender. For this role, Shah won the *Filmfare* Best Actor Award. Finally, the slum in which they stay is demolished and they all move on as the *chakra* (wheel) of life rolls on.

In Mrinal Sen's *Khandhar* (1984), an existentialist story reflecting loneliness and loss of hope, Shah portrayed a photographer who pretends to be the fiancé of a girl (Shabana Azmi) living with her aged mother in a ruined house in a village so that the old lady can die a peaceful death. (The real fiancé is married to someone else in a big city.)

Paar (1984), directed by Gautam Ghose, was set against the backdrop of feudal oppression. Shah appeared as a vengeful labourer, Naurangia, who kills a landlord's brother as the latter's men have murdered the benevolent schoolmaster of his village. Naurangia and his wife Rama (Shabana Azmi) flee the village but fail to find livelihood anywhere else. As the couple decides to return home, they are asked to drive a herd of pigs through a river to earn some money. The then pregnant Rama believes she has lost her baby while carrying out this difficult task. But the baby survives. Shah won kudos for his role and received the National Award for the Best Actor and also the Best Actor Award at the Venice Film Festival, 1985.

In Ketan Mehta's *Mirch Masala* (1985), set during the colonial era, Shah essayed the role of prurient, despotic tax collector who commands a village girl (Smita Patil) to sleep with him, but she manages to flee from his clutches. In the end, when he breaks into the place where several women (including Smita Patil) pound chillies to make masala, they, in a swift move, throw powdered chilli into his eyes.

In *Ek Pal* (1986), directed by Kalpana Lajmi, a bold film on woman's sexual autonomy, Shah was the sober but loving husband who accepts both his unfaithful wife (Shabana Azmi) and her baby after she has an affair with her former lover in his absence.

In Aruna Raje's *Rihaee* (1988), also an exposition on woman's right to motherhood, Shah appeared in the role of a seducer who makes a virtuous married woman pregnant. The woman refuses to comply with the diktat of the village elders asking her to forcibly terminate the pregnancy.

Apart from the above films, Shah also came up with riveting performances in Shyam Benegal's *Manthan* (1976), Ketan Mehta's *Bhavani Bhavai* (1980), Muzaffar Ali's *Umrao Jaan* (1981), Sagar Sarhadi's *Bazaar* (1982), Saeed Akhtar Mirza's *Mohan Joshi Hazir Ho!* (1984), Ketan Mehta's *Holi* (1984), Shyam Benegal's *Trikaal* (1985), Vijaya Mehta's *Pestonjee* (1988) and Girish Kasaravalli's *Ek Ghar* (1991).

Shah entered the mainstream cinema in 1980 with *Hum Paanch*, film maker Bapu's adaptation of the Mahabharata epic to the feudal milieu of rural India.

A number of 'commercial' films followed such as J. P. Dutta's *Ghulami* (1985), Subhash Ghai's *Karma* (1986) and Rajiv Rai's *Tridev* (1989) and *Vishwatma* (1992). In these movies, he was one among the many heroes.

In *Ghulami*, a Dharmendra–Mithun Chakraborty starrer, Shah played a police officer siding with his villainous landlord father-in-law causing much unhappiness to his wife (Smita Patil).

In *Karma*, he appeared along with Dilip Kumar, Jackie Shroff and Anil Kapoor in the memorable role of Khairu, a murderer convicted to death but selected to wage a war against Dr Dang (Anupam Kher), the head of an international terrorist organization. (For more details, see Chapter 5, Vol. 1.)

In *Tridev*, Shah appeared as a charming but reckless villager always ready to fight for the oppressed and helps Sunny Deol (a police officer) and Jackie Shroff (who wants to take revenge against the villain who has kidnapped his sister). The three of them combine their efforts and ultimately punish the villain.

Vishwatma presented him in the role of an upright Kenyan police officer of Indian origin who insists that the hero and his assistant (Sunny Deol and Chunky Pandey, policemen who have come to Kenya from India) in their mission to apprehend an elusive criminal must follow the Kenyan law.

Shah appeared as the 'solo' hero in Shekhar Kapur's *Masoom* (1983), Pankaj Parashar's *Jalwa* (1987), Gulzar's *Ijaazat* (1987) and Mahesh Bhatt's *Sir* (1993).

Masoom was a sensitive story about an 'illegitimate' child. Shah, his wife (Shabana Azmi) and two schoolgoing daughters are leading an ideal life in Delhi. One day, he comes to know that when he had a visited a hill station many years ago and had fallen in love with a local girl (Supriya Pathak, whom he had impregnated), she had given birth to a son. He then brings his son to his Delhi home, but his wife is not ready to accept him although his daughters are. The film's musical score by Rahul Dev Burman was one of its highlights. Shah received the *Filmfare* Best Actor Award for this film.

In *Jalwa*, he pitched in as a Bombay police officer who loses his brother to drugs and also witnesses the death of a friend. His investigation leads him to Goa, but the local police do not want him there. He on his own and with some help from the heroine goes after the villain (played by Tejeshwar Singh) and exposes a narcotics cartel.

Ijaazat, a love triangle, was based on *Jatugriha*, a novel by the noted Bengali writer Subhodh Ghosh and made into a Bengali movie in 1964 directed by Tapan Sinha starring Uttam Kumar and Arundhati Devi. In this sensitively made film, he has Rekha and Anuradha Patel for company. Composer Rahul Dev Burman came up with some melodious numbers sung by Asha Bhosle.

In *Sir*, Shah portrayed a professor living with his wife and his son. His son becomes the victim of a gang war shootout, in which many other innocent bystanders are also killed. He is shattered. His wife then walks out on him. He then decides to devote his life to his students. When he finds out that one of his students suffers from stammering, he wants to help her. She turns out to be the only child of the dreaded gangster, some of whose gang members were responsible for his son's death. Nevertheless, he attempts to bring about a truce between the rival gangs.

Shah broke away from his image as a 'serious' actor and indulged in several comic roles in films such as Sai Paranjpye's *Katha* (1983), the riproaring comedy *Jaane Bhi Do Yaaron* (1983), directed by Kundan Shah, Kawal Sharma's *Malamaal* (1988) and Ketan Mehta's *Hero Hiralal* (1988).

Katha, inspired by the popular parable of the hare and tortoise, was about two competing characters: the slow-but-sure upwardly mobile clerk (Naseeruddin Shah) and the easygoing but fast-working charmer (Farooque Sheikh). Both of them are out to win over the heroine's (Deepti Naval) heart.

In *Jaane Bhi Do Yaaron*, two professional photographers (Ravi Baswani and Naseeruddin Shah) set up a studio in an upmarket area of Bombay, but their venture fails to get going. They are disheartened. Fortunately, they are assigned a job by the editor of a magazine (Bhakti Barve) that seeks to expose the scandalous lives of the high and mighty. Along with the editor, they begin exposing the links between an unscrupulous builder (Pankaj Kapoor) and a corrupt municipal commissioner D'Mello (Satish Shah). During the course of their assignment, they discover that another shady builder (Om Puri) too is involved in the nefarious activities. In between Shah and Baswani enter a photography contest hoping to win the prize money. They take many photographs at different locations. On developing the negatives, in one of the photographs, they are amazed to discover a shooting scene. Upon magnifying the photograph they find that the killer is Pankaj Kapoor. They immediately return to the place (a garden) where they had taken that photograph and notice a body amidst the bushes. The body disappears suddenly but they manage to eventually trace it. The corpse is that of D'Mello. After a series of hilarious sequences, the duo manages to corner the villain. The dead body also plays a 'live' role in the fast-paced events!

In *Malamaal*, Shah inherits ancestral wealth on the condition that he has to spend a certain massive amount within a prescribed (brief) period.

In *Hero Hiralal*, Shah portrayed a happy-go-lucky autorickshaw driver from Hyderabad who is a diehard movie buff. He constantly spouts dialogues from various movies. He falls in love with an actress (Sanjana Kapoor) when a film unit comes to Hyderabad for shooting. When his love is spurned, he drives his auto to Bombay. He seeks out the heroine, but is rebuffed by her stepmother and the villain. Then, he meets Deepa Shahi (a publicity agent with daring plans). He tells her he is willing to commit suicide for love. She then comes up up the idea of a grand spectacle in which the hero would be enclosed in a sealed glass box, into which water would be slowly let in till the box becomes full: in other words, it would be a daredevil act in full view of the public. Eventually, love triumphs and the hero is saved from a watery death.

In international cinema, Shah has worked in the Ismail Merchant–James Ivory English-language film *The Perfect Murder* (1988, directed by Zafar Hai), in which he appeared as Inspector Ganesh Ghote, the fictional detective of H. R. F. Keating's novels. Stephen Norrington's *The League of Extraordinary Gentlemen* (2003) was a film (set during the Victorian times) based on the comic book series of the same name. Shah appeared as Captain Nemo, commander of the world's only submersible vessel, the *Nautilus*, who, along with a bunch of extraordinary people, has been commissioned to combat the threat of the evil 'Fantom', who is bent upon destroying the world. Apart from Shah, the film starred Sean Connery, Peta Wilson and Tony Curran. In *Monsoon Wedding* (2001) directed by Mira Nair, Shah played a typical Delhi-based Punjabi businessman, who is trying to organize his daughter's wedding on a grand scale. The whole family comes together from different parts of the world. All the resultant chaos, uncertainty, last-minute preparations and the undercurrents of family relationships are woven into the narrative.

In recent years, Shah has re-established his image as a highly commendable actor with five films in a row.

A part of *Dus Kahaniyan* (2007), 'Rice Plate', directed by Rohit Roy, is an interesting story about how real-life situations often make people from different communities appreciate the 'others'. In a railway canteen a staunch Brahmin lady (Shabana Azmi) orders a plate of rice and leaves the table to wash her hands. On return she finds a not-so-well-to-do Muslim (Shah) eating at her table. As she is hungry, she also starts eating but soon leaves in a huff. She then notices that she has left her luggage and handbag in the canteen and goes back to retrieve them. There she finds her belongings near a table and a plate of rice on top. Then she realizes that she was prejudiced and feels bad. Later, in the station, she offers a place to a Muslim family, which shows that she has changed her attitude.

Rahul Dholakia's *Parzania* (2007) was based on a heart-wrenching, real-life story of a Parsi family that becomes a victim of the 2002 Gujarat communal riots, in which hundreds of people (mostly Muslim) lost their lives apart from large-scale arson and destruction of property. Shah portrayed a shattered father who, along with his wife (Sarika), attempts to trace their missing son Parzan (Parzan Dastur) who has gone missing during the riots.

In *Khuda Kay Liye* (2007), the Pakistani classic directed by Shoaib Mansoor, Shah made his mark in a guest appearance as a wise maulana, who delivers in a court a highly spirited discourse on how the very tenets of Islam are being wrongly interpreted in the name of war and hatred, bringing the religion a bad name.

A Wednesday! (2008), directed by Neeraj Pandey, was a gripping story featuring a police commissioner (Anupam Kher) and an anonymous caller (Naseeruddin Shah) who threatens to carry out bomb explosions in several locations in Bombay in order to obtain the release of four Islamic militants. Shah uses state-of-the-art electronic equipment to keep the police on their toes. The two meet briefly when the police commissioner, after identifying the anonymous caller on the basis of a face sketch, offers the man a ride home and introduces himself. The film freezes momentarily just as the caller begins to smile and utter his name. The movie was packed with a slew of thrilling sequences, which kept the viewers guessing as to what was going to happen next.

Firaaq (2009), which marked the directorial debut of actress Nandita Das, presented a riveting narrative on the state of society in the aftermath of the 2002 communal violence in Gujarat. Shah appeared in the role of Khan Sahib, an optimistic elderly Muslim classical vocalist, who, shocked by the hatred and massacres around him, loses all hope. His deep faith in the power of music for arousing a sense of compassion and love in people is shattered. The film won several prestigious international awards.

Apart from the foregoing films, Shah has also made in his mark in a variety of roles. He played the villain in Rajiv Rai's *Mohra* (1994), his 100th film. Again, he played the villain with a dual identity of a ghazal singer and a Pakistani spy in John Mathew Matthan's *Sarfarosh* (1999). He appeared as Mahatma Gandhi in Kamalahasan's *Hey Ram* (2000). His role as the sozzled cricket coach in Nagesh Kukunoor's highly appreciated film *Iqbal* (2005) won him the National Award for best supporting actor.

The list of his films is a fairly long one. They include Mahesh Bhatt's *Naajayaz* (1995) and *Chaahat* (1996), Kaizad Gustad's *Bombay Boys* (1998), Rajkumar Santoshi's *China Gate* (1998), Sturla Gunnarsson's *Such a Long Journey* (1998), Nagesh Kukunoor's *Teen Deewarein* (2003), Farah Khan's *Main Hoon Na* (2004), Rakesh Roshan's *Krrish* (2006), Vishal Bharadwaj's *Omkara* (2006), Homi Adajania's *Being Cyrus* (2005), Rajat Kapoor's *Mithya* (2008), Shivam Nair's *Maharathi* (2008), Jagmohan Mundhra's *Shoot on Sight* (2008) and Raja Menon's *Barah Aana* (2009).

Shah made his directorial debut in *Yun Hota To Kya Hota*, released in 2006.

Although Shah steered his way competently through the 1980s and the 1990s into the new millennium as a highly reliable actor, he could not become a true indigenous hero in the mould of Dilip Kumar and Amitabh Bachchan.

Apart from his film career, Shah has also been an accomplished stage and TV actor. In 1977, he collaborated with Tom Alter and Benjamin Gilani to form a theatre group called Motley Productions. He has directed plays written by Ismat Chughtai and Saadat Hasan Manto. In 1988, he played the title role in the TV serial *Mirza Ghalib*, directed by Gulzar and, in 1989, he portrayed the Maratha King Shivaji in the serial *Bharat Ek Khoj* directed by Shyam Benegal. In 1998, he played the role of Mahatma Gandhi in the play *Mahatma vs. Gandhi*.

Om Puri

Most of what has been said about Naseeruddin Shah in the first paragraph about him holds equally true for another versatile actor – Om Puri.

Om Puri was born on 18 October 1950 in Ambala (then in Punjab and now in Haryana). After his initial studies in Punjab, he went on to join the National School of Drama, Delhi, and the Film and Television Institute of India (FTII), Pune. His career has run almost parallel with that of Naseeruddin Shah and the two of them have appeared together in a vast range of movies. Om Puri is known more as a character actor rather than a hero. He did appear as a hero in a few films, the notable ones being K. Hariharan and Mani Kaul's *Ghasiram Kotwal* (1976), B. V. Karanth and Girish Karnad's *Godhuli* (1977), Biplab Roychowdhury's *Shodh* (1981), Govind Nihalani's *Ardh Satya* (1983), Satyajit

Om Puri

Ray's telefilm *Sadgati* (1984), T. S. Ranga's *Giddh: The Vulture* (1984), Govind Nihalani's *Aghaat* (1985), Shyam Benegal's *Yatra* (1986) and *Susman* (1987), Basu Bhattacharya's *Aastha* (1987) and K. Hariharan's *Current* (1992).

His international ventures include Roland Joffé's *City of Joy* (1992), Udayan Prasad's *My Son the Fanatic* (1997, based on the novel by Hanif Kureishi), Damien O'Donnell's *East is East* (1999), John Duigan's *The Parole Officer* (2001) and Mike Nicol's *Charlie Wilson's War* (2007, in which he played the former Pakistani president Zia-ul Haq).

His roles as a character actor are too many to be included here, but most of them have been outstanding. For instance, in Govind Nihalani's *Aakrosh* (1980), Ketan Mehta's *Mirch Masala* (1985) and Govind Nihalani's *Dev* (2004, in counterpoint to Amitabh Bachchan).

Om Puri has played several roles for TV series as well, the most memorable one being in Govind Nihalani's *Tamas* (1987), set during the turbulent period of Partition.

Nana Patekar

Nana Patekar (born on 1 January 1951 as Vishwanath Patekar), with his powerful screen presence, accorded, in the post-Bachchan period, a much-needed fillip to the sagging image of the Indian film hero. He started as a Marathi stage actor

way back in 1968 and made his name in that field. In films he first appeared in Muzaffar Ali's *Gaman* (1978) in a stellar role. His role of a masochist-cum-sadist underworld don in Vidhu Vinod Chopra's *Parinda* (1989) set him on a firm footing. Soon he started bagging lead roles in which he defied, even if for a short period, the generic convention of the hero, infusing his

Nana Patekar

character with an aura of dignity and self-assurance rarely witnessed in our cinema.

In the Bombay-based crime films like N. Chandra's *Ankush* (1986) and *Pratighat* (1987), Patekar sought to rediscover the Maratha pride – not through the historicals like those produced by the Kolhapur studios in 1930s and 1940s – but through violent campaigns (including sloganeering) launched by Bombay's native working class to oust the 'outsiders' and to maintain the supremacy of the 'local' Maharashtrian criminals revered by the people. In *Prahaar* (1991, which he himself directed) too, he built up the fantasy of a military Pied Piper leading the street youth who are transformed into a 'glorious' army of bullies and who try to sort out the mess created by 'emasculated' people in the real world.

Krantiveer (1994, directed by Mehul Kumar), set against the backdrop of the 1993 Mumbai riots and a scathing attack on the decadent state of the nation and communal politics, presented Nana in a powerful role of a local thug who is finally transformed into a people's hero as he mobilizes slum dwellers to fight against communal hatred. He again won applause for his portrayal, in Gulzar's *Hu Tu Tu* (1996), of a politically sharp, outspoken cultural activist working among slum dwellers.

In *Ghulam-e-Mustafa* (1997), Nana appeared as Mustafa, an illiterate, but pious Muslim, who carries out his lone crusade against the criminalized and deeply corrupt society. He is not mean like the common criminal but actually principled, honest and strictly adheres to his own code of ethics, which forbids him to harm women, children and the common man. Because of this code, he is caught in the dilemma between morality and his lifelong allegiance to his godfather, Abba. Before being taken away to jail, a handcuffed Mustafa begins to offer *namaaz* (by kneeling down) for the well-being of the family, which he has supported, but Abba's hatchet man shoots him in his back. This scene was somewhat reminiscent of Mahatma Gandhi being killed by Nathuram Godse. *Ghulam-e-Mustafa* perhaps was the first film in Hindi cinema, which has shown, in a remarkable way, a full-blown and highly emotional interaction between the otherwise alienated Hindu and Muslim cultures.

Nana's achievements in the social genre have been equally impressive. In Arun Kaul's *Deeksha* (1991) he was a rebellious untouchable who demolishes the traditional Brahminical orthodoxy and releases an upper-caste boy from being ordained in the Brahminical order. In Partho Ghosh's *Agni Sakshi* (1996), Patekar essayed an extremely unconventional anti-hero – a middle-class sado-masochist male who has no other way to release his pent-up anger except through his brutal passion to disfigure the body and ruin the life of his wife. The film, for a change, projected a woman figure who, in view of her unending suffering, questions the very sanctity of marriage and leaves home with another man. In Sanjay Leela Bhansali's *Khamoshi – The Musical* (1996), Nana made his mark in the role of a deaf-and-dumb father unable to understand his daughter's (Manisha Koirala) obsession to become a classical singer.

In Anil Matto's *Yeshwant* (1997), he exhibited his histrionics as a diligent and honest police inspector who wants his illiterate wife (Madhu) to become highly educated and even qualify for the prestigious Indian Administrative Service (IAS); he succeeds in his efforts. However, he is framed by a drug dealer arrested by him, who also maligns Madhu by involving her in a sex scandal. Nana then kills the drug dealer and his minions.

Ab Tak Chhappan (2004, directed by Shimit Amin) marked the comeback of the artiste as a cynical, but upright police officer for whom death is as ordinary a matter as cooking food for the family. He is a crack shot who tracks down and kills fifty-six (hence the title) criminals with an impeccable, quick-fire professionalism. This movie was loosely based on the life of Daya Nayak, an 'encounter specialist' working for the Bombay Police.

In Prakash Jha's *Apharan* (2005), he appeared as Tabrez Alam, a powerful and influential minority leader who runs an empire based on murder, extortion, rape and kidnapping.

In Milan Luthria's *Taxi No. 9211* (2006), Nana appeared as a taxi driver. (For more details, see Chapter 9 under John Abraham.)

In the same director's *Hattrick* (2007), Nana featured as a bitter and cynical doctor who hates the mention of the word 'cricket'. One of his patients, Danny Denzongpa, turns out to be an ex-cricketer, who, despite many misunderstandings with the doctor, gradually manages to get rid of the latter's cynicism by awakening in him the spirit of the game and connecting him with the enthusiasm and the positive aspects of the world around him.

Gautam Ghose's *Yatra* (2007) was an offbeat film that sought to capture the making of literature-based cinema through a long-drawn-out process of links between the pen and the camera. Nana Patekar is a renowned writer, who meets a young film maker (Nakul Vaid) while travelling to Delhi to receive a prestigious award. Vaid is an admirer of his writing. They begin an intimate discussion on the writer's celebrated novel *Janaza* (funeral). The writer dwells on his personal experiences with the novel's protagonist, the nautch girl Lajvanti (Rekha), while the film maker presents a cinematic interpretation of the work. The writer, driven by the sentiments of past memories, starts a hectic search for Lajvanti and finally finds her. She has now taken the name Miss Lisa and sings popular songs from films. She renders some of the exquisite melodies from the past as an expression of reverence for the writer.

In *Welcome* (2007), directed by Anees Bazmee, he appeared as Uday Shetty, one of the three underworld dons (the other two were Saagar and RDX played, respectively, by Anil Kapoor and Feroz Khan) who wants to get his sister (Katrina Kaif) married into a respectable family. When her marriage is settled with a suitable groom (Akshay Kumar), chaos erupts due to his shady background.

In *The Pool* (2007), directed by the American film maker Chris Smith, Nana played the head of an affluent family who lives in a house with an opulent swimming pool, with which an eighteen-year-old hotel employee gets fascinated. The youngster offers his services to Patekar and through his interactions with the family, the latter's worldview begins to change and his future takes a different shape. The film won the Special Jury Prize at the 2007 Sundance Film Festival Utah, USA.

Dus Kahaniyaan (2007), an innovation in story telling on celluloid through an assemblage of seven directors, critically examined the recurrence of religious prejudices, marital discord, betrayal, loss of identity, uprootedness and alienation that characterize modern society. In the segment 'Gubbare' (meaning balloons), directed by Sanjay Gupta, the heroine (Anita Hassandani), while travelling with her husband (Rohit Roy) on a bus, gets into a quarrel with him. She moves away to occupy another seat and meets Nana Patekar, who is carrying eleven balloons. He explains that each time he and his wife have an argument, he would present her eleven balloons to placate her and she, in turn, would bake a cake for him. Later, Anita comes to know his wife is dead, but even then, he takes eleven balloons to her grave regularly. She then patches up with her husband.

In Sangeeth Sivan's *Ek – The Power of One* (2009), he appeared as a Cental Bureau of Investigation (CBI) inspector in pursuit of the hero (Bobby Deol) who is accused of assassinating a politician.

Nana Patekar's hero is cast in an entirely different mould from that of today's and yesterday's lead actors. He is cynical, street-wise, hyperactive and obsessed with destroying political and social hypocrisy. This rebel, in contrast with that of Amitabh Bachchan, does not bargain with the rich in terms of acquisition of wealth and power, but seeks to empower a society trapped by helplessness and facing total anarchy at the ground level. In his screen persona, Nana evokes the sophistication of the two Marathi stalwarts Baburao Pendharkar and Chandramohan and also that of Raaj Kumar and Sanjeev Kumar. With his sardonic smile, a deep-throated voice and unpredictable gestures and utterances, he casts a powerful spell over the audience.

Manoj Bajpai

Amidst the galaxy of today's stars, Manoj Bajpai (born on 23 April 1969) in Belwa, Bihar, represents the other India, i.e., Bharat, as this talented actor could rise to stardom despite his small-town background. A celebrity of the Delhi stage, who was rejected  thrice by the National School of Drama before his final admission, Manoj began his carrier in TV serials and bagged a small role in Shekhar Kapur's *Bandit Queen* (1994). Mahesh Bhatt gave him his first major break in *Tamanna* in 1997. However, it was Ram Gopal Verma's *Satya* (1998), a powerful and

Manoj Bajpayi

realistic depiction of the underworld, which shaped the screen persona of this formidable artiste. He immortalized the character Bhiku Mhatre, a typical underworld gangster, who branches out on his own after breaking away from the 'big guys'. He takes a newcomer (Satya) into the world of crime under his wing and grooms him as a gangster. The film brought out, through stark images, the ongoing turf war among Bombay's mafia dons.

Satya: A Review

The new Bombay of writers like Rohinton Mistry, Vikram Chandra and film makers like Sudhir Mishra, Vidhu Vinod Chopra and Ram Gopal Verma stands apart from the Mumbai of masala fare. Here, the images are stark, brooding and realistic with no compromises being made for the larger-than-life effect of the Salim-Javed and Amitabh Bachchan ilk. With no artificial colourings and no cardboard characters littered around, the images have a life-like quality, the characters are culled from the streets and the tensions are familiar, having already entered the public consciousness through newspaper reports and television headlines ...

Behind the superficial prosperity of the glittering metropolis, there lurks a desperation born out of a will to survive. In Verma's celluloid vision, the underworld is made up of small-timers like Satya who came in search of bread, butter and a life with decency and dignity. Bread and butter [are] permissible, but dignity? Now that's a rare commodity in the fabric of the bustling city. Self-respect is only for those who have crossed over into the nether world and thrive on sundry illicit '*dhandas*' [businesses]. For the rest, existence is allowed as long as they succumb to the extortionist demands of the small and big dadas ...

The remarkable balance which Verma strikes between crime and punishment, criminals and cops, lends the film a brilliant tenor. Both the cops and the criminals are depicted as victims of circumstances in Verma's Dostoevskian analysis ...

Source: *The Sunday Times of India*, 5 July 1998, New Delhi

In *Shool* (1999, directed by E. Nivas), Manoj portrayed the agony of an honest and intrepid police officer posted to a small town in Bihar as he treads a straight path despite the sleazy politics and the inevitable concomitant violence.

With his excellent comedy role, which was marked by down-to-earth spontaneity in Hansal Mehta's *Dil Pe Mat Le Yaar* (2000), Manoj announced his making of a complete actor. In this film, Manoj, like Raj Kapoor in *Shri 420* (1955) and *Jagte Raho* (1957), presented the ugly encounter of an innocent and honest outsider with the greed, deceit and hypocrisy engrained in a big city's culture. However, unlike Raj Kapoor's and Govinda's, this protagonist's experience is that of a lost world, where his cherished old values are shattered, leading to his irreversible alienation.

In Shyam Benegal's *Zubeida* (2001), set in the late 1940s, Manoj again made his mark in the role of a debonair maharaja not prepared to come to terms with the world beyond his decadent royal milieu.

In *Pinjar* (2003), the classic directed by Dr Chandraprakash Dwivedi and based on the famous Punjabi novel by Amrita Pritam, Manoj revealed his amazing acumen in interpreting the complex character of a poor, rural Muslim youth, who, in his obsession with a Hindu girl, finally realizes the tragedy of Partition in the form of the inhuman transaction of a woman as a commodity between the warring communities.

Manoj's indisputable talent has also been exploited in the emerging post-modernist genre of Hindi cinema in which the film makers seek to evolve radically different themes and narratives besides filming techniques to explore the human psyche and unusual behaviour patterns.

The actor played a full-blown psychopath in Rakeysh Omprakash Mehra's *Aks* (2001). (See Chapter 2 for more details.)

Road (2002, directed by Rajat Mukherjee), a rehash of *Duel* (1971), *Kalifornia* (1993) and *Joy Ride* (2001), projected him in the role of a pathologically sick man, a serial killer on the run who happens to take a ride in a car and torments his co-passengers (Viveik Oberoi and Antara Mali) with his irreverent behaviour and remarks. Despite Manoj's brilliant depiction of the character, this extremely negative role was not in keeping with his dominant screen persona of a disillusioned youth in search of his identity. The film therefore was a commercial failure.

In Ram Gopal Verma's *Kaun?* (1997), Manoj portrayed an individual who takes shelter in the house of a paranoid woman suffering from an acute neurotic disorder (à la Rajesh Khanna in *Ittefaq*, 1969).

Mehul Kumar's *Jaago* (2004), a lurid depiction of vigilantism, presented Manoj as an upright cop who join hands with the mother of child rape victim to eventually destroy all forms of evil plaguing a metropolis.

In Pankaj Parashar's *Inteqam: The Perfect Game* (2004), he essayed the role of a cynical, duty-bound cop, who tracks down a serial killer, a woman author (Isha Koppikar). She has been finishing off her victims in the same manner as described in her book, which has the same title as the film.

Deepak Tijori's *Fareb* (2005), a movie focusing on murky relationships in the corporate world, cast Manoj in the role of a married advertising executive who gets intimate with a high-class business woman after her husband is murdered. When Manoj decides to break off the relationship, she becomes vengeful and decides to destroy his life and acquires the ad agency where he works. Soon, Manoj is charged with her murder and his wife finally hires a lawyer to fight his case.

In the film *1971* (released in 2007), set against the backdrop of the 1971 Indo–Pak war, Manoj made his mark as one of the daredevil Indian prisoners of war who makes the most daring escape from a Pakistani camp to the Indian border.

In *Dus Kahaniyaan* (2007), Manoj, in the segment 'Zahir', directed by Sanjay Gupta, once again staged a nuanced performance in the role of a struggling writer, Sahil, who loses his mind after he makes a startling discovery about his love interest Sia, his attractive neighbour with whom he has been sexually involved.

Swami (2007), directed by Ganesh Acharya, focused on the rising aspirations of rural people to reap the benefits being offered by a globalized world. Swami (Manoj Bajpai) sells off his ancestral home in a village and moves to Bombay with his wife Radha (Juhi Chawla) and their son. He sends his son to a top-class public school but soon Radha falls seriously ill. While the husband starts working overtime to raise money for the operation, the wife spends it for buying a chair that Swami wants to possess so dearly. Radha dies and Swami slogs to meet her last wish to ensure that their son settles down in the USA.

In *Money Hai To Honey Hai* (2008, again directed by Ganesh Acharya), he appeared as a lottery winner who loses everything. (For more details, see Chapter 8, under Govinda.)

In Anand Kumar's *Jugaad* (2009), Manoj appeared as the CEO of an ad agency in Delhi that is forced to shut down due to a sealing drive ordered by a court. The film reveals how he uses his skills and resources to keep going despite various obstacles.

In Suparn Verma's *Acid Factory* (under production), Manoj is one of the five men who find themselves locked inside a factory and lose memories of their past.

Formally trained as a 'method' actor, Manoj is the master of precise intense underplay and later overplay, often released suddenly through a burst of emotions. Like Dilip Kumar, he often employs silence masterfully to convey his anguish and inner turmoil. Being cast in the Sanjeev Kumar mould, he evokes the grandeur and dignity of the original hero. However, amidst the plethora of new-age heroes, this serious contender for the position of the fourth-generation indigenous hero is gradually losing his place.

Kay Kay Menon

Kay Kay (Krishna Kumar) Menon, born on 23 August 1964, perhaps the most impressive actor who has emerged on the Indian screen in the new millennium, represents a new indigenous hero model in the making. An MBA from Pune University, he started his career in theatre productions and

gradually moved to television and finally to films. He made his debut with *Naseem* (1995) in the negative role of a religious fundamentalist. The film (titled *The Morning Breeze* in English) was written and directed by Saeed Akhtar Mirza. It was based on the Babri Masjid demolition by Hindu funda-mentalists on 6 December 1992 and recounts the traumatic experiences

Kay Kay Menon

of a young girl Naseem in the months leading up to the catastrophic event. (In the riots that followed, hundreds lost their lives and there was large-scale destruction of property.) Her ailing grandfather (Kaifi Azmi) dies on the day the Babri Masjid is destroyed. This film marked the only screen appearance of the legendary Urdu poet Kaifi Azmi (the father of Shabana Azmi).

Naseem was followed by Mahesh Mathai's *Bhopal Express* (1999). Set against the background of the gas tragedy that struck Bhopal in December 1984 (in which thousands died and thousands more were seriously affected), this human drama highlighted how large corporations operate, at times, callously and irresponsibly, and how the common people are the worst hit. This movie narrates the events as seen by a newly wed couple (Menon and Nethra Raghuraman) and their friends who are the victims of the tragedy.

Hansal Mehta's *Chhal* (2002) portrayed Menon as a CID officer torn between his professional duty and his love for a woman whose brother belongs to the underworld. He is assigned the task of penetrating a dreaded criminal group (posing as a gangster) but he falls in love with the sister of the don's henchman. He now makes a complete turnaround and develops sympathy for the gangsters, while they come to know about his true profession.

In Anurag Kashyap's *Paanch* (2003), a film highlighting the bizarre and anti-establishment lifestyle and thinking of today's youngsters, Menon came up with a powerful performance as Luke, the leader of a rock band who smokes pot, drinks rum and enjoys cutting Barbie dolls to pieces. The other members of the band are Shiuli (Tejaswani Kolhapure), a footloose girl who keeps on dating men, idiotic Pondy (Vijay Maurya), Murgi (Aditya Srivastava) and the muscular Joy (Joy Fernandes). They hatch a plot to get money for their band, which leads to much mayhem and violence. Their encounter with a cop (Sharad Saxena) was a major highlight of the film.

In Sudhir Mishra's *Hazaaron Khwaishein Aisi* (2005), a tribute to the cinema of realism, and set in the turbulent years of the late 1960s and 1970s, Menon as Siddharth epitomized the plight of the typical upper-class idealist youth of that period, who, despite being born to privileges and luxuries, were heavily influenced by Marxian ideals and political activism. Siddharth, the son of a judge and an alumnus of elite institutions, decides to go to a Bihar village to join a group that is working for the upliftment of peasants. His girlfriend (Geeta), on the other hand, goes off to England to do an MA. And his friend, Vikram (Shiney Ahuja), whose father is a Congressman of the old guard, who is also madly in love with Geeta, uses his connections to become a a fixer who amasses money and power at an alarming speed. The upheavals caused by the Emergency (June 1975 to March 1977), and its fallout, impact their lives negatively, and not one of the three emerges intact. Kay Kay performed, with brilliance, a very complex role depicting idealism, a longing for love and eventual downfall.

Anurag Kashyap's *Black Friday* (made in 2004, but released in India only in 2007 due to legal complications) – set against the backdrop of the Muslim backlash prompted by the demolition of the Babri Masjid in 1992 and based on S. Hussein Zaidi's book of the same name published in 2002 – enlisted Menon perhaps in his best role till date. The narrative was built around two key figures occupying two opposite ideological domains, each wanting to capture full control. Tiger Memon, the mafia don, plans and executes the bomb blasts by mobilizing a group of poor Muslim youth who have lost dear ones in the Hindu onslaught and by using his links with his boss Dawood Ibrahim in Dubai. Rakesh Maria (Kay Kay Menon), a sensitive and committed police officer (à la the upright cop Amitabh Bachchan in *Dev*; the character is based on the real-life cop who investigated the Bombay blasts case), launches a crusade to nab the culprits. As the symbol of a secular state and its law, he is not biased against a particular community. When he asks his team go to a Muslim locality to track down the suspects, he demands an assurance from his men that they would not hurt the religious sentiments of the people during the days of their fasting. Again, when he visits the locality, the Muslims invite him to share their meals at the end of fasting. He readily covers his head and, squatting on the floor, joins the community feast.

Silsilay (2005), an offbeat film directed by by Khalid Mohammed, was about the tensions and uncertainties in the life of today's high-society women. Adopting an episodic approach, the narrative tells the tragic story of its three protagonists: Zia (Bhumika Chawla), a successful Bollywood actress; Anushka (Riya Sen), middle-class girl working in the corporate sector; and Rehana (Tabu), a high-society housewife. Menon essayed the role of Anwar, the wealthy husband of Rehana but is obsessed with a sensuous air hostess Neeta (Celina Jaitley). Fed up with her husband's infidelity, Rehana walks out of his life. Zia also gets ditched by her boyfriend Neel (Rahul Bose), while Anushka parts ways with her lover, a rich playboy Nikhil (Ashmit Patel) and settles down with her office colleague Tarun (Jimmy Shergill). In the end, Rehana and Anushka come to the rescue of a pregnant Zia.

Menon has also appeared in several thematically important supporting roles but often with negative personality attributes.

In Ram Gopal Verma's *Sarkar* (2005), as the rebellious eldest son of the patriarch figure (Amitabh Bachchan), he won critical acclaim for his outstanding performance with an intensity and precision seldom seen in today's actors.

Chandan Arora's *Main, Meri Patni Aur Woh* (2005) presented him as the tall, smart and outgoing friend of a woman who is a good six inches taller than her ordinary looking husband (Rajpal Yadav), leading to unwarranted tensions between the couple.

Madhur Bhandarkar's *Corporate* (2006), a revelatory narrative highlighting the intrigues and immoral practices prevalent in today's business culture, cast Menon in the role of a company executive assigned to work on a government-funded soft drink project. His live-in partner uses her charms to seduce the rival company's employee to divulge the details of the project. Menon and his company then win the government contract.

In Reema Kagti's *Honeymoon Travels Pvt. Ltd.* (2007), an off-beat drama weaving together the experiences of six couples on their honeymoon and travelling in the same tourist bus, the young actor played an uptight and insecure Bengali man, very much in love with his beautiful, free-spirited wife, who takes on a bunch of robbers as she is a karate expert.

Anand Rai's *Strangers* (2007) presented Menon in the role of a management professional who meets a failed writer while travelling by train from Southampton to London. They start discussing their personal problems and find they are both victims of marital discord.

Anurag Basu's *Life in a Metro* (2007), a scathing attack on the prevailing culture of ambition, material success and debauchery in today's life in the metropolis, presented Menon again in a negative role of a success-driven husband whose indifferent attitude towards his wife (Shilpa Shetty) leads to bitterness and boredom in their relationship. Soon, he finds solace in Neha (Kangana Ranaut), a smart and ambitious girl. His wife starts an affair with another man.

Sirf (2008), directed by Rajaatesh Nayar, was an offbeat and engrossing commentary on the search for joy in the present-day materialistic world. It peeps into the lives of four couples from different strata of society. Gaurav (Kay Kay Menon) and Devika (Manisha Koirala) are a high-society couple with all the luxuries and yet they lack the zest for life. They, like other couples in the narrative, await some happening that will one day lead them to freedom from their mundane and unhappy existence.

Mumbai Meri Jaan (2008), a memorable film directed by Nishikanth Kamath, is set against the backdrop of the 11 July 2006 Mumbai train bombings. Instead of venturing into the political and communal roots of such tragedies, it focused on capturing their impact on the lives of common individuals. Kay Kay Menon again portrayed with his trademark finesse the role of Suresh, a Hindu fanatic who suspects every Muslim of being a terrorist, and who gets caught in the turmoil after he boards the second-class compartment of the ill-fated train whose first-class compartment is blown to bits by a bomb blast. However, in the end, he very ably overcomes his obsessive hatred when he realizes that terrorist attacks are carried out by those who are enemies of both the communities.

Shaurya (2008), directed by Samar Khan, had Menon in the small but pivotal role of Brigadier Rudra Pratap Singh, the archetype of an army officer – domineering and narcissist with a sense of sarcasm that reflects a self-perceived sense of righteousness.

In Arindam Nandy's *Via Darjeeling* (2008), inspired perhaps by Akira Kurosowa's masterpiece *Rashomon* (1950), Menon portrayed the flamboyant husband who goes missing during his honeymoon near Darjeeling just before the couple are about to return to Calcutta. The police inspector (Vinay Pathak), who investigates the case, finds that the wife (Sonali Kulkarni) has been complaining about a mysterious man stalking her for some time. The case remains unsolved. Two years later, the inspector relates this story while chatting with a group of friends, when each participant, governed by his own mental makeup and experiences, tries to decipher the mystery of the missing husband.

In Goldie Behl's *Drona* (2008, hero Abhishek Bachchan), Menon appeared as the villain – the evil sorcerer, Riz Raizada, a descendant of the *asuras* – who wants to get hold of a precious secret that will make him the master of the universe.

Manish Gupta's *The Stoneman Murders* (2009) portrayed Menon as a suspended policeman who wants to prove his capabilities so that he can be reinstated. He thinks he can do so by nabbing 'the stoneman' – a serial killer. However, he has to contend with the official police investigator (Arbaaz Khan) at virtually every stage. As the movie races towards its climax, the ending is something unexpected.

In Anuraag Kashyap's *Gulaal* (2009), Menon posted a brilliant performance in an anti-hero role as a vengeful Rajput chief who leads a separatist movement by mobilizing former princes and soldiers disillusioned with the treatment being meted to them by the Indian state. But eventually, he gets involved in murky and violent interclan enmity and in students' politics. He is eventually killed.

Indrajit Nattoji *Aagey Se Right* (2009) presents a satire on the chaotic times in present-day Bombay. The movie is about a terrorist falling in love and about the cop who is pursuing him losing his gun at a crucial moment.

Sankat City (under production), directed by Pankaj Advani, depicts a racy comedy about the occupational hazards of two small-time car thieves, Menon and Dilip Prabhawalkar, who happen to steal a Mercedes along with sum of Rs 10 million inside the car, which belongs to a vicious gangster/loan shark (Anupam Kher).

In David Dhawan *Hook Ya Crook* (under production), a comic thriller about cricket, Menon shares his space with John Abraham, Shreyas Talpade and Genelia D'Souza.

Arshad Warsi

Arshad Warsi, one of the most talented actors among today's breed, has made his mark both in serious and comedy roles. A natural actor to the core and with a variety of down-to-earth portrayals to his credit, he stands out in sharp contrast to the highly stylized reigning stars. He thus represents a continuity with the personas of Balraj Sahni and Sanjeev Kumar. However, as hero, his talent has not been fully exploited.

Arshad Warsi

Warsi was born on 19 April 1968 in Bombay. Unfortunately, he was orphaned when he was in his teens. In his younger days he was a keen student of drama and dance. He acted in several plays of the English Theatre Group in Bombay. He also became an accomplished dancer, winning a prize in a competition at the age of 21. He even set up his own dancing school. He also worked as a sales executive for some years, though he wanted to join the Indian Army.

Warsi made his debut in cinema in 1996 with Amitabh Bachchan's first production *Tere Mere Sapne* directed by Joy Augustine. He appeared as Balu, a smart cab driver who is asked by a disgruntled rich youth (Chandrachur Singh) to switch places with him. This man is in love with Balu's sister, Parvati (Priya

Gill). Balu in the end exposes his benefactor's manager who has been squandering his wealth. This role won for the actor wide appreciation and the attention of several film makers, who cast him in lead roles as well as supporting roles.

In K. Ravi Shankar's *Mere Do Anmol Ratan* (1998), a plot borrowed from the Raj Kapoor–Mehmood starrer *Parvarish* (1958), Warsi played a rich youth raised by a couple along with another lad, not knowing who is their real son.

He was also in the lead in Aziz Sejawal's *Hero Hindustani* (1998), a nationalist drama.

Trishakti (1999), directed by Madhur Bhandarkar and set against the backdrop of Bombay's gang wars, announced Warsi's long association with crime cinema. He made his mark as one of the three men who comes to the rescue of a don after he is attacked by a rival. The grateful don recruits them in his group but when his position is threatened by the trio, he gets them implicated in a crime.

In P. Vasu's *Hogi Pyar Ki Jeet* (1999), Warsi acted as an orphaned son who carries out his father's last wish: that is, he should marry the daughter of his (father's) tormenter and murderer.

However, these films largely had a lukewarm response at the box office and failed to establish him as the new face of Bollywood. It was the breakthrough shift to a perfect comic role in Rajkumar Hirani's *Munnabhai MBBS*, released in 2003, which brought Warsi into the limelight. The film also announced the arrival of a highly lovable comedian in Hindi cinema (à la Johnny Walker and Mehmood) after a long gap. The new jester with a matter-of-fact stupidity won the hearts of both the critics and lay audience with his role as 'Circuit', the chief disciple of the film's protagonist (Sanjay Dutt). He repeated the same feat in *Lage Raho Munnabhai*, the sequel to *Munnabhai MBBS*, released in 2006. The third film in the series, *Munnabhai Chale Amerika*, is eagerly awaited.

The post-Munnabhai period saw Warsi in several comedies: Priyadarshan's *Hulchul* (2004), Mahesh Manjrekar's *Vaah! Life Ho*

To Aisi (2005), David Dhawan's *Maine Pyaar Kyun Kiya?* (2005), Siddharth Anand's *Salaam Namaste* (2005), Vivek Agnihotri's *Chocolate* (2005), Rohit Shetty's *Golmaal* (2006), Indra Kumar's *Dhamaal* (2007) and Rohit Shetty's two films *Golmaal Returns* (2008) and *Sunday* (2008). Despite his 'supplementary' roles in these films, Warsi continues to explore his viability in lead roles.

Samar Khan's *Kuchh Meetha Ho Jaye* (2005) cast him as a belligerent airport manager who gets to meet his former sweetheart, now married, when the plane in which they are travelling gets stranded in a far-off place. Several other passengers too start contemplating on their predicament and reconsidering their life decisions while they await the news of the resumption of their respective flights.

Three films that have established Warsi as a highly promising hero are: Shashanka Ghosh's *Waisa Bhi Hota Hai* (2003), Kabeer Kaushik's *Sehar* (2005) and Raj Kaushal's *Anthony Kaun Hai?* (2006). All three were crime-oriented movies.

In *Waisa Bhi Hota Hai*, a gory tale about gang wars, he won kudos for his performance as a young man (Punit) who inadvertently gets caught between his allegiance to the underworld and his own police links. As he befriends a criminal from the gang led by Ganpat (Anant Jog), the other gang leader Gangu Tai (Pratima Kazmi) has him captured. When his policewoman fiancée, Agni (Sandhya Mridul), goes to arrest Gangu Tai, she finds out Punit is involved with Bombay's powerful mafia.

In *Sehar*, set against the backdrop of the cut-throat criminal politics in Uttar Pradesh, Warsi once again displayed his histrionics as an upright police officer who sets up a Special Task Force to deal with a criminal don. With the help of a physics professor (Pankaj Kapoor), he manages to track the cell-phone conversations, and thereby to identify the location of the criminals.

In *Anthony Kaun Hai?* Warsi played 'Anthony' aka Champ, a small-time crook based in Thailand who is an expert in forging passports and other documents. He carries out a meticulous plan to acquire a cache of diamonds that has been hidden by a magician (Raghuveer Yadav) in a prison compound. This movie has been inspired by Hollywood's *Who Is Cletis Tout?* (2001). Warsi was widely acclaimed for his performance.

He also played the lead in Ajay Chandok's *Kisse Pyar Karoon* (2009). He attempts to foil a scheming woman's plans to usurp his friend's wealth.

Apart from the foregoing films, Warsi has also made his mark in pivotal supporting roles.

He appeared as a TV journalist (who faces grave danger) in Kabir Khan's *Kabul Express* (2006). (For more details, see Chapter 9 under John Abraham.)

He played a highly committed footballer who is struggling to make his Southall club (facing closure) win a deciding match in Vivek Agnihotri's *Dhan Dhana Dhan Goal* (2007). (See also Chapter 9 under John Abraham.)

He portrayed the distraught brother-in-law of the hero, who has been killed by the mafia in Akashdeep's *Ghaath* (2000), another movie on gangsters.

Krazzy 4 (2008), a film about mental disorders, featured Warsi as a person diagnosed with intermittent explosive disorder, who explodes with sudden anger at the slightest provocation.

In S. Ramanathan's *Zamaanat* (2008), he was a poor college youth in love with a wealthy girl (Karisma Kapoor) who is falsely implicated in a murder. A blind senior lawyer (Amitabh Bachchan) leaves his life of seclusion and unravels the truth behind the murder.

In Neeraj Vora's *Short Kut: The Con Is On* (2009), Arshad Warsi appeared in a negative role. He played a deceitful junior artiste, who becomes a superstar by stealing a script penned by a struggling assistant director (Akshaye Khanna).

Rahul Bose

Rahul Bose, who has been termed as 'the superstar of Indian art-house cinema' is the poster boy of the post-modernist Generation-X cinema. This cinema, which arrived in the late

1990s, is hailed as a fine synthesis of the mainstream and the art-house streams. This new genre, a part of the rapidly expanding mall–PVR culture, seeks to capture the lives of ultra-modern, Internet-savvy and often high-society people trying to uphold their Western lifestyle and outlook within the framework of Indian values and conventions. This genre has also liberated the Indian film from its classical and post-classical cultural

Rahul Bose

and linguistic affinities, making it truly a global film addressed largely to the privileged urban youth.

Rahul Bose was born on 27 July 1967 in Calcutta. When he was young, his family moved to Bombay. He did his schooling from Cathedral and John Connon School there. He started acting at the age of six in a school play. He graduated from Sydenham College, Bombay, and performed on the Bombay stage in the plays *Topsy Turvy* and *There Are Tigers in the Congo*. He also performed abroad at the Leicester Haymarket in England where he starred in Tim Murari's *The Square Circle*. Inspired by his mentor mother, young Bose also became a boxing and rugby union player and participated in the Western India Championships, winning a silver medal in boxing. He also played cricket and was coached by the former Indian captain Mansoor Ali Khan Pataudi. Bose started his career as a copywriter and later became an executive in a renowned ad agency, but soon bid goodbye to the ad world to become an actor when film maker Dev Benegal offered him the lead role in *English, August*.

English, August, released in 1994, was about the growing alienation of an extremely Anglicized Indian Administrative Service (IAS) officer, nicknamed 'English, August', when he is deputed for a year's training to a small town. The man, whose world is centred around English poetry and literature and rock and jazz, undergoes a cultural shock as he tries to come to terms with the 'culturally inferior' grassroots milieu as perceived by him. The film was based on a novel of the same name authored by Upamanyu Chatterjee. It won the Best English Film Award at the 1995 National Film Awards and a Special Jury Prize at the 1994 Torino International Festival of Young (Italy). *English, August* was even acquired by Hollywood's 20th Century Fox.

In *Bombay Boys* (1998) directed by Kaizad Gustad, Bose appeared as Ricardo Fernandes, an Indian-Australian, who arrives in Bombay in search of his long-lost brother. He teams up with an aspiring actor from New York and a musician from London to explore what the city holds for them.

Bose's next film, *Split Wide Open* (1999) directed by Dev Benegal, was an offbeat film that sought to question the notions of morality amidst grinding poverty and deprivation in the backdrop of the water crisis in Bombay slums. Although the film was panned by critics, it was selected as the Indian entry for the 1999 Venice Film Festival. It won a Special Jury Award. Rahul Bose received the Best Actor Award at the 2000 Singapore International Film Festival.

In *Jhankaar Beats* (2003), directed by Sujoy Ghosh, Rahul Bose essayed the role of a headstrong advertising professional who is also a dedicated musician. He and his best buddy (Sanjay Suri) participate in Jhankaar Beats, an annual pop music contest. Both are diehard fans of composer Rahul Dev Burman and, after facing many setbacks, they are able to win the contest.

The foregoing films represented the making of what has been called the 'Generation-Next', and released the Indian film from the stranglehold of mainstream cinema.

Bose entered the world of art cinema in 2002 with Aparna Sen's *Mr and Mrs Iyer*, set against the backdrop of the contemporary hostile communal environment in the country. Bose appeared as a wildlife photographer, a Muslim nicknamed Raja, who unwittingly becomes the companion of the heroine, Mrs Iyer (Konkona Sen Sharma), travelling alone with her baby in a bus from a hill station to Calcutta. On the way, the two witness real-life communal carnage and mayhem.

In *15 Park Avenue* (2005), also directed by Aparna Sen, he essayed the role of Jojo, a weak-hearted character who backs out from a relationship with a girl Meethi (Konkona Sen Sharma) who is schizophrenic. He meets her after a gap of eleven years, leading to a further deterioration in her delusional behaviour. This movie was followed by *Anuranan* (2006), *Kaalpurush* (2008), *Before the Rains* (2008), *Antaheen* (2009) and *The Japanese Wife* (2009).

Anuranan, the directorial debut by Bengali film maker Aniruddha Roy Chowdhury, was a tribute to platonic love in today's modern world. The friendship between two couples, Rahul and Nandita and Amit and Preeti leads to a deeper bond between Rahul and Preeti. But this soulful love is misunderstood by Amit and others. The film won the Best Regional Film Award at the 54th National Film Awards.

In *Kaalpurush* (in Bengali), directed by Buddhadev Dasgupta, Bose appeared as an honest man troubled by a failed marriage. He seeks solace in the memories of his childhood by reconnecting with his long-lost father (played by Mithun Chakraborty). *Kaalpurush* won the National Award for the Best Film.

In Santosh Sivan's *Before the Rains*, set against the backdrop of a burgeoning nationalist movement in Malabar (now in Kerala), Bose appeared as an idealistic young Indian who is caught in a conflict between his ambitions for the future and loyalty to the past.

Antaheen (in Bengali), directed by Aniruddha Roy Chowdhury, was about human relationships being influenced by the Internet-created virtual world. Bose portrayed an upright but disillusioned police officer, who seeks solace in an online intense relationship with a young television journalist without knowing anything about her. When they unknowingly meet in connection with a controversial mega project, the lady later realizes some uncanny similarities between her anonymous chat friend and the person she met. But they don't meet after that, as she dies in a car accident.

Aparna Sen's *The Japanese Wife* (2009), made in English, Bengali and Japanese, featured Bose as a young village school teacher who develops a deep relationship with his Japanese pen friend (Chigusa Takaku) through letters, enters into a mail box marriage and remains loyal to her throughout his life, but actually never meets her.

Bose's entry into mainstream cinema began in 1999 with Govind Nihalani's *Thakshak*, also the first commercial venture of the celebrated film maker. He essayed the role of Sunny, the flamboyant and reckless grandson of the head of a business house, who is being trained to take over the business. His close buddy, Ishaan (Ajay Devgan), also from an affluent business family, rebels against the unlawful activities of his father. Ishaan falls in love with the heroine (Tabu) who witnesses Sunny's car killing many persons. Sunny asks Ishaan to choose between friendship and love. Ishaan goes along with Tabu and forsakes his friend.

With Sudhir Mishra's *Chameli* (2003), Bose got a firm foothold in Bollywood. In a well-crafted role, he portrayed a grieving man left alone after his pregnant wife dies in a car accident His life takes a new turn when he meets Chameli (Kareena Kapoor) a prostitute, who is worldly wise and practical in her approach to life.

Anant Balani's *Ek Din 24 Ghante* (2003) had the young actor in the role of a compulsive gambler who pretends to love a rich girl and tricks her into paying a huge amount that he owes to a casino owner. She discovers that he is cheating her and she eventually kills him. The film has been inspired by the 1998 German film *Run Lola Run*.

In *Mumbai Matinee*, Anant Balani's second venture in the same year, Bose appeared in the comic role of a 32-year-old man worried about his virginity. He becomes a sex symbol when a film maker casts him in the role of a love-maker. He later meets Sonali Verma (Perizaad Zorabian), a journalist, who helps him through his difficulties. Unfortunately, director Anant Balani died on 29 August 2003 before the film was released.

Rahul next opted to take up some films that didn't gel well with his image of a sensitive actor.

In *Pyaar Ke Side Effects* (2006) directed by Saket Chaudhary, Bose played a DJ in love with a girl (Mallika Sherawat) who has walked away from her marriage. But he suffers from the typical commitment phobia, which in the end is cured by his mother.

In Kittu Saluja's *Chain Kulii Ki Main Kulii* (2007), he appeared as the captain of the Indian cricket team who inspires Karan (Zain Khan) a thirteen-year-old highly talented orphan to fulfil his two dreams: one is to have parents and the other is to become a famous cricketer like Kapil Dev, one of the top players of his time who successfully led India to win the World Cup in 1983. The film was based on the 2002 Hollywood movie *Like Mike* and its title has been taken from the lines spoken by Amitabh Bachchan in the 1982 film *Satte Pe Satta*. Kapil Dev played a cameo in the film.

In Sanjay Chhel's *Maan Gaye Mughal-e-Azam* (2008), Bose played a R&AW (Research and Analysis Wing, India's external intelligence agency) agent who assists a group of actors attempting to prevent an underworld conspiracy from destabilizing the Indian Government. The drama troupe, while enacting a stage version of the classic *Mughal-e-Azam* (1960), had discovered this conspiracy. This movie was inspired by the cult film *Jaane Bhi Do Yaaron* (1983).

Dil Kabaddi (2008), directed by debutant Anil Sharma, highlighted the lives of modern-day married urban couples. Rishi (Rahul Bose) and Simi (Konkona Sen Sharma) are caught in a web of boredom, apart from their love becoming stale and their existence quite meaningless. They are tempted to enter into extra-marital relationships. The story line was apparently borrowed from Woody Allen's *Husbands and Wives* (1992).

Bose won a lot of accolades for his powerful presence in Samar Khan's *Shaurya* (2008) in the role of Major Siddhant Chaudhary, who has been appointed as the defence lawyer of a Muslim officer, Javed Khan, facing court-martial for shooting his commanding officer. He starts taking a keen interest in the case after meeting Kavya (Minissha Lamba), a journalist who demonstrates that the case is not as simple as it seems. He soon comes into direct conflict with his senior Brigadier Rudra Pratap Singh (Kay Kay Menon). *Shaurya* was 'inspired' by the gripping 1992 Hollywood movie *A Few Good Men*.

Bose has also acted in *A Mouthful of Sky* (1995), the first Indian serial in English produced by Doordarshan, the government-run TV channel. The serial was an exposition of the aspirations and anxieties of the post-independence generation of Indians caught up in the contradictions created by their Indianness vis-à-vis their Westernized outlook and lifestyle. The serial was jointly directed by Anant Balani, Mahesh Bhatt and Ajay Goel.

Bose made his directorial debut in 2001, even though he had then acted only in a few films, with *Everybody Says I'm Fine!* The film focused on the disturbed lives of Bombay's elite class seen through the curious mind-reading ability of a hairdresser. Bose won the John Schlesinger Award (runner-up) for best directorial debut at the Palm Springs (California) International Film Festival, 2003.

Apart from films, Bose is a committed social activist and an active rugby player. He has set up many NGOs, which have done a lot for society. In the wake of the 26 December 2004 Tsunami, he and his team worked to provide relief to the needy in the Andaman and Nicobar Islands.

Irfan Khan

Irfan Khan represents the transformation of a formally trained theatre artiste into a cinematically mature film actor. His cinema also marks an easy switchover from offbeat films (including foreign ventures) to mainstream melodramas. A complete actor par excellence, his portrayals, like those of Kay Kay Menon and Arshad Warsi, exhibit a wide diversity – from lead roles to villainous and comedy roles.

Irfan was born as Sahabzade Irfan Ali Khan on 30 November 1962 in Jaipur. He abandoned his postgraduate studies and joined the renowned National School of Drama (NSD), Delhi, in 1984. After completing his training at this institution, he appeared in TV serials like *Chanakya*, *Sara Jahan Hamara*, *Banegi Apni Baat*, *Chandrakanta*, *Star Bestsellers*, *Darr* (in which he played a psychopathic serial killer) and *Bhanvar*.

Irfan made his film debut in 1988 with Mira Nair's *Salaam Bombay* in a small role. Later he appeared in several critically acclaimed films including Basu Chatterjee's *Kamla Ki Maut* (1989), Govind Nihalani's *Drishti* (1990), Tapan Sinha's *Ek Doctor Ki Maut* (1991), Anjan Dutt's *Bada Din* (1998), Sturla Gunnarsson's *Such a Long Journey* (1998) and Akashdeep's *Ghaath* (2000).

Irfan's first film as hero was London-based director Asif Kapadia's *The Warrior* (2001). Inspired by the cinemas of Sergio Leone (known for his sphagetti Westerns) and Akira Kurosowa (*Seven Samurai*, 1954, and *Kagemusha*, 1980) and set in the feudal times in the deserts of Rajasthan, the film recounted the tragic tale of a cruel and fierce warrior named Lafcadia, who strives to give up his profession and wants to live in peace after an incident changes his approach to life. But a sadistic 'lord' (his patron) asks his followers to hunt him down and behead him when Lafcadia falls afoul of his patron. They behead a look-alike and also kill Lafcadia's son. A despondent Lafcadia keeps roaming from place to place, facing the wrath of the people whose lives he had destroyed. *The Warrior* was shown at many international film festivals and was greatly appreciated.

Irfan was also cast in Farida Mehta's *Kali Salwar* (2002), based on Saadat Hasan Manto's famous short story. This movie was followed by Asvin Kumar's short film, *Road to Ladakh* (2003), which also won plaudits at international festivals. The film is now being made into a full-length feature, again starring Irfan Khan.

In Tigmanshu Dhulia's *Haasil* (2003), he appeared in a negative role. In a powerful drama that unfolds against the backdrop of college politics in Uttar Pradesh, Irfan Khan played a belligerent student leader at loggerheads with his rival, Ashutosh Rana, who instigates a poor student (Jimmy Shergill) to commit a crime. Irfan also gets engaged to the student's sweetheart (Hrishita Bhatt).

Irfan next made a spectacular impact with Vishal Bharadwaj's *Maqbool* (2004), an adaptation of William Shakespeare's classic *Macbeth*. He essayed the title role as the right-hand man of Abbaji (Pankaj Kapoor), a powerful underworld don. Irfan Khan plots and carries out assignments with the help of his boss's mistress. She falls in love with Irfan and they plot to finish off Abbaji. Irfan kills his mentor when he is asleep. But later he too becomes a target of a faction of Abbaji's henchmen.

Irfan continued to excel in crime-oriented movies. Tigmanshu Dhulia's *Charas* (2004), a curious tale about the narcotics trade in an opium-growing region of India, which has enticed many foreigners, cast Irfan as a mysterious individual named 'Policeman' who has taken over control of the area. A London-based cop reaches this region to locate his British friend who has gone missing but becomes a target of the dreaded 'Policeman'.

Aditya Bhattacharya's *Dubai Return* (2005) cast the actor in the lead role as a small-time crook who fights to reinstate his position after he has made a big entry in the Bombay underworld with a shocking, high-profile killing, but his rival takes the credit for the deed.

In *The Killer* (2006), directed by Hasnain Hyderabadwala and

Raksha Mistry, he portrayed a suave businessman, who takes a cab driver hostage. Irfan is on a mission to kill various people who would testify against a dreaded don.

Gunasekhar's Telugu film *Sainikudu* (2006), a gory tale highlighting corruption in the upper echelons of public life, featured Irfan as the villain Pappu Yadav who siphons off government relief funds sent for the victims of a flood. Mahesh Babu, the protagonist, unleashes a crusade against him.

In the social genre, Irfan made his mark in films like Ishaan Trivedi's *7 ½ Phere* (2005), Himanshu Brahmbhatt's *Rog* (2005), Naseeruddin Shah's *Yun Hota To Kya Hota* (2006), Michael Winterbottom's *A Mighty Heart* (2007, in English), Kaushik Roy's *Apna Aasman* (2007), Anil Mehta's *Aaja Nachle* (2007), Anurag Basu's *Life in a Metro* (2007), Mira Nair's *The Namesake* (2007, in English), Nishikanth Kamath's *Mumbai Meri Jaan* (2008) and Jaideep Sen's *Krazzy 4* (2008).

7 ½ Phere, a true-to-life movie, addressed the problems created by modern gadgetry in today's society. Irfan, a TV photographer, surreptitiously captures on camera a wedding using hidden cameras, which leads to much chaos and embarrassment when telecast on a 'reality show'.

In *Rog*, he played a disturbed police officer who falls in love with a dead woman who was a breathtaking beauty when alive and whose murder he is investigating. He soon becomes a victim of suffering and anxiety.

Yun Hota To Kya Hota, a dig at the deep-rooted aspirations among many Indians to move over to, and settle down in, the USA, featured the actor as a troubled stock broker who leaves for this destination after being betrayed by his love interest. His departure is followed by several other aspirants desiring to make it to the US: a woman who is sick of her alcoholic husband; a brilliant student waiting for his father to die; and a housewife seeking to escape her domineering mother-in-law.

A Mighty Heart was based on the kidnapping and then the beheading of the *Wall Street Journal* reporter Daniel Pearl who went missing after interviewing an Islamic fundamentalist cleric in Karachi in early 2002. His wife Mariane Pearl's (played by Angelina Jolie) desperate search for her husband brings her to Pakistan. Irfan featured as a CID official. (Parts of the film were shot in India as Pakistan had refused permission.)

Apna Aasman had Irfan in the role the father of an autistic child. He and his wife are upset with their son and his inability to lead a normal life. However, he is good at arts. Anyway, Irfan gives his son a brain booster that has been developed by a maverick scientist believing that the ingredient can make him a genius. The son does become more intelligent but he is also very confused and remains aloof, with no emotional bonding with his parents.

In *Aaja Nachle*, Irfan portrayed a small-time goon, who, in the company of a local tomboy, an ex-MLA, a tea stall owner, a responsible government official, a struggling insurance agent and a vagabond, helps the NRI dancer (Madhuri Dixit) to revive the dance institution set up by her guru. (See also Chapter 8 under Akshaye Khanna.)

In *Life in a Metro*, Irfan appeared as a bridegroom selected by the heroine's younger sister through marriage portals, but the heroine does not like him. (See also matter under Kay Kay Menon.)

The Namesake (based on the bestselling novel with the same title by Jhumpa Lahiri) was about the cross-cultural experiences, including alienation, of Indian immigrants spread over two generations. This movie featured Irfan as Ashoke Ganguli, an NRI staying in the USA, who names his son (played by Kal Penn) Gogol after the famous Ukrainian author Nikolai Gogol. The lad is uneasy with his unusual name, as the family members keep coming to India, to maintain links with their cultural identity and Indian heritage. After he grows up, he falls in love with two women, while his parents struggle to come to terms with his American ways. Eventually, Ashoke dies of a massive heart attack and his wife Ashima (Tabu) sells off their suburban family house in the USA and returns to Calcutta.

Mumbai Meri Jaan (2008) portrayed Irfan as Thomas, a roadside coffee vendor, who is angry with the bourgeois attitude of the city. He is happy that the 11 July 2006 bomb blasts in local trains have shaken up the higher classes. Armed with this knowledge, he finds a way to strike back at the upper-class society, which refuses to accept him, by making hoax calls about hidden bombs at malls.

In *Krazzy 4*, Irfan was featured as a doctor, who is himself diagnosed with a compulsive personality disorder. He is obsessed with cleanlinees and wants to keep everything spic and span.

In Danny Boyle's runaway hit *Slumdog Millionaire* (2008), Irfan appeared as a policeman.

In Priyadarshan's *Billu* (2009), he played the title role with great panache. (For more details, see Chapter 8 under Shahrukh Khan.)

Other films of Irfan include Amol Shetge's *Gunaah* (2002), Amit Kimar's *The Bypass* (2003), Padam Kumar's *Supari* (2003), Madhur Bhandarkar's *Aan: Men at Work* (2004), Florian Gallenberger's *Schattan der Zeit* (2004, in German), Piyush Kumar's *Mr 100%* (2006), Tanveer Khan's *Deadline: Sirf 24 Ghante* (2006), Vic Sarin's *Partition* (2007), Wes Anderson's *The Darjeeling Limited* (2007) and Rohit Shetty's *Sunday* (2008).

In Suparn Verma's *Acid Factory* (under production), Irfan is one of the five men who find themselves locked inside a factory and have lost memories of their past.

***

Kamalahasan, Naseeruddin Shah, Om Puri, Nana Patekar, Manoj Bajpai, Kay Kay Menon, Arshad Warsi, Rahul Bose and Irfan Khan – despite their formidable screen presence and the quality of their cinemas – have been eclipsed by the reigning megastars. Their repository of talent is largely being invested in supporting (including comic and villainous) roles. Along with Amol Palekar, Raghuveer Yadav and Pankaj Kapoor, these actors represent many original traits of the indigenous identity of the Hindi film hero. Unfortunately, they look largely misfit in today's fragmented and distorted cinematic discourse unable to represent the hero's personality in all its dimensions.

Appendix

Amitabh Bachchan: Filmography*

1. Saat Hindustani (1969)

Type of film:	Social
Banner:	Naya Sansar
Cast:	Shahnaz, Madhu, Utpal Dutt, Madhukar, Anwar Ali, Amitabh Bachchan, Jalal Agha, Surekha, Sukhdeo, Prakash Thapa, Irshad, Panja Panjatan, Dina Pathak, A. K. Hangal, Anjali
Director:	K. A. Abbas
Story/script/ dialogues:	Madhukar
Music director:	J. P. Kaushik
Lyricist:	Kaifi Azmi
Cinematographer:	Ramchandra

2. Anand (1970)

Type of film:	Social
Banner:	Rupam Chitra
Cast:	Rajesh Khanna, Amitabh Bachchan, Sumita Sanyal, Ramesh Deo, Seema Deo, Johnny Walker, Dara Singh, Durga Khote, Lalita Pawar
Director:	Hrishikesh Mukherjee

---

*Does not include films in which Amitabh Bachchan put in a special appearance or a guest appearance or played a minor role.

Story/script/
  dialogues: Hrishikesh Mukherjee (story)
                    Gulzar (dialogues)
Music director: Salil Choudhury
Lyricists: Yogesh, Gulzar
Cinematographer: Jaywant Pathare

3. Reshma Aur Shera (1971)

Type of film: Social
Banner: Ajanta Arts
Cast: Sunil Dutt, Waheeda Rehman, Raakhee, Vinod Khanna, Jayant, Sulochana, K. N. Singh, Amrish Puri, Amitabh Bachchan, Padma Khanna
Director: Sunil Dutt
Story/script/
  dialogues: Ali Raza, Ajanta Arts Story Department
Music director: Jaidev
Lyricists: Balkavi Bairagi, Neeraj, Udhav Kumar
Cinematographer: Ramchandra

4. Pyar Ki Kahani (1971)

Type of film: Social
Banner: Vijayalakshmi Pictures
Cast: Amitabh Bachchan, Tanuja, Anil Dhawan, Farida Jalal, Bipin Gupta, Prem Chopra, Madhu Chanda, Agha, Mukhri, Mohan Choti, Pravin Paul, Yunus Parvez, Krishnakant, Birbal, Gulshan Bawra, K. N. Singh
Director: Ravikant Nagaich
Music director: Rahul Dev Burman
Lyricist: Anand Bakshi

5. Parvana (1971)

Type of film:	Social
Banner:	Shri Ambika Chitra
Cast:	Amitabh Bachchan, Navin Nischal, Yogita Bali, Om Prakash, Abhi Bhattacharya, Lalita Pawar
Director:	Jyoti Swaroop
Story/script/ dialogues:	Madhusudan (story) Agha Jani Kashmiri (dialogues)
Music director:	Madan Mohan
Lyricist:	Kaifi Azmi

6. Sanjog (1971)

Type of film:	Social
Banner:	Gemini Pictures
Cast:	Mala Sinha, Amitabh Bachchan, Aruna Irani, Madan Puri, Nazir Hussain, Ramesh Deo, Johnny Walker, Malika
Director:	S. S. Balan
Music director:	Rahul Dev Burman
Lyricist:	Anand Bakshi

7. Bansi Birju (1972)

Type of film:	Social
Banner:	P. V. Films
Cast:	Amitabh Bachchan, Jaya Bhaduri, Ramesh Deo, Nigar Sultana, Anwar Ali, Rajen Haksar, Yunus Parvez
Director:	Prakash Verma
Music director:	Vijay Raghav Rao
Lyricist:	Yogesh

8. Bombay to Goa (1972)

Type of film:	Social
Banner:	Mehmood Productions
Cast:	Amitabh Bachchan, Mehmood, Aruna Irani, Shatrughan Sinha, Anwar Ali, Mukhri, Lalita Pawar, Manorama, Manmohan, Keshto Mukherjee
Director:	S. Ramanathan
Music director:	Rahul.Dev Burman
Lyricist:	Rajinder Kishen

9. Ek Nazar (1972)

Type of film:	Social
Banner:	Amar Chitra International
Cast:	Jaya Bhaduri, Amitabh Bachchan, Nadira, Manmohan, Tarun Bose, Asit Sen, Sudhir, Raza Murad, Johnny Whisky, Rashid Khan
Director:	B. R. Ishara
Story/script/ dialogues:	B. R. Ishara
Music directors:	Laxmikant Pyarelal
Lyricist:	Majrooh Sultanpuri

10. Raaste Ka Pathar (1972)

Type of film:	Social
Banner:	Khosla Enterprises
Cast:	Amitabh Bachchan, Shatrughan Sinha, Laxmi Chhaya, Neeta Khayani, Prem Chopra, Bhagwan
Director:	Mukul Dutt
Music directors:	Laxmikant Pyarelal
Lyricist:	Anand Bakshi

11. Gehri Chaal (1973)

Type of film:	Social
Banner:	Chitralaya Pictures
Cast:	Amitabh Bachchan, Hema Malini, Jeetendra, Bindu, Prem Chopra
Director:	C. V. Sridhar
Music directors:	Laxmikant Pyarelal
Lyricist:	Rajinder Kishen

12. Bandhe Haath (1973)

Type of film:	Social
Banner:	Ralhan Productions
Cast:	Amitabh Bachchan, Mumtaz, Ajit, Ranjeet, O. P. Ralhan, Jagirdar, Kumud Chhugani, Anjana, Sardar Akhtar, Asit Sen, Madan Puri
Director:	O. P. Ralhan
Story/script/ dialogues:	O. P. Ralhan
Music director:	Rahul Dev Burman
Lyricist:	Majrooh Sultanpuri

13. Zanjeer (1973)

Type of film:	Social
Banner:	Prakash Mehra Productions
Cast:	Amitabh Bachchan, Jaya Bhaduri, Ajit, Bindu, Pran, Om Prakash, Iftekhar, Ram Mohan, Yunus Parvez, Purnima, Gulshan Bawra, Keshto Mukherjee
Director:	Prakash Mehra
Story/script/ dialogues:	Salim-Javed
Music directors:	Kalyanji Anandji
Lyricist:	Gulshan Bawra
Cinematographer:	N. Satyen

14. Abhimaan (1973)

Type of film:	Social
Banner:	Amiya Pictures
Cast:	Amitabh Bachchan, Jaya Bhaduri, Durga Khote, Bindu, Asrani, A. K. Hangal, David
Director:	Hrishikesh Mukherjee
Story/script/ dialogues:	Rajender Singh Bedi (dialogues)
Music director:	Sachin Dev Burman
Lyricist:	Majrooh Sultanpuri
Cinematographer:	Jaywant Pathare

15. Saudagar (1973)

Type of film:	Social
Banner:	Rajshri Productions
Cast:	Nutan, Amitabh Bachchan, Padma Khanna, Trilok Kapoor, Murad, Devkishan
Director:	Sudhendu Roy
Story/script/ dialogues:	Based on Narendranath Mitra's Bengali story *Rus*
Music director:	Ravindra Jain
Lyricist:	Ravindra Jain

16. Namak Haram (1973)

Type of film:	Social
Banner:	RSJ Productions
Cast:	Rajesh Khanna, Amitabh Bachchan, Rekha, Simi, Asrani, A. K. Hangal, Jayashree T., Om Shivpuri, Durga Khote, Raza Murad
Director:	Hrishikesh Mukherjee
Story/script/ dialogues:	Hrishikesh Mukherjee, Gulzar, D. N. Mukherjee
Music director:	Rahul Dev Burman
Lyricist:	Anand Bakshi
Cinematographer:	Jaywant Pathare

17. Kasauti (1974)

Type of film:	Social
Banner:	Lalit Kala Mandir
Cast:	Amitabh Bachchan, Hema Malini, Pran, Sonia Sahni, Ramesh Deo, Bharat Bhushan, Shubha Khote
Director:	Arvind Sen
Story/script/ dialogues:	Sudhir Kar
Music directors:	Kalyanji Anandji
Lyricists:	Anand Bakshi, Varma Malik, Indivar

18. Benaam (1974)

Type of film:	Social
Banner:	A. K. Movies
Cast:	Amitabh Bachchan, Moushumi Chatterji, Madan Puri, Prem Chopra, Iftekhar, Satyen Kappu, Shubha Khote, Dhumal
Director:	Narendra Bedi
Music director:	Rahul Dev Burman
Lyricist:	Majrooh Sultanpuri

19. Roti Kapda Aur Makan (1974)

Type of film:	Social
Banner:	Vishal Pictures
Cast:	Manoj Kumar, Zeenat Aman, Shashi Kapoor, Moushumi Chatterji, Premnath, Amitabh Bachchan, Madan Puri, Kamini Kaushal, Dheeraj Kumar
Director:	Manoj Kumar
Music directors:	Laxmikant Pyarelal
Lyricists:	Varma Malik, Santosh Anand

20. Majboor (1974)

Type of film:	Social
Banner:	Suchitra Films
Cast:	Amitabh Bachchan, Parveen Babi, Pran, Rehman, Satyen Kappu, Farida Jalal, Sulochana, Iftekhar, Sapru, Murad, K. N. Singh, Madan Puri, Tiwari, Anoop Kumar, Jagdish Raj, Master Alankar
Director:	Ravi Tandon
Story/script/ dialogues:	Salim-Javed
Music directors:	Laxmikant Pyarelal
Lyricist:	Anand Bakshi

21. Deewar (1975)

Type of film:	Social
Banner:	Trimurti Films
Cast:	Amitabh Bachchan, Shashi Kapoor, Nirupa Roy, Neetu Singh, Parveen Babi, Manmohan Krishna, Madan Puri, Iftekhar, Sudhir, Rajpal, Jagdish Raj, Kuljit Singh, Rajkishore, A. K. Hangal, Satyen Kappu
Director:	Yash Chopra
Story/script/ dialogues:	Salim-Javed
Music director:	Rahul Dev Burman
Lyricist:	Sahir Ludhianvi
Cinematographer:	Kay Gee

22. Zameer (1975)

Type of film:	Social
Banner:	B. R. Films
Cast:	Shammi Kapoor, Amitabh Bachchan, Saira Banu, Vinod Khanna, Indrani Mukherjee, Madan Puri, Ramesh Deo

Director: Ravi Chopra
Story/script/
dialogues: Salim-Javed
Music director: Sapan Chakravarty
Lyricist: Sahir Ludhianvi

23. Chupke Chupke (1975)

Type of film: Comedy
Banner: Rupam Chitra
Cast: Amitabh Bachchan, Dharmendra,
Sharmila Tagore, Jaya Bhaduri,
Om Prakash, Usha Kiran, David,
Keshto Mukherjee, Asrani
Director: Hrishikesh Mukherjee
Story/script/ Based on a story by Upendranath Ganguly
dialogues: D. N. Mukherjee and Gulzar (script)
Music director: Sachin Dev Burman
Lyricist: Anand Bakshi

24. Mili (1975)

Type of film: Social
Banner: Rupam Chitra
Cast: Ashok Kumar, Jaya Bhaduri, Amitabh
Bachchan, Aruna Irani, Usha Kiran,
Shubha Khote, Suresh Chatwal
Director: Hrishikesh Mukherjee
Music director: Sachin Dev Burman
Lyricist: Yogesh

25. Sholay (1975)

Type of film: Crime thriller
Banner: Sippy Films
Cast: Amitabh Bachchan, Dharmendra, Sanjeev
Kumar, Hema Malini, Jaya Bhaduri,

	Amjad Khan, A. K. Hangal, Satyen Kappu, Iftekhar, Leela Mishra, Vikas Anand, MacMohan, Keshto Mukherjee, Helen, Sachin, Asrani, Geeta Siddhaarth, Jairaj, Jagdeep, Jalal Agha, Om Shivpuri, Sharad Kumar, Master Alankar
Director:	Ramesh Sippy
Music director:	Rahul Dev Burman
Lyricist:	Anand Bakshi

26. Faraar (1975)

Type of film:	Crime thriller
Banner:	Alankar Chitra
Cast:	Amitabh Bachchan, Sanjeev Kumar, Sharmila Tagore, Master Raju, Sulochana, Rajen Haskar, Agha, Sajjan, Jayashree T.
Director:	Shankar Mukherjee
Music directors:	Kalyanji Anandji
Lyrics:	Rajinder Kishen

27. Kabhi Kabhie (1976)

Type of film:	Social
Banner:	Trimurti Films
Cast:	Waheeda Rehman, Amitabh Bachchan, Shashi Kapoor, Raakhee, Neetu Singh, Rishi Kapoor, Naseem, Simi, Parikshat Sahni
Director:	Yash Chopra
Music director:	Khayyam
Lyricist:	Sahir Ludhianvi

28. Hera Pheri (1976)

| Type of film: | Crime thriller |
| Banner: | Choudhry Enterprises |

Cast:	Amitabh Bachchan, Saira Banu, Vinod Khanna, Sulakshna Pandit, Padma Khanna, Pinchoo Kapoor, Dr Shreeram Lagoo, Jairaj, Urmila Bhatt
Director:	Prakash Mehra
Music directors:	Kalyanji Anandji
Lyricists:	Anjaan, Indivar

29. Do Anjaane (1976)

Type of film:	Social
Banner:	Navjeevan Films International
Cast:	Amitabh Bachchan, Rekha, Prem Chopra, Pradeep Kumar, Utpal Dutt, Lalita Pawar, Jagdish, Urmila Bhatt, Anoop Kumar, Abhi Bhattacharya (guest appearance), Mithun Chakraborty, Raj Mehra, Jagdeep
Director:	Dulal Guha
Music directors:	Kalyanji Anandji
Lyricists:	Varma Malik, Anjaan

30. Adalat (1977)

Type of film:	Social
Banner:	A. K. Movies
Cast:	Amitabh Bachchan, Waheeda Rehman, Neetu Singh, Hina Kausar, Kadar Khan, Anwar Hussain, Sujit Kumar, Suresh, Sapru, Pinchoo Kapoor
Director:	Narendra Bedi
Music directors:	Kalyanji Anandji
Lyricist:	Gulshan Bawra

31. Imaan Dharam (1977)

Type of film:	Social
Banner:	Suchitra Films

Cast: Amitabh Bachchan, Shashi Kapoor,
                       Rekha, Sanjeev Kumar, Amrish Puri,
                       Aparna Sen, Dr Shreeram Lagoo, Utpal
                       Dutt, A. K. Hangal
Director: Desh Mukherjee
Music directors: Laxmikant Pyarelal
Lyricist: Anand Bakshi

32. Khoon Pasina (1977)

Type of film: Social
Banner: Prakash Mehra Combine
Cast: Amitabh Bachchan, Rekha, Vinod
                       Khanna, Nirupa Roy, Aruna Irani, Asrani,
                       Ranjeet, Kadar Khan, Dev Kumar, Helen,
                       Bharat Bhushan
Director: Rakesh Kumar
Music directors: Kalyanji Anandji
Lyricist: Anjaan

33. Alaap (1977)

Type of film: Social
Banner: Rupam Chitra
Cast: Amitabh Bachchan, Rekha, Om Prakash,
                       Chhaya Devi, Manmohan Krishna, Farida
                       Jalal, Asrani, Lily Chakraborty, Benjamin
                       Gilani
Director: Hrishikesh Mukherjee
Music director: Jaidev
Lyricists: Dr Rahi Masoom Raza,
                       Dr Harivanshrai Bachchan

34. Amar Akbar Anthony (1977)

Type of film: Social
Banner: MKD Films

Cast:	Vinod Khanna, Rishi Kapoor, Amitabh Bachchan, Neetu Singh, Shabana Azmi, Parveen Babi, Nirupa Roy, Ranjeet, Mukhri, Jeevan, Pran, Helen, Nadira, Pratima Devi, Madhumati
Director:	Manmohan Desai
Story/script/ dialogues:	Mrs J. M. Desai (story), Prayag Raj (script) Kadar Khan (dialogues)
Music directors:	Laxmikant Pyarelal
Lyricist:	Anand Bakshi
Cinematographer:	Peter Pereira

35. Parvarish (1977)

Type of film:	Social
Banner:	MKD Films
Cast:	Amitabh Bachchan, Shammi Kapoor, Vinod Khanna, Neetu Singh, Shabana Azmi, Kadar Khan, Amjad Khan, Dev Kumar, Indrani Mukherjee, Hina Kausar, Master Ratan, Master Tito, Chand Usmani, Shaikh, Bhushan Tiwari
Director:	Manmohan Desai
Music directors:	Laxmikant Pyarelal
Lyricist:	Majrooh Sultanpuri

36. Ganga Ki Saugandh (1978)

Type of film:	Social
Banner:	Sultan Productions
Cast:	Amitabh Bachchan, Rekha, Amjad Khan, Pran, Bindu, I. S. Johar, Pran, Jeevan, Nana Palsikar, Satyen Kappu
Director:	Sultan Ahmed
Music directors:	Kalyanji Anandji
Lyricist:	Anjaan

37. Besharam (1978)

Type of film:	Social
Banner:	Navratna Films
Cast:	Amitabh Bachchan, Sharmila Tagore, Amjad Khan, Bindu, Helen, Nirupa Roy, A. K. Hangal, Devan Verma
Director:	Devan Verma
Music directors:	Kalyanji Anandji
Lyricist:	Yogesh

38. Kasme Vaade (1978)

Type of film:	Social
Banner:	Rose Movies
Cast:	Amitabh Bachchan, Raakhee, Neetu Singh, Randhir Kapoor, Amjad Khan
Director:	Ramesh Behl
Music director:	Rahul Dev Burman
Lyricist:	Gulshan Bawra

39. Trishul (1978)

Type of film:	Social
Banner:	Trimurti Films
Cast:	Waheeda Rehman, Amitabh Bachchan, Shashi Kapoor, Sanjeev Kumar, Hema Malini, Raakhee, Prem Chopra, Pamela Chopra, Poonam Dhillon, Sachin, Shetty, Yunus Parvez
Director:	Yash Chopra
Music director:	Khayyam
Lyricist:	Sahir Ludhianvi

40. Don (1978)

Type of film:	Crime thriller
Banner:	Nariman Films

Cast:	Amitabh Bachchan, Zeenat Aman, Helen, Pran, Iftekhar, Om Shivpuri, Jairaj
Director:	Chandra Barot
Music directors:	Kalyanji Anandji
Lyricist:	Anjaan

41. Muqaddar Ka Sikandar (1978)

Type of film:	Social
Banner:	Prakash Mehra Productions
Cast:	Amitabh Bachchan, Raakhee, Vinod Khanna, Rekha, Amjad Khan, Dr Shreeram Lagoo, Ranjit, R. P. Sethi, Madhu Malini, Nirupa Roy, Kadar Khan
Director:	Prakash Mehra
Story/script/ dialogues:	Laxmikant Sharma (story), Vijay Kaul, Kadar Khan (dialogues)
Music directors:	Kalyanji Anandji
Lyricist:	Anjaan
Cinematographer:	N. Satyen

42. The Great Gambler (1979)

Type of film:	Crime thriller
Banner:	C. V. K. Shastri
Cast:	Amitabh Bachchan, Zeenat Aman, Neetu Singh, Utpal Dutt, Prem Chopra, Sujit Kumar, Helen
Director:	Shakti Samanta
Music director:	Rahul Dev Burman
Lyricist:	Anand Bakshi

43. Jurmana (1979)

Type of film:	Social
Banner:	Shri Loknath Chitra Mandir
Cast:	Amitabh Bachchan, Raakhee,

	Vinod Mehra, Dr Shreeram Lagoo, Asrani.
	A. K. Hangal, Farida Jalal
Director:	Hrishikesh Mukherjee
Music director:	Rahul Dev Burman
Lyricist:	Anand Bakshi

44. Manzil (1979)

Type of film:	Social
Banner:	Shri Ambika Chitra
Cast:	Amitabh Bachchan, Moushumi Chatterji, Rakesh Pandey, Satyen Kappu, Vinod Pandey, A. K. Hangal, Dr Shreeram Lagoo
Director:	Basu Chatterjee
Music director:	Rahul Dev Burman
Lyricist:	Yogesh

45. Mr Natwarlal (1979)

Type of film:	Social
Banner:	Navjeevan Films International
Cast:	Amitabh Bachchan, Rekha, Amjad Khan, Rajni Sharma, Kadar Khan, Ajit, Yunus Parvez, Indrani Mukherjee
Director:	Rakesh Kumar
Music director:	Rajesh Roshan
Lyricist:	Anand Bakshi

46. Kala Patthar (1979)

Type of film:	Social
Banner:	Yash Raj Films
Cast:	Amitabh Bachchan, Shashi Kapoor, Raakhee, Shatrughan Sinha, Neetu Singh, Parveen Babi, Prem Chopra, Parikshat Sahni, Romesh Sharma, Poonam Dhillon, Manmohan Krishna, Iftekhar, Madan Puri, Yunus Parvez

Director: Yash Chopra
Story/script/
  dialogues: Salim-Javed
Music directors: Rajesh Roshan, Salil Choudhury
                      (background music)
Lyricist: Sahir Ludhianvi
Cinematographer: Kay Gee

47. Suhaag (1979)

Type of film: Social
Banner: MKD Films
Cast: Amitabh Bachchan, Rekha, Shashi
                      Kapoor, Parveen Babi, Amjad Khan,
                      Nirupa Roy, Kadar Khan, Jeevan, Ranjeet
Director: Manmohan Desai
Music directors: Laxmikant Pyarelal
Lyricist: Anand Bakshi

48. Do Aur Do Paanch (1980)

Type of film: Crime thriller
Banner: Devar Films
Cast: Amitabh Bachchan, Shashi Kapoor, Hema
                      Malini, Parveen Babi, Kadar Khan, Lalita
                      Pawar, Dr Shreeram Lagoo
Director: Rakesh Kumar
Music director: Rajesh Roshan
Lyricist: Anjaan

49. Dostana (1980)

Type of film: Crime thriller
Banner: Dharma Productions
Cast: Amitabh Bachchan, Zeenat Aman,
                      Shatrughan Sinha, Prem Chopra, Amrish
                      Puri, MacMohan, Sudhir, Sudha Chopra

Director: Raj Khosla
Music directors: Laxmikant Pyarelal
Lyricist: Anand Bakshi

50. Ram Balram (1980)

Type of film: Crime thriller
Banner: Navjeevan Films International
Cast: Amitabh Bachchan, Dharmendra, Zeenat
                     Aman, Rekha, Ajit, Helen, Prem Chopra,
                     Sujit Kumar, Utpal Dutt, Amjad Khan
Director: Vijay Anand
Music directors: Laxmikant Pyarelal
Lyricist: Anand Bakshi

51. Shaan (1980)

Type of film: Crime thriller
Banner: Sippy Films
Cast: Sunil Dutt, Amitabh Bachchan, Shashi
                     Kapoor, Raakhee, Shatrughan Sinha,
                     Parveen Babi, Bindiya Goswami, Johnny
                     Walker, Kulbhushan Kharbanda, Mazhar
                     Khan, MacMohan, Sudhir, Yunus Parvez,
                     Bindu
Director: Ramesh Sippy
Music director: Rahul Dev Burman
Lyricist: Anand Bakshi

52. Barsaat Ki Ek Raat (1981)

Type of film: Social
Banner: Shakti Films
Cast: Amitabh Bachchan, Raakhee, Utpal Dutt,
                     Amjad Khan, Prema Narayan
Director: Shakti Samanta
Music director: Rahul Dev Burman
Lyricist: Anand Bakshi

53. Naseeb (1981)

Type of film:	Social
Banner:	MKD Films
Cast:	Amitabh Bachchan, Hema Malini, Shatrughan Sinha, Rishi Kapoor, Reena Roy, Kim, Pran, Jeevan, Amrish Puri, Kadar Khan, Amjad Khan, Shakti Kapoor, Prem Chopra, Lalita Pawar, Jagdish Raj
Director:	Manmohan Desai
Story/script/ dialogues:	Prayag Raj (story), K. K. Shukla (script) Kadar Khan (dialogues)
Music directors:	Laxmikant Pyarelal
Lyricist:	Anand Bakshi
Cinematographer:	Jal Mistry

54. Laawaris (1981)

Type of film:	Social
Banner:	Prakash Mehra Productions
Cast:	Amitabh Bachchan, Zeenat Aman, Amjad Khan, Ranjeet, Bindu, Dr Shreeram Lagoo, Suresh Oberoi, Jeevan, Preeti Sapru (special appearances: Raakhee and Om Prakash)
Director:	Prakash Mehra
Music directors:	Kalyanji Anandji
Lyricists:	Anjaan, Prakash Mehra

55. Silsila (1981)

Type of film:	Social
Banner:	Yash Raj Films
Cast:	Amitabh Bachchan, Shashi Kapoor, Jaya Bachchan, Rekha, Sanjeev Kumar, Sudha Chopra (special appearances: Kulbhushan Kharbanda and Devan Verma)

Director:	Yash Chopra
Story/script/ dialogues:	Preeti Bedi (story), Sagar Sarhadi (script and dialogues)
Music directors:	Shiv Hari
Lyrics:	Javed Akhtar, Rajinder Kishen, Hassan Kamaal, Nida Fazli, Dr Harivanshrai Bachchan
Cinematographer:	Kay Gee

56. Yaraana (1981)

Type of film:	Social
Banner:	A. K. Movies
Cast:	Amitabh Bachchan, Neetu Singh, Amjad Khan, Tanuja, Kadar Khan, Aruna Irani, Jeevan, Ranjeet, Bharat Bhushan, Lalita Pawar
Director:	Rakesh Kumar
Music director:	Rajesh Roshan
Lyricist:	Anjaan

57. Kaalia (1981)

Type of film:	Crime thriller
Banner:	Bobby Enterprises
Cast:	Amitabh Bachchan, Parveen Babi, Pran, Asha Parekh, Raza Murad, K. N. Singh, Amjad Khan, Kadar Khan
Director:	Tinnu Anand
Music director:	Rahul Dev Burman
Lyricist:	Majrooh Sultanpuri

58. Satte Pe Satta (1982)

Type of film:	Comedy
Banner:	Uttam Chitra

Cast: Amitabh Bachchan, Hema Malini, Sarika,
                    Vijayendra, Ranjeeta, Amjad Khan, Shakti
                    Kapoor, Sudhir, Paintal, Aradhana, Prem
                    Narayan, Madhu Malhotra, Kanwaljeet,
                    Asha Sachdev, Sachin
Director: Raj N. Sippy
Music director: Rahul Dev Burman
Lyricist: Gulshan Bawra

59. Bemisaal (1982)

Type of film: Social
Banner: Shri Loknath Chitra Mandir
Cast: Amitabh Bachchan, Raakhee, Vinod
                    Mehra, Aruna Irani, Sheetal, Om Shivpuri,
                    Devan Verma
Director: Hrishikesh Mukherjee
Music director: Rahul Dev Burman
Lyricist: Anand Bakshi

60. Desh Premi (1982)

Type of film: Social
Banner: S. S. Movietone
Cast: Amitabh Bachchan, Hema Malini, Uttam
                    Kumar, Sharmila Tagore, Navin Nischal,
                    Parveen Babi, Shammi Kapoor, Premnath,
                    Kadar Khan, Prem Chopra, Amjad Khan,
                    Jeevan, Madhu, Parikshat Sahni
Director: Manmohan Desai
Music directors: Laxmikant Pyarelal
Lyricist: Anand Bakshi

61. Namak Halal (1982)

Type of film: Social
Banner: Choudhary Enterprises

Cast:	Amitabh Bachchan, Shashi Kapoor, Smita Patil, Parveen Babi, Waheeda Rehman, Om Prakash, Ranjeet, Satyen Kappu
Director:	Prakash Mehra
Music director:	Bhappi Lahiri
Lyricist:	Anjaan

62. Khuddar (1982)

Type of film:	Social
Banner:	Yokohama Productions
Cast:	Amitabh Bachchan, Vinod Mehra, Sanjeev Kumar, Parveen Babi, Bindiya Goswami, Prem Chopra, Tanuja, Mehmood
Director:	Ravi Tandon
Music director:	Rajesh Roshan
Lyricist:	Majrooh Sultanpuri

63. Shakti (1982)

Type of film:	Social
Banner:	M. R. Productions
Cast:	Dilip Kumar, Amitabh Bachchan, Smita Patil, Raakhee, Amrish Puri, Kulbhushan Kharbanda
Director:	Ramesh Sippy
Story/script/ dialogues:	Salim-Javed
Music director:	Rahul Dev Burman
Lyricist:	Anand Bakshi

64. Nastik (1983)

Type of film:	Social
Cast:	Amitabh Bachchan, Hema Malini, Pran, Amjad Khan, Devan Verma, Nalini Jaywant
Director:	Pramod Chakravarty

Music directors: Kalyanji Anandji
Lyricist: Anjaan

65. Andha Kanoon (1983)
Type of film: Social
Banner: Shri Eswari Productions
Cast: Amitabh Bachchan, Hema Malini, Rajnikant, Reena Roy, Madhavi, Prem Chopra, Amrish Puri, Pran, Danny Denzongpa, Madan Puri
Director: T. Rama Rao
Music directors: Laxmikant Pyarelal
Lyricist: Anand Bakshi

66. Mahan (1983)
Type of film: Social
Banner: Satya Chitra International
Cast: Amitabh Bachchan, Ashok Kumar, Waheeda Rehman, Zeenat Aman, Parveen Babi, Amjad Khan, Mukhri, Kadar Khan, Shakti Kapoor, Aruna Irani
Director: S. Ramanathan
Music director: Rahul Dev Burman
Lyricist: Anand Bakshi

67. Pukar (1983)
Type of film: Social
Banner: Rose Movies
Cast: Amitabh Bachchan, Zeenat Aman, Randhir Kapoor, Tina Munim, Prem Chopra, Dr Shreeram Lagoo, Om Shivpuri, Sujit Kumar
Director: Ramesh Behl
Music director: Rahul Dev Burman
Lyricist: Gulshan Bawra

68. Coolie (1983)

Type of film:	Social
Banner:	MKD Films
Cast:	Amitabh Bachchan, Waheeda Rehman, Rati Agnihotri, Rishi Kapoor, Kadar Khan, Shoma Anand, Om Shivpuri, Suresh Oberoi, Nilu Phule, Amrish Puri, Mukhri
Directors:	Manmohan Desai, Prayag Raj
Music directors:	Laxmikant Pyarelal
Lyricist:	Anand Bakshi

69. Inquilab (1984)

Type of film:	Social
Banner:	Shri Eswari Productions
Cast:	Amitabh Bachchan, Sridevi, Kadar Khan, Utpal Dutt, Shakti Kapoor, Ranjeet, Iftekhar, Satyen Kappu
Director:	T. Rama Rao
Music directors:	Laxmikant Pyarelal
Lyricist:	Anand Bakshi

70. Sharabi (1984)

Type of film:	Social
Banner:	Choudhary Enterprises
Cast:	Amitabh Bachchan, Jaya Prada, Pran, Om Prakash, Ranjeet, Satyen Kappu, Deepak Parashar, Suresh Oberoi, Mukhri
Director:	Prakash Mehra
Music director:	Bhappi Lahiri
Lyricists:	Prakash Mehra, Anjaan

71. Mard (1985)

Type of film:	Social
Banner:	MKD Films and Aasia Films

Cast:	Amitabh Bachchan, Amrita Singh, Nirupa Roy, Dara Singh, Prem Chopra, Goga Kapoor, Bob Christo, Satyen Kappu
Director:	Manmohan Desai
Story/script/ dialogues:	Prayag Raj (story), K. K. Shukla (script) Inder Raj Anand (dialogues)
Music director:	Annu Malik
Lyricists:	Rajinder Kishen, Prayag Raj, Indivar
Cinematographer:	Peter Pereira

72. Giraftaar (1985)

Type of film:	Crime thriller
Banner:	Ramraj Kalamandir
Cast:	Amitabh Bachchan, Rajnikanth, Kamalahasan, Poonam Dhillon, Madhavi, Nirupa Roy, Kadar Khan, Ranjeet, Shakti Kapoor, Aruna Irani, Kulbhushan Kharbanda
Director:	Prayag Raj
Music director:	Bhappi Lahiri
Lyricist:	Indivar

73. Aakhri Raasta (1986)

Type of film:	Social
Banner:	Lakshmi Productions
Cast:	Amitabh Bachchan, Jaya Prada, Sridevi, Anupam Kher, Sadashiv Amrapurkar, Bharat Kapoor, Dalip Tahil, Om Shivpuri
Director:	K. Bhagyaraj
Music directors:	Laxmikant Pyarelal
Lyricist:	Anand Bakshi

74. Shahenshah (1988)

Type of film:	Social
Banner:	Film Vision
Cast:	Amitabh Bachchan, Meenakshi Sheshadri, Amrish Puri, Pran, Aruna Irani, Prem Chopra, Kadar Khan, Jagdeep, Rohini Hattangadi
Director:	Tinnu Anand
Music directors:	Amar Utpal
Lyricist:	Anand Bakshi

75. Ganga Jamuna Saraswati (1988)

Type of film:	Social
Banner:	Ramraj Kalamandir
Cast:	Amitabh Bachchan, Jaya Prada, Meenakshi Sheshadri, Mithun Chakraborty, Amrish Puri, Nirupa Roy
Director:	Manmohan Desai
Music director:	Annu Malik
Lyricists:	Prayag Raj, Indivar

76. Jadugar (1989)

Type of film:	Social
Banner:	Prakash Mehra Productions
Cast:	Amitabh Bachchan, Jaya Prada, Amrish Puri, Amrita Singh, Aditya Pancholi, Pran, Raza Murad, Bharat Bhushan, Satyen Kappu
Director:	Prakash Mehra
Music directors:	Kalyanji Anandji
Lyricists:	Prakash Mehra, Anjaan, Javed Akhtar

77. Main Azaad Hoon (1989)

Type of film:	Social
Banner:	Nadiadwala Sons

Cast:	Amitabh Bachchan, Shabana Azmi, Manohar Sngh, Anupam Kher, Ajit Vachhani, Sudhir Pandey, K. K. Raina, M. K. Raina, Avtar Gill, Javed Khan
Director:	Tinnu Anand
Music directors:	Amar Utpal
Lyricist:	Kaifi Azmi

78. Toofan (1989)

Type of film:	Social
Banner:	MKD Films and Aasia Films
Cast:	Amitabh Bachchan, Meenakshi Sheshadri, Amrita Singh, Farooque Shiekh, Kamal Kapoor, Raza Murad, Pran, Sushma Seth, Zarina Wahab
Director:	Ketan Desai
Music director:	Annu Malik
Lyricists:	Prayag Raj, Indivar, Gulshan Bawra
Cinematographer:	Peter Pereira

79. Aaj Ka Arjun (1990)

Type of film:	Social
Banner:	BMB Films
Cast:	Amitabh Bachchan, Jaya Prada, Anupam Kher, Radhika, Kiran Kumar, Suresh Oberoi
Director:	K. C. Bokadia
Music director:	Bhappi Lahiri
Lyricist:	Anjaan

80. Agneepath (1990)

Type of film:	Social
Banner:	Dharma Productions
Cast:	Amitabh Bachchan, Mithun Chakraborty, Danny Denzongpa, Neelam, Madhavi,

Rohini Hattangadi, Tinnu Anand,
Archana Puran Singh, Alok Nath

Director:	Mukul S. Anand
Story/script/ dialogues:	Santosh Saroj
Music directors:	Laxmikant Pyarelal
Lyricist:	Anand Bakshi
Cinematographer:	Pravin Bhatt

81. Hum (1991)

Type of film:	Crime thriller
Banner:	Romesh Films
Cast:	Amitabh Bachchan, Kimi Katkar, Rajnikanth, Anupam Kher, Danny Denzongpa, Kadar Khan, Govinda, Deepa Sahi, Shilpa Shirodkar, Romesh Sharma, Annu Kapoor
Director:	Mukul S. Anand
Story/script/ dialogues:	Ravi Kapoor (story), Mohan Kaul (script) Kadar Khan (dialogues)
Music directors:	Laxmikant Pyarelal
Lyricist:	Anand Bakshi
Cinematographer:	W. B. Rao

82. Ajooba (1991)

Type of film:	Costume drama
Banner:	Filmwalas
Cast:	Amitabh Bachchan, Dimple Kapadia, Shammi Kapoor, Rishi Kapoor, Sonam, Amrish Puri, Saeed Jaffrey, Jairaj, K. N. Singh, Dara Singh, Sushma Seth
Director:	Shashi Kapoor
Music directors:	Laxmikant Pyarelal
Lyricist:	Anand Bakshi
Cinematographers:	Sergei Anufriyev, Aleksandr Kovalchuk, Peter Pereira

83. Akalya (1991)

Type of film:	Crime thriller
Banner:	M. R. Productions
Cast:	Amitabh Bachchan, Shashi Kapoor, Jaya Prada, Amrita Singh, Jackie Shroff, Meenakshi Sheshadri, Aditya Pancholi, Helen, S. M. Zaheer
Director:	Ramesh Sippy
Story/script/ dialogues:	Salim Khan
Music directors:	Laxmikant Pyarelal
Lyricist:	Anand Bakshi

84. Indrajeet (1991)

Type of film:	Social
Banner:	Rose Movies
Cast:	Amitabh Bachchan, Jaya Prada, Kumar Gaurav, Neelam, Saeed Jaffrey, Sadashiv Amrapurkar, Kamal Kapoor, Kadar Khan
Director:	K. V. Raju
Music director:	Rahul Dev Burman
Lyricist:	Gulshan Bawra
Cinematographer:	Peter Pereira

85. Khuda Gawah (1992)

Type of film:	Social
Banner:	Glamour Films
Cast:	Amitabh Bachchan, Sridevi, Danny Denzongpa, Nagarjuna, Vikram Gokhale, Shilpa Shirodkar, Kiran Kumar
Director:	Mukul S. Anand
Story/script/ dialogues:	Santosh Saroj Rajkumar Bedi
Music directors:	Laxmikant Pyarelal
Lyricist:	Anand Bakshi
Cinematographer:	W. B. Rao

86. Mrityudaata (1997)

Type of film:	Social
Banner:	Amitabh Bachchan Corporation Ltd (ABCL)
Cast:	Amitabh Bachchan, Karisma Kapoor, Dimple Kapadia, Arbaaz Khan, Paresh Rawal, Ashish Vidyarthi, Mukesh Rawal
Director:	Mehul Kumar
Music directors:	Anand Milind
Lyricist:	Sameer

87. Major Saab (1998)

Type of film:	Social
Banner:	ABCL
Cast:	Amitabh Bachchan, Ajay Devgan, Sonali Bendre, Nafisa Ali, Mohan Joshi, Ashish Vidyarthi, Kulbhushan Kharbanda
Director:	Tinnu Anand
Story/script/ dialogues:	Robin Bhal (story, script) Santosh Saroj (dialogues)
Music director:	Anand Raj Anand
Lyricists:	Dev Kohli, Anand Raj Anand
Cinematographer:	Ravi K. Chandran

88. Lal Badshah (1999)

Type of film:	Social
Banner:	B. M. B. Productions
Cast:	Amitabh Bachchan, Manisha Koirala, Shilpa Shetty, Mohan Joshi, Raghuvaran, Nirupa Roy
Director:	K. C. Bokadia
Music director:	Aadesh Srivastava
Lyricists:	Shayam Raj, Maya Govind, Gauhar Kanpuri
Cinematographer:	Peter Pereira

89. Kohram (1999)

Type of film:	Social
Banner:	Mehul Movies
Cast:	Amitabh Bachchan, Nana Patekar, Tabu, Danny Denzongpa, Jaya Prada, Mukul Dev, Jackie Shroff, Kabir Bedi
Director:	Mehul Kumar
Music directors:	Dilip Sen, Sameer Sen
Lyricists:	Anand Bakshi, Dev Kohli, Sameer

90. Hindustan Ki Kasam (1999)

Type of film:	Social/war
Banner:	Devgan Films
Cast:	Amitabh Bachchan, Ajay Devgan, Manisha Koirala, Sushmita Sen, Prem Chopra, Navin Nischal, Farida Jalal, Kadar Khan, Gulshan Grover, Shakti Kapoor
Director:	Veeru Devgan
Music director:	Sukhvinder Singh
Lyricist:	Anand Bakshi

91. Bade Miyan Chhote Miyan (1999)

Type of film:	Comedy
Banner:	Epic Enterprises
Cast:	Amitabh Bachchan, Govinda, Anupam Kher, Paresh Rawal, Asrani, Raveena Tandon, Madhuri Dixit
Director:	David Dhawan
Music director:	Viju Shah
Lyricist:	Sameer

92. Suryavansham (1999)

Type of film:	Social
Banner:	V. S. Films

Cast:	Amitabh Bachchan, Soundarya, Kadar Khan, Anupam Kher
Director:	E. V. V. Satyanarayana
Music director:	Annu Malik
Lyricist:	Sameer
Cinematographer:	Gopal S. Reddy

93. Mohabbatein (2000)

Type of film:	Social
Banner:	Yash Raj Films
Cast:	Amitabh Bachchan, Aishwarya Rai, Shahrukh Khan, Uday Chopra, Jimmy Shergill, Shamita Shetty, Jugal Hansraj, Kim Sharma, Preeti Jhangiani, Anupam Kher, Amrish Puri
Director:	Aditya Chopra
Music directors:	Jatin Lalit
Lyricist:	Anand Bakshi
Cinematographer:	Manmohan Singh

94. Aks (2001)

Type of film:	Crime thriller
Banner:	ABCL
Cast:	Amitabh Bachchan, Manoj Bajpai, Nandita Das, Raveena Tandon, Amol Palekar, K. K. Raina, Tanvi Azmi
Director:	Rakeysh Omprakash Mehra
Music director:	Annu Malik
Lyricist:	Gulzar
Cinematographer:	Kiran Deohans

95. Ek Rishta (2001)

Type of film:	Social
Banner:	Cineyug
Cast:	Amitabh Bachchan, Raakhee, Akshay Kumar, Juhi Chawla, Karisma Kapoor, Mohnish Behl, Alok Nath
Director:	Suneel Darshan
Music directors:	Nadeem Shravan
Lyricist:	Sameer
Cinematographer:	Sameer Reddy

96. Kabhi Khushi Kabhi Gham (2001)

Type of film:	Social
Banner:	Yash Raj Films
Cast:	Amitabh Bachchan, Jaya Bachchan, Shahrukh Khan, Kajol, Hrithik Roshan, Kareena Kapoor, Farida Jalal, Alok Nath
Director:	Karan Johar
Music directors:	Jatin Lalit, Sandesh Shandilya, Aadesh Srivastava
Lyricists:	Anil Pandey, Sameer
Cinematographer:	Kiran Deohans

97. Aankhen (2002)

Type of film:	Crime thriller
Banner:	V. R. Pictures
Cast:	Amitabh Bachchan, Akshay Kumar, Paresh Rawal, Arjun Rampal, Sushmita Sen
Director:	Vipul Shah
Music directors:	Aadesh Srivastava, Jatin Lalit
Lyricists:	Prasoon Joshi, Praveen Bhardwaj, Aatish Kapadia, Nitin Raikar
Cinematographer:	Ashok Mehta

98. Hum Kisi Se Kum Nahin (2002)

Type of film:	Comedy
Banner:	Epic Enterprises
Cast:	Amitabh Bachchan, Sanjay Dutt, Ajay Devgan, Aishwarya Rai, Paresh Rawal, Annu Kapoor
Director:	David Dhawan
Music director:	Annu Malik
Lyricist:	Anand Bakshi
Cinematographer:	Manmohan Singh

99. Kaante (2002)

Type of film:	Crime thriller
Banner:	Pritish Nandy Communications Ltd
Cast:	Amitabh Bachchan, Sanjay Dutt, Suniel Shetty, Kumar Gaurav, Lucky Ali, Mahesh Manjrekar
Director:	Sanjay Gupta
Music director:	Anand Raj Anand
Lyricists:	Anand Raj Anand, Vishal, Lucky Ali, Dev Kohli
Cinematographer:	Kurt Brabbee

100. Armaan (2003)

Type of film:	Social
Banner:	Aarti Enterprises
Cast:	Amitabh Bachchan, Anil Kapoor, Gracy Singh, Preity Zinta, Anupam Kher, Randhir Kapoor
Director:	Honey Irani
Story/dialogues	Honey Irani (story) Javed Akhtar (dialogues)
Music directors:	Shankar Ehsaan Loy
Lyricist:	Javed Akhtar
Cinematographer:	S. Ravi Verman

101. Baghbaan (2003)

Type of film:	Social
Banner:	B. R. Films
Cast:	Amitabh Bachchan, Hema Malini, Salman Khan, Paresh Rawal, Lillete Dubey, Mahima Chaudhary, Sharad Saxena, Aman Verma, Saahil Chadha, Suman Ranganathan, Rimi Sen, Samir Soni
Director:	Ravi Chopra
Music director:	Aadesh Srivastava
Lyricist:	Sameer
Cinematographer:	Barun Mukherjee

102. Boom (2003)

Type of film:	Crime thriller
Banner:	Kazaid Gustad Films
Cast:	Amitabh Bachchan, Jackie Shroff, Javed Jaffrey, Gulshan Grover, Madhu Sapre, Padma Lakshmi, Katrina Kaif, Zeenat Aman
Director:	Kazaid Gustad
Music directors:	Sandeep Chowta, Punjabi M. C., Talveen Singh
Lyricist:	Arshad Sayed

103. Aetbaar (2004)

Type of film:	Social
Banner:	Bhatt Films
Cast:	Amitabh Bachchan, Bipasha Basu, John Abraham, Supriya Pilgaonkar, Tom Alter
Director:	Vikram Bhatt
Music director:	Rajesh Roshan
Lyricist:	Dev Kohli
Cinematographer:	Pravin Bhatt

104. Deewar – Let's Bring Our Heroes Home (2004)

Type of film:	Social
Banner:	Vinod Doshi Films
Cast:	Amitabh Bachchan, Sanjay Dutt, Akshaye Khanna, Amrita Rao, Tanuja, K. K. Menon, Raghuveer Yadav
Director:	Milan Luthria
Music director:	Aadesh Srivastava
Lyricist:	Nusrat Badr
Cinematographer:	Nirmal Jani

105. Lakshya (2004)

Type of film:	Social/war
Banner:	Excel Entertainment and Motion Pictures
Cast:	Amitabh Bachchan, Hrithik Roshan, Preity Zinta, Om Puri, Amrish Puri, Boman Irani
Director:	Farhan Khan
Music directors:	Shankar Ehsaan Loy
Lyricist:	Javed Akhtar
Cinematographer:	Christopher Popp

106. Khakee (2004)

Type of film:	Crime
Banner:	Rajkumar Santoshi Films
Cast:	Amitabh Bachchan, Ajay Devgan, Akshay Kumar, Aishwarya Rai, Tusshar Kapoor, Atul Kulkarni, Lara Dutta
Director:	Rajkumar Santoshi
Music director:	Ram Sampat
Lyricist:	Sameer
Cinematographer:	K. V. Anand

107. Dev (2004)

Type of film:	Social
Banner:	Govind Nihalani Films
Cast:	Amitabh Bachchan, Fardeen Khan, Kareena Kapoor, Om Puri, Amrish Puri, Milind Gunaji, Rati Agnihotri
Director:	Govind Nihalani
Music director:	Aadesh Srivastava
Lyricists:	Nida Fazli, Govind Nihalani
Cinematographer:	Govind Nihalani

108. Veer-Zaara (2004)

Type of film:	Social
Banner:	Yash Raj Films
Cast:	Shahrukh Khan, Preity Zinta, Rani Mukherji, Kirron Kher, Divya Dutta, Boman Irani, Anupam Kher, Amitabh Bachchan, Hema Malini
Director:	Yash Chopra
Music directors:	Madan Mohan, Sanjeev Kohli
Lyricist:	Javed Akhtar
Cinematographer:	Anil Mehta

109. Black (2004)

Type of film:	Social
Banner:	Applause Bhansali Productions
Cast:	Amitabh Bachchan, Rani Mukherji, Shemaz Patel, Ayesha Kapoor
Director:	Sanjay Leela Bhansali
Music director:	Monty*
Cinematographer:	Ravi K. Chandran

*Songless film; only background music.

110. Ab Tumhare Hawale Watan Saathiyo (2004)

Type of film:	Social/war
Banner:	Movie World
Cast:	Amitabh Bachchan, Bobby Deol, Akshay Kumar, Divya Khosla
Director:	Anil Sharma
Music:	Annu Malik

111. Ek Ajnnabi (2005)

Type of film:	Social
Banner:	G. S. Entertainment
Cast:	Amitabh Bachchan, Arjun Rampal, Perizaad Zorabian, Rucha Vaidya, Vikram Chatwal
Director:	Apoorva Lakhia
Music director:	Vishal Shekhar
Lyricists:	Sameer, Jaydeep, Vishal Dadlani, Lalit Tiwari
Cinematographer:	R. J. Gururaj

112. Waqt: The Race against Time (2005)

Type of film:	Social
Banner:	Blockbuster Movie Entertainment
Cast:	Amitabh Bachchan, Akshay Kumar, Priyanka Chopra, Boman Irani
Director:	Vipul Shah
Music director:	Annu Malik
Cinematographer:	Santosh Thundiiayi

113. Bunty Aur Babli (2005)

Type of film:	Crime
Banner:	Yash Raj Films
Cast:	Amitabh Bachchan, Abhishek Bachchan, Rani Mukherji, Raj Babbar
Director:	Shaad Ali
Music directors:	Shankar Ehsaan Loy
Lyricist:	Gulzar
Cinematographer:	Aveek Mukhopadhyay

114. Viruddh (2005)

Type of film:	Social
Banner:	ABCL and Satyajeet Movies
Cast:	Amitabh Bachchan, Sharmila Tagore, John Abraham, Sanjay Dutt, Anusha Dhandekar, Prem Chopra, Sharad Saxena
Director:	Mahesh Manjrekar
Music director:	Ajay Atul
Cinematographer:	Vijay Arora

115. Sarkar (2005)

Type of film:	Crime
Banner:	K Sera Sera
Cast:	Amitabh Bachchan, Abhishek Bachchan, Kay Kay Menon, Supriya Pathak, Katrina Kaif, Tanisha
Director:	Ram Gopal Verma
Music directors:	Bapi Tutul/Amar Mohile
Lyricist:	Sandeep Nath
Cinematographer:	Amit Roy

116. Baabul (2006)

Type of film:	Social
Banner:	B. R. Films
Cast:	Amitabh Bachchan, Salman Khan, Rani Mukherji, Hema Malini, John Abraham, Om Puri
Director:	Ravi Chopra
Music director:	Aadesh Srivastava
Cinematographer:	Barun Mukherjee

117. Kabhi Alvida Na Kehna (2006)

Type of film:	Social
Banner:	Dharma Productions
Cast:	Amitabh Bachchan, Shahrukh Khan, Rani Mukherji, Preity Zinta, Abhishek Bachchan, Kirron Kher, Arjun Rampal
Director:	Karan Johar
Music directors:	Shankar Ehsaan Loy
Lyricist:	Javed Akhtar
Cinematographer:	Anil Mehta

118. Darna Zaroori Hai (2006)

Type of film:	Social
Banner:	K Sera Sera
Cast:	Amitabh Bachchan, Riteish Deshmukh, Anil Kapoor, Mallika Sherawat, Manoj Pahwa, Suniel Shetty, Sonali Kulkarni, Arjun Rampal, Bipasha Basu, Rajpal Yadav, Makrand Deshpande, Isha Koppikar, Randeep Hooda, Zakir Hussain, Nisha Kothari, Mohit Ahlawat
Directors:	Ram Gopal Verma, Manish Gupta, Sajid Khan, Jijy Philip, Prawal Raman,

J. D. Chakravarthy, Vivek Shah

Music directors: Salim Merchant, Sulaiman Merchant,
                          Amar Mohile
Cinematographer: Kiran Reddy

119. Family – The Ties of Blood (2006)

Type of film: Social
Banner: ABCL
Cast: Amitabh Bachchan, Akshay Kumar,
                          Bhumika Chawla, Aryeman Ramsay,
                          Shernaz Patel, Sushant Singh,
                          Gulshan Grover
Director: Rajkumar Santoshi
Music director: Ram Sampat
Cinematographer   Ashok Mehta

120. Nishabd (2007)

Type of film: Social
Banner: RGV Film Company
Cast: Amitabh Bachchan, Jiah Khan, Revathi,
                          Shraddha Arya, Aftab Shivdasani
Director: Ram Gopal Verma
Music directors: Vishal Bhardwaj/Amar Mohile
Lyricist: Munna Diman

121. Cheeni Kum (2007)

Type of Film: Social
Banner: Gautam Kumar
Cast: Amitabh Bachchan, Tabu, Paresh Rawal,
                          Zohra Sehgal, Swini Khera
Director: R. Balakrishnan
Music director: Ilayaraja
Lyricist: Sameer
Cinematographer   P. C. Sriram

122. Ram Gopal Verma Ki Aag (2007)

Type of ilm:	Crime
Banner:	K Sera Sera
Cast:	Amitabh Bachchan, Mohan Lal, Ajay Devgan, Nisha Kothari, Sushmita Sen, Rajpal Yadav, Gaurav Kapoor
Director:	Ram Gopal Verma
Music directors:	Bappi Lahiri, Ganesh Hegde, Amar Mohile, Prasanna Shekhar, Nitin Raikwar
Lyricists:	Sajid Farhad, Nitin Raikwar, Shabbir Ahmed
Cinematographer	Amit Roy

123. Eklavya: The Royal Guard (2007)

Type of film:	Social
Banner:	Vinod Chopra Productions
Cast:	Amitabh Bachchan, Saif Ali Khan, Sanjay Dutt, Vidya Balan, Jackie Shroff, Boman Irani, Jimmy Shergill, Rima Sen, Sharmila Tagore, Parikshat Sahni
Director:	Vidhu Vinod Chopra
Music director:	Shantanu Moitra
Cinematographer	Nataraja Subramanian

124. Bhootnath (2008)

Type of film:	Horror
Banner:	B. R. Films
Cast:	Amitabh Bachchan, Aman Siddiqui., Juhi Chawla, Shahrukh Khan, Rajpal Yadav
Director:	Vivek Sharma
Music director:	Vishal Shekhar
Lyricist:	Javed Akhtar
Cinematographer	Vishnu Rao

125. Sarkar Raj (2008)

Type of film:	Social
Banner:	Z Picture Company
Cast:	Amitabh Bachchan, Abhishek Bachchan, Aishwarya Rai, Dilip Prabhawalkar, Victor Banerjee, Tanisha Mukherjee, Supriya Pathak
Director:	Ram Gopal Verma
Music director:	Amar Mohile

126. God Tussi Great Ho (2008)

Type of film:	Social
Banner:	Eros Entertainment
Cast:	Salman Khan, Priyanka Chopra, Amitabh Bachchan
Director:	Rumi Jaffrey
Music director:	Sajid Wajid
Cinematographer	Ashok Mehta

127. The Last Lear (2008)

Type of film:	Social
Banner:	Arindam Chowdhury (producer)
Cast:	Amitabh Bachchan, Preity Zinta, Arjun Rampal, Divya Dutta, Shefali Shah
Director:	Rituparno Ghosh
Music directors:	Raja Narayan Dev and Sanjoy Das
Cinematographer	Aveek Mukhopadhyay

128. Zamaanat (2008)

Type of film:	Social
Banner:	S. Ramanathan (producer)

Cast:	Amitabh Bachchan, Vijayshanti, Arshad Warsi, Karisma Kapoor, Anupam Kher, Tinnu Anand, Shivaji Satham, Sharad Saxena, Baby Sana
Director:	S. Ramanathan
Music director:	Viju Shah
Cinematographer	Y. N. Murali

Index